CHUCK LONG

Go Hawks!

Chuck Long

AARON PUTZE

CHUCK LONG

DESTINED FOR GREATNESS

bpc

Business Publications Corporation Inc.

Chuck Long: Destined for Greatness is published by
Business Publications Corporation Inc., an Iowa corporation.

Copyright © 2017 by Aaron Putze.

Reproduction or other use, in whole or in part, of the contents
without permission of the publisher is strictly prohibited.

ISBN-13: 9780996521352
Library of Congress Control Number: 2017958783
Business Publications Corporation Inc., Des Moines, IA

bpc

Business Publications Corporation Inc.
The Depot at Fourth
100 4th Street
Des Moines, Iowa 50309
(515) 288-3336

DEDICATION

Dedicated in loving memory of our fathers:
Charles Long and Edward Schmalen.
They were destined for greatness in their public
relations and farming professions, respectively, and
more than delivered with positive, upbeat attitudes
and strong work ethics.

CONTENTS

The Kid Was A Winner

BY MARC HANSEN

Long ago, when I was covering Chuck Long and the Iowa football team for the *Des Moines Register*, I asked Hayden Fry a question: Did the Hawkeye coach ever worry that maybe he was putting too much pressure on his young quarterback by proclaiming this relatively unheralded rookie "destined for greatness"?

I thought it was a decent question. No disrespect intended. I mean, the young man, while a proven leader and a solid citizen from a wonderful family, hadn't exactly filled the sky with footballs at Wheaton North. In fact, every one of his pass completions supposedly ended up on his highlight reel during the college recruiting process.

The kid was a winner, no doubt. He led his team to the state championship, dodging game MVP honors by completing one of four passes for negative yardage, causing only Northwestern, Northern Illinois and Iowa to flock to his doorstep. His first recruiting call came around Thanksgiving of his senior year, right about the time most prospective college students are making a decision.

Yep, destined for greatness. In those days, Division I universities were granted ninety-five football scholarships -- compared with the eighty-five today, and Chuck was one of the last Hawkeye prospects offered that year.

Not surprisingly, the Texan who would eventually become the winningest football coach in Hawkeye history, glared at me (not for the first time). Too much pressure?

"You gotta' be kidding me!" Hayden explained with a shake of his head.

End of interview. Being a quick study, I took that as a "no." I can't remember if the "conversation" occurred after a win or a loss -- probably the former because there weren't many setbacks across Chuck Long's glorious college playing career. What Fry saw in practice every day, of course, was a rangy young quarterback with a big heart, a cool head, uncanny instincts and, as it turned out, one of the most accurate throwing arms in the history of college football.

"When I arrived at Iowa the fall of my freshman year," Chuck once told me, "I don't think anybody was too excited. I don't think I was high on any recruiting analyst's lists."

True. That fall, the Hawkeyes signed the nation's No. 1 junior college quarterback prospect, Cornelius Robertson. If anything, it made Long even more determined to prove himself.

After becoming the starter in the fall of 1982 following his freshman redshirt year, Chuck was yanked after the Hawkeyes were blown out by Nebraska in the season opener. The following week, backup quarterback Tom Grogan -- who beat out Robertson for the No. 2 spot -- got the start against Iowa State.

But after another loss, Chuck was back in the lineup -- this time for good -- leading Iowa to a 17-14 victory over Arizona. The Hawkeyes would win eight of their final 10 games, including a Peach Bowl victory over Tennessee.

Because he also took two snaps in the 1982 Rose Bowl during his redshirt season, he ended up playing in an unprecedented five bowl games. In the 1984 Freedom Bowl, he set another record, torching Texas for six touchdown passes, while throwing for 461 yards in a 55-17 rout, despite a steady rain throughout the game.

After the '85 season, the oldest son of Charles and Joan Long won the Maxwell Award as the best player in the country and the Davey O'Brien Award as the country's best quarterback. To this day, No. 16 still belongs on the list of the top college passers ever. If it weren't for the freak phenomenon that was Bo Jackson, one of the greatest athletes of all time, Long would have run away with the 1985 Heisman Trophy. As it was, after throwing for almost 3,000 yards and 26 touchdown passes, he finished only 45 points behind the Auburn running back in the closest vote ever.

A remarkable career.

The only sad part of the Chuck Long story is that his dad, who passed away in 2008, isn't here to relive it in Aaron Putze's engaging book. If there was a Most Valuable Parent Award in college sports, Charlie Long would have been in the running. He was calm, low-key, quick with a smile. Never way up, never way down. A lot like somebody else.

Hard to believe, but more than thirty years have slipped away since the oldest of Joan and Charles Long's three sons guided the Hawkeyes to the Rose Bowl.

Former Illinois coach Mike White once said Long (and his coach) played a role in the evolution of the college passing game by opening the air-traffic lanes in what once was perceived as a three-yards-and-a-cloud-of-dust conference.

And while I still don't think the question that set Hayden off those many years ago was that crazy, I do think this aptly titled book is one every Hawkeye diehard would enjoy.

ACKNOWLEDGEMENTS

Writing a book takes more than a subject and author. It requires a tremendous supporting cast. We had them.

God bless our families – our wives Lisa and Crystal and our children. They were patient and understanding while we were involved in research, interviews, meetings, writing and editing. Their encouragement and understanding made the book possible. For that we're eternally grateful.

Heartfelt appreciation to:

- Carol Bodensteiner, Marc Hansen, Van Harden and Keith Wendl for meeting with Aaron early in the process. You answered every question and encouraged us to follow through on the idea of telling this incredible story.

- And an additional shout-out to Marc Hansen for the helping hand with editing. You're a true professional and respected colleague.

- Dale Arens, University of Iowa Assistant Athletic Director, Trademarks and Licensing and Steve Roe, University of Iowa Assistant Athletics Director, Communications for their input and expertise every step of the way.

- Photographer Bob Rasmus for providing some incredible images to accompany this inspirational story.

- Publisher Ashley Holter of Write/Brain for shepherding this project through from concept to reality.

- Our many friends and family in Wheaton, Waukee and West Bend and on the stops along the way in Iowa, Michigan, California, Oklahoma and Kansas. It's been a rewarding and memorable journey!

- Everyone who offered words of encouragement along the way. It was much-needed wind in the sails, particularly when the hours grew long. We'll forever be grateful.

AARON PUTZE

CHUCK LONG

DESTINED FOR GREATNESS

Chuck Long:
a story so obvious it was almost overlooked

The story of Chuck Long was an obvious one. So obvious no one had written it.

How Chuck's accomplishments managed to fly under the radar for so long is itself a story. It's a testament to an athlete who competed at the highest level and succeeded in a way that no one, including members of his own family, could have imagined.

Perhaps this fact alone—that one of the most successful athletes in the history of Hawkeyes football never sought the attention or accolades he earned—speaks volumes about the humble person Chuck Long is.

The story of the boy from Wheaton, Illinois—the grade school star of "The Tot Lot" who grew up to throw for miles (literally) as a collegiate and pro quarterback—seems too good to be true. But it's not, even though it took Chuck a bit of convincing to tell it.

I recall broaching the idea with Chuck in early 2015 just after he was named executive director of the Iowa Sports Foundation (ISF). As communications director for the Iowa Soybean Association (ISA), a farmer-led organization located in Ankeny, Iowa, and an ISF presenting sponsor, I took note of the news. Sure, as a lifelong Hawkeyes fan, the chance to visit with someone as synonymous with the program as farming is with Iowa was a notable opportunity. But more to the point, capturing some thoughts from Chuck and his plans as ISF's new leader was important to share with ISA members.

Chuck promptly replied to my request for a telephone interview, and we were soon chatting. After our ninety-minute conversation, I scanned my eight typewritten pages of notes in awe.

I mean, how often does a seventeen-year-old kid in his first year as a starter under center win a 4A state high school football title (completing just one of four passes for minus three yards in the championship game to boot)?

Or, after averaging just a handful of throws per game as a two-year high school starter for a team that took pride in pounding the run, be offered a full-ride scholarship to play Big Ten quarterback?

Who could imagine being new on campus yet proclaimed by your head coach with the southern drawl and the last name Fry that you're "destined for greatness"? And who loses his lunch (literally) on his head coach during his first collegiate start—and gets benched as a result—only to one day compete in five college bowl games and finish second in the Heisman Trophy competition?

What if a kid whose first love was basketball would one day hold the University of Iowa football records for career pass attempts (1,203), yards passing (10,461), completions (782), and touchdown throws (74)?

These unique events and accomplishments are vintage Chuck Long.

But dig a little deeper, and you begin to understand the depth and talent of a person who, after being dismissed out of high school by all but three Division I football programs for not looking the part of a strong-armed QB, goes on to:

- Throw for more than two hundred yards in twenty-seven collegiate football games and over one hundred yards in forty-two of his last forty-five games
- Hold Iowa's single-season completion percentage mark (67.1 percent) and the Big Ten records for touchdown passes in a game, season, and career
- Rank third in NCAA history with career passing efficiency and sixth in passing yards
- Toss an NCAA record twenty-two straight pass completions (at Indiana in 1984)

- Be selected a three-time consensus first team all–Big Ten pick and recognized as one of just nine Hawkeyes football players to be recognized on Kinnick Stadium's Wall of Honor
- Be selected the overall no. 12 pick by the Detroit Lions in the 1986 NFL draft.

"Chuck," I asked a couple weeks following our conversation and after whittling down eight pages of notes into an eight-hundred-word column, "have you ever considered putting some of these stories down on paper?"

"It's no big deal," was his nonchalant reply. "Not now anyway. Maybe sometime. Later, maybe."

Mm, no.

Chuck's story needed to be told. After all, no one affiliated with those glory years of Hawkeyes football (1981–85) or his time as a Wheaton North Falcon and Detroit Lion was getting any younger (or memories any sharper).

And while Chuck's accomplishments on the football field were the stuff of legends, a more important story emerged when taking inventory of his life and career. It was his qualities as a person that jumped off the pages—a storyline that came to life through interviews with family, neighbors, coaches, and teammates, and observed in our time together traveling to interviews and conversing on the backyard deck.

Chuck's five years at Iowa were an almost mythical period in the history of Hawkeyes football, unforgettable moments that took place during a time when many families connected to farming were being crushed under the massive weight of a rural economic meltdown.

Authoring a book wasn't in my plans. But sometimes you ask a simple question and life takes an unexpected turn. Chuck Long is indeed a special person with a life story jam-packed with memorable moments, outstanding achievements, and an interesting cast of characters.

An obvious story for sure. And one I'm honored to help share.

—AARON PUTZE

Everyone loved Chuck Long.
He proved that in his playing career, coaching career,
and as a student at the University of Iowa. Chuck did
all the right things, and he's still doing that today as an
announcer for the Big Ten Network and in his work
with the Iowa Sports Foundation. I just can't put into
words how much I love Chuck Long and what he did
not only for Iowa but for every team
he's been associated with.
He's a real winner.

— HAYDEN FRY

CHAPTER 1

First and Long

"I enjoy people who give all their effort. I've always enjoyed underdogs—guys who weren't supposed to win but did."
— CHUCK LONG

Oct. 19, 1985 (Saturday)
2:30pm
Kinnick Stadium, Iowa City, Iowa

Clouds hang thick and low atop Kinnick Stadium, and the air is heavy and closes around you like a blanket. Portable sunshine provided by Oskaloosa, Iowa's own Musco Lighting casts a warm and mystical glow over the University of Iowa landmark named after its most celebrated athlete and the more than sixty-six thousand fans that fill it.

The top-ranked Iowa Hawkeyes football team, led by quarterback Chuck Long, is playing host to heated rival and no. 2-ranked Michigan Wolverines. It's a collision of college football goliaths, the first time since 1948 that no. 1 and no. 2 have butted heads. It's a sure-to-be slobber-knocker. Fans are in a fever pitch, embracing the falling temperatures and pesky drizzle.

It's a matchup Chuck relishes.

Just nine months earlier, the blond-haired gun-slinging signal caller from Wheaton North (Illinois) spurned the National Football League for a fifth year under center for the Hawkeyes. He took a pass (pun intended) on being a first-round draft pick and the seven-figure pay that would have accompanied it. He remained a Hawkeye for a moment like this—the opportunity to take the field on one of the loftiest collegiate sports stages, competing in front of the passionate Iowa fans he adored and with an inside track to a Rose Bowl berth hanging in the balance.

The campus was juiced in the week leading up to the nationally televised game.

And rightly so.

Iowa, fresh off a hard-fought 23–13 win over the Wisconsin Badgers in Camp Randall Stadium, is perched atop the Associated Press poll for the third consecutive week. Michigan, featuring the nation's fiercest defense and an offense led by hard-nosed and workmanlike quarterback Jim Harbaugh, has come calling after thumping the Michigan State Spartans 31–0 in East Lansing.

Now, with just minutes remaining until kick, electricity courses through Kinnick. The amperage begins with the fans in the bleachers, moves across the cool turf, channels up the brick-lined tunnel, and spills into the Hawkeyes locker room where the team paces with calm resolve and quiet anxiousness simultaneously.

Flanked by teammates and fellow quarterbacks Mark Vlasic and Chuck Hartlieb, Chuck senses the enormity of the occasion. He embraces it. He soaks it in.

It's arguably the most anticipated and significant contest in Iowa Hawkeyes football history and one that the agricultural state desperately needs to go its way. Farmers, the backbone of Iowa's economy and character, are hurting. Many are being bludgeoned by one of the worst economic downturns to grip the tight-knit, mostly rural state since the Great Depression. They need a lift.

Chuck is ready for this moment. His meticulous preparations, paired with a quiet confidence that has followed him from his time as a boy in Wheaton to one of the biggest college football stages in America, serve him well. In fact, he revels in the opportunity.

Now, with ball in hand, eyes closed, and the tremor of the anxious crowd vibrating within the bowels of Kinnick, Chuck mentally simulates game time. He visualizes defensive alignments. He anticipates the tendencies of the defensive backs. He rehearses how he'll attack the defensive stunts and blitzes that are sure to come.

He knows his teammates share his confidence, thanks to a quality week of practice and the swagger that accompanies being college football's top dog.

But tension also lingers in the Hawkeyes locker room, a fact not lost on its mustachioed, swashbuckling head coach, Hayden Fry.

In his seventh year at Iowa, the colorful and energetic product of Eastland, Texas, has a pedigree perfect for the game of college football and coaching the young men who play it.

Once a Division I standout himself,[1] Fry served in the US Marines, earning the rank of captain before leading several universities to college football relevancy, including Southern Methodist and North Texas.

In 1979, Fry took the reins of a hapless Iowa program at the urging of Bump Elliott, its athletic director and former coaching adversary (Fry's SMU Mustangs lost to Elliott and the Michigan Wolverines 27–16 in his first season in Dallas in 1963).

Hayden Fry quickly brought a winning attitude and bowl victories to Iowa City.

Just like Chuck, Fry didn't shy from big moments. He welcomed them with enthusiasm. On occasions such as this, his experience in the trenches and ability to motivate men to accomplish great things served him well. So, too, did his fascination with the human psyche and his master's in behavioral psychology earned from Baylor University.

Not one for delivering long-winded pep talks, Fry drew upon an assortment of jokes and off-the-cuff analogies that amused players, fans, and media alike. His mission was to loosen his team up just before leaving the locker room, firmly believing that you play better if you play loose.

---

[1] Hayden Fry played multiple positions for the Odessa, Texas, High School football squad (1943–46), including safety and quarterback. In his senior season, Fry led Odessa to fourteen consecutive wins and the state high school football championship. He went on to play quarterback at Baylor University, graduating in 1950 with a degree in psychology.

Fry himself never passed up on the chance for shenanigans, even prior to kickoff of one of the most anticipated and meaningful games in Iowa history. The Texas native and riverboat gambler had some fun with Michigan head coach Bo Schembechler during pregame drills by positioning one of his offensive linemen not skilled in long-snapping near him. The lineman hiked the ball to the Iowa punter again and again and again, failing miserably each time. After watching the debacle unfold before him, Schembechler couldn't contain himself. "Fry, come over here," he yelled, "and tell me what in the world you're having this guy do? You can't tell me you're going to have this guy snap to your punter!" To which Hayden Fry shouted back with a broad grin, "We don't plan on punting today."

Now the locker room is quiet. The lights are dimmed so players can be alone in their thoughts, visualizing the big stage and the big plays they're about to make. The lights come back on, Hayden Fry cuts loose with one more joke and a yalp, and the Hawkeyes catapult out of the locker room and onto the national and international stage.[2]

From the opening kick, all-out war ensues. Michigan's hallmark bend-but-don't-break defense continually befuddles Iowa's potent, lethal, and clock-eating offense led by the one-two punch of Chuck Long and running back Ronnie Harmon.

Iowa's defense warms to the task, keeping Michigan off balance with superb play of its own.

Jarring hits, missed opportunities, and the enormity of the outcome taxes and vexes fans, exhausts players, and frustrates coaches.

The night grows long.

As temperatures fall and blackness envelopes the stadium, Michigan wills its way to a 10–9 lead. A missed field goal by Iowa kicker Rob Houghtlin at the 7:33 mark of the fourth quarter adds to the misery of Iowa fans and the drama of the epic clash. The Hawkeyes' defense is called on yet again to rise to the challenge and send the Wolverines' offense to the sidelines.

---

[2] In addition to an announced attendance of 66,350, millions more, including members of the US armed forces, watched the game on television and heard the broadcast on Armed Forces Radio. A writer in the *Detroit Free Press* best described the wide interest in the game, calling it a "mid-season bowl game."

And it responds.

Iowa regains possession at its own twenty-two-yard line. Just 5:27 hangs on the clock.

With his team trailing by one point and the will of the Hawkeyes faithful pressing down from above, Chuck gathers himself under his trusted center, Mark Sindlinger. He exhales and makes time slow down. He scans the field from sideline to sideline. He looks at the clock and then forward, directly into the teeth of the nation's top-ranked defense.

Time to play ball for a quarterback who has made a career of reading defenses and then shredding them.

Undeterred by the pressure, drama, and ice-cold drizzle, the six-foot-four quarterback, possessing a quick-fire release and uncanny accuracy, marches Iowa a grueling sixty-six yards. Along the way, several third-down plays—all of them crucial—are converted.

Now, with the Hawkeyes stalled at Michigan's twelve-yard line and facing fourth down, Hayden Fry signals timeout. Without hesitation, he points in the direction of another Illinois product, placekicker Rob Houghtlin.

As sixty-six thousand-plus raucous fans rise to their feet, the sophomore takes his position just outside the nineteen-yard line. He bends down, places the tee on the right hash mark, and holds the pose for what seems an eternity.

Mentally, Rob is picturing the sequence of steps needed to successfully launch a twenty-nine-yard field goal into the fog-laden air and through the goalposts. And him into Hawkeye lore.

A whistle blows. The timeout ends. The game clock reads :02.

The Hawkeyes' play-by-play duo of always-animated Jim Zabel and his beloved color man, Eddie Podolak, peer down from their lofty perch. Both have persevered through losing seasons accompanied by all-out tail-kickings. Now they bask in the spoils of a nationally recognized football program. Both are hoarse and exhausted after three hours of air time. But they are ready to proclaim the outcome of one of the most significant calls in the history of Iowa athletics, whatever it might be.

Both teams, mentally and physically torched, crouch low in the trenches for one last play. Hawkeyes holder and backup quarterback Mark Vlasic kneels near the tee that Houghtlin has strategically positioned. He looks to the center, then to Houghtlin, then back to the center, then to Houghtlin, then to the center. He freezes briefly, then gives the signal.

The ball is snapped and placed on the tee with the precision of a laser-guided missile. Houghtlin goes in motion, his right foot connecting flush with the cold, wet pigskin. The football launches with conviction toward the goalposts standing tall behind the north end zone. Fans filling every nook of Kinnick hold their collective breath, craning their necks as their eyes trace the flight of the football the moment it's airborne.

Chuck doesn't turn his back on what is unfolding in front of him, nor does he close his eyes. He doesn't put his head in a towel or cross his arms or hang onto the shoulder of another player.

After throwing for nearly 270 yards on the afternoon and scrambling for his life more times than he can count, Chuck looks dead straight ahead with confidence. He knows Houghtlin will perform, just as he has so many times before during the season.

As a pair of zeroes appear on the scoreboard, the football disappeared into the raucous throng, and the lead changes for the fifth and final time.

Iowa 12. Michigan 10.[3]

Chuck Long raises his arms. So does Rob Houghtlin.

History made.

Pure bedlam.

And validation yet again for a quarterback who, before even taking one snap for the now-undisputed no. 1 team in the nation, was tabbed by his coach as "destined for greatness.

---

[3] Iowa ran eighty-four offensive plays to Michigan's forty-one. Chuck Long's 268 yards passing helped the Hawkeyes win the yardage battle by a remarkable 422–182. Iowa also dominated time of possession for 38:05 to Michigan's 21:55. One week later, when asked about the heartbreaking defeat, Jim Harbaugh said, "It felt like someone reached in and pulled everything out" when Houghtlin's field goal went through the uprights.

GOLDEN AGE OF BEING A HAWKEYE

"The name meant nothing to me," recalled longtime KCRG-TV (Cedar Rapids) sports director John Campbell when asked about the first time he heard that the Hawkeyes had landed Wheaton North High prep Chuck Long.

A native of Oskaloosa and graduate of DePauw University in Greencastle, Indiana, Campbell had returned to Iowa in 1979 to join the KCRG team after a stint at WBAY-TV in Green Bay, Wisconsin. His arrival coincided with the naming of Hayden Fry as head football coach of the Iowa Hawkeyes.

"There hadn't been much buzz around the Iowa football program for quite some time," Campbell said. "I remember walking into my first Iowa Hawkeyes football media day, looking around at the players and seeing just one or two NFL bodies…that was it. The cupboard was bare and I was shocked by that."

But change was afoot in Iowa City. "Obviously Hayden did a great job of building the program and did it very quickly by taking kids that didn't have a pro body and making solid college football players out of them."

When the Iowa football program announced that Chuck Long had accepted its scholarship offer: "All I thought was wanting to get good video of the kid," Campbell said. "So when he took the field for his first snap against Northwestern his freshman year, I began creating a file of video and finding out a little about him and his background.

"Of course, Coach Fry had that famous line about Chuck that he was 'destined for greatness,' and that changed everything. Hayden was the great psychologist, so if he said that, he was trying to make everyone believe that about Chuck. But who could argue? After all, Hayden saw him every day in practice and those of us in the media didn't, so folks decided to go with Hayden on that one."

Campbell, who retired from full-time sports reporting for KCRG in 2012, said he wasn't around Iowa City during the bleak years but sure heard about them.

"I followed the Hawkeyes while in Wisconsin. My mom would send me a copy of the Des Moines Register's 'Big Peach' or I'd go out and find a hill somewhere and listen to Jim Zabel on the replay."

Speaking of Zabel, Campbell's appreciation and admiration for the legendary voice of the Hawkeyes, who passed in 2013 at the age of ninety-one, never waned.

"Back in the day, he'd do a Hawkeyes basketball game one night and then a Cyclones basketball game the next, then Drake University and on and on. I'll always remember those Saturday nights in central Indiana because I'd do whatever I could to catch the AM signal so I could listen to Jim Zabel. He was the best at calling a game and had a profound impact on me, personally and professionally."

Charles Franklin "Chuck" Long Jr. was born Feb. 18, 1963, in Norman, Oklahoma, the first of three sons to parents Charlie and Joan Long.

The young family lived in a quaint neighborhood just down the street from the University of Oklahoma, where Charlie and Joan first met.

Charlie Long was a natural athlete. A native of Norman, he led his high school team to the state basketball title in 1956. As a college student, Charlie turned his attention to a career in journalism and public relations. After graduating, he went to work at the Norman Transcript, the hometown newspaper.

Admired by his peers and recognized for his love of people, Charlie Long bled Sooner red and followed Sooner football with an eagle eye. He possessed an infectious sense of humor, was always ready with a story, and was a good father. In time, these qualities would prompt his oldest son to play college football for a colorful and charismatic coach who exhibited many of the same characteristics.

Joan Long was also a native Oklahoman. After attending the prestigious Wellesley College in Massachusetts, she transferred to the University of Oklahoma, where she earned a degree in medical technology. She was an honor student at both schools.

Charlie and Joan married in 1961. Just two years later, they welcomed a baby boy into the world and named him Charles Franklin, or "Chuck" for short.

A little more than three years later, a second son, David, was born.

When Chuck was four, Charlie accepted a job with The Quill, a magazine for professional journalists in Chicago. The move to the Midwest came as a surprise to many, including Joan.

"Being from Norman, Charlie had lived around Sooner football his whole life and absolutely loved it and the community," she recalled. "I'm not sure whatever prompted him to move away. Then again, it was a good offer, so away we went."

The Chicago suburb of Wheaton was an ideal setting for the Longs, and the family quickly put down roots. When Chuck was eight, the couple's third son, Andy, arrived. Born with cerebral palsy, the good-spirited, kind-hearted, and energetic boy participated in every family activity and became one of the most popular and beloved residents of Wheaton.

"It was a happy, normal home with the boys always on the go," said Joan Long. "They were always busy and involved in all kinds of things."

But, she quickly added, never did she or Charlie place expectations on them.

"Charlie played all kinds of sports with the boys when they were growing up, but he never got on them. Instead, he was always teaching.

"And that was the thing about Charlie. He loved to teach. If the neighborhood kids were playing a game of baseball, there's a good chance he was right in the middle of it giving pointers on how to hit, run, field, and throw.

"Charlie loved being their teacher. But he enjoyed being a father more."

There was a playground near the Long family home, which suited Chuck perfectly. He was happiest when he was able to bounce something. Or hit something. Or throw something. Or jump over something. Anything that required energy, dexterity, and physical ability.

If a game was being played in the neighborhood, Chuck was there. If there wasn't a game being played, he organized one. If there was a team to be part of, he joined it. If there wasn't a game that caught his fancy, he invented one. He even laced up skates and learned to play ice hockey on a pond not far from the family's front door.

"It was a very normal life for the boys, and they loved it, just a lot of carefree days," Joan Long recalled fondly. "He was out playing something all the time. Didn't matter the day or the season. They would play football in the snow. And they nearly wore the tires off their bicycles. They rode them everywhere."

Not much for watching TV, Chuck would take to the phone to encourage his buddies to play some ball. His home away from home was the playground. By the time Chuck began grade school, little league baseball came calling.

"A lot of the neighbor friends played at that playground every day after school and throughout the summer," Joan Long said. "And wherever those kids were, there was Charlie. He would coach them on the empty lot, and the kids really took to it. Even when Chuck was in little league, he preferred playing with neighborhood friends and with his dad.

"He sure enjoyed that," she added, "although I'm pretty sure Charlie loved it even more."

He did, because Charlie Long was indeed a self-described "sports nut." Yet he never pushed sports on Chuck, saying that he wanted his son to "live his own life" and develop his own personal love for athletics.

Chuck's years at Hawthorne Elementary in Wheaton were equally all-American. He got good enough grades, caused only a bit of mischief from time to time (as most kids that age are prone to do), and continued to gravitate to all things sports.

"It didn't matter what it was," said Joan Long. "Baseball, football, hockey, basketball, whatever. If it bounced, rolled, moved, or could be hit or thrown, Chuck was right there in the middle of it. He just loved to play."

Hawthorne Elementary was also the place where Chuck met Lisa Wells.

Born in Oak Park, Illinois, Lisa and the Wells family moved to Wheaton when the little girl with the big smile and spunky personality was five.

Just like Chuck, the brown-haired, brown-eyed girl never sat still, preferring dance and cheerleading. Although they both knew of each other and their paths crossed on occasion, they didn't share a classroom until sixth grade. After that, they quickly became acquainted.

Chuck and Lisa shared a close group of friends throughout junior high, jamming to "We're an American Band" by Grand Funk Railroad, "Free Bird" by Lynyrd Skynyrd, and "Bad, Bad Leroy Brown" by Jim Croce while grabbing Slurpees at the 7-Eleven. If they weren't hanging out at nearby Kelly Park, they were at the movie theatre watching *Jaws, Grease,* and *Rocky.*

In August before their freshman high school year at Wheaton North, Lisa Wells and her best friend competed for a spot on the flag girl squad. While they were practicing their skills in the school parking lot, members of the Falcons' football team, including Chuck, were sweating through early-season drills not far away.

"Soon, just after football practice ends, here comes Chuck walking along with the varsity quarterback, Rick Johnson," Lisa Long recalled. "Chuck was just thrilled that he was carrying on a conversation with him. I mean, Chuck was riding a bicycle to and from school while Rick was driving a Corvette—big difference.

"Of course, all the guys stopped to look at the flag girls. That's when Rick asked who I was. Chuck's reply? 'Oh, that's Lisa Wells.' And before I knew it, he was trying to impress Rick by saying that he could introduce us. I couldn't believe it! Seriously? But that was Chuck being Chuck. To this day, he still denies it, no doubt just trying to save face. I mean, really, trying to pawn me off just to look cool?"

The ploy didn't work.

Rick Johnson was quickly a thing of the past. When Chuck and Lisa turned sixteen the summer before their junior year, they were a pair.

Their first "official" date was to a local restaurant where Chuck admittedly wore too much cologne in addition to a silk shirt with a too-large collar.

"Not sure about the cologne, but she really didn't like the seventies-style shirt," Chuck recalls to this day with a laugh.

Wheaton North High School fielded competitive football squads but struggled to stand out in a football-crazy Chicago metro that routinely birthed three-, four-, and five-star preps.

Perhaps that was because Falcons head coach Jim Rexilius preferred teaching the fundamentals and seeing his players execute them. He also favored quickness over bulk, "particularly if the kid has heart," he said.

While high-flying, pass-happy offenses were trending among high school programs, Rexilius wasn't a believer. Never one for following the herd, the hard-nosed, player-friendly coach preferred a punishing running game.

And, boy, the team could run, a fact not lost on Chuck Long.

After playing sophomore ball for the Falcons, the lanky seventeen-year-old junior stood an impressive six feet three inches and was quickly making a name for himself. A letter-winner in baseball and basketball, Chuck had turned his attention to football. Soon he found himself involved in a spirited battle for the Falcons' starting quarterback.

His competition: none other than the coach's son.

But it didn't last long. Chuck quickly earned the role of lead signal caller and, with expectations running high, led the Falcons onto the field for the 1979 season opener versus Forest View High.

The Falcons opened the scoring when Chuck hit receiver John Flaherty for a fifty-five-yard touchdown. Forest View answered with a punishing run game of its own to tie the game. Wheaton North edged into the lead again 13–7 courtesy of a touchdown run and missed extra point. But Forest View responded with a running touchdown followed by the all-important extra point to take a 14–13 lead.

The score held. And in his first start as a high school quarterback, Chuck Long was the losing quarterback.

Undeterred, Rexilius stuck with his starting signal caller and featuring the run. The Falcons won their next game. And the next. The team continued to run. And won again. And then ran more. In fact, most box scores found Chuck attempting less than five throws per contest. The formula worked. The Falcons won again. And again. And then again.

"And this went on and on, and they won all the rest of the games that year," Joan Long said. "I remember telling Charlie at one of those games, 'You know, Chuck looks pretty good out there.' And Charlie looked at me and said, 'He sure does.' It was just like that every game his junior season. The wins just kept coming."

To the surprise of the Falcons faithful, the greater Chicagoland sports press, and even the Long family, Chuck's junior year continued into the playoffs and eventually a berth in the state championship game versus LaSalle-Peru.

Despite being the underdog and a quarterback performance that, when the final horn sounded, read one of four passes for minus three yards, Wheaton North accomplished the unthinkable.

The Falcons capped a 12–1 season with a 14–6 victory over LaSalle-Peru and hoisted the 1979 4A Illinois state football championship trophy.

It was the school's first.

"I passed four or five times a game that season. Truth be told, my attempts my entire junior year were some quarterbacks' attempts for a game," Chuck recalled. "Did I want to throw the ball a lot more? Sure. But we ran the ball and played great defense. I learned a valuable lesson that year, and that was the concept of team; that it's not all about stats but about being part of a system and a group of guys that put what was best for the team ahead of any personal ambitions."

Chuck's junior season as a Wheaton Falcon was both surprising and unforgettable. And he was just getting started.

Winning a high school state football championship in 1979 was as unexpected as finding oceanfront property in Wheaton.

And just as memorable.

Chuck's senior season as starting quarterback of the Falcons was equally entertaining but also bittersweet.

The team rolled through the regular season and playoffs undefeated, earning a second consecutive trip to the 4A semifinals.

But the outcome was different. Rather than advancing to the championships, the Falcons were upended in the semifinals by DeKalb 12–6.

Season over.

Career over.

Yet Chuck made his starts count. In two seasons, Chuck lost just two games—his first and last start. Sandwiched in-between were twenty-three victories, two state football playoff berths, and a state championship.

In addition to his success on the football field, Chuck also lettered in basketball and baseball. He earned all-DuPage Valley Conference honors in basketball and baseball and was named to the all-state football team in 1980.

While Chuck handed the ball to a trio of talented Falcons running backs, just a handful of collegiate recruiting letters trickled in. No one was surprised that Chuck flew under the radar. Coach Rexilius wasn't much for passing, so few schools noticed the quarterback, including big-name programs. But a few letters did arrive from universities in need of a quarterback, including one from coach Bill Mallory at Northern Illinois and another from Northwestern Wildcats head coach Dennis Green.

Then a third appeared, postmarked "Iowa City." It featured the signature of a wily and charismatic coach. His name was Hayden Fry.

"They stepped off the plane, and their eyes got big as saucers. I tried to make the best of it. I told them, 'Hey, fellas, people spend thousands of dollars to come up here and learn how to ski.' But they didn't buy it. They got right back on the plane and went home to Texas."

Iowa coach Hayden Fry recalling his hopefulness that a half-dozen members of the North Texas State football team would follow him to Iowa upon his taking the Hawkeyes job. The new coach arrived in Iowa City on a cold-as-the-arctic day in December 1978. They were not impressed and returned to Texas. Hayden Fry stayed.

("Every day's Fry-day in Iowa to Hawkeye faithful," David Casstevens, Dallas Morning News, Dec. 21, 1981)

It was 1980, and Hayden Fry was in his second season at the helm of a beleaguered Iowa football program. He was committed to doing the unthinkable and what many fans and pundits considered impossible: restoring pride and respect in a program that had become the doormat of the Big Ten Conference.

How bad were the Hawkeyes?

When Hayden arrived in 1979 after six seasons as coach of North Texas University—a mid-major school located just north of Dallas-Fort Worth—

he inherited a program that hadn't seen a winning record in seventeen consecutive seasons. Mingled within that abysmal stat were three one-win seasons (1965, '67, and '71). The nearly two-decade losing streak also included an 0–11 campaign in 1973.

Iowa's last taste of success prior to Hayden Fry's arrival: a 38–12 victory over California in the 1959 Rose Bowl.

Fry's arrival in Iowa City brought renewed optimism. The energetic and enthusiastic son of a farmer was known for his winning pedigree, including the unconventional schemes he had perfected while coaching six-player football in the US Marines.

In six years at the helm of the North Texas Mean Green (the university adopted the name in recognition of their alum, four-time Super Bowl champ and Pittsburgh Steelers great Mean "Joe" Green), Hayden Fry compiled an impressive 40–23–3 record.

Prior to North Texas, he turned in an eleven-year run as head coach of the Southern Methodist University (SMU) Mustangs. While the results were mixed (forty-nine wins, sixty-six losses, and one tie), he led the team to three postseason berths, including a victory in the 1968 Astro-Bluebonnet Bowl.

Fry's decision to leave his beloved home state of Texas to take a job in Iowa City was born largely out of frustration. Unable to earn bowl bids at North Texas, Fry relished the chance to coach in a premier conference that could compete on the nation's biggest stage.

He also enjoyed challenges and taking chances.

While at SMU—and what he would one day reference as his greatest head coaching accomplishment—Hayden Fry was the first to offer an African American athlete a scholarship in the Southwest Conference.

The young man was Jerry LeVias.[4]

Acutely aware that the team hadn't had a winning season for quite a while, Hayden was intent on changing that. It was also important to Hayden that the team bring in the very best players it could.

The five-foot-nine, 160-pound LeVias was a gifted playmaker and could play multiple positions as a member of the SMU squad including running back, quarterback, wide receiver and punt and kick returner.

Most importantly, Hayden also recognized LeVias as a "great person."

"Jerry was unbelievable," Fry recalled years later. "To make a long story short, we won a Southwest Conference championship Jerry's sophomore year, and he was right up in the top ten, if not the top five, in the nation in pass receiving, number of passes caught, touchdowns, punt returns, and kick returns. And he was an all-American academically. You name it, Jerry achieved it."

Hayden Fry's moxie and judge of character and talent were indeed revolutionary. And they would transform the fortunes of a Hawkeyes program many had long written off as a perennial loser.

Oddly enough, Iowa City was an attractive destination for Hayden Fry. And the man offering him a job was Iowa's popular and highly respected athletic director, Bump Elliott. Not only was he a compelling personality, Elliott was also a fellow former US Marine.

Having arrived in 1970 after coaching ten years at the University of Michigan, Elliott quickly established a reputation for hiring good people and empowering them to develop and lead winning programs. Ironically, it was also Elliott who, as head coach of the Wolverines, handed Hayden Fry his first loss at SMU, a 27–16 defeat to open the 1963 college football season.

Elliott's respect in the fraternity of college athletics was well-deserved, and deep down, Hayden Fry relished the chance to come to Iowa City.

He got his wish.

---

[4] Hayden Fry called the recruitment of Jerry LeVias—even with the hate mail and threatening phone calls that accompanied it—a highlight of his successful and distinguished career. "It opened the door for all of the fine black athletes who had been leaving Texas and going to the Pacific Coast or the Big Ten or somewhere else where they could play," he said. LeVias graduated from Southern Methodist and quickly made his mark in the NFL, playing for the Houston Oilers and San Diego Chargers. He retired from the league after the 1974 season and began his professional career in energy and retail. He also served underprivileged children by helping them receive an education and job training in his hometown of Houston. Fry says he and LeVias have had "a wonderful relationship through the years, and we've been great friends. Jerry will always be an inspiration to me, and I hope I am to him, too."

In December 1978, Fry was named Iowa's twenty-fifth head football coach. In his first two seasons, he compiled a 9–13 record, including a respectable 8–8 in the Big Ten.

One of Fry's most redeeming qualities was his belief that football was a game to be enjoyed. So, when his coaching staff took the helm of a program, it was tasked with making the sport fun for players.

And his assistant coaches had to be the very best. Hayden's philosophy was you win when players believe in their coaches – when they trust the men who are holding the clipboards, devising the schemes, conjuring up game plans and encouraging them to perform at a high level.

"I never hired an assistant coach in my life unless I was completely convinced that he was motivated to be a head coach," Hayden mused. "Then I knew he would see his players graduate and stay out of trouble and do all those things that a head coach should do."[5]

The approach worked at SMU and North Texas. And, in just two years at Iowa, Hayden's winning recipe was manifesting itself in better play and more competitive games.

Many people noticed, including Chuck Long.

A believer in good coaching, Chuck relished the prospects of playing Big Ten football and benefiting from the talented staff Hayden was assembling.

Coaches will tell you the third year at any school is a pivotal one, and that was certainly true for Iowa. To take the next step, Fry had a three-point plan: hire great coaches, field a talented defense and solid special teams, and, above all, recruit an elite quarterback (or, as he called it, the "carburetor of the football machine").

With his first two losing seasons at Iowa and the 1981 campaign knocking on the door, Fry and his quarterback coach, Bill Snyder, needed to establish a tradition of winning. To make that happen, significant upgrades were needed,

---

[5] Hayden Fry's ability to hire quality assistant coaches became legendary. Twenty-nine assistants he hired while serving as head coach at SMU, North Texas, and Iowa became head coaches in either college or professional football. "My father had a lot of words of wisdom," Fry recalled. "When I was nine or ten years old, he told me, 'Son, I don't know what you're going to become or do when you grow up, but if you're going to be successful, if you're going to be a winner, you gotta surround yourself with winners.'" In 2015, two of the nation's top college football coaches—Oklahoma University's Bobby Stoops and the University of Iowa's Kirk Ferentz—were former assistant coaches of Fry's.

particularly on the offensive line. The improvements were necessary to plow wide holes in defensive fronts and keep the quarterback upright.

Fry needed a new O-line coach to get the job done, and to the surprise of many, he looked east to the Steel City for his guy.

It was 1980, and Kirk Ferentz was working as a graduate assistant offensive line coach at the University of Pittsburgh. It was a remarkable year for the Panthers. Coached by Jackie Sherrill and led by quarterback Dan Marino, the squad finished the season with an 11-1 record and no. 2 national ranking.

Not a bad place to be for the Royal Oak, Michigan, native who starred as a prep on the gridiron for Upper St. Clair High School near Pittsburgh before playing college football as a linebacker at the University of Connecticut. There he eventually become captain and earned all-academic honors while earning a degree in English Education.

After a two-year stint as an English literature instructor and defensive coordinator at Worcester Academy in Massachusetts, Ferentz returned to his home state and went to work for Coach Sherrill.

Pitt's offensive line, under the direction of coach Joe Moore, was the nation's premier unit. While Marino earned accolades, the O-line reveled in doing the dirty work. Led by all-American center Russ Grimm, the unit kept Marino upright while plowing big holes for running back (and eventual first-round NFL draft pick) Randy McMillan.

Fry liked what he saw in the graduate assistant and in the spring of 1981 placed a call to Ferentz inviting him to Iowa City to interview for the offensive line coaching job.

Ferentz was intrigued but figured it was only right to seek Joe Moore's blessing before making the 1,300-mile round trip to Iowa City. Just the thought of doing so, however, made him uneasy. Would Moore take his interest in applying for employment elsewhere as a sign of disrespect? Would looking for a job cost him the one he had?

Ferentz ultimately summoned the courage to speak with Joe. Sort of.

He raised the idea very cautiously; said he was thinking about the offensive line coach position that had been posted in Iowa City; that it would be a good opportunity for the right person; that maybe he should throw his name into the hat for consideration...

Moore stopped him cold.

"C'mon, Kirk. You're thinking about it?" he asked with more than a hint of sarcasm. "You're thinking about interviewing for that job? When I was your age, I would have crawled to an interview like that. And here you are telling me that you might apply? Who are you kidding?"

Such was Joe Moore—honest and to the point.

It was the sendoff Kirk Ferentz needed to interview with confidence.

Perhaps it was the ingenious O-line schemes run by Pitt. Or the 11–1 season the Panthers had just completed, punctuated with a 37–9 thumping of no. 18 South Carolina in the Gator Bowl. Or both.

Regardless, several films of the Pitt team in action had made their way to Iowa City long before Kirk Ferentz arrived in Cedar Rapids for the interview. The schemes that fueled the dominant Pitt Panthers team play ignited Hayden Fry's curiosity. It was an area Iowa needed to strengthen. Perhaps Kirk Ferentz was just the guy for the job.

Several days later, Ferentz met with Hayden Fry.[6] The conversation began with small talk—weather, family, and the latest football gossip. After that, Ferentz accompanied Fry to the staff room where he was put through a rigorous evaluation that included recognizing offensive and defensive sets, describing run and pass blocking schemes, and explaining teaching techniques.

Fry hit the ground running and never let off the gas throughout the conversation. The interview was thorough and tough. But the conversation was comfortable. Personalities clicked. No question went unasked or unanswered.

While Ferentz was being chauffeured back to Cedar Rapids for the flight home, Fry and quarterbacks coach Bill Snyder consulted. It didn't take them long to agree they had found their man. An untested and unproven graduate assistant from Pitt would soon be offered the position of Hawkeyes offensive line coach.

Soon after returning to Pittsburgh, Ferentz gave a full account to Joe Moore. When he finished describing the interview in detail, Moore didn't skip a beat. "Congratulations," he said. "You got the job."

Twenty-four hours earlier, a job Kirk Ferentz didn't care to get was now one he craved.

The very next day, Coach Fry called and offered him the position. Ferentz immediately accepted, telling Fry that he relished the opportunity and the challenge. [7]

Less than one month after the job was posted, the position was filled.[8] Kirk Ferentz dove head-first into the Hawkeyes playbook and began training men just a few years his junior on the fundamentals of offensive line play.

A BIG FAN

There are few people who speak more highly of Kirk Ferentz than Chuck Long.

---

[6] Kirk Ferentz recalls three interviews in his life. The first was with Hayden Fry. The second was with University of Maine athletic director Kevin White and the third with Bill Belichick of the New England Patriots. "With Bill, he just stoned you in an interview—no feedback, no response, nothing. I died a million deaths with him," Ferentz recalled. But Hayden Fry was different. "From the moment you met him, it was like you had known him for twenty years. It was like he was your uncle. He was just very comfortable." When Ferentz interviewed in 1981 for Iowa's offensive line coach, Fry met him wearing blue jeans and smacking bubble gum. "He asked during the interview how I was doing and what my momma thought about me interviewing for the position. And I was like, 'Coach, I'm twenty-five years old—I don't have to ask my mom.' You just had to control all the stuff he threw out at you, but it was a good interview, a lot of fun, and just one of those things that clicked from the very start."

[7] "It's amazing how quickly things can change," Ferentz recalled about his job interview. "Funny thing was that I was indifferent when I came to Iowa City for the interview. But at the end of the day, I had never wanted anything more than the chance to come and coach at Iowa. Fact is, Hayden was the only guy in America who would have interviewed me and given me a shot like that. But that was Coach Fry."

Both arrived in Iowa City in 1981, a commonality that fostered a kindred spirit between the offensive line coach and freshman quarterback that remains intact more than thirty-five years later.

"One of the things I tell people about my early years at Iowa was the great staff," Chuck said. "Just consider the coaches from the 1982–84 teams that have been or will be in the College Football Hall of Fame: Hayden Fry, Barry Alvarez, Bill Snyder, Bob Stoops, and Kirk Ferentz.

"When I was playing for the Detroit Lions, I was often asked what made Iowa such a successful football program and if there was one significant staff member," said Chuck. "And I would say, 'Yes, Kirk.' They asked why, and I said I believed that a team goes as far as its offensive line will take you. If you have a tough O-line, your team follows suit. There may be a rare occasion when that doesn't happen. But the hire of Kirk Ferentz was one of Iowa's most significant. Kirk changed the dynamic of our team by dramatically improving our offensive line play. And when that happened, we vaulted up the polls."

———————————

With lackluster interest from other major conference schools, Chuck eagerly traveled to Iowa City to join other recruits for a campus visit.

He found the facilities more than adequate and the location was nearly ideal, given the relatively short drive from Wheaton.

[8] Chuck Long said one of the best examples of the genius of Hayden Fry was his hire of Kirk Ferentz as offensive line coach. Many raised their eyebrows, said Chuck, given Ferentz's youth and inexperience, and no third-year coach would make such a long shot hire today. But Fry saw something in Ferentz, who was being tutored by renowned offensive line coach Joe Moore (1932–2003) at the University of Pittsburgh. Moore built the line that protected college football superstar Dan Marino and is considered to this day to be the best to ever coach the O-line in college. Ferentz served nine years as offensive line coach at Iowa and then took the head coaching position at the University of Maine. He coached for the Cleveland Browns and Baltimore Ravens before being named the University of Iowa's twenty-sixth head football coach in 1998.

But it was a conversation over dinner at a downtown Iowa City eatery that sealed the deal between the coach and recruit.

From the very start, the chemistry between Hayden Fry and Chuck Long was unmistakable.

Chuck swore Fry saw a lot of himself in the Wheaton North product. After all, Fry had been a seventh-string quarterback at Baylor and worked his way up to be one of the school's most prolific signal callers.

And Fry saw in Chuck a steady leader who had a spark and winning pedigree.

Joan Long also knew that Chuck was impressed.

"When he went to visit Iowa, he absolutely loved it," she said. "He decided right then and there that he wanted to play for the Hawkeyes."

The Iowa staff was equally high on Chuck and saw him as a decent fit for a program on the rise. Although Chuck ran multiple yet basic versions of the option for Wheaton North, Hayden Fry and Bill Snyder quickly learned that he was an outstanding leader who possessed a strong albeit raw arm.

It was a simple evaluation, Fry later admitted, one that included watching a few reels of game film and visiting with Chuck personally.

"He was so intelligent, so smart, and a real gentleman," Fry recalled. "A quarterback is the coach on the field, so when it comes to the guy calling the plays, you have to have a man that the other players highly respect and do what he says. I knew Chuck could be that quarterback."

Snyder also recognized Chuck's intangibles—qualities that don't show in the box score.

"He was a young guy who perfectly fit the principles and values of our program at Iowa, which centered around caring for and helping to guide young people to be successful in life," he said. "Chuck was intelligent and caring, he possessed tremendous poise, was a great teammate and leader, and set a wonderful example for everyone around him."

Ferentz, who was just getting settled in, was also impressed by the "skinny kid who at the time looked like he was about fifteen years old."

Chuck was sold. So were Charlie and Joan.

"Charlie loved Hayden Fry. He knew he was a good coach," Joan Long said. "Charlie completely forgot about the Sooners when Chuck became a Hawkeye. In fact, from the moment Chuck was recruited by Iowa, he wanted to move to Iowa City."

But not everyone shared Chuck's enthusiasm for becoming a Hawkeye.

"Chuck had some teachers tell him that he wouldn't play if he went to Iowa; that he would be nothing more than a bench warmer and a warm body on the practice field," said Joan Long. "But he dismissed that and paid no attention to it. He just moved on. He was good at that, too."

Chuck's high school counselor wasn't sold and tried to convince him not to go to the Big Ten, Chuck recalled.

"Told me more than once that I wouldn't make it. That was one of several times when I was reminded I was the underdog."

But being encouraged to set his sights on smaller schools was the fuel that lit Chuck's fire to be a Big Ten starting quarterback. It was the edge he was looking for and an early lesson about the importance of perseverance; of doing something that others said couldn't be done; of taking the road less traveled to realize a dream; of going all in when others encouraged a safer, more secure route.

Despite the doubters, Chuck was convinced he would succeed.[9]

The learning curve, however, would be steep.

Sept. 21, 1981

Dear Charles and Joan:

All of the coaches and players sincerely appreciate your nice note of congratulations on the win over Nebraska. Chuck is a winner, and we are

extremely pleased with the progress he has made this fall. The future looks very
bright for him academically and athletically. Hope to see you the next time you
come to town. Best personal regards to you and your fine family.

Sincerely,

Hayden Fry

Head Football Coach

The University of Iowa

Hawkeyes fans were optimistic that the 1981 football campaign would represent a much-needed turning point for a program plagued by two decades of losing.

A 41–0 trouncing of Michigan State to punctuate a 4–7 1980 season offered tangible hope. So, too, did a relatively deep unit that included several talented recruits, chief among them a blond, curly-haired quarterback from Wheaton, Illinois.

Yet no one could have predicted the shot across the college football bow that would take place in the 1981 season opener for Iowa—a clash with the mighty Nebraska Cornhuskers in Kinnick in front of more than sixty thousand fans.

The Cornhuskers, led by stoic head coach Tom Osborne, were a confident bunch coming off a 10–2 1980 season that included a 57–0 thrashing of Iowa in Lincoln and a 31–17 win over Mississippi State in the Sun Bowl. They entered the game ranked no. 7 nationally and were legit championship contenders.

But on this day, Sept. 12, 1981, Iowa's offense, with just twenty-eight yards passing, managed to claw out enough points thanks to a salty defense that contained an explosive Nebraska offense led by Davenport

---

[9] Chuck asked for no. 12—the number he wore at Wheaton North—when he arrived at Iowa. "I'll always remember Ron Fairchild, the equipment manager for the Hawkeyes, when I told him I wanted [it]," he recalled. "He just looked at me, paused for a second, and responded deadpan, 'Number twelve is taken. Quarterback Pete Gales has it. You'll get sixteen.' I wore number sixteen my entire career at Iowa and for the Detroit Lions, too, so that ended up being a good call by Ron."

(Iowa) Central High's Roger Craig and all-American-to-be running back Mike Rozier.

When a furious flurry of fourth-quarter drives deep into Iowa territory by the Cornhuskers was turned away—thanks in large part to Nebraska's fifth turnover of the day with just 2:51 remaining—and the final horn sounded, the black and gold celebrated the most unlikely of victories and one of the most celebrated in the school's history: a 10–7 win over one of the nation's most elite and prestigious college football programs.[10]

And in the process, Iowa said "hello" to college football relevance.

But the young Hawkeyes squad had a lot to learn.

So did Chuck, who watched the herculean effort by Iowa unfold from the sidelines.

"He's as fundamentally sound as any freshman quarterback I've ever been associated with," Hayden Fry said in an interview with the *Iowa City Press-Citizen*. "For a freshman, he makes me smile all over."

High praise indeed for a quarterback who was sixth on the Iowa quarterback depth chart behind starter Peter Gales, backup Gordy Bohannon, and reserves Tom Grogan, Denny Klaperich, and Dave Chambers.

After the stunning victory over Nebraska, Iowa traveled to Ames to face the Iowa State Cyclones. Coached by Donnie Duncan, the Cyclones were striving to regain their winning ways. Following back-to-back 8–4 seasons in 1977–78, they had struggled to a 3–8 campaign in 1979 and rebounded to finish 6–5 in 1980.

Iowa State opened the 1981 season at home with a 17–13 nonconference victory over West Texas A&M. One week later, a confident Hawkeyes squad arrived in Ames. Sixty minutes of football later, Iowa was on the wrong side of a 23–12 score and for the second consecutive year did not lay a hand on the Cy-Hawk Trophy. The coveted piece of hardware stayed in Ames.

---

[10] Nebraska finished the 1981 regular season 9–2, earning a berth in the Jan. 1, 1982, Orange Bowl. They lost to no. 1-ranked Clemson 22–15. Running back Mike Rozier played two more seasons at Nebraska, earning all-American honors in '82 and '83.

The seesaw season was just getting started.

The following week and for the second time in their first three contests, Iowa hosted a top ten team when UCLA came to Iowa City. A 20–7 win over the no. 6 Bruins on Sept. 16 earned the Hawkeyes a no. 18 national ranking.

The following week, Iowa traveled to Evanston, Illinois, where they trounced coach Dennis Green's Northwestern Wildcats 67–0.[11] Chuck saw his first playing time of the season, completing his only pass attempt for fourteen yards. That pasting was followed by wins against Indiana in Iowa City and an impressive 9–7 defeat of no. 5 Michigan in Ann Arbor thanks to three field goals off the foot of kicker Tom Nichol.

With its win over the Wolverines—its first since 1962—Iowa zipped to no. 6 in the polls. Next up was a home date versus Minnesota.

The high-flying Hawkeyes were quickly grounded. The Golden Gophers dealt the Hawkeyes a crushing defeat of 12–10, returning to Minneapolis in possession of the coveted Floyd of Rosedale trophy.[12]

One week later, Iowa was handed its third defeat of the season, a 24–7 setback on the road versus Illinois (the Fighting Illini were a scrappy squad that would ultimately finish 7–4, good for a three-way tie for third place in the Big Ten Conference).

---

[11] Iowa's matchup versus Northwestern was the first time Chuck returned to his home state of Illinois as a college quarterback. The Wildcats were coached by Dennis Green and played located in Dyche Stadium just thirty-eight miles from Wheaton North. The home turf turned into a house of horrors for Northwestern as Iowa thumped the Wildcats 67–0. Green, who was just one of three coaches to have recruited Chuck, penned this letter to Joan and Charlie Long following the defeat (dated Oct. 13, 1981):

Dear Joan and Charles Long:

As you know, we are extremely excited about Chuck, and we really feel that he's going to be a tremendous quarterback. His performance in our game last week against Iowa has proven that to be the case. I hope that everything is going well for him there. I'm sure it is, because Iowa is a fantastic university. We at Northwestern have a long road to success, but I feel the road is worth traveling. Thanking you again, and tell Chuck that I wish him the best.

Sincerely,

Dennis Green
Head Football Coach
Northwestern

Green was a respected and well-liked coach who was hired by Northwestern in 1981 as only the second African American head coach in Division I-A history. The Wildcats finished 0–11 in Green's first season. He coached five seasons at Northwestern—the same five years that Chuck Long played quarterback at Iowa—compiling a 10–45 record (7–37 in the Big Ten). After a three-year hiatus from coaching following the 1985 season, Green coached the Stanford Cardinals for three seasons before embarking on a successful thirteen-year NFL head coaching career.

That loss didn't sit well with Hayden Fry and the boys, who stood 5–3 overall and 3–2 in the Big Ten with just three regular season games remaining.

Rather than default to its losing ways, a determined Hawkeyes football team featuring a balanced attack on both sides of the ball righted the ship. The team ended the regular season with three lopsided wins, defeating Purdue, Wisconsin, and Michigan State by a combined score of 86–21.

And in the season finale versus the Spartans—a 36–7 thumping in Kinnick—the Hawkeyes earned the ultimate prize and an unthinkable achievement prior to the season's kick. The win over Michigan State, coupled with a stunning victory by Ohio State over Michigan, sent roses raining onto the Kinnick turf. Iowa had earned a trip to Pasadena to take on the high-powered Washington Huskies Jan. 1 in the sixty-eighth playing of the Rose Bowl. [13]

On Nov. 24, just three days after their regular season finale, offensive coordinator Bill Snyder wrote Charlie and Joan Long:

Now that our regular football season has concluded, I want to let you know again how much we appreciate Chuck and all that he has contributed to the resurgence of the football program here at the University of Iowa.

I know that his preparation for the Rose Bowl will carry the same dedication it has throughout the year. He has worked hard, always done his very best, and has proven to be a quality young man both on and off the field.

We are very proud of him and his achievements, and we thank you for allowing him to be a part of our program.

With warm personal regards,

Bill Snyder

---

[12] Floyd of Rosedale is a bronze trophy in the shape of a pig awarded to the winner of the Iowa-Minnesota football game. It was introduced in 1935 when the governors of both states agreed that the winner would receive a prize hog from the losing governor's home state. Following a hard-fought 13–6 victory in the inaugural "trophy" game, the Gophers were presented an Iowa hog from Rosedale Farms. One year later, a bronze version of the swine was created after it was decided that trading a live pig back and forth was not very practical.

[13] Iowa and Ohio State finished tied for the 1981 Big Ten regular season title. Given that they did not play each other in the regular season, Iowa was awarded the Rose Bowl berth since Ohio State had most recently appeared in "the granddaddy of them all."

Unfortunately for the Hawkeyes, the team's third appearance in "the granddaddy of them all" (and their first since 1959) was a forgettable one.

Iowa's offense tallied just 264 yards of offense—including eleven rushing yards by Chuck Long on two attempts—but was unable to land a scoring punch. And its defense, one of the Big Ten's best, was befuddled. Led by freshman Jacque Robinson's 142 rushing yards and another 142 yards passing by quarterback Steve Pelluer, Washington dominated Iowa, winning 28–0.

Ironically, and unbeknownst to the Hawkeyes faithful who dejectedly exited the Rose Bowl in the fading twilight of the New Year's Day defeat, the lopsided affair would one day be part of an NCAA record for most bowl game appearances by a college quarterback.

It would also ignite a fire within that same college quarterback to do whatever it took to return the Iowa Hawkeyes to Pasadena, even if it meant wearing the Hawkeyes uniform for more than four years.

Even before the Hawkeyes took the field versus Washington in the 1982 Rose Bowl, sports writers and fans were looking ahead to the team's prospects for the next season.

"The Hawkeyes face a rebuilding task in 1982: a huge chunk of that defense will be gone, and several key spots on offense will be vacated after this season," wrote *Quad City Times* sports editor Gary Richards. "But the future isn't exactly bleak. Chuck Long and [wide receiver] Dave Moritz are two insurance policies against Iowa folding in '82."

With the departure of senior quarterbacks Pete Gales and Gordy Bohannon, a contest for the starting spot was in the works between Chuck Long and Tom Grogan.

If there was a favorite, it wasn't hard to tell.

"Chuck's among the best five high school quarterbacks in the country," the coach proclaimed to anyone who would listen.

Asked for a reply, Chuck said tepidly, "I don't know about that."[14]

Sports reporters were split on their opinion of Iowa's long-term offensive prospects.

"Unless a junior college quarterback is recruited, Long looms as the favorite to win the No. 1 job in the spring," Richards penned. "Tom Grogan, now the third-team signal caller, appears the man to beat out, but Long has the credentials to do just that."

Al Grady, sportswriter for the hometown *Iowa City Press-Citizen,* was less optimistic and hinted at additional competition for the team's top signal caller.

"The quarterback spot is obviously a question mark and wide open at this time," Grady opined in a Nov. 25, 1981, column. "Chuck Long, a freshman this year, may be the heir-apparent, but Tom Grogan will argue that point and so may Dennis Klapperich.

"Fry says he definitely hopes to recruit a top-notch junior college quarterback who can both run and throw and also will be looking for an outstanding high school prospect. At any rate, Iowa is going to start with an inexperienced quarterback and that is not good news."

Sports pundits also predicted that, depending on his personnel at quarterback, Hayden Fry would expand the offensive playbook given the loss of defensive personnel. To make that happen, he would need to add firepower at quarterback.

There were quiet doubts within the Iowa football coaching ranks about the solidity of the QB position. Not surprisingly, some of the apprehension included Chuck's ability to lead a Big Ten football program as an inexperienced sophomore-to-be.

That was particularly true for Bill Snyder, who had accompanied Hayden Fry to Iowa in 1979 after three years as his assistant at North Texas State. Now serving as Fry's offensive coordinator and trusted advisor, Snyder

---

[14] Iowa's 8–4 record for the 1981 season and a berth in the 1982 Rose Bowl brought high expectations for the 1982 campaign. "It was a powerful motivator," Chuck recalled. "I was going to work hard during the off season and do everything I could to be the team's starting quarterback. I didn't want to let Hayden Fry down for the faith he had placed in me."

encouraged his boss to go after a junior college quarterback to bridge the inexperience gap.

Outwardly, Chuck took the high road: "I think we'll have a good recruiting year," he told reporters when asked about Iowa's quarterback depth—or lack of. "I'll be working hard for the next season because this season was basically a learning year for me. I should know the offense pretty well, and I'll give it my best shot next spring."

But inside, Chuck's psyche was churning.

Snyder, a respected offensive mind, was a well-known proponent of junior college recruiting. It was also becoming obvious that the coaches, despite their glowing endorsements, did not believe Chuck was the near-term answer. College football is much more sophisticated than high school, making the learning curve tougher to grasp, not to mention the need to earn the respect of teammates.

For that reason, Fry and Snyder nabbed two highly regarded quarterback recruits, Cornelius Robertson and Mark Vlasic.

Robertson was a much-heralded product from Compton, California, with the tools and experience to step in and immediately fill the shoes of Bohannon and Gales. The physically gifted athlete completed 329 of 629 (52 percent) for 4,898 yards at Compton, including an impressive average of fifteen yards per completion.

Pennsylvania native Mark Vlasic was a high school football standout with equally strong credentials. The six-foot-three multisport star passed for more than 1,200 yards during his final two years at Pennsylvania's Center High and was the prototypical pocket passer whose game was ideally suited for Big Ten play.

"I was a skinny kid with a weak arm fighting through my freshman year just trying to grasp the system," Chuck recalled. "Here I was going from throwing five to six times a game in high school to trying to understand a collegiate passing game. I was struggling to catch up to the pace of the college game. Naturally, one would have some doubts about what the future holds."

But that would soon change in the warm embrace of the California sun.

CHAPTER 2

Destined for Greatness

"He's looking great. He should've started last year."

GORDY BOHANNON,
Iowa's starting quarterback most of the 1981 season,
when asked to analyze the play of Chuck Long
in the team's first spring 1982 scrimmage
(Cedar Rapids Gazette, *April 25, 1982*)

Monday, April 12, 1982
Hawkeyes football press conference
Iowa City

"I don't believe I have ever seen a performance like the one Chuck Long showed us Saturday in his initial outing," exclaimed a beaming Hayden Fry to a room packed to the rafters with sports reporters.

"I am amazed at how the young man ran the offense—not only in the sharpness of his passing, but in the poise he showed while he was being battered, his command of the field in his running, his presence in the huddle. It was simply an exceptional performance."

Sincere and objective scouting or wishful thinking? No one knew for sure with just one month remaining before Iowa's spring, intra-squad football game and four months until the start of running another Big Ten Conference gauntlet.

Chuck's line in the team's first spring scrimmage was borderline perfection: fifteen completions on sixteen attempts for 171 yards.

"I felt really excited about it," Chuck said when asked to summarize his performance. "I surprised myself. Of course, I had some help. The receivers were open and the line did a real fine job for the first scrimmage. In high school, we didn't throw that much. I threw more in scrimmage last Saturday than in any game in high school. That was fun."

With the search underway for a new Hawkeyes signal caller, the speed of Chuck's maturation as a college football player couldn't have been better timed—or more unexpected. This was, after all, the same Chuck Long who had completed just one pass—on one attempt versus Northwestern—the previous year while spending the majority of the season mired sixth on Iowa's quarterback depth chart.

Succeeding as a college football player wasn't an option for Chuck. He was committed to making the most of the opportunity he had been given, due in part to the financial boost a scholarship could bring. It was this dedication that drove Chuck to endure and even excel as a member of Iowa's scout team his freshman year.

Often the unsung heroes of any successful team, scout teams are comprised of practice squad players that emulate the play style of opposing teams. In doing so, the rest of the team can anticipate the opponents' play calls and defense, thus being better prepared for game-time action.

As famed NFL Green Bay Packers coach Vince Lombardi often said, "Practice does not make perfect. Only perfect practice makes perfect." Solid scout teams help make perfect practice, and the results show up on game day.

Chuck's reps on the scout team were a painful but valuable experience. The extra snaps, licks, bruises and throws would prove invaluable. And nowhere was this truer than during the two weeks of practice in Pasadena leading up to Iowa's 1982 Rose Bowl matchup against Washington.

Although it was grueling, Chuck would admit many years later that it was on the practice field in Pasadena where the college game of football began to click. Chuck's confidence rose with the experience, and it showed, with his performance continually improving when facing off against Iowa's first team defense.

The maturation and improvement wasn't lost on Lon Olejniczak, a Decorah native and Hawkeyes junior letterman who played receiver and punt returner.

"You've been tearing it up out here," he confided to the freshman QB at the conclusion of another grueling session under the warm Pasadena sun. "Who knows, you may actually have a future here at Iowa."

But just several weeks removed from the Rose Bowl, Iowa signed flashy junior college quarterback Cornelius Robertson.[1]

"We never recruit a junior college player unless we have a desperate need," Hayden Fry said when asked to explain the team's interest in the transfer.

The Compton Community College product was California's top-ranked junior college quarterback. The lightning-quick human highlight reel had completed an astounding 329 of 629 passes for almost five thousand yards during his time at Compton. His impressive resume wasn't lost on Hawkeyes fans, who figured that the heralded JC transfer would pick right up where Bohannon and Gales left off.

The move didn't shock Chuck. But it did pinch his psyche. The message sent by Fry and Snyder was that they didn't believe Chuck was the quarterback answer for the next two years, prompting them to travel 3,600 miles round trip to lure Robertson to the Hawkeye State.

And as if one quarterback recruit wasn't enough, Fry also nabbed Pennsylvania prep Mark Vlasic of Center High School in Center Township. The broad-shouldered quarterback was a prototypical pocket passer, strong on his feet and wielding a cannon for an arm. In other words, Vlasic was the perfect weapon for rugged Big Ten play and a near mirror image of Chuck.

News about Robertson and Vlasic caused a stir on campus and throughout the Hawkeyes football fan base. The program was trending upward, and the once-apathetic fans now craved more wins, more Big Ten championships, and more trips to Pasadena.

---

[1] Chuck wasn't thrilled when he picked up the morning newspaper on a cold January day in Iowa City and read that Cornelius Robertson was on his way to Iowa. "They really built him up," he confided to Bob Pille of the *Chicago Sun Times* in a Sept. 1, 1982, interview. "Passed for the junior college record of five thousand yards or something at the time. You hear about these California quarterbacks—that's where all the quarterbacks come from—and I was a little worried to read all about this junior college transfer coming in."

For Chuck, the arrival of Robertson added fuel to his motivational fire. He intended to be Iowa's starting quarterback. So while others went to downtown Iowa City to partake of the nightlife, Chuck set about improving his craft, working on throwing mechanics and spending extra time in the gym. His regimen included lengthy sessions jumping ropes, lifting weights, and running. He was also a frequent visitor to the Iowa fieldhouse where he immersed himself in studying game film to better understand defensive tendencies and Iowa's passing scheme.

By the time April arrived and spring was in full bloom—and for the first time since arriving in Iowa City—Chuck's personal doubts about his ability to lead the Iowa football program were superseded by a humble and quiet confidence, a byproduct of hard work, preparation, and advice from his parents to focus on getting a little bit better every day.

On April 21, 1982, Hayden Fry gave notice that Chuck was leading the pack in the quest to be Iowa's starting quarterback.

No one was more surprised than Chuck, even with a top-notch early-spring team scrimmage where he completed fifteen of sixteen passes for 171 yards on a cool, blustery day in Iowa City.

He had anticipated an all-out battle for quarterback. With Fry's early announcement, Chuck's focus on winning the starting job intensified. He also put pressure on himself to perform at a higher level.

"The offense is going to have to carry a bigger share this fall than it did last year," said Chuck, referencing the success of a defensive unit that had propelled the team to its Rose Bowl appearance. "If I'm under center, you'll see a lot more drop-back action, maybe some more shotgun. I like to run the shotgun. It gives me more time to set up and look at things. But if the passing isn't there, I'll run. I've always liked to run. I'll pull it down if I have to."

A couple of weeks later, Hayden Fry announced that Chuck would indeed be the starter when the season kicked. Chuck validated his coach's decision with a "sparkling performance" (Fry's words) during a two-hour scrimmage. He completed twenty-five of thirty-one passes for 357 yards and two touchdowns while rushing for twenty-seven yards on eight carries, including a nine-yard touchdown scamper.

Game on.

———————

With Robertson nursing a knee injury sustained during spring practice, Chuck's steady approach under center quickly became a calming force for a team on the cusp of cementing a winning brand.

Despite his youthful appearance and stature, Chuck had hit on an electric 78 percent of his pass attempts (sixty-three of eighty-one) during spring ball while demonstrating a cool command of the offense. He also displayed an adeptness at reading defensive pass coverages and taking charge in the huddle.

Outwardly, Fry did his best to manage expectations and throw off the scent of the opposition by fretting over the team's inexperience, particularly at quarterback.

"I told someone if we could get our schedule changed where we could play against our number two and number three defenses, I'd say he [Long] could be a pretty good quarterback," Fry told reporters. "That's all we have to base Chuck on right now, and I don't know how good of a barometer it is of his ability."

Perhaps that stoic assessment was revised just a few days later when, in the team's final spring scrimmage, Chuck completed ten of sixteen passes for ninety-seven yards while guiding the first-team blacks to a dominating 38–10 victory over the reserve whites in front of a sun-drenched Kinnick crowd of 21,500. In the mix was an eleven-yard touchdown strike to tight end Mike Hufford.

"I was a little nervous at the start, knowing all those fans were watching me," Chuck admitted when asked about his comfort level as Iowa's new starting quarterback. "It was good, sound football, and we played good ball control football. But I know things will be different this fall when we have to open things up and there are a few more fans in the stands."

Hayden Fry could find few negatives in his postgame assessment of a busy spring that concluded with twenty allotted practices.

"Long has improved his knowledge of the game and has made very few mistakes" he said. "The highlight of practice has been Chuck."

Sports writers were busy pecking away at their typewriters, composing their annual spring assessments of the team and predictions for the season. Much of the ink they devoted to the Hawkeyes had something to do with the team's untested sophomore-to-be quarterback.

Among them was veteran sports writer Al Grady. The columnist had followed the hometown team for nearly thirty years for the *Iowa City Press-Citizen*. Like Hayden Fry, Grady was sold on Chuck's ability to lead the team.

"Chuck Long does, indeed, look like a good quarterback," he wrote in his spring game recap on May 4, 1982. "He handles himself well from a technical standpoint. His handoffs are good and so are his fakes. He's not afraid to run the football. He seems to know when to throw the football and when not to. He seems very willing to eat the football and take a loss, if necessary, rather than risk an interception. He throws a very catchable ball, and almost every pass he's thrown all spring has been on target."

However, Grady added that it was both "very difficult and very unfortunate" to have to open the fall campaign with an untested quarterback, especially in Lincoln versus the Nebraska Cornhuskers.

"And that's what Iowa must do, whether the quarterback is Chuck Long or Tom Grogan or someone else," Grady wrote. "What you would like is a confidence builder. Nebraska can be a confidence crusher, and we can only hope for the best in that department.

"I think the most realistic expectation of the fans for the 1982 football team would be that it can have a winning season for the second year in a row and establish a strong foundation for 1983 and 1984," Grady added.[2]

Despite the crowded field of quarterback suitors taking snaps in spring ball, Chuck indeed stood out from the crowd, throwing for nearly one thousand yards while completing 78 percent of his pass attempts.

Truth be told, Chuck had serious doubts when spring practice opened whether he had what it took to be a Big Ten quarterback. Unfamiliar situations can quickly overwhelm the psyche of the inexperienced. It's often what you don't know that can cause anxiety and frustration, and that certainly was true for Chuck.

These feelings eased with a taste of success in practices and scrimmages. But the confidence came with an asterisk: every completed throw and yard gained were against Iowa reserves.

No one knew that better than Chuck Long and Hayden Fry. But as sure as Iowa can grow soybeans and corn, Fry and quarterback coach Bill Snyder had a knack for developing young men into talented Division I football players.

Would Chuck Long be one of them?

Hayden Fry sure seemed to think so.

———————————

"A lot of athletes don't know how to win. I look upon coaching just like it's an accelerated course in calculus or physics. You have to teach a football team the characteristics of winning. You can go back to George

---

[2] Al Grady, respected sportswriter and Hawkeyes enthusiast, passed Dec. 15, 2003, at the age of seventy-six. A native of Kalona, Iowa, he was both a fan and a critic of the Iowa Hawkeyes for more than a half century. He began writing about Hawkeyes athletics in 1944, working as sports editor and sports columnist for the *Press-Citizen* from 1951 to 1987. He spent fifteen years in semiretirement, writing a column for the Voice of the Hawkeyes magazine, several books about Iowa athletics, attended virtually all the weekly press conferences for football and men's basketball, and hosted a weekly television show called Sports Opinion that aired on Iowa City's public access channel. Grady received numerous offers while writing for the *Press-Citizen*. He declined them all, citing the Hawkeyes beat as his "dream job."

Washington or Abraham Lincoln or Winston Churchill
and move right on up to Arnold Palmer and Jack
Nicklaus. There are basic qualities that each
winner has."

HAYDEN FRY
("1982 another success for Fry psychology,"
Buck Turnbull, Des Moines Register, *Dec. 19, 1982)*

As the days in America's heartland grew shorter and with another
harvest season knocking on the door, the leader of Iowa's football program
was brimming with confidence as he groomed his group of young men to
be winners.

Chuck Long was his special project.

"He's a unique guy for not having played," said Fry when he greeted
the press on August 17, just weeks before Iowa's 1982 season opener
versus the Nebraska Cornhuskers. "He's had as fine a spring as any
freshman I've ever seen. Yet it's just really hard to evaluate Chuck because
he's only gone against our number two or three defenses. A lot of passers
look pretty good in pregame warm-ups, but when the bullets start flying
they don't throw too well.

"But I don't think Chuck's that kind of guy. I think Chuck is for real."

And then, without skipping a beat, he voiced a one-sentence
Constitution that would ignite a new generation of Hawkeyes success.

"I just believe he's one of those people destined for greatness."

Destined for greatness? Chuck Long, the lanky, curly blond-haired
sophomore-to-be quarterback who had yet to start a college football game?
The kid who hadn't notched one accomplishment as a Hawkeye to earn his
"three hots and a cot"?

The proclamation surprised almost everyone, including Chuck.

"I think he's exaggerating," he calmly replied when asked by sports
writers to comment on Fry's lofty prediction. "I haven't stepped on the field
yet. I have a lot to prove. The entire offense has a lot to prove."

Despite Chuck's efforts to deflect the "destined for greatness" tag, it did little to throw off the scent of inquiring reporters who weren't bashful about sharing their opinions.

"Chuck Long may be great someday, but few quarterbacks are great as sophomores," wrote Gary Richards of the *Quad City Times.*

However, a *Cedar Rapids Gazette* headline sang the QB's praises: "Fry says he's 'destined for greatness'—This Hawkeye quarterback has come a 'long' way fast."

Veteran *Gazette* sports reporter Don Doxsie took note of Chuck's quick ascent to the starting job, given that the Wheaton North prep "didn't exactly fill the air with passes.

"He has come a long (pardon the pun) way in the past year," he wrote. "At the Hawkeyes' 1981 preseason press day, he was an obscure freshman who sat in the bleachers and watched as the media hounds sniffed around his older teammates.

"At Monday's 1982 media day, it was Long who was one of the main attractions as dozens of reporters clamored around him."

The media's rhetorical carousel wouldn't end any time soon because Hayden Fry wasn't about to renege on his prediction with the season opener at no. 3 Nebraska just three weeks away.

"He acts like he's played first team all along. He's had as fine a spring training as any quarterback I've ever seen. He has great poise, ability, good selection on reading defenses, and uncanny accuracy. He's just a unique guy for not having played. He's one of those unusual people who's destined for greatness."

Hype? Hope? Honesty? No one knew for sure.

Glowing endorsements aside, the coach didn't mince words about which side of the ball he expected to carry the team, at least in the season's early going. He thought the team could contend, but only if the defense played to its potential.

"We always are a good defensive team. That's my trademark," he said. "Everybody thinks of me as a flamboyant coach who likes to throw the ball.

Well, I've always said you win first with defense, then great kicking.[3] That's been true since the time of Knute Rockne and Pop Warner. And the third way you win is by running the ball on offense, not passing it."

If those words made Chuck wince, no one was the wiser.

"Coach Fry talks a lot," he said. "He can exaggerate things. I haven't stepped on the field yet. I haven't proven myself.

"I'm trying to keep the pressure off now so that I can prepare for the first game as much as I can. I have confidence in myself and confidence in the team. I treat it [the starting role] as a challenge. I just want the team and the fans to have confidence in me."

In less than one month, that confidence would be shaken to the core by two teams clad in red.

Hayden Fry was a farm boy at heart, so he knew and respected the inner strength that came from working hard and sweating even harder.

His roots were planted in the rust-colored West Texas soil. He was raised on a farm, and both his mother (one of seven siblings) and father came from farming backgrounds. His grandpa served as a Texas Ranger who, when off duty, set out into the countryside to lasso wild horses, selling them for $5 each.[4]

As a US Marine, Hayden Fry had also learned the importance of not settling for anything less than 110 percent.

These qualities, combined with natural charisma, a psychology degree, and a knack for knowing the Xs and Os of football, made him an astute judge of character and football IQ.

---

[3] Waterloo, Iowa, native Reggie Roby played for the Hawkeyes from 1979 to 1982. Despite his strong arm and experience as a quarterback, Hayden Fry converted him into a punter and kicker. As a senior, Roby led the nation in punting with a 48.1-yard average. His 45.4-yard career average as a Hawkeye remains a school record and one of college football's best. He went on to have a successful sixteen-year pro career, often wearing a watch during kicks to gauge their hang time. A father of six, Reggie passed Feb. 22, 2005, of a heart attack. He was just forty-three.

[4] The Texas Rangers were founded in 1823 by Stephen F. Austin. The agency originally employed ten men who served as rangers to protect more than six hundred newly settled families who had arrived in Texas following the Mexican War of Independence. Placed under financial constraints by the Great Depression, the agency underwent several reorganizations, including a merger with the Texas Highway Patrol in 1935. Today, the Texas Rangers are protected from being disbanded by statute.

And everything he knew to be true about winning football made him a big fan of his newly named starting quarterback. Chuck exhibited an inner strength and excelled in every respect on a checklist of attributes that mattered to the coach, from his professional association with teammates and getting good grades to having athletic ability and a great personality. Chuck was also a great listener and applied what the coaches taught on the sidelines to his performance on the practice field.

"Chuck Long's not only a great football player but a great human being," Hayden Fry said. "He's going to do great things as a Hawkeye."

FARMING: IOWA FOOTBALL'S BREAD AND BUTTER

If you're a University of Iowa football player or coach, you'd better appreciate agriculture.

"It was one of the first things Hayden told us," said Chuck. "I remember him telling me, 'Charlie, to get in good with Iowa you have to get in good with the farmers first. They are the backbone of the state. If they love you, everybody else will.'"

That's one reason why so many people loved Hayden, Chuck said.

"His appreciation of farmers was genuine, and he always wore it on his sleeve. He truly loved the farm community.

"Hayden reasoned that Iowans would come to see you play if they love you, not just because you win. There's a big difference there with Iowa fans. If you're competitive and they love you, they'll show up."

And that's important, Chuck said, especially during the lean years.

"If you stumble and have some losing seasons—and you will—you better be relating to the fans and have them on your side. Because you're going to need their loyalty when the wins don't come."

"Chuck Long is indeed a confident young man, far from boastful, but confident that good things can happen again to the Iowa football team. The confidence will come in handy as the Hawks tackle a tough slate, starting Sept. 11 at Nebraska."

CRAIG COOPER, *QUAD CITY TIMES*, AUG. 29, 1982

The sophomore quarterback Hayden Fry had called "a pleasant surprise," having "unbelievable command presence in the huddle," and being "destined for greatness" was just moments away from falling hard as he led the Iowa Hawkeyes into Memorial Stadium in Lincoln for its 1982 season opener.

Ranked no. 3 in the nation and picked to win the Big Eight Conference, the Nebraska Cornhuskers didn't need any added motivation to come out fast and mad against the young Hawkeyes. Just one year earlier, Coach Tom Osborne's squad had been upset 10–7 in Iowa City.

To say that the Hawkeyes' backers were a bit pessimistic about the team's chances to handle Nebraska's explosive offense and hard-hitting defense would have been an understatement.

"Memorial Stadium and the Huskers have the capability of chewing an inexperienced quarterback up and spitting the remains into Cornhusker Highway," wrote Craig Cooper of the *Quad City Times*. "Losses are not quickly forgotten by Nebraska players or fans, and Iowa beat Nebraska in the opener last season."

Chuck was determined not to let the energetic and enthusiastic Cornhuskers crowd rattle him.

"I've been thinking about it all summer long and all fall. I definitely will be a little nervous going into the game, but I'm glad we're playing them," he said. "It will be a challenge."

In addition to being a sophomore quarterback, Chuck also proved to be prophetic.

With on-field temperatures soaring well into triple digits, Nebraska dominated from the opening kick. By the time patrons vacated their seats for a halftime visit to the concessionaires, the Huskers had rolled to a commanding 28–0 lead.

And they weren't about to take their foot off the gas.

Fueled by a potent running attack and stifling defense, Nebraska took out its frustration with the previous year's loss by outplaying the Hawkeyes. Iowa avoided a shutout by mustering a fourth-quarter touchdown—against the Cornhuskers' reserves, no less.

Final score: 42–7 Nebraska.

"It seemed like they were all over us all day, blitzing and stunting, and they disguised it well," Chuck said. "I think the biggest thing was our inability to pick up the blitzes or call the plays that would have gotten us out of trouble."

Iowa, almost to a fault, stuck with its run-first game plan throughout most of the first half. The idea: establish the run to set up the play-action-pass and have the defense (the team's strength) keep the game close.

But any idea of a Hawkeyes upset quickly evaporated on the scorching artificial turf as the Cornhuskers blistered Iowa on both sides of the ball. In the blink of an eye, Nebraska stormed to a 21–0 lead. They stretched it to 28–0 when, in the closing minutes of the first half, defensive end Wade Praeuner scooped up an errant snap and rumbled to the end zone for an easy six.

And all of this before Iowa could tally a first down.

Iowa's attempt to open up the offense and play more relaxed in the second half had little impact. Nebraska continued to roll, racking up nearly six hundred yards of total offense for the game, cruising to the thirty-five-point victory.

Just how bad a day was it for Iowa and Chuck's debut as a Hawkeye?

- During the first half, Iowa netted just one yard on nineteen plays, with its only first down coming on a seven-yard scramble by Chuck as time expired in the second quarter.

- For the game, Nebraska outgained Iowa by nearly 250 yards on the ground and another seventy by air.

- In his first start, Chuck finished five of seven for thirty-one yards and one interception.

- Iowa's performance was so poor that even Chuck got sick to his stomach in the fourth quarter, removing himself courtesy of a self-imposed timeout so he could lose his lunch on the sidelines—on Coach Fry. Chuck eventually blamed the episode on a combination of heat exhaustion and overindulging during the pregame meal.[5]

- Chuck was eventually pulled from the game, giving way to backups Tom Grogan (four of ten, fifty-five yards) and Cornelius Robertson (one of four, seven yards).

As a reward for his performance in Lincoln, Chuck was officially benched.

Junior signal caller Tom Grogan was named Iowa's starter for the following weekend's contest versus the Iowa State Cyclones in Iowa City.

The results were equally abysmal.

With nearly sixty thousand fans jamming Kinnick and Tom Grogan taking the snaps, Iowa's offense was again a no-show. Iowa fell flat on offense for the second consecutive week, losing 19–7.

---

[5] Chuck Long will forever remember his first start as an Iowa Hawkeye. "It was a very hot day in Lincoln… nearly 120 degrees on the field," he recalled. "So hot you could see heat waves bouncing along the fake turf. So we're getting crushed 42–0 in the fourth quarter, and I've been getting pummeled the entire game. On top of the scrapes and bruises, my stomach is boiling, and I'm feeling absolutely awful due to eating too much in the pregame meal.

"I just had to get off the field, so I called a timeout with not much time on the clock so I can get to the sidelines. I no sooner get there than I'm greeted by Coach Fry, who's just fuming.

"And as always, he's wearing his signature white pants and white shoes. He yells, 'Charlie, why in the world are you calling a timeout? Keep the clock running and let's get to the dang locker room.' No sooner did he get done giving me the riot act when I proceeded to throw up all over his white pants and shoes. He just looked down, then looked at me, and said, 'Charlie, you're benched.' And he indeed benched me right on the spot.

"I'll continue to tell this story to parents and to young kids or grandkids as motivation to always look up, to not worry about the first time and falling short, but to remember that even if you hit bottom in the first go-around, that there's no place to go but up. Just keep plugging away. And to remember to always have an extra pair of pants and shoes with you when you're on the road. Hayden was sure glad he did!"

Despite riding the pine, Chuck stayed positive. "I was a little bit depressed when I found out I wasn't going to start," he said. "It really didn't have any effect on me though. I just wanted to win the game."

Hayden Fry took out his frustration on reporters following the loss, calling them and their questions too negative.

But Chuck would have none of that. "I think the quarterbacks are in a situation where they have to carry a lot of weight," he said. "When the team's messing up or something's not happening, people blame the quarterback. I'm ready to accept that.

"I don't think the media or the fans have put too much pressure on us," Chuck added. "We have a good line, but it's just a matter of putting everything together. It seems like one position breaks down on every play, including quarterback."

Others suggested that Hayden Fry was about to burn the playbook and shuffle the starting lineup to ignite an offensive spark.

"Iowa coach Hayden Fry is putting out a 'help wanted' sign," wrote AP sports writer Chuck Schoffner. "He's going to try to find some speedy wide receivers in an effort to revive the Hawkeyes' offense which was listless for the second straight week.

"At the same time, the Iowa coach said he still has faith in quarterbacks Tom Grogan and Chuck Long who have struggled in the first two games. He said it's going to take some time before the offense becomes a polished unit."

Gus Schrader of the *Cedar Rapids Gazette* asked, "Where's the pizzazz?" Several fans, he wrote, had asked why Iowa played so conservatively in the 19–7 loss versus the Cyclones.

"They recalled Hayden Fry was the coach who came to Iowa promising 'We'll use a lot of wild stuff. We'll run the Statue of Liberty out of our own end zone. Sometimes we'll line up with no backs behind the quarterback.' He said his Hawks would 'run one play up the middle and then have the band play Auld Lang Syne.'"

So what kind of offense should Iowa run—meat and potatoes or gadgetry and tomfoolery? Was Tom Grogan the answer at quarterback or should the youthful Chuck Long be starting? Was Iowa's offense that anemic or were the defensive units of Nebraska and Iowa State that good? Would Iowa's offensive line gel and provide consistency so the team could put points on the board?

A college football season that had been greeted just two weeks earlier with a renewed sense of purpose and optimism was now teetering on the brink with more questions than answers.

Two games. Two losses.

And a date in the desert with the Arizona Wildcats just six days away.

HOLY CRAP

"That's what we were thinking after starting the 1982 season 0–2 and with a trip upcoming to Arizona," admitted Kirk Ferentz thirty-four years later during a conversation in the comforts of his spacious Iowa football office located across the street from Kinnick Stadium.

Chuck Long's sophomore season, he said, was a special and historic year.

"It was one of my favorite years coaching at Iowa—and I've had a lot of them," Ferentz said with a wry smile. "We were 3–3 and then things took off. I tell people we have a job because of the turnaround that season. And to think it began with the win over the Wildcats."

Not only was the team 0–2, Ferentz added, but it was an ugly 0–2. Having Chuck begin his Hawkeyes career with a road game versus Nebraska was not ideal. The team then struggled against in-state rival Iowa State, amassing just 107 yards of offense.

"It was a little dicey at that point, and we were all wondering about our chances to figure things out," Ferentz recalled. "So we went down to Arizona, and for obvious reasons, they were probably a little overconfident. We got Ronnie [Harmon] more involved in the offense, and he started playing out wide a bit and catching some balls, and we did some things to open the offense. It was a critical game."

Sure, there were big wins in 1981 that started the momentum for a winning tradition, Ferentz said, including victories on the road versus Michigan and at home against Nebraska. But Ferentz touted the win against Arizona in the third week of the 1982 campaign as perhaps one of the most important in the program's history and the catalyst for establishing a winning tradition.

———————————

Despite the season's ugly start, the Iowa Hawkeyes remained a confident bunch.

And Chuck returned to the starting lineup.

"The two losses to open the season have done nothing to shake the confidence of Chuck Long, designated starting quarterback this week for the Iowa football team," reported Craig Cooper of the *Quad City Times*. "The sophomore from Wheaton, Ill., believes it is only a matter of time before the Hawks break loose offensively. They will get their next chance Saturday night against Arizona in Tucson."

Chuck also took the high road, placing the burden for better performances by the team on himself and the Hawkeyes offense.

"The quarterback situation has to be more stable," Chuck confided. "From game to game, Tom [Grogan] and I will probably both play, but if you go into each game with a little consistency, it's a start."

Hayden Fry also stuck to his word and made lineup changes leading up to Iowa's prime time showdown vs. 1–1 Arizona. J. C. Love-Jordan, who missed the entire 1981 season due to injury, would open at wingback. His backup would be Ron Harmon, a six-foot-one, 195-pound freshman from Laurelton, New York. Joel Hilgenberg was moved ahead of Bill Bailey at center.

The head coach didn't mince words when explaining his decision to reinsert Chuck as starting quarterback. "Because he's going to progress more," he said matter-of-factly.

With its confidence on shaky turf, the Hawkeyes took the field in the desert at 9:30 p.m. Iowa time against the Wildcats as a six-point underdog.

Most agreed with the Vegas odds-makers. Earning its first victory of the season so far from home seemed like a long shot. Traveling west to play under the lights rarely turned out well for Iowa football teams, and history was likely to repeat itself. The speedy Arizona squad was playing its third consecutive home game of the young season that had included a hard-fought home opener loss (23–13) to the no. 1-ranked Washington Huskies.

But on a ninety-degree evening in Tucson, Hayden Fry and his Iowa Hawkeyes defied the odds and resurrected a season teetering on the brink.

The Wildcats struck first, driving eighty yards on sixteen plays to take a 7–0 lead early in the second quarter. Iowa answered when Chuck hit Love-Jordan on a nine-yard scoring strike. But just as quickly, the Hawkeyes relinquished the lead just before half and went to the locker room trailing 14–7.

Iowa rallied in the third quarter when Chuck connected with wide receiver Dave Moritz on a fourteen-yard touchdown pass to tie the game. The seesaw affair continued well into the fourth quarter as both teams played field position, favoring their defense to force a game-winning play.

But Iowa broke through. With the prospect of an 0–3 start staring them squarely in the face, Iowa took possession deep in its own territory late in the fourth quarter. Chuck proceeded to march the Hawkeyes on a seventy-eight-yard, eleven-play drive that ended with a twenty-yard field goal by kicker Tom Nichol with just 2:20 remaining on the clock.

Iowa's heralded defense then did its part, holding the speedy Wildcats scoreless in the final two-plus minutes on its way to a second-half shutout. Iowa won, 17–14.

In his second collegiate start, Chuck finished eighteen of twenty-seven for 187 yards while accounting for forty-three of the team's 244 yards rushing (almost equaling their output in their first two games versus Nebraska and Iowa State combined).

Iowa skeptics quickly returned to being cheerleaders.

- "What a truly effective game plan Iowa's football Hawkeyes employed Saturday evening in their 17–14 conquest of the University of Arizona in Tucson," wrote Doug Newhoff of the *Waterloo Courier.* "What Iowa did to the 'Cats was straightforward enough. Long came out throwing, and none of his eight first-half passes hit the turf. Seven were completed to Iowa receivers and one to an Arizona defender."

- "Iowa rolled up a whopping 431 yards in this one and made coach Hayden Fry look like a good prophet, for he has been saying the Hawkeyes aren't that bad offensively after playing to excellent defensive clubs in Nebraska and Iowa State," noted Gus Schrader of the *Cedar Rapids Gazette* (Schrader had predicted a Wildcats win).

- "Iowa became a football team, and sophomore Chuck Long demonstrated all the savvy of a reborn Johnny Unitas Saturday night in a 17–14 upset victory over Arizona that dispelled any notion that someone had burned the Hawkeyes' offensive playbooks," opined *Des Moines Register* staff writer Ron Maly. "It was a sensational turnaround for Long and other members of Iowa's offense. Long was definitely the best passer on the same field on which the Wildcats' heralded Tom Tunnicliffe performed."

Every win in college football is a big one. But this one, on this night, and the fashion in which it was won, was truly momentous for Iowa.

While fans whooped and cheered the win, little did they know that history would one day record the victory as one of the program's most significant—a major turning point from years of mediocrity and irrelevancy to a sustained period of winning seasons and a steady diet of bowl appearances. Had they lost the game, who knows what Iowa's fortunes would have been for the remainder of the season or the season after that…

"That game became our template for success," Chuck would one day recall. "I'll never forget the jubilation of that locker room. We tasted victory, and we liked it. We liked it a lot."

Hayden Fry was a relieved head coach following the thrilling come-from-behind win over Arizona that for the first time in the young season revealed the team's mental mettle and resiliency.

"Chuck Long played a super game. He played maybe as good a game as any quarterback I've ever had from an all-around standpoint," said a beaming Fry. "He made a few mistakes, but that was to be expected. We took a gamble on naming him our number one quarterback and on the offensive strategy, and it all turned out real good."

Fry then tabbed Chuck as his starting quarterback for the remainder of the season.

Good for Chuck. Bad for Northwestern.[6]

In the Hawkeyes' Big Ten opener—a homecoming game, no less—the Hawkeyes offense found the end zone in the game's opening minute and proceeded to pound the Wildcats 45–7. Chuck continued to improve. After missing on his first two attempts, he connected on the next nine and finished nine of eleven for 131 yards and two touchdowns before taking an early shower in the third quarter.

"I really enjoy throwing the ball," Chuck said after another solid performance. "It's fun. We didn't throw in high school because we didn't have to. But you have to throw in the Big Ten, and I welcome the challenge."

The thumping at the hands of a confident Chuck Long was Northwestern's thirty-eighth straight defeat in Big Ten play. For the black

---

[6] Chuck Long's first two wins as the Iowa Hawkeyes' starting quarterback came in back-to-back weeks and were both against Wildcats—first a 17–14 upset against the Arizona Wildcats Sept. 25, 1982, in Tucson followed by a 45–7 romp over Northwestern in Iowa City.

and gold, the convincing win was just what it needed to build its fledgling confidence as the team prepared for a third consecutive road game, this one in Bloomington, Indiana.

The Hoosiers, led by head coach Lee Corso, were a pesky bunch, routinely finishing middle of the pack in the competitive Big Ten. Iowa's 42–28 win the previous year was solid, but no one believed this year's tussle would be as lopsided. Indiana, like Iowa, owned a 2–2 record. Its resume included wins versus Northwestern and Syracuse and losses—both on the road—to no. 19 USC and Michigan.

On this day, Iowa wouldn't let Indiana get back on the winning track. Running back Eddie Phillips rushed for two touchdowns, and Norm Granger caught a sixty-three-yard scoring strike from Chuck to help Iowa edge the Hoosiers 24–20 in a shootout. Chuck finished twelve of seventeen for 186 yards.

"It looks like Iowa has found its quarterback," said Corso.

With the victory, Iowa was officially on a roll. And as it found its groove, so did Chuck. At the season's five-week mark, the sophomore quarterback was the nation's most efficient passer, completing a remarkable 70 percent of his throws.

But those statistics and the growing buzz in Hawkeye Nation meant nothing to the Michigan Wolverines when they came calling on Iowa City one week later.

Ready to atone for a 9–7 upset at the hands of Iowa in the Big House the previous season, Bo Schembechler and his maize-and-blue-clad Wolverines were undefeated in Big Ten play and a seven-point favorite. The veteran coach praised Iowa's newfound running game and "that young quarterback" and big offensive line.

When the teams met on the field in Iowa City, the up-and-coming Hawkeyes could offer little resistance to a powerful Wolverines squad that featured a balanced run-pass combination led by quarterback Steve Smith. A missed scoring opportunity in the first half and fumbles deep inside both teams' territories helped Michigan race to a 22–0 lead by the end of the third quarter.

When the final horn sounded and the last of the remaining Hawkeyes faithful made their way to the exits, Iowa was on the losing end of a 29–7 score.

"It was like puncturing a balloon and watching the air escape," wrote Mark Dukes of the *Cedar Rapids Gazette* in his game-day postmortem.

That's how Chuck assessed the damage of a second-quarter fumble just six inches outside Michigan's goal line that prevented Iowa from being the first to score. Not one to turn down a gift, the Wolverines had seized the momentum by marching the length of the field, turning the costly miscue into seven points.

"After that, especially at the start of the second half, we got deflated," Chuck said. "We weren't together, and we showed signs of inexperience."

With 14:13 to go in the game, Iowa shot itself in the foot again when Chuck and running back Norm Granger bungled a handoff. Michigan capitalized yet again, building a 22–0 lead. Fry placed the blame on Granger, saying he had lined up in the wrong spot because he hadn't practiced all week.

But it was Chuck who, despite throwing for 220 yards on thirty-two pass attempts, shouldered the blame.

"That was my fault," he said. "I thought Norm would be on the right, but he ended up on my left. I tried to force the ball to him."

In the team's weekly press conference three days later, the sting of the loss was still evident. Hayden Fry, the often jovial head coach, turned testy when pressed by reporters as to whether the team's next two games—Minnesota and home versus Illinois—represented another crossroads for his team.

"I'm in no mood for funny questions or expert prognostications," he snapped. "Just like I said before the season, we're taking it one game at a time. Nobody can predict the Big Ten race. I've got a crippled football team that gave their best yesterday but got beat by a fine football team."

With the loss, Iowa stood at 3–3 at the midway point of Fry's third season. It had been a rough and tumble ride featuring a sluggish start, a three-game winning streak, and a demoralizing loss at the hands of Michigan. Such was life in the Big Ten.

But Chuck Long and the Hawkeyes would not shrink in the face of adversity.

If there was a hangover from the loss against Michigan, it quickly faded on the artificial turf in Minneapolis as Iowa plowed its way to a 21–16 victory.

After a five-year hiatus, the coveted Floyd of Rosedale trophy was returning to Iowa City.

A euphoric Hayden Fry was ready to make the most of the moment, appearing in the postgame news conference wearing a straw hat, red flannel shirt, and bib overalls.

"These are my Iowa clothes," he said with a grin. "All you great Minnesota writers, radio people, and TV…I didn't want you to look like liars, so I've got my clod clothes on. We're taking Floyd home where he belongs. Sooooey, pig, sooooo-ey."

Fry's antics were actually a dig at Minnesota coach Joe Salem. Reporters had quoted Salem as saying he hated Iowa. Salem had also worn bibs to practice in the week leading up to the game, supposedly to fire up the Gophers, a team that had bested Hayden Fry during his first three seasons at Iowa.

During the Hawkeyes' weekly press conference in Iowa City the previous Tuesday, sports writer Al Grady of the *Iowa City Press-Citizen* had asked Fry why he never ran the quarterback sneak.

The coach's reply was short and to the point: "Well, we just don't run it."

At least not until Saturday when Chuck scored on a quarterback sneak versus the Golden Gophers.

When pressed on his sudden appreciation for the QB sneak—the first he had called in twenty-one years—Hayden Fry didn't miss a beat. "I knew ol' Smokey Joe would be listening and hear us say we don't run the QB sneak," he quipped. "After all, he has a pipeline down here and knows just about everything we say or do by reading the papers. So it seemed like a perfect time to try it. And we did. And Chuck scores."

And what about the bibs and flannel shirt?

"Shoot, I like to do things with a little flair. It was good fun," he boomed. "I figured if we were going to take Floyd home, I better dress for the occasion."

Iowa was back on the winning track. And the "destined for greatness" tag Hayden Fry had hung on Chuck before the season began was also starting to stick.

One week after its hard-fought victory over Minnesota, Iowa edged the Illinois Fighting Illini 14–13 before nearly sixty thousand delirious fans at Kinnick. The winning score came on an eight-yard touchdown pass from Chuck to freshman running back Ronnie Harmon. The team's record stood at 4–1 in the Big Ten and 5–3 overall. The team also trailed the undefeated Michigan Wolverines by just one game in the race for Big Ten Conference champion.

After eight games, Chuck Long had established himself as a legitimate college football quarterback, completing nearly 70 percent of his passes on the season (82–125) for 918 yards while tossing five touchdowns and eight picks. Brigham Young's Steve Young held the top spot nationally.[7]

But as had been the case all year, just as the spotlight began to warm on Chuck and the Hawkeyes, the team cooled.

A Hawkeyes visit to West Lafayette was a forgettable one. Just a week following the win over Illinois, Iowa was blitzed by the Purdue Boilermakers 16–7. Almost everyone on the team, including Chuck, used the word "flat" to describe the team's performance.

"They played a good game," he said, "and we just weren't making things happen in the first half. Even when we got down 16–0 at the half, I thought we could come back and score two touchdowns and a field goal to win. We got the touchdown, but the clock ran out on us after that.

"We aren't thinking of any bowls," Chuck added. "We just want to win the last two games and have another winning season."

And with that, the Hawkeyes hosted Wisconsin for its season finale in Kinnick. And just like after the losses against Iowa State and Michigan, the squad rebounded and notched a decisive win by doubling up the Badgers 28–14.

Chuck's stat line was workmanlike: fourteen of twenty-two for 177 yards. He also scored two touchdowns, both on one-yard quarterback keepers, a play that hadn't even been in Iowa's playbook until three weeks earlier.

With the victory, Iowa clinched a second straight winning season, quite an accomplishment after nineteen consecutive losing campaigns. The last time Iowa had strung together two consecutive seasons where they won more than they lost was 1960–61.

Just one Big Ten game remained for the confident 6–4 Hawkeyes—a road trip to East Lansing to tussle with the Michigan State Spartans.

"According to the expressed sentiments of many impatient Iowa football fans, Chuck Long went from budding prodigy to king-sized flop and back to promising young quarterback during the first three weeks of the season," wrote *Des Moines Register* staff writer Bob Dyer. His gradual growth as a field leader, Dyer wrote, "is a major reason why Iowa has won six of its last eight games and is one victory away from a berth in the Peach Bowl."

---

[7] Brigham Young quarterback Steve Young held the top spot among total offense leaders, passing and rushing for 2,013 yards and accounting for 335.5 yards per game. Initially, Young struggled managing BYU's option offense, so much so that the coaching staff considered moving him to defensive back. He eventually settled in the QB role, setting an NCAA single-season completion percentage record his senior year (71.3 percent) before signing a record ten-year contact with the US Football League's Los Angeles Express in 1984 worth a scintillating $40 million. The following year, he was signed by the NFL's Tampa Bay Buccaneers in a USFL and CFL supplemental draft. Labeled a "bust" by NFL scouts, Young was traded to the San Francisco 49ers in 1987 to serve as a backup to Joe Montana. In four seasons as a backup to Montana, Young threw twenty-three touchdown passes and just six interceptions.

Somehow, some way, the Chuck Long-led Hawkeyes could clinch no worse than third place in the Big Ten with a victory Saturday at Michigan State.

"We've turned it around one hundred percent," Chuck said. "Deep down inside, we knew we were better than what we showed the first two games. We just didn't have the right combinations."

With just one regular season game left to play, Chuck had completed 116 of 179 passes for 1,267 yards and eight touchdowns. His 64.8 completion percentage made him a cinch to break Randy Duncan's one-season school mark of 58.8 set in 1958. He also needed just eighty-one yards to move into third place in yards passing in a season behind Gary Snook (1964) and Larry Lawrence (1969).

Chuck was growing up quickly as a Big Ten quarterback, learning by doing. As he gained on-the-job experience, his poise and confidence grew. He was also becoming more astute at deciphering defensive schemes, anticipating the tendencies of teammates, and establishing a feel for clock management and field position

"It comes with experience," Chuck told reporters. "I was hesitant at first, but we've run the plays so many times in practice and in games that it's become second nature."

Hayden Fry was also reveling in the team's success.

"Iowa is for real," he said. "Last year and this year laid the foundation for Iowa to be looked at by [Michigan Coach Bo] Schembechler—and some of those other fellows who looked down their noses at us—as being competitive. It shows that we will battle and be a top-division team."

The Spartans were a team in turmoil. At 2–8, veteran coach Frank "Muddy" Waters had already been fired with one game left to play (i.e., a dead man walking). The unique circumstances made Hayden Fry restless.

The firing, he said, "creates a whole new emotional atmosphere" surrounding the game. "I can't control the emotions of the people up there, but I'll try to do something with the emotions of our people here. They don't perform or function as smoothly when pressure is on them. They play better when they're relaxed."

For most of the game, Iowa played as though it didn't have a care in the world, jumping out to a 24–3 halftime lead. Then, with a Peach Bowl berth hanging in the balance, the Hawkeyes played tentative in the second half, giving up fifteen unanswered points. But an interception by senior safety Bobby Stoops with thirty seconds remaining halted a Spartan drive and sealed Iowa's second consecutive bowl appearance.

"Thank God for Bobby Stoops," a relieved Hayden Fry exclaimed just moments before accepting an official bid from the Peach Bowl's selection committee. "I never dreamed before the season that we could do this well. I can't say enough good things about this football team."

The Atlanta Journal's Thomas Stinson agreed.

"As the Hawkeyes have assembled back-to-back winning records for the first time in more than 20 years, Long has filled a major role, operating a multiple pro set offense well enough to finish fourth in Big Ten total offense," he penned in his Dec. 29, 1982, column. "Said Fry, 'He sure knows how to hurt certain defenses,' which may be as startling a statement as the one above, considering Long had thrown just one varsity pass when the season started."

Now it was off to Georgia to take on the Tennessee Volunteers in the fifteenth edition of the Peach Bowl played in Atlanta-Fulton County Stadium.[8]

"On a muggy August day in Iowa City, Hayden Fry predicted greatness for quarterback Chuck Long," *Quad City Times* sports editor Gary Richards wrote following the marquee matchup.

"And on a chilly December afternoon in Atlanta, Long lived up to that prediction."

---

[8] Atlanta-Fulton County Stadium was built in 1966 and was the home for Major League Baseball's Braves. For twenty-five years, it was home to the Braves and the NFL's Atlanta Falcons. One of the more notable sporting achievements that took place in the stadium was on April 8, 1974, when Atlanta's long-ball hitting outfielder, Hank Aaron, became baseball's all-time career home run leader when he connected on his 715th "tater." The stadium was imploded in 1997.

CHAPTER 3

Peaches and Gators

Dec. 1, 1982

Mr. & Mrs. Charles Long:

It seems appropriate at this time of the year to properly thank you for allowing Chuck to be a member of our 1982 Iowa football program. But more importantly to tell you how proud we are of him and how very much we appreciate his dedication, loyalty, fortitude, and hard work. The routine of a major college student-athlete is not an easy one, with so many demands placed upon his time. As in many cases, the individual rewards are not that great, therefore it takes a very special individual to be part of this and share in the achievement of common goals.

Chuck is a special person to us. We are grateful for the many unselfish sacrifices he has made here. I know that you are equally as proud, and rightfully so. Thank you again.

Very sincerely,

Bill Snyder

Offensive Coordinator

After beginning the 1982 season 0–2, no one anticipated Iowa would be playing on New Year's Eve.

Not even Chuck.

"I didn't expect a seven–four season because we had such a young team, but to have the success we've had this year, I think it shows even better things ahead," he told reporters just days before Iowa matched wits with the 6–4–1 Tennessee Volunteers in the Peach Bowl.

The season had been a learning experience for Chuck, beginning with the opening smackdown by the Nebraska Cornhuskers that included a second-half trip to the bench thanks to a bad combination of overindulgence in the pregame meal and heat exhaustion.

"To a certain extent, it [being benched] opened my eyes," Chuck told Iowa Sports Desk correspondence George Kunke II. "We kinda came in to the season with…maybe a little too much confidence.

"When we played Nebraska, it opened my eyes especially. Getting benched helped me…think about what I did wrong and what I needed to do to get my confidence back."

Coming off a Rose Bowl loss to the Washington Huskies, Chuck saw the Peach Bowl as an opportunity for the Hawkeyes to redeem themselves on the national stage against a Tennessee team led by head coach Johnny Majors.[1]

"I don't think the Peach Bowl people could have chosen two better teams," Chuck said.

The Vols were confident and athletic adversaries, with jet-propelled wide receiver Willie Gault. The senior preseason all-American and soon-to-be first-round NFL draft pick was a world-class hurdler in track who had nabbed nearly fifty catches on the year and was a prolific punt and kick returner.

Tennessee also boasted a formidable defense led by future NFL Hall-of-Famer Reggie White and hometown boy Michael Cofer. And for good measure, Majors had two of college football's most skilled position players at the ready: kicker Fuad Reveiz and punter Jimmy Colquitt.

---

[1] Majors, like Chuck Long, was an all-American and runner-up for the Heisman Trophy (1956). As a player for the Volunteers, he was a triple-threat tailback and went on to play in the Canadian Football League. Following his playing days, Majors held several college football head coaching positions, starting with Iowa State University (1968), where he compiled a 24–30–1 record in five years and two bowl appearances (Sun and Liberty). Majors amassed a career coaching record of 185–137–10.

CHUCK LONG: DESTINED FOR GREATNESS

Iowa, playing in back-to-back bowl games for the first time in team history, also had weapons.

For a second consecutive season, the Hawkeyes' defense—led by tackle Mark Bortz, strong safety Bobby Stoops, and freshman linebacker Larry Station—set the pace in the Big Ten in both total defense and rushing defense. Punter Reggie Roby was the nation's leader with a 48.1-yard-per-boot average. Running backs Owen Gill and Norm Granger along with Chuck Long at quarterback and wide receiver Ronnie Harmon provided enough offensive firepower to stress opposing defenses.

The much-anticipated matchup between Iowa and Tennessee didn't disappoint.

Chuck Long came out firing, connecting on his first eleven passes. Pinpoint accuracy resulted in three second-quarter touchdown strikes, propelling Iowa to a commanding 21–7 halftime lead.

The Volunteers added six points to start the third quarter only to fall behind 28–13 after a seventy-five-yard drive by Iowa that ended with a two-yard touchdown plunge by running back Eddie Phillips.

Undeterred, Tennessee struck again quickly on a nineteen-yard TD snare by Gault. A twenty-seven-yard Reveiz field goal cut the Iowa lead to 28–22 with just 4:55 to play.

That's as close as the opponent got, thanks to valiant stands by the Iowa defense—one at its own eight-yard line with 3:29 left and again in the final minutes when the squad sacked Vols quarterback Alan Cockrell twice and forced two incompletions.

"A season that started with a whimper ended with a bang for Iowa quarterback Chuck Long," noted Associated Press sportswriter Chuck Schoffner after the quarterback's sizzling performance.

Chuck's stat sheet sounded far more accomplished than the work of a sophomore completing just his first full season under center.

He set two Peach Bowl records—total yards (306) and total yards passing (304)—while hitting on nineteen of twenty-six passes for three touchdowns. Completing his first eleven pass attempts bested his own record of nine against Northwestern in week four of the season. He was also named the game's co-MVP with Iowa defensive lineman Clay Uhlenhake and earned the CBS-TV team of sportscasters' (led by the venerable Verne Lundquist) most outstanding player recognition. The award, sponsored by Chevrolet, netted the university $1,000 for its general scholarship fund.[2]

"I was thinking before this game back to September and the Nebraska game," Chuck said in his postgame reflections.[3] "We've come such a long way as a team. We showed that we can pull together at the right time, and that's the sign of a winner. Even though we're a young team, right now I think we're playing like a senior team."

Gary Richards, sports editor for the *Quad City Times,* in summarizing Iowa's Peach Bowl triumph, noted that Chuck usually spoke in terms of the team instead of himself, which was one reason why he was accepted as the leader of the offense.

"The greatness label hung around him before the season could have been a rock around his neck," Richards penned. "But it didn't drag Long down. If anything, it was a goal to reach, and steps in that direction have been taken."

And just one day later, Richards added another "Peach Bowl leftover" with a prediction: "If Fry has his way and if backup quarterback Cornelius Robertson agrees, Robertson will be playing a different position next season. Wide receiver is a possibility."

---

[2] The Fox Valley Sports Journal quietly reported on the fanfare surrounding the award announcement. "When the game [Peach Bowl] had ended and the team was gathered along the sidelines minutes after the victory had been gained, the announcement on the field was made that Long was Chevrolet's outstanding player," the paper reported. Chuck was surprised and modestly accepted the award.

[3] During the loss to Nebraska in Chuck's sophomore season, Fry yanked the QB toward him when he arrived on the sidelines and gave him the tongue lashing Chuck knew he had coming after failing to execute the proper play. The chewing out didn't last long, observed Gary Richards of the *Quad City Times.* "I grabbed him pretty good just to get his attention," Fry said. "I looked at Chuck and he just smiled back at me. He knew what he had done wrong. But if I'm mad at somebody and he agrees with me, what can you do?" Fry asked rhetorically. "Not stay mad," Richards answered.

A PEACHY WIN

Iowa's Peach Bowl victory meant a lot to Chuck. "We had been fighting and scratching all year long and trying to win," he recalled. "I remember that week of preparation was really good, felt good in practice. It all clicked that week and came together. The game plan was solid. No one expected us to win. After all, Tennessee had Willie Gault and Reggie White."

The bowl victory was especially meaningful for Chuck because it was Hayden Fry's first bowl victory and Iowa's first since 1959.

"I still wasn't quite sure of my place in the football world until that win," Chuck said. "I had not yet had the hot game because we hadn't thrown the ball a ton. But we were motivated to win a bowl game given that we had lost the previous year.

"When we beat a SEC team and one that had more talent than we did, we knew we could play with anyone and could beat anyone in the country," he added. "It was another turning point for a program on the rise."

Chuck and his girlfriend, Lisa Wells, had gone their separate ways after high school—geographically speaking, that is.

Lisa Wells had considered several universities while she and Chuck were preparing to graduate from Wheaton North. Making the list were Iowa State University (ISU), Eastern Illinois, and Wisconsin. She chose ISU, a beautiful, tree-filled campus nestled in the welcoming community of Ames, Iowa located just a short drive north of Des Moines and about two and a half hours west and north as the crow flies from Iowa City.

While Chuck accepted a scholarship to play football at the University of Iowa, Lisa Wells pursued a degree in Cyclone Country. Yet that didn't keep her from traveling to Iowa City nearly every weekend her first semester to see Chuck and cheer on the Hawkeyes.

ISU made total sense for her academically. The school boasted a well-respected fashion merchandising program that came highly recommended by her father, a retail professional by trade. But logistically, ISU was simply too far away from Iowa City. Lisa Wells wanted to experience the energy and excitement of Hawkeyes football and the buzz that accompanied the team's 1981 Rose Bowl berth.

It was "too much fun" to be with Chuck, she confided, and to experience his maturation as the Hawkeyes' quarterback was something far too thrilling to miss.

Immediately following her freshman year at ISU, Wells transferred to Iowa, majoring in early childhood education. So there she was, now a junior-to-be at the University of Iowa, reunited with Chuck, Iowa's starting quarterback, who'd appeared in the team's first bowl game in more than twenty years as a freshman and was now a Peach Bowl victor.

Life was good.

And it was about to get even better.

"He was just great. And he's only a sophomore. He will only get better."

HAYDEN FRY

Hawkeyes head coach quipping about the performance of Chuck Long and his prospects for future success following Iowa's 28–22 win over the Tennessee Volunteers in the 1982 Peach Bowl

It was springtime in Iowa City, and the Hawkeyes were soaring high in preparation for the 1983 season that would kick off Sept. 10 in Ames versus the Cyclones.

"Crying towels and talk of so-so records have vanished from this Big Ten university that, not long ago, was in football's soup line during a nineteen-year period that was without a winning record," wrote *Des Moines Register* staff writer Ron Maly. "It was during that awful era that Iowa often was included in the Bottom Ten nationally. Now the Hawkeyes are in everybody's top 20 and Fry doesn't mind it one bit."

Iowa's 28–22 Peach Bowl win over Tennessee was already a distant albeit pleasant memory for a squad that was growing up and getting hungrier with each taste of success. Chuck's confidence was building, and enthusiasm was growing in a college town quickly acquiring an appetite for winning and trips to warm destinations in December and January.

Just one year ago, Hayden Fry had made a proclamation that sounded as odd as Iowa farmers growing potatoes and cucumbers instead of corn and soybeans.

"Listeners were stunned. Those who had upper plates saw them drop out of their mouths. The same with those who had lower plates," wrote the *Register's* Maly. "The only words that should be wasted on sophomores, after all, are supposed to be 'young,' 'untested' and 'green.' Let's see, wasn't it Woody Hayes who once said a coach can figure on losing one game for every sophomore he starts?

"But Fry has been coaching football teams long enough to know the difference between a so-so quarterback and an extraordinary one."

True. Fry wouldn't have made the "destined for greatness" proclamation unless he truly believed it. And he did.

Many coaches get tied up in the Xs and Os of the offense and defense in football. Not Fry. He preferred to delegate these details to capable assistants. Doing so allowed him to look at the bigger picture, promote team chemistry, and accentuate individual strengths of his players to the benefit of the collective good. Hayden Fry had earned a master's degree in behavioral psychology at Baylor University. The education, combined with natural instincts, provided him unique insight into what made people tick…their sensitivities, strengths, and weaknesses. He quickly applied his education to his time in the US Marine Corps[4] and as a college football coach.

He also kept a close eye on his assistants and evaluated their interaction with players. He demanded his assistant coaches remember that the players they mentored were not machines. They were human beings with opinions, feelings, and egos. Precision didn't matter to Hayden Fry. Results did. And if an assistant coach went too far in emphasizing mechanics over individuality, Fry let him know.

That included offensive coordinator Bill Snyder. He had joined Fry on the North Texas State coaching staff in 1976, and the two had forged a strong relationship. Always the teacher, Fry had gone over the techniques of throwing the football with Snyder while also encouraging a hands-off approach regarding Chuck's raw mechanics. It was results that mattered to Hayden, not appearances.

During a spring practice session, Fry observed Snyder criticizing Chuck for throwing wobbly passes, even if the toss was completed. It didn't take Fry long to approach him.

"Coach Snyder, leave the kid alone; don't say anything else to him," the former marine instructed.

"He didn't turn his thumb down when he released the ball, he over-strided and wound up too much," Snyder replied tartly.

"Coach Snyder, remember, the result is what's important," Fry scolded. "He's completing every pass. Leave him alone."

The blood vessels began rising in Bill Snyder's neck and face. But he didn't respond, instead moving elsewhere on the practice field to observe other offensive drills.

It was the last time he ever corrected Coach Snyder, Fry one day recalled with a wry chuckle. "But it was also the last time he ever corrected Chuck Long."

Fry's reprimand of an assistant was a sign that the program was growing in maturity. And it was quickly forgotten as there was work to do to prepare for

---

[4] Hayden Fry joined the US Marine Corps in 1952 after a stint as an American history teacher and assistant football coach at Odessa (Texas) High School. It was during this time that a young Fry met and befriended George H. W. Bush, who, in 1988, was elected the forty-first president of the United States.

another grueling Big Ten campaign. The talented and deep Hawkeyes would start the season with two road games—at Iowa State and Penn State. Additional road dates included Illinois, Michigan, Wisconsin, and Michigan State. Making the trip to Iowa City were Ohio State, Northwestern, Purdue, Indiana, and Minnesota.

Chuck's off-season preparation manifested itself in a calm confidence that was noted by reporters focused on the Iowa program.

"Long not only acts like an All-America type, he looks like an All-America type," wrote Gary Richards of the *Quad City Times*. "He stands 6-foot-4, has blond hair and is almost always neatly attired. His manner is humble and his cooperation fine. He'll answer questions for hours at a time and then stop to answer one more as he heads out the door."

Fry, too, was walking tall and talking enthusiastically about the team's prospects.

Outwardly, he brushed off the team's no. 18 preseason rank, calling it "coffee talk." But inwardly, he relished the prospects of what his high-powered offense could achieve, especially when combined with a stalwart defense that had grown into one of the Big Ten's most prolific units.

"Most balanced offense I've had," Fry boasted.

His words would prove prophetic.

"It's always good to get good publicity and good press. I like to block both the negative and the positive dealings with the press out of my head because I feel I know what I can do on the field. I have confidence in myself in what I can do. I really don't need anybody else to give me praise or give me some negative effects."

CHUCK LONG
sophomore quarterback, Iowa Hawkeyes, in a conversation with Iowa Sports Desk correspondent George Kunke II (Feb. 5, 1983)

"Drought ends for Hawkeyes, 51–10" read the headline splashed across the Sept. 11, 1983, edition of the *Des Moines Register's* "Big Peach."

The perennial in-state grudge match had not been much of a contest, at least recently, with the Cyclones winning three straight and five of the last seven.

But on this day, Sept. 10, 1983, the Iowa offense ran all over Iowa State, racking up twenty-three first downs to the Cyclones' eleven, rushing for 257 yards, and amassing another 278 through the air on its way to the lopsided win.[5]

"Chuck Long is a very gifted athlete who is a deceptive runner, too. He is extremely knowledgeable and understands the game very well," Snyder said of his offensive leader. "He's a gifted young man who has some very intrinsic traits—those other qualities such as leadership capabilities. He's an extremely tough youngster."

That toughness was on display again one week later when Chuck and the thirteenth-ranked Hawkeyes traveled to University Park, Pennsylvania, and left as 42–34 winners over the Penn State Nittany Lions who, just one season earlier, had finished as college football's national champion.

The football game resembled a track meet. Iowa's offense gobbled up large chunks of real estate—586 yards to be exact—including 348 by air and 242 via the ground. Penn State coach Joe Paterno had led the Nittany Lions for eighteen years, and only Boston College had gained more yards (656) in a single game. Chuck's 345 yards passing was also a school record.

"Long's performance Saturday was typical of his play," Fry said in postgame comments. "He'll continue to get better. He also has a good supporting cast."

Just two weeks into the season, Chuck had connected on twenty-nine of forty-seven passes for 549 yards and three touchdowns. He had yet to throw an interception.

The 2–0 start—both road wins—rocketed Iowa up the national polls. Now no. 7, the Hawkeyes relished their home opener against the no. 3 Ohio State Buckeyes led by quarterback Mike Tomczak.

---

[5] The 51–10 blowout of Iowa State in 1983 began a streak of fifteen consecutive wins by Iowa in the in-state rivalry. The Hawkeyes outscored the Cyclones 590–206 during the same stretch.

As did fans. For the first time in a long time, a positive energy bounced around campus and the city, spilling into the farm fields and surrounding communities. Iowa had the makings of a program on the rise, and the optimism was contagious. The state's identity rose and fell with the success of its university football programs. And everyone took note of the wins that were coming more frequently in Iowa City.

Most conversations about the program's place in the national college football conversation usually began with a reference to its quarterback.

"Nobody in college football has more poise," said Hayden Fry when asked by reporters to explain the team's quick start. "Most unflappable guy I've ever seen. He can be turned upside down, free flipped, blindsided, and never gets ruffled, never says anything to the guy who didn't block or dropped a pass. As soon as he makes a mistake, he's aware of it. I don't have to tell him."

After being benched the previous season versus Iowa State, the Hawkeyes were 10–2 with Chuck under center.

Nolan Zavoral, sports editor for the *Iowa City Press-Citizen,* critiqued Chuck closely. After every start, the veteran reporter was more and more impressed with what he saw.

In a 42–34 win over Penn State, for example, Chuck completed sixteen of thirty passes, including two for touchdowns, and scored once himself on a five-yard keeper while throwing no picks. Yet with a genuine, and sometimes maddening reserve, Zavoral noted, "Long recognized his teammates rather than basking in the glow of the team's early success."

True to form, Chuck deflected the praise, passing it along to deserving teammates.

"My receivers—give credit to them. A [touchdown] ball Eddie [Phillips] caught…some that Dave Moritz caught…they weren't great balls but those guys got them," Chuck said.

"Which is the way Long is and always has been in an Iowa uniform," Zavoral observed. "Low-key, self-effacing. The boy next door comes to play a little game of football. Long wears neatly pressed slacks, a dark sport coat, and white shirt open at the neck. The forehead offers the only clue that Long did something other this afternoon than go to the library and study. On his forehead is a dark red stain of a mark from the way the helmet fits and the way other opposing players tend to rap on it."

While Chuck took the lofty rankings and the opportunity to face Tomczak on home turf in stride, local media pounced on the storyline like it was their last meal.

"Chuck Long and Mike Tomczak are supreme quarterbacks (both are juniors, by the way) and rate among the nation's very finest. If they are now golden boys, living portraits of the all-American youth, it is because they have exceeded what was expected of them," Brian Chapman of the *Cedar Rapids Gazette* penned.

He recited Chuck's modest upbringing, and although he performed well as a starting high school quarterback, he was chased by few college recruiters.

According to Taylor Bell of the *Chicago Sun-Times:* "No one expected Long to go to Iowa. People were surprised a Big Ten school would want him. Everyone knew he had great leadership, brains, and was a take-charge guy— all of that. But they questioned if he had the tools."

Added the *Chicago Tribune's* Jerry Schnay: "Chuck Long was an excellent athlete in a program not suited to showcase his talent while Tomczak starred in a program to do just that. We all knew Chuck was a good athlete, we just weren't sure how good he was."

Chapman even tracked down Wheaton North coach Jim Rexilius, who offered a firsthand assessment that mirrored what observers had come to understand and what Coach Fry saw that most other college recruiters hadn't.

"He could run the ball, throw the ball, run the option—do whatever we wanted him to do. What I remember about Chuck was his coolness on the field. I don't remember him fumbling the ball or throwing a bad pass."

Joan Long, Chuck's mom, also offered an enlightening perspective when asked by Chapman if she and her husband were ever unhappy with Rexilius' offensive tactics. "Since he passed so seldom, he had to be more accurate," she reasoned. "Each pass had to count. He ran a lot, which toughened him. I read a quote by Fry where he said Chuck's running in high school helped him adjust to the Big Ten."

Sports writers didn't leave an angle unexplored as the Iowa-Ohio State grudge match loomed.

Some local reporters were authoring retrospectives, reintroducing Chuck to the Iowa faithful. Others were announcing Chuck to college football fans nationwide as the Hawkeyes rose in the polls.

After a shaky inauguration to big-time college football, Chuck was earning rave reviews from writers just starting to pay attention.

"Iowa quarterback Chuck Long looks like a man who has been throwing a football all of his life," wrote Tim May of the Columbus Dispatch. "He can fade into the pocket and hit a sprinting target 50 yards up the field. Or he can roll right and hit an out-cutting target 25 yards away. Or can soft-touch a flip to a back zipping through linebacker land. Just give him the ball and let him fire. He's a natural."

Chuck used the opportunity to heap praise on his coach while emphasizing his love for Iowa City and Hawkeyes fans.

"Coach Fry sold me on the program. He told me he was going to turn the program around, and over a period of three years he has. I'm just glad I came here, to be a part of it," he told May. "I have a good school in Iowa, and things have worked out really well. I just want to keep doing what we're doing.

"I think Iowa has arrived ever since Coach Fry and his staff have been here," Chuck added. "It took them three years to turn it around and take this team to the Rose Bowl. Sometimes I have to just pinch myself, I feel so good. I never dreamed I'd be in a spot like this. I'm just one of the more fortunate ones."

Finally, after a week of intensive practices, interviews, and hype, game day arrived. On Sept. 24, Kinnick was filled to the brim with more than sixty-six thousand fans. Among them, Ohio Gov. Richard Celeste, who had taken office just eight months earlier. Having correctly predicted the Buckeyes' ten-point win over no. 2 Oklahoma the previous week (Ohio State prevailed 24–14), Celeste took his home-state team by fourteen over Iowa while declaring the day as "Beat the Iowa Hawkeyes Day."

But on this day, in Iowa's house, and in front of a regional television audience, it took more than a declaration to blunt Iowa's success. For the first time in twenty-one years, Iowa brought down the vaunted Buckeyes 20–14 behind the strong arm and heady play of Chuck Long.

And some riverboat gambling by Hayden Fry.

Clinging to a 13–7 lead with the clock fading and dusk enveloping over Kinnick, Chuck settled under center with the sideline marker reading third down and six yards to go on Iowa's own twenty-seven-yard line.

Rather than play it safe and let Reggie Roby boom one into another zip code, Hayden Fry and Chuck Long had other plans.

With his quarterback still somewhat green against Big Ten defenses, Fry often deferred to his more experienced receivers to help Chuck call plays at the line of scrimmage. It was a complicated matrix of moves and motions dictated by defensive alignments, time, down, and distance. If, for example, a receiver thought a stop-and-go would be successful, he would give a subtle nod of the head to the quarterback.

With the outcome of the game hanging in the balance, the Hawkeyes broke huddle and spread the field. Trusted receiver David Moritz took his position opposite talented Buckeyes defender Shaun Gayle. As Chuck prepared for the snap, he scanned the line, his receivers, and defensive alignment. In a millisecond, he picked up the slightest nod from Moritz—the nonverbal cue that the route would be a risky stop-and-go; all Chuck had to do was sell it with a pump fake and then deliver a strike on time downfield.

And that's just what he did. Upon securing the snap, the Hawkeyes quarterback retreated from his center with the poise more fitting of a senior signal caller and zipped a perfect pass in stride to a streaking Moritz.

The trusted and sure-handed teammate had found a seam in the airtight Buckeyes defense, and Chuck had noticed. Moritz reached high, secured the throw, and darted seventy-three yards to pay dirt.[6]

Ohio State added a late touchdown of their own, but it wasn't enough. Iowa intercepted a Tomczak pass on the last play of the game to seal Ohio State's fate. When the clock drained to zeroes, delirious Hawkeyes fans poured onto the field and tore down the north goalposts.

"What a fantastic game," Hayden Fry yelped to quote-hungry reporters once the dust had settled and night descended on Iowa City. "I think everybody would have been ready to string me up if that long pass hadn't worked. But I'm sure Ohio State didn't think we'd do it. They probably thought we'd run the ball and then have to punt, so they'd get the ball back. Instead, I gambled, and it worked."

The lightly recruited Iowa quarterback had also made another statement on the Kinnick turf, outplaying Tomczak. The Ohio State signal caller had come into the game ranked no. 1 nationally in passing efficiency. Chuck was third. The stat line, however, read in the Iowa quarterback's favor. Chuck finished sixteen of twenty-six for 276 yards, two TDs, and just one interception. Tomczak found the going much harder, completing just thirteen of thirty-four passes for 125 yards and one touchdown. He was intercepted three times.

"Football is a funny game," Tomczak said. "Yes, it's a hard pill to swallow. We needed a big play in the second half and didn't get it. Iowa is a good club and is going to win a lot of games."

"They really knocked us down with that long touchdown pass; it was just a tremendous play," conceded Ohio State head coach Earle Bruce who, prior to this day, had never lost to Fry (including a stint at Iowa State).[7]

"It was a rock 'em game," he added. "Chuck Long came up with the big play when it was needed, and he delivered."

———————

Three games. Three wins. And a no. 4 national ranking.

Not a bad start to the 1983 season.

———————

[6] Just before Chuck took the snap on the touchdown play, Buckeyes defender Shaun Gayle gave the boy from Wheaton a wink. "At first I thought that was kind of crazy, but in a split second, I'm like 'OK, Shaun, let's see if you can stop us.'" Since Moritz was older than Chuck, he wasn't about to second-guess his receiver. "I wasn't going to tell him no—and sure enough the play worked and allowed us to ice the game. It was a special moment." Gayle was drafted the following spring by the Chicago Bears. He played eleven NFL seasons in the Windy City and a twelfth for the San Diego Chargers. He holds the NFL record for returning the shortest punt for a touchdown, a five-yard scamper versus the New York Giants in the 1985 playoffs.

"Ohio State and Michigan have always been the stud teams in the Big Ten, so to beat one of them is really big," said Dave Moritz, Hawkeyes split end and one of Chuck's favorite targets, after the team's statement win over no. 3 Ohio State.

A resounding victory on a big stage against a perennial college football powerhouse provided instant national credibility for Iowa. Just twenty-one days after the season had kicked, the Hawks had leapfrogged twelve spots in the Associated Press poll, trailing only Nebraska, Texas, and Arizona. The no. 4 ranking was the Hawkeyes' highest since October 1961.

Now, with the target squarely on their back, the Hawkeyes returned to the road, traveling to Illinois to play the Fighting Illini. The Big Ten title aspirant was a formidable foe and still in a bad mood following a tough-luck 14–13 loss the previous season in Iowa City.

"They kicked our butts," announced Illinois middle linebacker Mike Weingrad, fresh off his team's 20–10 win over no. 19 Michigan State in East Lansing. "We can't wait to get back at them."

Des Moines Register staff writer Bob Dyer aptly described Iowa's return to Champaign as "walking into a hornets' nest." A capacity crowd of more than seventy-one thousand was expected, with about seventy thousand of them cheering on the 2–1 home team.

"Illinois goes completely berserk on defense," said an understandably concerned Hayden Fry. "They try to put the hurt on you, and they're pretty successful at it. I believe Illinois will bring out the best in my players."

Cedar Rapids Gazette prognosticator "Scoop Longshot" was plenty confident one day prior to the game.

"It's about time somebody took the fight out of the Fighting Illini," Scoop boasted. "And it will probably take somebody like the Hungry Hawks of Humble Hayden to do it. The Hawks' offensive linemen haven't shaved for a few weeks now but they should make things pretty hairy for the Illini defense

---

[7] Earle Bruce was 2–0 against Hayden Fry prior to the Sept. 24, 1983, loss in Iowa City. Bruce played fullback at Ohio State and was an accomplished collegiate head coach, succeeding Woody Hayes at the helm of the Buckeyes in 1979. As a head coach, Bruce spent time at Iowa State University (1973–1978) and the University of Northern Iowa (1988). He compiled a 154–90–2 career record as a college football head coach.

this week. They'll open plenty of holes for Norm 'The Lone' Granger and hold out Mark Butkins and the boys long enough for Chuck 'Throw It' Long to fire a few scoring passes to Dave 'Good Mitts' Moritz.

"Me and the ol' crystal ball figure the score should be about 35–14."

Ol' Scoop figured wrong.

Illinois ran over the Hawkeyes literally and figuratively. The team rolled up nearly 475 yards of offense behind the strong arm of quarterback Jack Trudeau,[8] forced two fumbles, snagged two interceptions, and sacked Chuck Long seven times for more than half a football field (fifty-five yards).

The outcome was never in doubt against an Iowa squad that was outplayed, outhustled, and outcoached. Illinois built a 24–0 lead just one minute into the second quarter and limited Iowa and its potent offense to just two legitimate scoring chances.

"I told the team afterward that no one will go through the Big Ten undefeated," Hayden Fry said.[9] "I'd rather lose big than drop a heartbreaker at the wire. There won't be any second-guessing today. We just got whipped.

"I don't know what happened to us," the bewildered coach added. "They beat us bad. It was not a good day for the Hawks."

Chuck had been hounded throughout the afternoon by a relentless Illinois pass rush. By the time he hit the showers, he had completed just twelve of twenty-seven passes for 224 yards.

"No one has been chased as much as Long since the last Smokey and the Bandit sequel," remarked one sports reporter.

Hayden Fry tried to put the team's first setback of the season in perspective.

"You try to be realistic. Nice things were being written, and we were deserving. But it's another plateau of pressure," he said. "Recognition and awards are a two-bladed knife. When you earn something, there is added responsibility from the public and the media to uphold that image. With

---

[8] Trudeau took the starting reins of the Illini his sophomore season and never relinquished them. As a sophomore, Trudeau outplayed Iowa's Chuck Long. He torched the Iowa secondary for 286 yards in a 33–0 rout. The 10–1 Illini advanced to the Rose Bowl that same season, losing to UCLA 45–9.

it comes added stress, pressure, and emotion to return to that level of recognition. It's an extremely difficult thing to do for the coaches and players and even the media and fans.

"Saturday was something they couldn't experience in the classroom," he added. "If they examine what happened, it will be far more valuable to them in life. Life is emotional highs and lows. Normally you handle the highs better than the lows, but you better be prepared either way."

With the stinging loss against Illinois behind them, Hayden Fry vowed to learn from mistakes made in the days leading up to Iowa's trip to Champaign.

Following the Hawkeyes' 20–14 upset win over Ohio State, the veteran coach—who served on the United Press International board of coaches—divulged he had voted his team all the way up to no. 2 behind Nebraska.

"There were two mistakes last week," Hayden Fry confided. "I disclosed my vote for the Hawks, which I've never done before, and being a superstitious guy, I don't want to repeat that.

"And we were covered by a very excellent article in Sports Illustrated. I have had that happen before, and we've always lost the next week."[10]

Superstitions aside, what Iowa needed was just what the schedule offered—a pair of games on the home turf including Oct. 8 against 1–3 Northwestern followed by the 1–3–1 Purdue Boilermakers.

The Wildcats were the first victims. Dennis Green[11] and his squad offered little resistance as the Hawkeyes took out their frustrations from being shut out the previous week, rolling up large chunks of yardage in an eventual laugher.

"NU offensive as Iowa sets offensive mark in 61–21 win," read the headline in the following day's Chicago Sun-Times.

---

[9] The 1983 Illinois Fighting Illini did not lose a game in the Big Ten, becoming the first team at the time to defeat all nine conference opponents in a single season.

The fifteenth-ranked Hawkeyes broke an impressive seventeen records on the day. Chuck passed for 420 yards, raising the school passing mark he already held (he threw for 398 versus Penn State earlier in the season), and set a team record for total offense by an individual (398 yards). The team's 713 yards of total offense set a Big Ten record. Backup quarterback Tom Grogan also got into the act after Chuck left the game with eleven minutes remaining, connecting on an eighty-six-yard touchdown strike, a Kinnick Stadium record.

In Hayden Fry's five games as Iowa head coach versus Northwestern, the Hawkeyes had won 'em all by a combined score of 253–37.

"We had a down week against Illinois, and we had something to prove offensively," Chuck said after his record-setting performance. "It feels good to be part of all of the records. We always had the capability of having a good offense. It's just a matter of proving it from week to week."

Even Northwestern's head coach was complimentary of Iowa's effort.

"They were too tough, too strong," said Green. "We were obviously handled very easily by a very good football team. And Chuck is fabulous. He's been one of my favorite people since I tried to recruit him. He just loved Northwestern, but he loved Iowa more. When he made his decision, I just shook his hand because I love Iowa, too. He's very poised—he's a super quarterback."

After his big day versus Northwestern, Chuck sat atop the nation's quarterbacks in offensive success. For the season, he had completed eighty of 133 attempts for 1,469 yards and eight touchdowns. Chuck was also second nationally in total offense with 289 yards a game and was named the Associated Press' Midwest Player of the Week on offense for his performance versus the Wildcats.

---

[10] Many teams and athletes believe an appearance on the cover of Sports Illustrated invites bad luck. The urban legend states that individuals or teams appearing on the cover will subsequently be jinxed. There are numerous examples to support the claim. There are just as many that debunk it.

[11] Green, a native of Harrisburg, Pennsylvania, had deep roots with the University of Iowa. He attended the university, graduating cum laude with a degree in finance. He played running back for the Hawkeyes and served as an assistant coach (1974–76).

One week later, the Hawkeyes beat the Purdue Boilermakers in a driving rainstorm 31–14. While Chuck passed for more than two hundred yards for the seventh consecutive game, Iowa's performance was largely lackluster. Purdue tallied ten more first downs (28–18) and was outgained by just twenty-five yards.

"Did you ever think you'd see the day Iowa would win like this and look so bad?" Fry asked in the postgame news conference. "It was unbelievable."

Now, with a record of 5–1 and confidence restored, no. 12 Iowa turned its attention to one of its most daunting and anticipated assignments of the season: a nationally televised matchup versus tenth-ranked Michigan in the Big House.[12]

And the press, as it usually does, wasted no time fanning the competitive fires. Much of the pregame banter focused on Iowa's dramatic improvement under the steady hand of Hayden Fry.

Frank Broyles, the Arkansas athletic director who had served as Hayden Fry's backfield coach while at Baylor before hiring him on his coaching staff in Arkansas, called the turnaround in Iowa City a "near miracle."

Iowa had, after all, experienced nineteen nonwinning seasons prior to Fry's arrival.

"Hayden is a remarkable person," Broyles told *Des Moines Register* staff writer Ron Maly. "He's turned three football programs around from zero. Maybe Bear Bryant turned three programs around, but not many others. Some have turned around two, but not three."

Broyles said Fry's secrets in breathing life into a Hawkeyes program that once was close to being dead are "perseverance, imagination, creativity, and motivation."

Michigan coach Bo Schembechler also piled on the praise, but wasn't exactly thrilled about the team's return to relevance.

---

[12] The Big House is aptly named. Located in Ann Arbor, Michigan, it's the largest stadium in the United States and second largest in the world. Built in 1927 at a cost of less than $1 million, its official seating capacity is 106,701 (but has hosted crowds in excess of 115,000). Iowa Stadium in Iowa City opened in 1929. In 1972, it was named Kinnick Stadium in honor of Iowa Hawkeyes football player and 1939 Heisman Trophy winner Nile Kinnick, who died in service during World War II. Kinnick Stadium seats 70,585 (2006-present).

"Iowa's resurgence under Fry has been a tremendous thing for the school and is great for the conference, but I don't like it worth a damn," he said. "I wouldn't have believed Fry could turn the program around that quickly. Iowa is a good team and well coached.

"It will be the best team we've played so far," he added. "Iowa's improvement this year is directly responsible to the better play of their quarterback. Chuck Long has been exceptionally good, and that's the strength of their team. The way they throw the ball is miraculous."

Hayden Fry also admitted to being surprised by the team's improvement in a place considered by most in college football to be a coach's graveyard.

Bo Schembechler once said a college football program couldn't be built in five years, but Fry did it in three, and he wasn't afraid to remind his coaching rival.

"I guess ol' Bo is wrong," he quipped to reporters in one of numerous pregame press conferences.

That said, Fry admitted to never having a timetable for rebuilding programs.

"There are always a lot of variables. I did everything I could to change the minuses to pluses—the uniforms, the way the players conducted themselves in the classroom as well as on the field, having them say 'yes, sir,' 'no, sir,' and 'thank you,'" he said. "I wanted them to take pride in their academic responsibilities as well as their bodies. I think the key is starting with the individual. Collectively you get a team. Not many coaches do that. They get too caught up in dealing with the Xs and Os and 'Let's run off tackle and pass.' They forget they're dealing with human beings and sensitivities."

Iowa's turnaround had become a national story, evident by the increased attention of bowl officials and television networks.

Six games into the season, major bowls were taking a liking to the Hawkeyes. Orange Bowl executives were floating a possible Iowa-Nebraska matchup while the Cotton Bowl made no secret of their admiration of Hayden Fry.

"An outstanding quarterback is always a good draw," said Jim Brock, the bowl's executive director. "Chuck Long is that kind of draw, but it really starts with Hayden. He's a national figure, and he's done a tremendous job at Iowa. Everybody knows Hayden; he'd be great from a media standpoint."

The American Broadcasting Company (ABC) also liked Iowa's growing popularity, a fact that didn't go unnoticed by Fry.

"It's a real credit to our program that ABC has picked our game for a national telecast," he crowed. "Notre Dame and Southern California are playing on the same weekend, but it's our game that's on the tube.

"At $100,000 for a thirty-second commercial, the network has to have a real good game. And if they'd make me out a check for part of that amount, I'd feel even better."

Royalty checks and bowl game invitations aside, there was a game to be played.

The top twelve college football matchup didn't disappoint the 104,559 fans that packed the Big House on a gloomy, rainy day in Ann Arbor.

Iowa trailed 6–3 at halftime after only a trio of field goals could dent the scoreboard, including a record-breaking fifty-six-yarder by Hawkeye Tom Nichol—Iowa's only score.

But the team rallied in the second half, scoring ten points in less than four minutes to tie the hard-hitting contest 13–13.

With just 1:30 remaining in the game, Iowa drove deep into Wolverines territory for what appeared to be a game-winning kick attempt. But sure-handed Owen Gill, who rushed for 120 yards on twenty carries on the afternoon, fumbled after a jarring hit by Michigan's Carlton Rose. Wolverine Rodney Lyles recovered, and Michigan quickly chewed up yardage and the clock, settling at Iowa's twenty-eight-yard line. Enter Michigan walk-on senior kicker Bob Bergeron, who proceeded to nail a line drive forty-five-yard field goal with just eight seconds remaining on the clock.

Michigan 16. Iowa 13.

"The other team was just eight seconds better," said an upset Fry. "You certainly have to give Michigan credit for moving the ball down into position for the field goal. Not too often is a coach proud in defeat, but I don't believe I've ever been prouder than I was today. I really feel bad because our guys showed a lot of character and fight in the second half. They played with as much heart as any team I've been associated with."

The game was a challenge for Chuck, too, as he battled the nation's no. 2 defense. He finished just nine of eighteen for ninety-one yards.

"They did a good job," said the Big Ten's top passer and the nation's no. 2. "They say the rain hurts passing more than running, but that's no excuse because my receivers made some great catches.

"We're still in the [Big Ten] race," he added, "but we just have to get some help from somebody."

The loss was a punch to the gut of a Hawkeyes team striving for a Rose Bowl berth.

But in usual Hayden Fry fashion, he was determined to see the positive in disappointment.

"Hell, it isn't the end of the world," he said. "We have only two losses. Penn State lost its first three, and now they're on a roll and talked about for a bowl game. We still have an opportunity for a truly outstanding season."

While Hayden Fry was busy making lemonade out of lemons, the game's outcome tarnished the team's overall resume and credentials.

And that of individual players, including Chuck.

Buck Turnbull of the *Des Moines Register* was one of the first to take notice in a story headlined, "No justice: Hawks' Long left off all-America list."

"Iowa quarterback Chuck Long must be wondering what a guy has to do to get some respect," he wrote. "He's become the Rodney Dangerfield of college football. After all, Long is the Big Ten's leading passer—as he has been all season—and he ranks fourth nationally. His team has won five of seven starts, stands sixth in the country in total offense and is 17th in both wire service polls this week.

"Yet here comes the all-America checklist in the mail from the Football Writers Association of America, normally an astute group of observers, and nowhere is the name of Chuck Long to be found."

But Turnbull also recognized that the person who was least concerned by the obvious slight was…Chuck.

"Things like this don't worry me too much," Chuck said. "If we have a good season and somebody has a good year, then he's going to be recognized."

Then, in typical Chuck Long fashion, he changed the subject by placing the emphasis of the story somewhere else.

"I'm sure picking all-American teams can get involved in a lot of politics. I'm mainly concerned about how successful our team is during the season and going to a bowl game."[13]

A propensity for putting team first and rebounding from stinging defeats had become a trademark of Hayden Fry's Hawkeyes. Within hours of leaving Ann Arbor, Iowa focused on its next opponent.

Too bad for the Indiana Hoosiers. Shortly after the game kicked, Indiana's fate was sealed. Iowa jumped out to a 21–0 first-quarter lead on its way to thrashing the Hoosiers 49–3 behind another strong performance by Chuck.[14] He finished the day sixteen of twenty-five for 233 yards, leaving him just 103 yards shy of the Hawkeyes record for most passing yards.

Many people were disappointed he didn't surpass the mark. But not Chuck.

"No, I'm not disappointed at not breaking the record. It will be sweeter to break it on the road," he said. "I know it's going to come sooner or later."

Then he shifted the focus to someone else: "I was pleased to see Dave Moritz break the records for receiving, as he's a fine receiver and deserves it. Indiana was worried about Dave today, and that gave us some underneath routes today."

But try as he might, Chuck was not able to distract the cadre of sports writers covering Iowa Hawkeyes football from the fact that an Iowa quarterback was on the precipice of setting multiple records in the team's next game.

No. 15 Iowa's opponent was Wisconsin, and Chuck needed to pass for about the length of a football field to catch Larry Lawrence's 1969 mark

---

[13] Chuck did what he could to duck the weekly quarterback comparisons. As Buck Turnbull of the *Des Moines Register* noted, Chuck didn't get too worked up about trying to outshine a rival quarterback week after week. That included an Oct. 29, 1983, matchup versus Indiana led by sophomore quarterback Steve Bradley. Chuck and Bradley ranked 1–2 on the Big Ten season for yards gained passing (Chuck with 1,776 and Bradley with 1,607). "Bradley is a good quarterback, and Indiana throws a lot," Chuck told Turnbull. "But I don't want to get caught up in any passing duel. I'm not worried about that as much as just winning the game."

of 2,086 yards of total offense in a season. He also needed just eighteen completions to break Gary Snook's record of 280 pass completions in a career and thirty-seven yards to eclipse Snook's 3,738 yards passing in a career.

"Naturally, the one least excited about Chuck Long breaking the record appears to be Chuck Long," wrote *Iowa City Press-Citizen* sports writer Dave Hyde.

But records are made to be broken, especially by someone with the arm strength, mobility, and pocket awareness of Chuck Long.

In a 34–14 win over the Badgers at Camp Randall Stadium in Madison, Wisconsin, Chuck Long inked his name in Hawkeyes lore by setting six Iowa records and tying another.

Chuck began the game with eleven consecutive completions. When he exited late in the fourth quarter, he had amassed 231 yards on sixteen of twenty-one passing against the nation's thirteenth-ranked pass defense.

"He gains confidence with every game," remarked Iowa Hawkeyes tight end Mike Hufford. "I just never thought he could be this good. But now he comes out there and points people in the right directions and has everything under control. He's unbelievable."

Wisconsin's Brian Marrow, cornerback and tri-captain, was succinct in his assessment: "He's the best quarterback our secondary's played against all season. He's just good. There's not much more you can say."

KINDRED SPIRITS

Kirk Ferentz will forever admire Hayden Fry for his ability to spot talent that everyone else missed.

---

[14] Leading 42–3 with seven seconds remaining, Iowa's third-string quarterback Cornelius Robertson lofted a ten-yard touchdown pass to reserve receiver Scott Helverson on the last play of the game. Indiana head coach Sam Wyche was not amused. As soon as the game ended, Wyche marched his players out to the middle of the field, telling them to look around and remember the scene. *Des Moines Register* staff writer Buck Turnbull reported on the development, with Wyche saying he hoped to pay Iowa back for the indignity someday. He never did. Wyche coached just one year at Indiana (finishing 3–8) before being named head coach of the Cincinnati Bengals in 1984, a position he held for eight years.

"Someway, somehow, Hayden and Bill Snyder saw something in Chuck Long that other guys didn't see," said a relaxed Ferentz during a conversation in his office lounge shortly after the 2015 Hawkeyes completed a 12–0 regular season and Rose Bowl appearance.

"Chuck didn't have many scholarship offers, yet he ends up being one of the most prolific quarterbacks to ever play in the Big Ten. Go figure."

Hayden Fry's knack for spotting diamonds that just needed a bit of polishing rubbed off on his coaching assistants, including Ferentz.

"Whether it's Chuck, Dallas Clark, or Bob Sanders, seems we've had a lot of those stories here at Iowa," Ferentz continued. "The common denominator is guys who love football, are really team oriented, and tough and competitive with a lot of upside. Coach Fry and Coach Snyder identified that in Chuck, and the rest is history."

Chuck often said that he and Ferentz enjoyed a "kindred spirit" during their time together at Iowa. And it continues today.

"Neither of us had much of a resume when we arrived together at Iowa, not unlike the entire coaching staff at the time," Ferentz recalled. "When I left Iowa to coach at Maine and as an assistant with the Cleveland Browns, I thought a lot about what made it a special time. It started with the staff. Coach Barry Alvarez was the first guy I met when I arrived at Iowa; he had been a very successful high school coach in Mason City [Iowa] before coming to the Hawks. There was Bill Snyder, who was at Austin College before joining Coach Fry at North Texas and then coming along with him to Iowa."

Also on Fry's staff was Bill Brashier, who, as the story goes, was on Fry's North Texas State squad and convinced him to take the Iowa job when he received the offer in 1979 (Fry was also considering offers from Oklahoma State and Ole Miss).

"Bill Brashier is a hall of fame coach and in my opinion one of the best assistants not to be a head coach," Ferentz said. "Same goes for Carl Jackson. There really wasn't a guy on the staff in those early years who had a resume, but that's what made Coach Fry so special—his ability to see things in people that maybe they didn't see. It's fair to say that the commonality is that we all loved football and got the value of teamwork."

And reflecting again on those five memorable years with Chuck calling the signals, Ferentz smiled.

"Sure, it's important to have a good offensive line, but I can tell you, to be a good offensive line, it helps to have a good quarterback."

"The bowls involve so much politics. It's like lobbying in Congress. There's a lot of behind-the-scenes talking. You never know right down to the last minute. Every year there are two or three teams playing in bowls where nobody guessed they would be."

HAYDEN FRY
Iowa coach responding to postseason play speculation following the team's 34–14 triumph in Madison.

With a record of 7–2 and just two games remaining in the regular season, Iowa was thick in bowl conversations while Chuck's adventures at quarterback were becoming the stuff of legend.

"Hawks soar with Long's air express," proclaimed the *Daily Iowan*.

"Long sets records, Iowa sails," announced the Nov. 6, 1983, *Des Moines*

Register headline following Chuck's commanding performance at Camp Randall in Madison, followed by the subhead, "Quarterback nearly perfect on his passing in first half."

"If things keep up, they may have to rename the Iowa football record book 'The Chuck Long Story,'" quipped *Cedar Rapids Gazette* sports writer Don Doxsie in a Nov. 6 story headlined "'Chuck Long Story' gets new chapters."

"After all, the Iowa quarterback's name probably appears in there more often than anyone's after erasing another handful of records in the Hawkeyes' 34–14 conquest of Wisconsin Saturday."

In the second quarter of the contest, Chuck surpassed Randy Duncan's record for touchdown passes in a season (eleven) and finished the day by topping Hawkeyes legend Eddie Podolak's career yards in total offense (3,796).

"There is more within reach," Doxsie wrote. "Long needs only three more completions to set the Iowa career record of 230 to get the single-season mark. If he faces many more teams like Wisconsin, there might be bigger records in sight."

The Wisconsin State Journal headlined its postgame coverage of the Badgers' debacle, "A Long afternoon, indeed." Tom Butler, the paper's sports reporter, wrote, "Iowa held all the trump cards and quarterback Chuck Long played them like a master as the Hawkeyes scored on four of their first five possessions and trounced the Badgers 34–14."

Al Grady of the *Iowa City Press-Citizen* was also impressed with Chuck's performance against the Badgers.

"The word all-American is overused because, after all, there are only two or three all-American quarterbacks, depending upon which publication or news association you might read, or believe, or agree with," he wrote. "But that one Saturday was bona fide all-American. He might have had one also at Penn State, but I was unable to get to that one."

Grady, well-versed on the historical roots of Iowa football, called Chuck the best quarterback to wear the Hawkeyes uniform since Randy Duncan, who came in second in the Heisman Award voting in 1958.

"On Saturday, Long was in complete control of the football game from Strike One until he left the game late in the third quarter," he wrote. "His poise; his confidence; his leadership; his unerring accuracy; his ability to find an open receiver; his cunning ability to scramble, to avoid the rush, to complete the pass while (and after) being hit; and his faking and ball handling cut Wisconsin to pieces and simply carved the heart out of the Badger defense.

"Long probably won't make many all-America teams this year, if any, but put him in your future book, pray for him to stay healthy, and look ahead to three more games this year and next season with a smile."

While those buying ink by the barrel were opining at great length about Chuck's success, his parents, Joan and Charlie, were taking it all in stride.

Just hours before kickoff in Madison, *Iowa City Press-Citizen* sports editor Nolan Zavoral met up with the couple to gauge their reaction as they tailgated with friends and family.

"Well, for one thing, Chuck has always had this air of confidence about himself," Charlie Long said. "It was an inward thing he always had. He never strived for attention. He felt secure with himself, I think. I guess because he was the oldest [of three boys]."

Joan Long was equally candid.

"Well, that, and Chuck was always a gifted athlete," she said. "If you'll pardon a mother for saying so, but he was. He was always the first one taken when the kids chose up sides for a game or something. He was always the tallest. The confidence couldn't have come without that."

Joan and Charlie Long told Zavoral that as a youngster Chuck was always on the phone, lining up games with his pals. Snow, sleet, rain—the elements didn't matter.

"Chuck played on. And always from his own interest," Charlie Long said.

"He would practice all day," Joan Long added. "Whatever it took to be good, he'd do. You know, the extra things. Like playing when the snow was high."

While reporters continued to tell the Chuck Long story, others were looking for comparisons between the 1983 and 1968 Hawkeyes.

"The styles between the two teams are very similar because both teams had the ability to run and pass," said Hawkeyes alum Eddie Podolak when asked by *Cedar Rapids Gazette* sports writer Brian Chapman. "I'm very impressed with the way the current team varies its offensive attack every week according to the character of the defense they play. They can feature power one week, finesse the next. It doesn't seem to matter what type of defense they face."

Podolak also admitted that the '68 team was more predictable than the 1983 edition.

"We came out and did three or four things, all developed off three or four basic plays. Of course, defenses were far more basic then."

Riding a wave of success and with national attention affixed on East Lansing, Iowa took the field Nov. 12, 1983, to take on the 4–4–1 Michigan State Spartans.

On a day when the offense didn't show, Iowa was fortunate that the defense did and made just enough plays to claim a 12–6 victory.

"The Iowa offense didn't hit on all cylinders Saturday, but the defense came through with a 'Mr. Goodwrench' rescue just before the warrant on a juicy bowl bid ran out," wrote Gus Schrader of the *Cedar Rapids Gazette*.

"Yes, it was good to have our defense come through today, as our offense has won some big games for us," admitted Hawkeyes strong safety Mike Stoops, whose sixth interception of the season and the subsequent sixty-yard run back in the third quarter helped spurn another Spartans scoring opportunity and flipped field position in favor of the visiting team.

The win improved Iowa to 8–2 on the season, but it came with a price.

Chuck suffered a high ankle sprain in the contest and two days later was modeling a cast. Hayden Fry announced his quarterback would be a no-show for practice during the week, adding that Chuck was "very questionable" for seeing playing time in the team's season finale versus the 1–9 Minnesota Golden Gophers.

Fifth-year senior Tom Grogan would be under center for the Hawkeyes if Chuck wasn't at full strength, Fry added. Cornelius Robertson and fourth-string signal caller Mark Vlasic could also see playing time.

The game, to be played in Kinnick, would serve as a prelude to another bowl appearance—Iowa's third in as many years.

"Right now, we're in a holding pattern until the bowl people tell us which ones are open," said Fry, acknowledging such suitors as the Gator, Sun, and Holiday. "Last year we had our choice of five bowls. This year, we already contacted some of the bowl people and told them we won't be available for their games. I won't mention names. That wouldn't be fair, and we're just honored to have the chance to be considered."

Talk about a nice problem to have.

By Wednesday, Hayden Fry told a flock of reporters that Chuck's status was still up in the air.

"It's very, very doubtful he'll play. The decision will not be made until game time. Right now I'm thinking Tom Grogan will start at quarterback and Corny Robertson will be number two," he said.

One day later, Chuck's status for Saturday's game versus Minnesota was revealed. He would sit.

But Iowa didn't miss its no. 1 signal caller.

The Hawkeyes steamrolled the Golden Gophers 61–10 behind senior tailback Eddie Phillips (172 yards rushing) and sophomore wingback Ronnie Harmon, each tallying three touchdowns in the rout. Senior fullback Norm Granger added 123 yards while tailback Owen Gill rushed for 104 more. No such records were kept, but *Des Moines Register* staff writer Bob Dyer ventured it might be the first time Iowa ever had three players rush for more than one hundred yards in the same game.

Shortly after the game, it was announced that the Hawkeyes would meet up with Florida in the Gator Bowl Dec. 30 in Jacksonville, Florida. Hayden Fry's buttons were poppin'.

"I'm really proud about our players, our staff, and our students. They made it a fine year," he said. "To go 9–2 and have a chance to go 10–2 and play a team like Florida in one of the best bowls of the country is super. I think we can play with anyone in the country, and we look forward to playing Florida."

The same could be said for the Gators, led by head coach Charley Pell and offensive coordinator Mike Shanahan, who respected Iowa's resume and its quarterback. What impressed them particularly was the way Iowa ended the season rolling up nearly 660 yards of offense despite Chuck watching most of the game from the sideline.

"They are versatile in so many ways. What makes their offense so tough to stop is that they move the football with a fine balance of running and passing," said Pell, who had previously served as head coach of the Clemson Tigers. "Everything Iowa did was good, but it's hard to tell just how good they are without their top man [Long] in there. Any time an offense moves the way Iowa did, it gives you an idea of how strong they are."

"What impresses me most about Chuck is that he does well in the national stats and we don't feature the passing game. It's one thing to be high in the national stats when a team builds its offense around a quarterback, but when you have a balanced offense like we do, it's quite an accomplishment."

HAYDEN FRY
in an interview with sports columnist Greg Larson
(Florida Times-Union, *Jacksonville, Dec. 28, 1983*)

Many people were taking note of Iowa's starting quarterback, and not just for his athletic ability. They were recognizing the man who wore no. sixteen for his character and charisma.

"Judging from the editing job Chuck Long has done on Iowa's passing records over the past two seasons, one would guess his most valuable asset would be his strong right arm," wrote *Cedar Rapids Gazette* sportswriter

Don Doxsie in a 1983 Christmas Day column. "But ask Long's strongest supporters about him and they don't talk about his arm. They mention his head…and his heart."

Dave Moritz, one of Chuck's favored targets, credited Chuck for his ability to read defenses. "He sees openings that other quarterbacks don't. Like last year in the Peach Bowl, there was something like sixteen times that he audibilized and changed the play at the line of scrimmage. And he called a play that worked and gained positive yardage fifteen times. That's pretty good when you can guess right fifteen out of sixteen times."

Hayden Fry had long credited Chuck for his strong intellect, which was born out of hours upon hours of watching film. But he also confided in Doxsie that he admired Chuck's inner strength.

"He's the most unflappable young man I've ever coached," Fry said in an interview. "He's always the same. His expression never changes. He never gets excited."

Those characteristics don't show up on stat sheets, particularly when you're an option quarterback on a high school team that rarely throws the ball and has a power run game and stout defense. Yet Fry gave him a scholarship anyway.

"And it was evident Fry knew he had something special before Long had even started a game at Iowa," Doxsie wrote. "Prior to the 1982 season, he told the news media that the then untested sophomore was 'destined for greatness.' Long had thrown exactly one pass in his college career to that point and Fry's comment drew some snickers.

"Now, 23 games, 17 victories, 34 touchdowns and 4,112 passing yards later, nobody is snickering…at least not the opponents."

In the lull between college football's final regular season game and the start of bowl season, sports writers go searching for any angle they can find to fill pages. Writing for the Sporting News, the *Des Moines Register's* Bob Dyer noted that the days leading up to the Gator Bowl provided the perfect opportunity to assess college football's crop of quarterbacks and tab the three best performers.

Scott Stankavage of North Carolina and Randy Wright of Wisconsin made the list.

So did Chuck Long.

"At first, they seemed like the Odd Couple," wrote Dyer. "Skeptics wondered why Hayden Fry, the supposedly pass-happy coach of the Iowa Hawkeyes, would recruit Chuck Long, a wishbone quarterback being sought by few schools."

You couldn't blame Dyer for his skepticism. Chuck Long threw only ninety-two passes his senior year at Wheaton North.

Fry's 1968 Southern Methodist team threw nearly that many in a wild game against Ohio State, Dyer noted.

Yet Fry insisted it was "football's version of love at first sight."

"The first time I met Chuck I was impressed," Fry admitted to Dyer. "He was a big, good-looking fellow who was fast and had a strong arm—a winner. Everything about him was first class."

Three years later, Chuck Long was making Hayden Fry look like a genius.

"No longer a diamond in the rough," Dyer wrote, "the polished junior now rates as a crown jewel among Big Ten quarterbacks."

What made Chuck a formidable foe, Dyer figured, was his ability to direct a balanced attack that ranked among the nation's most prolific while flourishing within a system that gave him a tremendous amount of freedom.

Chuck Long went from budding prodigy to king-sized flop to promising quarterback all in a three-week span when he first came to Iowa, Dyer added. "That might at least cause a 19-year-old brief bouts of bewilderment, but Long remained calm. Deep down inside, he knew he was better than those first two games."

"He has great poise, ability, good selection on reading defenses, and uncanny accuracy," Fry said to Dyer.

When told of his coach's assessment, Chuck just grinned and retorted, "I think he's exaggerating."

Then again, maybe not.

EARNING HIS WAY

Hayden Fry's respect for Chuck Long showed early in the quarterback's Iowa career.

"He was truly outstanding in every respect," said Fry from his home in Mesquite, Nevada. "He excelled at throwing the football, making the right plays.

"As coach, I called all the plays from the sidelines. But I quickly gained so much respect for Chuck that I did something I had never done before. When he got to the line of scrimmage and looked at the defense, if he didn't think the play would work, he had what I called 'check with me,' meaning he could change the play into what he thought would be a winner.

"And he just did a fantastic job with it through the years. It was the reason he broke so many records in the Big Ten and why we did really well in the bowl games. His ability to read defensive schemes and his personality; it's hard to describe, really."

"He fascinates everybody around him. He never gets excited, never gets his head down after a loss, never gets big-headed. You just know from being around Long, whether it's on the football field or in a bull session, that here's a guy who can't miss. There are no flaws in his armor."

HAYDEN FRY
describing his starting quarterback to Bob Dyer of the Sporting News *(Dec. 5, 1983)*

According to NCAA statistics, Chuck Long was going to be the top returning quarterback in the nation when the next college football season came calling.

Like signal caller Wayne Peace at Florida, Chuck had broken almost every Iowa passing record, and many observers were anticipating a spirited matchup between the two all-Americans.

Chuck wasn't among them.

"I'm not going to get caught up in something like that," Chuck told Greg Larson of the Florida Times-Union. "Contests like that can hurt a team sometimes. I could pass for five hundred yards and we could lose the game. I'd feel awful about that. I'd feel a lot better if I passed for only fifty yards and we won.

"In looking at the films, Florida has been a team that does not give up the big play very often," Chuck added. "This could hurt us. You have to earn everything you get against Florida. I think we're going to have to be more patient against Florida than we've been at times this season."

But Chuck had plenty of experience at being patient, Larson observed.

"He had to harness his strong arm as a high school quarterback at Wheaton North," he wrote. "Because he was obscured by the grind-it-out system, Long was recruited heavily by only three schools. He didn't have to think long about accepting Iowa's offer over those from Northwestern and Northern Illinois."

Hayden Fry, whose theory had always been to recruit players from winning teams as opposed to players who often appeared to have more talent on losing teams, never wavered in his pursuit of Chuck Long, Larson wrote.

"He led his team to a state championship and the semifinals," Fry said. "Players on these teams know what it takes to win."

––––––––––––––

"It's difficult when the coach says good things about you, and you try to live up to that. But I just tried to ignore it. And I knew I could play. It's just a matter of going after it and doing it."

CHUCK LONG
on coach Hayden Fry's praise leading up to the Hawkeyes' matchup against the Florida Gators in the 1983 Gator Bowl ("Fry says Hawkeyes quarterback is a Long shot for the 1984 Heisman," Clyde Bolton, Birmingham News*)*

The days leading up to the Gator Bowl featured weather…well, fit for gators! Heavy rain and cold temperatures (lows near ten degrees) wiped out practices, forcing teams inside for conditioning and to fine-tune game plans.

"Iowa-like" weather—overcast with highs in the thirties—was predicted at game time.

Hayden Fry and Florida coach Charley Pell put on their best game faces.

"We're just not looking at weather being a factor in the football game," Pell said. "We'll just crank up the heaters and put up with it. That's all we can do."

Fry tried to make lemonade out of lemons. "I personally have never gone into a ball game, be it an all-star game, a bowl game, or as an assistant coach, as concerned about the lack of preparation," he said. "But that doesn't mean we're gonna lose the football game. It does mean that we've left a lot of work undone that we planned to do."

Yet the coach strived to keep the team loose and wasn't afraid to let reporters know that he was enjoying the ride, too.

"I don't have to coach to eat," said Hayden, adding that he had oil investments just in case coaching the Hawkeyes didn't work out. "That makes all the difference in the world. I just go out and have fun."

Chuck downplayed the game's significance and his duel with Florida's talented QB, Wayne Peace.

Like Chuck, Peace had thrown for more than two thousand yards and completed more than 60 percent of his pass attempts on the season. Both held most of their school's passing records and were all-conference selections.

The lack of practice time for both teams, not to mention subfreezing game-time temperatures and blustery winds, took their toll once the game kicked. Iowa and Florida misfired often, committed turnovers, and struggled to establish running games.

Iowa was especially prone to miscues.

Chuck threw four interceptions.

Kicker Tom Nichol botched a kick attempt in Iowa's own end zone, and the Gators bit, cashing in a defensive touchdown.

Multiple drives into Florida territory failed to net the Hawkeyes a touchdown.

Add them all up, and it equaled a 14–6 loss for Iowa in a game contested before a record crowd of 81,293 fans (every one of them chilled to the bone thanks to minus-thirteen-degree windchills throughout the game, one of the coldest ever experienced in Florida).

"We just didn't play well enough to win," said Fry. "We have no alibis, no excuses. Florida did a heck of a job against us, and I'm sure Charley Pell is shaking his head that he was able to win with a high- powered offense that scored only one touchdown. We have a high-powered offense and couldn't even score a touchdown. The Gators had the best team on the field tonight."

Chuck, who finished the game thirteen of twenty-nine for 167 yards, didn't argue with his coach's assessment and praised the play of Florida's stout secondary.

"Florida played a heck of a defense. You've got to give their defense a lot of the credit. They took us completely out of the game."

Cedar Rapids Gazette sportswriter Don Doxsie had paid close attention to Chuck from his vantage point inside Gator Bowl Stadium (hopefully while standing near a portable heater). He marveled at what he saw, relaying it to Iowa fans in a New Year's Day column that read like something out of Dr. Seuss: "They took away his audibles, they took away his practice time, they took away his favorite receiver. They may have even taken away a little of his pride in the third quarter when a few Iowa fans started to chant for backup quarterback Tom Grogan.

"But they didn't steal Chuck Long's spirit."

IF THE LABEL FITS...

"Winners handle winning with class," said Lisa Long, reflecting on the life and career of her husband, Chuck. "They handle the highs and lows.

"What's so great about the 'destined for greatness' title to this book is that everything that happened to Chuck was so out of the blue. When Coach Fry hung that on Chuck, it was like, 'What did he just say?' Now it seems like people are throwing around that prediction all the time.

"But when Coach Fry said it, he did so at a time when coaches didn't say things like that. I can remember our reaction. We took it seriously while Chuck just kind of swept it away."

Then there was Bill Snyder. He, according to Lisa Long, was more of a realist than his head coach.

"He's a lot like me. I would dial it down, and he would, too," she said. "But there was a turning point sometime in that 1984 season where it was, 'Oh, wow, I do think there's something special here...maybe not the whole 'destined for greatness' tag, which is a bold, crazy thing. But we kind of got started thinking that perhaps the NFL was a possibility even though at that time quarterbacks from Iowa didn't get drafted in the NFL.

"But we were wrong. Hayden was right."

CHAPTER 4

Producing and Pondering

"NCAA Move Will Give Long Fifth Year as Hawk"

"BIG PEACH" HEADLINE
(Des Moines Sunday Register, *Jan. 29, 1984*)

It's 1984. Ronald Reagan is re-elected in a landslide over Walter Mondale, a gallon of gas costs $1.10, and the Soviet Bloc is boycotting the Olympic Games in Los Angeles.

The first Apple Macintosh is sold, Wham! is crooning "Wake Me up before You Go-Go," and Sony and Philips sell the first commercial CD players. Prime time TV features Magnum, P.I. and Dynasty while Ghostbusters, Beverly Hills Cop, and Indiana Jones and the Temple of Doom are packing them in at the local movie theatre.

And Chuck Long is making the most of summer at his home in Wheaton, Illinois, by throwing two hundred to three hundred passes several days a week in preparation for his fourth season as a Hawkeye.

"I haven't been passing every day," he tells Ron Maly of the *Des Moines Register*. "Arms weren't made to be throwing footballs around all the time. I've been filling out my workout cards and sending them back to Coach Fry. You can't lie, because they test all of us when we get back to Iowa City for practice."

Chuck was relishing the return for his senior season.

But would it be his last?

Maybe. Maybe not.

Eight months earlier—just weeks after the Hawkeyes' loss to Florida in the Gator Bowl—delegates to the National Collegiate Athletic Association's (NCAA) convention gathered in Dallas.

One item of business on the agenda was clarifying confusion surrounding the status of "redshirting," a practice allowing collegiate athletes the option of delaying one of their four years of eligibility.

The NCAA had banned redshirting of freshmen in 1980 but reversed itself in 1982 after a two-year trial. The move was retroactive, impacting players who hadn't played in any varsity or junior varsity games as freshmen.

However, the approval of the little-noticed amendment made an exception for an undetermined number of Division I athletes who had played in two or fewer games in 1980 and 1981.

On Jan. 29, 1984, a trio of *Des Moines Register* reporters broke the news. Rick Brown, Marc Hansen, and Michael Wegner surmised, as was being rumored, that one of the players impacted was Chuck Long, quarterback, Iowa.

Those with firsthand knowledge of the amendment, including the dean of the University of Minnesota's law school, were confident Chuck was one of several athletes who would receive an additional year of eligibility. Chuck had played only sparingly his freshman year, including a token appearance in a 64–0 drubbing of Northwestern and a loss against the Washington Huskies in the 1982 Rose Bowl.

University of Iowa athletic director Bump Elliot, when asked immediately following the NCAA's announcement if the amendment's passage would impact Chuck, only hinted at the possibility that the quarterback would qualify for an additional year should he choose to exercise the option.

The rule change and its potential impact on his Iowa career had Chuck's mind racing.

"I've heard rumors, but I don't think they're true," he told reporters as the reality of the NCAA's decision began to sink in. "I don't know much about it. The coaching staff hasn't indicated anything to me. Maybe it's true and they're going to surprise me."

Within hours, the new NCAA rule allowing Chuck and several other collegiate athletes to count 1981 as a redshirt year was the talk of the town. It didn't take Hawkeyes fans long to connect the dots and begin contemplating the possibility of two more years with Chuck Long as their starting quarterback.

By mid-March, Chuck was seriously considering a return to Iowa City for a fifth season.

"I'd say right now I'm leaning toward taking another year because I need that fifth year to graduate," he said while enjoying spring break at the family's home in Wheaton. "But I see all the money people are making in the US Football League, so you never know."[1]

A crowd of more than thirty-one thousand filled sun-drenched Kinnick for the team's spring game April 28, 1984. They wanted to be entertained, and they were.

Chuck was an efficient twenty of twenty-eight for 187 yards while running backs Owen Gill and Ronnie Harmon zigzagged across the turn for decent chunks of yardage. Fullback Fred Bush even got into the act, topping the rushing chart with forty yards (Harmon and Gill had thirty-two and twenty-six respectively).

"They did a lot of dancing out there, didn't they?" Chuck asked reporters following the game. "We only ran about one-fourth of our running plays, but we don't want to show a lot right now. We'll be a lot more wide open next fall. Winning 24–0 is more of a confidence builder for the summer than anything else. The thing I liked best about our offense is the ball control we showed."

While Chuck was basking in the glow of a solid, injury-free scrimmage, his coach wasn't as impressed.

---

[1] The US Football League launched in 1983. It was the brainchild of David Dixon, a New Orleans businessman who saw a market for professional football while the National Football League was between seasons. Despite a somewhat successful launch, attendance was fickle at best, and the league was soon hemorrhaging money. Dixon's dream was short-lived: the USFL folded in 1985.

"The offensive line made a lot of progress this spring, but it didn't show," he grumbled. "They did as poor a job blocking for our running game as they have all spring. I think it eventually will be a very good offensive line, but we'll have to see some improvement."

That was Hayden Fry. Never satisfied. Always motivating. Always thinking about ways to get better.

With the team's ascension to national prominence, many were taking an interest in the ol' coach and his unique antics.

"Only Shirley knows for sure the exact routine her husband Hayden Fry follows each morning," wrote Mark Dukes of the *Cedar Rapids Gazette*. "But chances are that even before he pulls up his slick gray cowboy boots, reads his Good Morning Friend, and puts on his sunglasses, the Iowa coach probably is thinking about football.

"And the feeling here is that he ponders unfulfilled goals more than the mountains already climbed," Dukes added. "He doesn't necessarily think about the Hawkeyes' three straight winning seasons, three straight bowl trips, five straight first division Big Ten finishes, his 65.8 winning percentage against the league or the security of his job."

True Hayden.

"We've worked hard to become winners, very hard," said the Texas native on the eve of another grueling Big Ten campaign. "But we're not there yet. Each morning when I wake up, I'm motivated because I know there's more to do."

———————

Hayden Fry and his coaching staff were laying the foundation for a winning Hawkeyes football program.

And they were doing it one man at a time.

One of them was nose guard Hap Peterson.[2]

---

[2] Hap Peterson arrived in Iowa City in 1981 and, like Chuck, played in five bowl games after opting for a fifth year of eligibility after an NCAA ruling in 1984 changed the status of redshirting. He was a Hawkeyes captain in 1985, sharing MVP honors with twelve of his senior teammates and earning honorable mention all-American status by the Associated Press. Peterson is the godfather to Chuck's son Nathan.

A Chicago native and son of a US Marine, Hap grew up around sports. His father, Howard, a graduate of Morningside in Sioux City, Iowa, played professional football for the New York Giants before going to work for farm equipment manufacturer International Harvester. [3]

Howard Peterson's success with the company required frequent moves. The last was to Bettendorf, Iowa, a bustling city of thirty thousand nestled in southeast Iowa adjacent to the banks of the Mississippi River and just sixty miles from Kinnick.

Hap Petersen made a name for himself on the Bettendorf High wrestling mat and football field. As a senior, Petersen won the state heavyweight wresting title with a 30–0 record and anchored the defensive line on the state football championship runner-up (losing to Newton in the season finale).

Given the family's proximity to Iowa City, Howard Petersen was a Hawkeyes season ticket holder. Despite Iowa's dismal showing on the gridiron, he wouldn't hesitate to ask his son, "Hey, wouldn't it be great to play at Iowa?"

"Pops, these guys are terrible," Hap Petersen would reply as if trying to dodge his father's not-so-subtle nod to being a Hawkeye.

But as if on cue, Iowa assistant coach Carl Jackson was soon hard at work recruiting the all-conference high school wrestler and football player. A memorable visit by Hayden Fry to the Peterson home sealed the deal. [4]

For Hap Petersen, the opportunity to play for coaches who were honest, direct, and optimistic was too good to pass up—not to mention for a team that was just a stone's throw from his family's front door.

---

[3] In the early 1830s, inventor Cyrus Hall McCormick founded the International Harvester Company (IH) when he produced and patented a horse-drawn grain reaper. Fueled by quality products and the mechanization of farming, IH became one of the leading domestic manufacturers of agricultural machinery, trucks, and construction equipment by the mid-1900s.

[4] Hap Petersen will never forget when Hayden Fry, accompanied by assistant coach Carl Jackson, made his one and only recruiting visit to the Peterson home in Bettendorf:

"So my dad was this no-nonsense guy. Been a marine. Played professional. He understood what it took to win and to be a good leader. But the truth of the matter was that my mom had this little schnauzer dog named Sam. And Sam hated everyone. He'd bark like hell at anybody who came in the door.

"Well, Hayden came into my house, and Dad gave up his chair, which he never did because no one else ever sat in Dad's chair. But Hayden sat down, and Dad sat on the couch. And Sam came right up and, without skipping a beat, jumped up and sat on Hayden's lap and made himself super comfortable. My mom looked at my dad and said, 'Oh heck yeah, he's going to Iowa.' True story. Keep in mind this is the same dog that barked like hell and woke the whole household anytime I came home past curfew."

Very quietly, Hayden had assembled a deep and talented coaching staff that included Jackson, Barry Alvarez, Dan McCarney, Bill Snyder, Bob Stoops, Bill Brashier, and Kirk Ferentz. They were a confident bunch and dedicated to turning the beleaguered program around. In turn, the players believed in them. That combination had Iowa well on its way to achieving national relevance.

Iowa's notoriety as a farming state was also a plus for the defensive standout. Petersen grew up around farming, moving from farm town to farm town as his father was transferred to new IH equipment dealerships. He embraced hard work as a kid, weeding soybean fields, detasseling corn, and baling hay. He got so good at these chores that his father often recommended his employment to area farmers. Being around farms and working for farmers galvanized Hap Petersen's appreciation for the profession and what farming meant for the fans who filled Kinnick for each home game.

For Hap Petersen, the stars were aligned to accomplish great things. His freshman class was composed of humble, hardworking young men.[5] Among them was a relatively inexperienced and largely unknown quarterback from Wheaton, Illinois.

Like Chuck Long, Hap Petersen and many of his comrades came from similar backgrounds and were raised in households where parents guided, influenced, and encouraged. They were solid, well-grounded individuals whose athletic talent was surpassed by a relentless work ethic.

Many of the boys were also "earthy folks" who understood what it meant to pull together as a team and play as a team. They were a band of brothers and leaders who wanted to be part of something special by turning around an Iowa program that had been largely irrelevant for nearly two decades.

Hayden Fry and his staff knew the game of football. But they knew even better the power of positive thinking and how to motivate young men. They encouraged players to do their part to the best of their abilities. By bringing

---

[5] "Hayden had an opportunity to choose anybody he wanted to wear the Hawkeyes uniform that year," said Hap, "but for some reason, he saw something in us kids, chose us, and it all came together. That's the magic of Hayden Fry."

their lunch pails to the practice field each day and working together, they could accomplish things as a team that they, and the fans, could have never imagined.

Almost immediately, the Hawkeyes were doing the unthinkable. In Chuck's first game ever in Kinnick, Iowa defeated seventh-ranked Nebraska in the team's 1981 season home opener.[6]

By 1984, Hayden Fry made it abundantly clear that a person had far more ability than he gave himself credit for. Placing young men in the right position and right frame of mind made the sum of the parts far more effective than any individual.

With each win, the positivity became infectious. When two people began believing they could be great, then it became three, then four, then eight, and, eventually, the entire team.

"On defense, if you weren't part of every tackle on every play, you were letting people down," Hap Petersen recalled. "We were eleven people to the ball. Everyone on target. If I didn't get to the quarterback or cause some disruption in his throwing motion or his dropping back, then I was putting my defensive backs on an island. I took as much responsibility as the guy covering them. It was that approach that made the team special.

"Everyone had an appreciation for their job. I knew everything that the linebacker and defensive end and cornerbacks and safeties had to do. I also knew what I had to do. This was instilled in us by some truly special coaches who we were extremely fortunate to be around when they were young in their careers."

And the less they saw of Hayden Fry on the sidelines during the game, the better.

Really.

"We had a competition on our side of the ball versus the offensive side of the ball," Petersen said. "Our whole goal was to keep Hayden down on the other end of the sidelines. When he came down on our end of the ball or our end of the sidelines, we knew we were in deep you-know-what because he had no business on our end of the sidelines. We all talked about this a lot as

---

[6] "I'd like to say that I knew something about it, but it was just lucky," Chuck recalled. "It was a feel about the kind of mojo around the program. Truly one of the best sports environments I've been around in my life."

players. So did the coaches. They told us to get our asses in there and do our jobs so Hayden didn't come down on our end, because if he did, it would only be trouble.

"As a result, we took intense ownership of our individual performances, and that effort transcended to the team level," Petersen said. "Those are amazing life lessons that people don't generally get exposure to. But we did playing for Coach Fry and a truly outstanding coaching staff."

———————————

"It's kind of a sad situation this year," said Iowa ticket manager Jean Kupka. "We have too many orders for the seats we have. We expect to return about four thousand orders. Last year, we returned about three thousand.

"We've been sold out for four years, but people continue to increase their orders," she added. "Many of them are people who have not ordered before. I apologize to the people. We don't like to return them. It seems the demand increases each year."

That's a nice problem to have for a football program that struggled for almost twenty years to get fans to care.

As the appetite grew for tickets, so did Hayden Fry's expectations for Chuck Long.

While Kupka and her staff of eight managed more ticket requests with the help of a new computer system, Fry ratcheted up the Heisman hype for his quarterback. In fact, the coach rarely made a public appearance without first talking about his quarterback and the Heisman Trophy.

Chuck, as was his nature, took the praise and accolades in stride.

"I don't feel any special pressure going into the season because I'm being mentioned as a Heisman Trophy candidate," he told Ron Maly of the *Des Moines Register*. "It's quite an honor just to be listed by Coach Fry as a legitimate candidate. But even though it's a compliment, I still have to prove myself on the field.

"And I'm not going to be thinking about the Heisman Trophy during the season," he added with total sincerity. "I just want to perform up to my abilities and hope we can show the nation that we're a team to be reckoned with and get back to the Rose Bowl."

Pure Chuck.

With kickoff to the 1984 season rapidly approaching, other names were being floated as Heisman contenders, including quarterbacks Bernie Kosar (Miami) and Doug Flutie (Boston College); running backs Bo Jackson (Auburn), Napoleon McCallum (Navy), Keith Byars (Ohio State), D. J. Dozier (Penn State); and Bill Fralic, offensive tackle from Pittsburgh.

Stiff competition, to say the least.

No quarterback had won the Heisman Trophy since Auburn's Pat Sullivan in 1971.

But Chuck Long had the credentials. Over the past two seasons, he had thrown for nearly 4,300 yards and twenty-five touchdowns. He had finished second nationally the previous year in passing efficiency and first in yards per completion (10.3).

Yet Chuck still figured he was…well, a long shot.

"I'd say my chances are pretty slim because only one player in a million gets it," Chuck said. "Plus, a quarterback hasn't won it in a long time. I'm just honored to be in the running.

"It's more a matter of opinion on who thinks which player is good," he added. "Those things are never right anyway. I'd rather not be named in preseason; I'd rather earn it by the end of the year."

Another Iowa State Fair had concluded. Children were preparing to return to school. The days were growing cooler and shorter.

And Hayden Fry was restless.

It was September, and just one week remained until the Hawkeyes played host to the Iowa State Cyclones in the season's opener.

"I think back five years ago, and things have changed considerably here, mostly for the better," he mused in his weekly news conference. "We go into the season highly rated, and I think we'll possibly have a good year. But I'm a little uptight because of the high expectations."

In fact, Hayden Fry wasn't afraid to say the expectations were too high: "We have a major overhaul to do on the offensive team," he said as if wearing a chip on his shoulder. "To say that this can be done overnight is ridiculous. It remains to be seen if we can get ready in time.

"We are going into this season highly ranked...but this team hasn't played a game yet. They haven't proven anything. I've felt better going into a season mainly because the competition wasn't so tough."

Home games included Iowa State, Penn State, Illinois, Michigan, Wisconsin, and Michigan State. Iowa would travel to Ohio State, Northwestern, Purdue, Indiana, Minnesota, and, oddly enough, Hawaii for its season finale Dec. 1.

Even the Cyclones, a team that Iowa had manhandled 51–10 the previous year, had Hayden Fry reaching for the Rolaids.

"They brought in fifteen junior college players. We haven't been able to evaluate them, but we know they'll be stronger," he groused to sports editor Steve Batterson of The Daily Iowan.

The Nittany Lions were another sore subject for the coach.

"Penn State came on like gangbusters last season. Remember, they scored thirty-six points against us when their offense supposedly hadn't jelled."

And don't forget about the Buckeyes. And the Fighting Illini.

"Ohio State will be looking to pay us back, and we know how Illinois put a knot in our head. We're concerned with the whole season but especially with the first four games."

After listening to the ol' coach, you'd think Iowa was on the verge of going winless.

While Hayden Fry fretted, Chuck played it cool.

"Sure, we're rated high," he said of the tenth-ranked Hawkeyes, "but if we go in with a cocky attitude, we'll probably get it deflated pretty quick. If we go in with a low-key attitude thinking that we've got to work hard, we'll be OK. Right now, we're only 0–0–0 with twelve games to go."

He also downplayed the need for an inexperienced offensive line to keep him upright.

"My strength is in throwing the ball downfield," he said. "I pose a better threat throwing the ball on the run or scrambling around. I feel I'm a good pocket passer but not a pure drop back quarterback. I like a little movement and don't want to stay in the pocket and take the sack."

Fry countered by putting the pressure back on the O-line.

"Chuck is so fluid and easygoing, he doesn't really look like he's that outstanding until you look at his stats," he said. "He just doesn't throw bad passes. Every time Chuck throws the ball, we expect it will be on target. It would be tragic if our linemen didn't develop to give Chuck the protection that he needs to throw the ball."

In the team's season opener versus the Cyclones, Hayden Fry and his tenth-ranked Hawkeyes could take a break from worrying.

The offensive line executed well against an Iowa State defense that lined up in multiple formations and blitzed often.

They did everything well but tackle.

"The line saw it all today and did a good job of picking up everything the defense came at them with," Chuck said following a 52–21 romp in front of more than sixty-six thousand fans. "We were a little frustrated early, but we were really a big play offense today. That's something we haven't been before. We've never really had an offensive show like we had today."

Less than eight minutes into the second half, Iowa had surged to a 52–7 lead. But before Chuck was pulled with seven minutes remaining in the third quarter in favor of reserve quarterback Mark Vlasic, he had amassed a workmanlike stat line: ten of seventeen for 217 yards and four touchdowns (on tosses of fifteen, sixty-three, three, and sixty-eight yards). He threw just one interception.

"I'm sure [Boston College quarterback and Heisman candidate] Doug Flutie and others didn't come out that early," Fry said. "I'm not trying to get Chuck Long the Heisman and we won't run up his stats for that. My only concern is winning, and fortunately, I've got a quarterback who feels the same way."

The defense also rose to the occasion in the Hawkeyes' season opener. "Our game plan was to go for the big play on defense, and you couldn't have written the script any better," said Fry after his squad forced an astonishing eight turnovers.

"We obviously had a bundle of mistakes early, but not many coaches can gripe about fifty-nine points, and I can't either," Fry told Mark Dukes of the *Cedar Rapids Gazette* after the team notched its eighth consecutive home victory. "I knew if we'd stick to our knittin' that sooner or later we'd pop one. Fortunately, we popped more than one."

But Fry warned that the team still had a long, long way to go before facing talented Penn State.

"They've been national champs, they've gone to bowl games for seventeen or eighteen straight years, they have a great coach, and everything about Penn State is quality."

The blowout rocketed the Hawkeyes up five spots in the AP poll, settling at no. 5 with the twelfth-ranked Nittany Lions ready to invade Kinnick.

As was sometimes his way, Joe Paterno played possum as game day approached. Just one year earlier, Iowa had claimed a 42–34 win in Happy Valley, and the veteran coach was determined to avoid a repeat performance. "We're not anywhere near good enough to be in a league with Iowa right now," said Paterno. "I think Iowa has to be one of the best—I don't know, five, six, four, eight—teams in the nation. I don't think there's much comparison at all between us and Iowa. Iowa is much better than we are."

As a headline in the Sept. 12 *Cedar Rapids Gazette* proclaimed, Hayden Fry "wasn't buying Paterno's act."

"I've never heard so many good things said about the Hawkeyes," he laughed after listening to Paterno gush. "If Joe ever gets out of coaching, maybe we can hire him to take [sports information director] George Wine's job."

On the other hand, Fry added, "Have you ever recalled Penn State not having the finest football team? Just a year ago, they were national champs. No need me talking about Penn State no matter what Coach Paterno says. He always has a fine, fine football team.

"Plus," Fry chuckled, "they play William & Mary next week and Herbert and Lucille the week after."

So on a day with momentum on the side of Iowa, the talented and opportunistic Nittany Lions took the air out of the Hawkeyes' sails. A rugged defense accompanied by a resolute offense combined to do just enough to claim a 20–17 victory.

"What Paterno brought with him to Kinnick Stadium Saturday was not a bunch of pussycats but a pride of hungry and opportunistic Nittany Lions who put a bite on the Hawkeyes," wrote *Des Moines Register* staff writer Bob Dyer.

It was Iowa's first home loss since 1982 and a shock to the Hawkeyes' system. Chuck Long, sacked six times and on the run most of the game, passed for just 189 yards on the day, completing only five passes in the first half before finishing a pedestrian sixteen of twenty-seven.

"Honestly, we had a lot of chances to win the game today," said a dejected Hayden Fry in postgame remarks. "We just made a lot of mistakes. That pretty much sums up the ball game. We had four fumbles, and they all were critical."

So, too, was Iowa's failure to execute on a fourth-down-and-one from the Penn State twenty-nine with less than two minutes remaining in the fourth quarter. A pitch from Chuck Long to running back Ronnie Harmon began with great promise but came up short by the nose of the football to net Iowa a new set of downs. Penn State quarterback Doug Strang then ran out the clock to preserve the win.

"I think the blocking was there, and everybody said I made it, but they marked it short," the junior running back said. "When I look at the films, I probably should have gone outside with the run. But that's history now."

The loss sent Iowa backward in the polls to no. 14.

"The Hawkeyes did it all Saturday, mixing in almost every type of screwup this side of the Three Stooges," wrote an unapologetic Don Doxsie of the *Quad City Times*. "There were fumbled punts, bumbled snaps, blown assignments, interceptions, penalties. And most of them came at bad times at bad places on the field."

Ouch.

Oh, and just in case some were thinking the Hawkeyes were national championship material… well, that went out the window along with back-to-back wins against Penn State.

"If I were coaching at Texas or one of those other schools with a long-established program, I might have been thinking of a national championship," Hayden Fry said with an aura of reality. "But our program is still at its infancy. We've got to learn to walk before we can run.

"Anyone who dreams of a national title, well, they've got to be a little crazy in the head," added the psychology major-turned-football coach.

Now the battered Hawkeyes had to hit the road, this time for Columbus, Ohio, and the no. 5 Buckeyes, led by powerful and shifty tailback Keith Byars. This Heisman Trophy candidate wasn't lacking in confidence.

"There's no doubt in my mind I'll win [the Heisman Trophy]," said the junior from Dayton, Ohio, following his team's 44–0 whitewash of Washington State the previous week. "I don't want to wait until my senior year. I want to be a two-time winner."

The words didn't escape the ears of the Hawkeyes coaching staff, who were more than eager to pass them along to the team's defensive unit.

"I'm kind of surprised he'd say that," said Hawkeyes safety Mike Stoops. "I wouldn't expect anyone to make that kind of statement, especially someone from a class program like Ohio State."

Then again, if the shoe fits, wear it.

Iowa, a 20–14 victor over the Buckeyes the previous year, had seen Byars for only one half before he was forced to leave the game with a leg injury. Byers had tallied ninety-eight yards rushing despite that limited appearance.

The 233-pound back picked up right where he left off, rumbling for touchdown runs of fifty and seven yards, catching a fourteen-yard touchdown pass, and completing his first throw, a thirty-five-yarder. The Heismanesque performance in front of 89,733 fans (the second-largest attendance in team history) helped pace the Buckeyes to a 45–26 win over an outmanned Iowa squad.

"Byars gave a super performance," Hayden Fry conceded. "He certainly didn't do anything to hurt his chances for the Heisman Trophy."

The game also continued an ominous trend for the Hawks. Similar to its home loss versus Penn State, Iowa was the giver of extra possessions to the dangerous Buckeyes. Four more turnovers—two fumbles and two Chuck Long interceptions—created yet another uphill challenge that proved too steep to climb.

"What can I say, turnovers hurt us," Chuck said. "We outrushed them, we outpassed them, and we ended up losing the game. The thing you look at there is the turnovers. They hurt us last week, and they hurt us this week. We just have to concentrate. There's nothing we can do different in practice. We just have to learn to hold onto the ball."

Bill Happel, one of Chuck's favored receiving targets, tried to stay positive and keep the turnover bug in perspective.

"You know, a lot of breaks went against us," he said. "We just have to keep working, and things are bound to turn our way. We just can't let it get us down."

Byars, who just one week earlier had predicted he'd carry the Heisman Trophy back to Columbus in December, struck a humbler note following his performance against the Hawkeyes.

"I'm going to put what happened each week behind me so I can go out and play my best on the field," he said.

No doubt the young man had received a talking to by his head coach.

"I told Keith he's going to have to prove how good he is on the field, not in talking to the press," said Earle Bruce. "He could turn off as many people as he turns on with that kind of talk."

While Byars was getting a lesson in humility, others were talking about Iowa's inability to hold onto the ball and eliminate mistakes. Turning the corner is always easier said than done, especially when a 3–1 Illinois team awaits in a game that would be nationally televised.

Led by fifth-year head coach Mike White, the Fighting Illini were flying high after a 10–2 1983 season (including a 33–0 whitewash of Iowa in Champaign) and a 40–7 thumping of the Michigan State Spartans the previous week. They were the winners of twelve consecutive Big Ten games and, led by quarterback Jack Trudeau, stood 3–1 on the season.

"The question now is what the losses back to back versus Penn State and Ohio State mean to Iowa's season, and where the Hawkeyes go from here," wrote sports columnist Al Grady of the *Iowa City Press-Citizen*. "It's a direct reversal from last year when successive somewhat surprising wins over Penn State and Ohio State thrust Iowa into the national limelight and into a no. 3 ranking nationally. Then came the big thud at Illinois."

After tasting victory in its season opener, Iowa's record was now turned inside out. With a mark of 1–2, the Hawkeyes were desperate for a win.

"We were embarrassed last year," Chuck said. "We got beat up pretty bad. They caught us at a bad time. We're gonna be hungry."

"I'm optimistic about our future. Our luck will change."

HAYDEN FRY
(Sept. 29, 1984)

Hayden Fry didn't like to lose. But when he did, it was used as a teaching moment.

The name of the game was continually improving as a team.

Sometimes losses could be valuable learning opportunities, said Hayden, especially when you were trying to turn a losing program into a winning one, as was the case when he arrived in Iowa City in 1979.

"You can get so satisfied with winning. Wins can make you forget that you may have gotten a few breaks or the other team may have helped beat themselves," the wise coach said in a Dec. 12, 2015, conversation from the comfort of his home in Mesquite, Nevada.

"Winning can camouflage a lot of things. But in losses, you have to analyze all the mistakes you made and things you could have done better. You analyze the weak points and you focus on putting new plays into the system that can work."

Fry, who won more than 230 college football games as a head coach, liked a good, hard-fought, well-played game as much as the fans, especially when the Hawkeyes were victorious. Turnovers and blown assignments, however, were another matter. Nothing good came from giving the opposition more possessions or chances to make a play.

"The most important thing in football is not to beat yourself," he said. "Eliminate the interceptions, the fumbles, blocked punts, and missed tackles. The way to do that is by understanding the things that you either can't coach or to avoid calling plays the player doesn't have the ability to execute. First rule of thumb is to not put players in a position where they can't succeed.

"You have to be smart by not asking your players to do something they really don't have the ability to do," Fry added. "Or, if you have assistant coaches or even as the head coach, don't spend time teaching something that you really don't know how to teach. You have to get that out of your system. You have to be very honest and down to earth and analyze what the team can do best and what we must stop doing that's hurting us."

According to Fry, players like Chuck Long transitioned this philosophy from the playing field to their personal lives, jobs, and professions.

Fry's advice: never put yourself in a position you're not capable of managing.

"Apply this approach to your personal life—your financial investments, your family, a lot of major decisions in your life. You'll find a lot of things you learn in football can help you win in all walks of life."

THE LITTLE THINGS

John Streif arrived on the University of Iowa campus in 1966 as a student. After a brief stint with the Detroit Lions and West Point Academy, the native of Manchester, Iowa, was named Iowa's assistant athletic trainer in 1972. Forty years later, in 2012, he retired from the position.

Not a bad run. And with his extended tenure as a Hawkeyes insider, he has more than a few memories. Like those years at Iowa and the first time he met Hayden Fry.

"I was here during a lot of losing years. My first year on the job was with coach Ray Nagal, and he was followed by Frank Lauterbur and then Bob Commings," said Streif, ticking them off with the same ease as wrapping a bum ankle. "They were all good people, too, and they wanted to win, just like Hayden."

But there was something different about the Texan and his unique ability to relate to people: he could see the humanity in football.

"The other coaches wanted to win so badly. And when it came down to the hard times and the tough times, they concentrated even harder on the Xs and Os and winning games," Streif said. "When you do that, you can often forget the little things.

"But from the very beginning, that guy [Hayden Fry] had leadership ability and discipline and made our young people concentrate on the little things. Like how you treat people, handle the media and the law enforcement people in our community, how to dress and wear a hat, and how to handle the silverware in the dining room.

"Those young people got that same lecture and that same stuff for four or five years and probably didn't want to hear it, but they needed it," Streif said with confidence. "That's what made Coach Fry so special. It was his attention to detail and the little things in his program that he never forgot. And he was a lot like Chuck; he surrounded himself with great people.

"He knew what he was doing. I have the highest and utmost respect for him. I always will."

Hayden Fry's upbeat approach served him well as the Illinois game loomed. When asked if it qualified as a "must win," Fry stayed even-keeled.

"I think what you must do is do your best. That's the way I coach. I will say this: it's time we stop losing. But that's up to my players. My eligibility is gone."

By now teams were wise to Chuck Long. They respected him so much that they weren't about to let the four-year quarterback's arm beat them. Even an arm that was still physically wounded after sustaining a bruised shoulder in the team's opener versus the Cyclones.

That was just fine with Hawkeyes running back Ronnie Harmon. The native of Queens, New York, had been a consensus all-city football player at Bayside High School and continued to showcase his offensive attributes at Iowa.

And at no time was that more evident than when Illinois came calling Sept. 29, 1984, in front of a raucous record crowd of 66,322 in Kinnick.

Needing to right the ship after consecutive losses to Penn State and Ohio State, Harmon provided the spark Iowa sorely needed. The 196-pound junior running back chewed up nearly his weight in yards (191) and scored three touchdowns, propelling the Hawkeyes to a 21–16 homecoming victory.

The performance ranked Harmon eighth in Iowa's record book for single game rushing total (Eddie Podolak held the top spot, netting 286 in seventeen attempts versus Northwestern in 1968) and earned him United Press International's Midwest Offensive Player of the Week.

"That was a beautiful victory on national TV," Fry exclaimed in his postgame comments. "That just goes to show that you've got to have faith and believe. After we had two chances for chip shot field goals and we had passes intercepted, I said, 'Lord, if you let us get down there again, we're going to run it.' He must have put his hand on our backs, because I haven't seen such beautiful blocking like that in the second half in a long time."

Iowa's running game rolled over Illinois, netting 313 yards, including 115 from Owen Gill. Most impressive was Iowa's last drive of the game. Leading by just five points with 6:18 on the clock, Iowa's Gill ran for more than half a football field as the Hawkeyes ran out the clock on fourteen consecutive running plays.

Meanwhile, Chuck finished seven of fourteen for seventy-three yards.

No one was more pleased with his passing performance on that Saturday than Chuck, considering that the previous year versus Illinois, he had been twelve of twenty-seven and sacked seven times.

"I think a lot of people are wrapped up in stats, but they will come," Chuck predicted. "The most important thing is to win the game. I'd feel sick to my stomach if I threw for three hundred yards and we lost the game."

Just ask Jack Trudeau, QB for Illinois, who completed twenty-six of thirty-three passes for 230 yards but left the field on the losing end of the scoreboard.

"I had a sick feeling after this loss," he said. "We're very disappointed because this was our first Big Ten defeat in two years."

Chuck's slim numbers weren't a fluke. Hayden Fry said the game plan was to control the ball, even knowing that it would hurt his quarterback's stats.

"I had a long talk with him and he said, 'Whatever it takes to win,'" Fry said.

"To me, this was great because it was a win over my home state, and it was on national TV," Chuck added. "Stats don't matter, but wins do."

With one-third of the season in the books, Iowa now embarked on a four-game midseason stretch that included road trips to Northwestern (a team Fry called "vastly improved" from the previous season) and no. 14 Purdue. Then a home date versus the Michigan Wolverines followed by a visit to pesky Indiana.

It was a four-game stretch that saw Iowa outscore its opponents 121–26.

The first victim was Northwestern. Despite pregame comments of being "worried" about the Wildcats' year-over-year improvement, Hayden Fry's Iowa Hawkeyes once again demolished the team from suburban Chicago 31–3 in front of a crowd of 36,500 in Evanston (many of them clad in black and gold).

Iowa pounced quickly on the outmanned Cats, taking a 21–0 lead by early in the second quarter on three touchdown runs by Harmon. He finished with 121 yards (his third consecutive one hundred-yard game) and caught six passes for another sixty-four.

The Hawkeyes set a school record in the contest by holding Northwestern to just forty-nine yards in total offense (besting sixty-seven yards allowed against Kansas State in 1955). Three Wildcats quarterbacks managed just seven completions in twenty-six attempts on the afternoon,[7] with the team's only score coming on a forty-nine-yard field goal in the second quarter.

Hayden Fry and Chuck Long, much like Green, were far from enthusiastic about the team's offensive performance. The Wildcats sacked Chuck six times for eighty-five yards. Yet somehow, someway, Chuck still managed 263 yards on nineteen of twenty-eight passing.

"This has been my roughest day as a player," Chuck confided shortly after the final gun. "We were kind of lax out there, and we weren't as emotional as we should have been. … It was just one of those days that happen. I'm glad it happened against Northwestern rather than against Ohio State or Michigan."

Fry was equally chagrined and oddly succinct with the six sacks allowed by Iowa. "We certainly didn't play good football," he said. "We're just not doing a good job of protecting Chuck. However, it was our best defense in years. They played like they did at the end of last season. I don't even need to look at the statistics."

That assessment changed one week later when Iowa took the field in West Lafayette, Indiana, against the Big Ten-leading Boilermakers—a destination Iowa had not won at since 1956 when then-head coach Forest Evashevski led the Hawkeyes to the slimmest of victories, 21–20.

Fry scoffed at a Purdue "jinx" in the days leading up to the much-anticipated matchup.

"Team members change, coaches change, we just don't put anything into that," he said in advance of a critical showdown that would pit Iowa's vaunted ground game against Purdue's air attack led by junior quarterback Jim Everett whom Fry called "one of the school's all-time greats."[8]

"Purdue is hungry. They remind me a lot of us in my freshman year," added Chuck.

With representatives of the Liberty, Holiday, Florida Citrus, and Sun Bowls watching from the stands above and a capacity homecoming crowd rocking the stadium, the Hawkeyes stormed into West Lafayette and ripped the no. 14 Boilermakers 40–3.

---

[8]Hayden Fry shared a different perspective following Iowa's lopsided win in West Lafayette. "I'd be telling a story if I said the coaches completely overlooked the fact that Iowa hadn't won here in twenty-eight years," he said in his postgame news conference. "But we didn't play it up much. I tried it once before, and Mark Herrmann [a former Purdue quarterback] put a knot on our heads."

[7]Northwestern starter Sandy Schwab sustained a bruised shoulder in the third quarter and exited the game. Top reserve Mike Greenfield was inserted by coach Dennis Green only to be taken out in the fourth quarter. Green, according to sports editor Steve Batterson of the *Daily Iowan*, said the freshman quarterback was hit so hard "he couldn't remember his locker combination following the game."

Chuck, who had made no excuses about his subpar season leading up to game time, lit up the Purdue defense (that included cornerback Rod Woodson, who would one day graduate from Purdue for an NFL career possessing thirteen Boilermaker records), hitting on seventeen of twenty-one throws (80 percent) for 369 yards.

The Heisman-like performance also included four touchdowns coming on strikes of fifty-one, fifty-six, thirty-one, and thirty-eight (including one courtesy of the flea-flicker). Sophomore wide receiver Robert Smith, who wasn't even listed on the Hawkeyes' two-deep depth chart, was on the receiving end of three of them. On the day, Iowa's offense rolled up nearly five hundred yards on Boilermakers sod.

"It's sure one of the better days I've had," Chuck quipped. "My arm felt better than it ever has, and I could feel in pregame warm-ups that it was going to be a good day."

A bit of an understatement considering he was pulled with one minute remaining in the third quarter for backup Mark Vlasic in a game versus the Big Ten's no. 1 pass defense (the Boilermakers came into the game allowing a measly 168.4 yards in the air per contest).

"He was brilliant on a wet, gray afternoon," observed Ron Maly of the *Des Moines Register*. "He riddled Purdue's secondary and wound up with the second-biggest day of his career."

Hayden Fry's goal, he said, was to score early and often to deflate the homecoming crowd of more than sixty thousand.

"We wanted to get the crowd out of the game and let them do something with those yellow towels besides wave them and also keep that choo-choo quiet," said Fry, referring to the Boilermakers' traditional locomotive that sounded off when the home team scored touchdowns.

"We're in the middle of it [Big Ten race] for going to a big bowl game," he added with a sly grin, "particularly that one out west."

> "As for shaking hands after a game, there's no rule
> that requires it. It's just a matter of sportsmanship.
> Some don't want to do it, but I'm a different
> personality. I don't think it's good for players to see
> their coach not wanting to shake hands with the other
> guy. My gosh, it's still a game."

HAYDEN FRY

*after Purdue coach Leon Burtnett went to the locker room without
shaking the Iowa coach's hand following the Hawkeyes' 40–3
win in West Lafayette ("Iowa, Fry get big victory but no hand from
Burtnett," Des Moines Register, Monday, Oct. 15, 1984)*

It's fun when you're in the thick of a conference race. For Iowa, the experience was still fresh enough to be special.

The Hawkeyes were accomplishing all sorts of firsts, and it took the crafty penmanship of *Iowa City Press-Citizen's* Al Grady to make sense of it all by noting that when Hayden Fry arrived in Iowa City, the Hawkeyes hadn't...

- Won at Purdue since 1956
- Beaten Purdue here or there or anywhere since 1960 (Iowa had now won three of its last four skirmishes against the Boilermakers)
- Had a winning season since 1961
- Won at Michigan since 1958
- Been to a bowl game since 1959
- Beaten Ohio State since 1962 and
- Had a one thousand-yard rusher in a season

"That list of negatives we used to talk about is being narrowed down and down and down,"

Grady penned. "And say, while I think about it, there is one more jinx of sorts that Hayden and his boys might want to attend to. Michigan hasn't lost in Iowa City in 22 years and only once in 11 times in history."

That was music to the ears of a Hawkeyes fan base that had become used to having little to say the Monday preceding a college football Saturday and little to look forward to for the upcoming Saturday.

With the win over Purdue, Iowa vaulted back into the Big Ten fray and returned to the Associated Press college football rankings at no. 18. The team was also coming home to Iowa City to complete the final contest of a midseason four-game stretch.

And what better matchup to get the juices flowing for Hawkeyes fans than the much-despised Michigan Wolverines led by the one and only Bo Schembechler?

"Iowa is formidable," Schembechler bellowed. "They're big, physical, experienced, and free of injury. I can't believe what they did to Purdue."

With a share of the Big Ten Conference lead up for grabs, the sound of the 11:00 a.m. kickoff nationally televised by CBS came as music to the ears of the more than sixty-six thousand fans in the stands in Kinnick.

The contrast between the two teams was palpable—the surging, up-and-coming Hawkeyes led by a relatively obscure, fresh-faced quarterback from Wheaton versus the Michigan Wolverines, the stalwarts of the Big Ten with a grumpy head coach, a battle-tested QB in Jim Harbaugh, and backed by one of the largest and most fiercely loyal fan bases in the country.

Only on this day, Russell Rein would be taking the snaps for Michigan instead of Harbaugh, who had been injured two weeks prior in a 19–7 setback versus Michigan State. His absence was devastating for Michigan and cast a cloud over its offense thicker and darker than the low skies that brought light rain and fog to Kinnick at kickoff.

The one-dimensional Wolverines were sitting ducks for Iowa's defense. The Hawkeyes stunted and confused Rein while putting the kibosh on the visitors' ground game. In what CBS-TV announcers Brent Musburger and Ara Parseghian described as a defensive masterpiece, Michigan could muster only 117 yards before a last-gasp drive chewed up another seventy, eventually stalling at Iowa's eleven-yard line with just thirty-two seconds remaining.

Meanwhile, Iowa's offense rolled. Ronnie Harmon opened the scoring with a three-yard run followed by Tom Nichols' field goals of twenty-nine and forty-six yards. Leading 12–0 at the end of the third quarter, Iowa sealed Michigan's fate in the final frame scoring on a ten-yard scamper by Owen Gill[9] and a two-yard scramble by Chuck Long.

When the horn sounded, Iowa had handed Schembechler his worst loss in sixteen years as Wolverines head coach, first shutout in seven years, and first loss at Kinnick. And it was the first time Iowa had blanked Michigan in fifty-five years.

Final score: Iowa twenty-six. The Wolverines zip.

The fourth straight victory for Iowa came as representatives of seven postseason bowls sat high atop Kinnick.

"Just another day at the office," said Chuck, who was fourteen of twenty on the day for a workmanlike 146 yards. Meanwhile, running backs Owen Gill and Ronnie Harmon had combined for another 148 by ground.

"What a great game," Hayden Fry proclaimed at the start of his postgame news conference. "It was one of the most satisfying victories I have ever been associated with, against one of the best football programs in the country. Bo was at a disadvantage with his number one quarterback hurt, and we took advantage."

"We had a beautiful game plan and our defense was superb," added Chuck. "When you blank Michigan, it's a great tribute to your defense and its coaches. Our defense definitely deserved the most valuable player award today."

Bo Schembechler wasn't as impressed. "They're good but not quite that good. Not good enough to shut us out," he snorted.

The victory was only Iowa's second win over Michigan ever in Iowa City, the other coming in 1962 when the Hawkeyes cruised 28–14 over the Wolverines. It was also the first time Michigan had been shut out since 1977

---

[9]Owen Gill was a four-year letterman for the Hawkeyes from 1981 to 1984. When he finished his career at Iowa, Gill was the university's career rushing leader with 2,556 yards. The Brooklyn, New York, native ranks among Iowa's top ten in career rushing yards and career rushing touchdowns (twenty-two). He competed in four bowl games while a Hawkeye, including the 1982 Rose Bowl, and shares the Iowa record for rushing touchdowns in a game (four in a win over the Iowa State Cyclones as a junior).

and the third consecutive game where Iowa's defense kept its opponent out of the end zone.

"Feeling desperate Saturday, maybe Michigan broke out its Rose Bowl offense a few months early," penned *Des Moines Register* columnist Marc Hansen. "Either that, or the Hawkeyes uncloaked a defense worthy of the Rose Bowl, not to mention a rounded offense that looked like something the Wolverines have come up (and fallen down) against on many a New Year's Day.

"Hard to tell which way to look at Iowa's 26–0 victory. But whatever their vantage point Saturday, 66,000 Kinnick Stadium eyewitnesses saw the game of the decades."

"Those polls are ridiculous. I feel like writing to United Press International and saying I don't want to be associated with its dumb poll."

HAYDEN FRY

after his team could manage no better than no. 17 after its fourth straight win—a 26–0 blowout of the Michigan Wolverines to earn Iowa a share of the Big Ten lead with a record of 4–1 ("Fry irked with polls; calling voting 'guesswork,'" Ron Maly, Des Moines Register, Oct. 24, 1984)

At 5–2 and tied atop the Big Ten standings with Ohio State at 4–1, the winning pieces of a memorable 1984 season were falling into place.

But Hayden Fry, as he was known to do, poured a cold dose of reality on expectations.

"The players are getting a chance to read some real nice press clippings, but all those things aren't going to win the next ball game," he said. "We've still got to tee it up and earn it."

Four conference games remained against teams with a combined record of 10–18: Indiana (0–7), Wisconsin (4–3), Michigan State (3–4), and

Minnesota (3–4). The Hawkeyes would then close out the regular season with a Dec. 1 road trip to Hawaii, whose record seven games into the season stood at 4–3.

"We haven't been on this plateau very long," said Fry when asked if Iowa was taking the final lap of the season in a slow jog. "We'll just work into the psychology of it. I've read a lot of books on learning how to win—even things from Sigmund Freud and Dale Carnegie and others—and I believe all you can do as a human being is try to improve.

"So we're just going to keep it simple. I'm not a very intelligent guy, but I make an effort to improve myself and strive for that each day. If we can maintain consistency, perhaps eventually we can reach the place where we'll think even an eight–three record has been a poor year."

A second trip to the state of Indiana in just three weeks would find no. 17 Iowa taking on the Hoosiers. Though the Hoosiers were winless on the season, Hayden Fry left nothing to chance.

"I'm just like an old mule with blinders on when it comes to looking at other teams," he muttered. "All I can see is the next one. And I'm sure Indiana is just lickin' their chops. They've greatly improved their defense. The only thing that looks bad about them is their record."

A raucous, red-clad crowd greeted Iowa in Bloomington on game day. The Hoosiers, led by coach Bill Mallory (the team's third coach in three years), were underdogs, but statistics can be deceiving. Six of its seven losses were by nine points or less (or an average of 6.3 to be exact).

Nearly thirty-eight thousand fans were ready to rumble, hopeful that they'd witness an Iowa letdown.

They almost got their wish.

With star Iowa running back Owen Gill left behind in Iowa City nursing a bruised kidney sustained in the team's win against Michigan, Chuck and Iowa's offense put just enough points on the board thanks to a last-minute defensive stand. The Hawkeyes prevailed in a squeaker, 24–20.

The back-and-forth contest included more twists and turns than a blockbuster movie script fresh out of Hollywood.

Harmon ran for more than 160 yards, but Indiana's defense made him earn every one.

Despite nursing a swollen elbow—a medical condition that had appeared out of nowhere the Thursday prior to game day—Chuck connected on twenty-two consecutive passes. The output was an NCAA record formerly held by Brigham Young's Steve Young.[10] The first in the streak occurred with less than three minutes to play in the first quarter; the last came at the 10:53 mark of the fourth quarter when Chuck was intercepted by Indiana's Jeff McGain.

And that's when things got hairy for the no. 17 team in the land.

Trailing by just four points and with plenty of time on the clock, a determined Indiana team was in business. Behind a solid performance by quarterback Steve Bradley (he finished the game nineteen of thirty-one for 263 yards), the Hoosiers marched deep into Iowa territory.

With just minutes to play, Indiana faced a first-and-goal from Iowa's seven. After giving up five yards on first down, the Hawkeyes braced for the Hoosiers' best effort as the team lined up for a second-and-goal on the two-yard line. In what Fry would later call one of the greatest defensive performances he had witnessed, Indiana failed to convert on three consecutive plays, the last being from the five-inch line.

An interception by Iowa's Devon Mitchell on Indiana's final possession as the clock wound down put the game on ice and allowed Iowa to escape in a thriller.

---

[10]Chuck's record-setting performance proved that you don't have to be flashy to be effective. His twenty-two straight completions (doubling his previous best of eleven, which he did twice) ranged from a seven-yard loss on a check-down to running back Ronnie Harmon to a twenty-five-yard gainer to receiver Bill Happel. His twenty-one passes covered 176 yards, an average distance of less than 8.2 yards. As reported by John Millea of the *Cedar Rapids Gazette,* Chuck broke the Big Ten mark of consecutive completions (fourteen by Illinois' Tony Eason against the Iowa Hawkeyes in 1982) when he connected with Happel for a fifteen-yard gain with 5:30 remaining in the third period; he then snapped Steve Young's record on a nine-yarder to Jonathan Hayes on the first play of the fourth quarter.

Interestingly, East Carolina quarterback Dominique Davis holds the NCAA record for most consecutive completed passes in a game during an October 2011 contest against Navy. Davis hit on all twenty-six of his throws during the first half, breaking the record of twenty-three held by Tee Martin of Tennessee (1998) and Aaron Rodgers of California (2004). Combined with ten completions to end his previous game versus Memphis, Davis' streak of consecutive completions reached thirty-six over the span of two games.

Chuck finished the game twenty-six of thirty for 227 yards. The first and last of the twenty-two consecutive completions were caught by Ronnie Harmon, the first for eight yards and the last for a loss of one.

"I told Coach Mallory he has a super team," said Hayden Fry. "They could go undefeated the rest of the way. Indiana's one of the finest teams we've played. We were not flat; we were battling for everything we're worth. We had the greatest goal line stand I've ever seen."

The loss sent Indiana to 0–8.[11] The win catapulted Iowa to 6–2 overall and 5–1 in the Big Ten, good enough for the outright conference lead thanks to Ohio State's loss to Wisconsin. The Buckeyes, Wolverines, and Boilermakers were log-jammed in a tie for second with records of 4–2.

Wisconsin, Iowa's next opponent, was in the fifth spot with a record of 5–3 overall, 3–3 in the Big Ten. And they were ready for a tussle with the country's no. 17 college football team.

With just three games remaining on its Big Ten schedule, Iowa was in the enviable position of controlling its own destiny. Wins to close the season over Wisconsin, Michigan State, and Minnesota would capture the conference title and punch Iowa's ticket to Pasadena and another Rose Bowl berth, the second in Hayden Fry's short tenure in Iowa City.

It was the best of times in Iowa City.

But they wouldn't last.

"Long powers Iowa; Hawkeyes are alone in first."

So proclaimed the headline in Sunday's (Oct. 28, 1984) *Chicago Tribune*. It was just the kind of bulletin board material needed for a team like Wisconsin that stood 3–3 in the Big Ten Conference and 5–3 overall.

---

[11]The Hoosiers, under first-year head coach Bill Mallory, went winless in 1984, finishing the season 0–11. Three of the losses were by four points or less; six by seven points or less. Following the loss to the Hawkeyes, Indiana mailed it in, losing their last three games (versus Ohio State, Illinois, and Purdue) by a combined score of 115–38. Two years later, Mallory righted the ship, taking Indiana to six bowl games over an eight-year stretch (1986–93).

It was also bad karma considering the fate that had awaited other Big Ten teams that had ascended to the conference perch. Illinois, Ohio State, Michigan, and Purdue had all found themselves in first place, only to tumble in the week that followed.

To make the predicament even dicier, Hayden Fry owned a 5–0 mark against Wisconsin as skipper of the Hawkeyes. Meanwhile, Badgers boss Dave McClain was 0–6 versus Iowa. As if that wasn't bad omen enough, the Hawkeyes were also banged up. Chuck's elbow, which had swelled to the size of a grapefruit due to an infection just two days prior to the Indiana game, was still sore but being treated with antibiotics. Owen Gill remained out of action with a bruised kidney. Ronnie Harmon was withheld from practice with muscle spasms in his back and neck following the hard-fought win against Indiana.

"You know how good Wisconsin can be," warned sports columnist Al Grady of the *Iowa City Press-Citizen* in sizing up Iowa's next opponent.

Hawkeyes fans were about to be reminded.

It was a game that Chuck would one day recount as the most physical of his collegiate career. Not that both teams didn't see it coming.

"It's gonna be a game of line-'em-up, knock-'em-down football," predicted Badgers linebacker Craig Raddatz. "We'll have to be ready for some heavy hitting, because in my mind Iowa's always the most physical team we play."

Wisconsin jumped on Iowa quickly with a methodical game plan that included hard-nosed running and tenacious defense.

After a twenty-five-yard field goal by kicker Todd Gregoire midway through the first quarter, the Badgers tacked on another seven in the opening frame thanks to the first of four interceptions of Chuck and a one-yard run by Marck Harrison.

With 6:41 remaining in the first quarter, Wisconsin led 10–0. Hawkeyes faithful sat in stunned disbelief as the Badgers rolled behind the play of three soon-to-be first-round NFL draft picks Al Toon, Richard Johnson, and Darryl Sims.[12]

Then, all-out trench warfare ensued as Iowa's defense knuckled down and its offense began to eat one hard-fought yard after another. The hits on both sides of the ball were crisp but jolting as Iowa clawed and kicked to maintain its precarious conference lead while Wisconsin aimed to steamroll its way back into title contention.

In a game fitting for the Big Ten and national television (CBS broadcast the matchup), the momentum seesawed, as did the emotion. And as the game wore on, so did the tension as Hawkeyes fans willed the home team back into the fray.

After being shut out in the first half (on just forty-five yards of total offense), Iowa responded with a solid drive midway through the third quarter, setting up a twenty-six-yard field goal by Tom Nichol. The Hawkeyes then drew even less than four minutes into the fourth quarter when Chuck dove into the end zone on a one-yard keeper.

Then, disaster.

On a second-and-eight deep in Iowa territory, running back Ronnie Harmon got sandwiched between two Badgers linemen as he took to the open field on a pass play. He went down in a heap. A collective gasp immediately filled the stadium, then silence.

Medical professionals quickly responded, and players huddled around their fallen colleague as a helpless head coach looked on. Shortly thereafter, the worst of fears were confirmed as a stretcher was brought onto the field. Harmon had suffered a broken tibia and fibula. His day, and season, were finished.

"You could hear the snap," said Badgers cornerback Averick Walker. "I was behind the play and saw him cut back. Sims and Melka made the tackle, and his ankle just got caught up. His leg was twisted one way and his foot was torn the other.

---

[12]The 1984 Badgers squad was loaded on both sides of the ball. Eight teammates were selected in the 1985 NFL draft. Joining Toon, Johnson, and Sims were Dan Turk, Ken Stills, Kevin Belcher, and James Melka. Toon, drafted tenth overall by the New York Jets, played in three Pro Bowls and was selected as the 1986 AFC Player of the Year.

　　　　　　　　　　　　　　CHUCK LONG: DESTINED FOR GREATNESS

"I'd never seen anything like it before," he added. "He was in excruciating pain. He was trying not to cry but he was really yelling."

As the reality of the injury settled over the more than sixty-six thousand somber Hawkeyes fans, the situation quickly went from bad to worse. On the very next play, Chuck lay motionless on the turf after sustaining a wicked hit on a nine-yard gainer.

In addition to a diagnosed concussion, Chuck sustained a badly bruised knee, forcing him to the sideline. His day, like Harmon's, was finished.

The loss of Iowa's two most explosive and prolific offensive weapons cast further doubt over the prospects of a season that, less than three hours ago, had brimmed with unlimited potential, not to mention the fragrance of roses.

With a Big Ten win (or loss) hanging in the balance and Chuck Long and Ronnie Harmon as spectators, Iowa managed to continue the drive, consuming a precious six and a half minutes of game time. The change in field position allowed the Hawkeyes to pin the Badgers on their own seven-yard line. Iowa's defense did the rest.

When the horn sounded, "there were no winners, just survivors," wrote Dave Hyde of the *Iowa City Press-Citizen*. Final: Wisconsin 10, Iowa 10.

Chuck's line: ten of twenty-three for 111 yards and four interceptions.

Chuck left the locker room that day on crutches but was quick to predict that he would take the field the following Saturday against Michigan State.

"Just a bruise on my left knee," he said. "A minor injury. I may be out for a few days, but I think I'll be back by midweek. They played good defense. Good against the run, and they had tall defenders who were hard to see over," he added.

Hawkeyes safety Mike Stoops, like every Hawkeye that day, was physically spent.

"I really don't know how to feel," he mustered. "Both teams played tough defense, and we really had to fight for our lives for a tie after we spotted them ten points."

The team may have been a bit overexcited when the game began, Stoops admitted. Seemed that way, given the fact that the Hawkeyes gave up ten points in the opening quarter, only to pitch a shutout the rest of the way while holding the Badgers to just fifty-four yards of total offense.

Hayden Fry summed up the afternoon perfectly: "Wisconsin won the first half. We won the second."

The tie, Iowa's first in twelve years, kept the Hawkeyes in contention for a post–Big Ten season trip to Pasadena and the Rose Bowl.[13]

Despite the tie, Iowa remained in the driver's seat for a one-way ticket to Pasadena. Wins over Michigan State and Minnesota to close out its conference schedule would clinch the league title for the Hawkeyes.

At 5–1–1 on the season, Iowa relished the opportunity to stay put in Iowa City for a second consecutive week. The Spartans were 5–4, yet posed a formidable foe for an Iowa squad nursing injuries and egos. The bumps and bruises and highs and lows of the 1984 season had made for an unforgettable ride for the team with the only assurance being that more twists and turns lay ahead.

Terry Edward Branstad was nearing the midway point of his first four-year term as the Hawkeye State's thirty-ninth governor.

The farm boy hailed from Leland, Iowa, a tiny, rural community nestled just a few miles south of the Minnesota border. He was also a football enthusiast, having played offensive and defensive line and linebacker in high school.

Much like Chuck Long, Branstad possessed a quiet yet confident demeanor. And just like Chuck, his relentless work ethic had allowed him to accomplish much, not the least of which was being elected governor at age thirty-six following a four-year term as Iowa's lieutenant governor under Gov. Robert D. Ray.[14]

The son of Rita (Garland) and Edward Arnold, Branstad received his undergraduate degree at the University of Iowa. He then earned a law degree

---

[13]The 1984 college football season included just eighteen bowl games, beginning with the California Bowl on Dec. 15 and concluding Jan. 1 in New Orleans with the Sugar Bowl. Others included the Cherry (Pontiac, Michigan), Aloha (Honolulu), and Bluebonnet (Houston). In 2015, forty postseason college football games were played.

from Drake University Law School in Des Moines and was drafted, serving in the United States Army from 1969 to 1971 as a military policeman at Fort Bragg.

As a boy, Branstad was given a great deal of responsibility. It was the 1950s, and there was plenty of work to do on the Winnebago County farm. Like others its size, the 144-acre livestock and grain farm had yet to make the full transition from horsepower to steel. A lot of labor was required to make a farm run. As a child, there were always chores for young Terry to do. At the top of the list were weeding the soybean fields, caring for the family's chickens, pigs, sheep, and cattle, and helping reap and store the hay and straw off an additional eighty acres the family custom farmed.[15]

And if all that wasn't enough to keep him out of trouble, there were always things that needed doing on Grandma and Grandpa's hundred-acre farm located just across the gravel road.

It was the need and expectation to be responsible and grab the lunch bucket and go to work each day that prepared Branstad to one day embrace the rigors of endless campaigning and the relentless demands of serving as Iowa's chief executive officer.

And just like Chuck, mentors also played a key role in shaping his destiny. For Chuck, it was his father, Charlie, and high school football coach Jim Rexilius. For Branstad, it was his teachers, who motivated him to pursue a career in public service.[16]

Governors have a lot in common with quarterbacks. They must be team leaders, make decisions on the fly, and not be afraid of mistakes. When things go well, there are many people and departments to give credit to. When things go south, they often shoulder the blame…alone.

---

[14]Branstad was elected governor of Iowa in November 1982. He was the youngest chief executive in Iowa's history. When he left office, he was the state's longest-serving governor. After spending time in private business and serving as president of Des Moines University, Branstad was re-elected governor in November 2010 and again in 2014. In spring 2016, he became the nation's longest-serving governor (twenty-two years). In December 2016, he was nominated by President Donald Trump to serve as US ambassador to China and confirmed by the US Senate in the summer of 2017.

[15]As with any occupation, there were jobs the governor enjoyed the least while growing up on the farm. "We had chickens and we had to clean the chicken barn, which wasn't fun," he recalled. "Also, we didn't have running water in the chicken barn, so we had to carry water down there. The eight-gallon cream cans and five-gallon buckets of water were heavy to tote. At least it was downhill from the pump to the livestock barns."

Branstad was quick to credit his competitive spirit for opening doors and reaching goals.[17] From a distance, he saw those same attributes in his alma mater's ascendance on the gridiron and the characteristics of Iowa's starting quarterback.

Rather than fear scrutiny, Branstad, like Chuck, embraced it. The doubters held little influence over the chief of state's approach to governing. In fact, they only empowered him. The key to keeping one's head above water, whether on the football field or dealing with one of the worst natural disasters ever to hit Iowa,[18] was staying focused on the job at hand and dismissing those lacking solutions or pedaling negativity.

Staying focused was key for Branstad as he plunged headfirst into the second half of his inaugural term as governor. While the Hawkeyes were the heartbeat of the state's sports world and continuing to improve, the state's economic well-being was in retreat. The unemployment rate was high and ticking higher, and fissures in the bedrock of Iowa's economy—the all-important farming industry— were appearing due to slumping commodity prices and ballooning interest rates. Economists were sounding the alarm, and for good reason. A decline in purchases by US ag trade partners combined with massive debt loads that farmers had accumulated during better times—debt that would soon need to be serviced—were putting the financial squeeze on many hardworking farm families.

Not possessing a magic wand, Branstad instead focused on listening to better understand the scope and scale of the growing economic crisis and what could be done to help. He assembled a team to lend a hand. He reached

---

[16]"I had great teachers," Branstad admitted in an interview for this book just weeks before he became the nation's longest-serving governor. "They inspired me. I really give them credit for why I'm governor. They encouraged me and made me want to go into a career in public service."

[17]Branstad campaigned for Iowa governor in 1982, 1986, 1990, 1994, 2010, and 2014. He has never lost an election.

[18]It was dubbed "The Flood of '93." Intense rain throughout North Central Iowa over the span of several weeks caused the Des Moines and Raccoon Rivers to swell. Saylorville Lake, a critical reservoir located less than ten miles north of the capital city's downtown and fed by the Des Moines River, quickly filled beyond capacity, requiring the emergency spillway be opened. Catastrophic flooding occurred in downtown Des Moines and the convergence of the Des Moines and Raccoon Rivers. Des Moines' water and wastewater utilities were overwhelmed. Residents of Des Moines were without running water and functioning toilets for nearly two weeks. Des Moines Water Works CEO L. D. McMullen, Gov. Robert D. Ray, and Lt. Gov. Terry Branstad were credited for helping lead Des Moines and the state through the tragedy.

out to banks and lenders, encouraging them to work with farmers to ease the financial crunch. Trading partners were courted and urged to buy Iowa-grown commodities. Crisis hotlines were established to help farmers and their spouses talk through the pain, angst, and despair.

Yet thousands of Iowa farm families remained crushed by piles of debt and record supplies of corn, soybeans, pork, and beef that no one needed.

Although 116 miles separated Kinnick Stadium from Terrace Hill, Hayden Fry also recognized the suffering being endured by many of his loyal fans and resolved to do something about it.

Despite the tie with Wisconsin, the Hawkeyes dropped only one spot (no. 18) in the Associated Press rankings.

Hayden Fry and his coaching staff had all the right pieces in the right places for the 1984 season's homestretch. Unfortunately, many players were banged up heading into an important clash with Michigan State.

Ronnie Harmon was out for the season with a broken leg.

Chuck was hobbled by a bruised knee.

Others nursed aches and pains resulting from the wear and tear of another strenuous and hard-hitting college football season.

Without Harmon, Iowa's offensive scheme was dealt a serious blow. Much of what the Hawkeyes did when they had the football revolved around the junior running back.

Chuck's questionable status wasn't helpful, either.

"Right now, I really anticipate that it will be Chuck Long in the pregame warm-ups," Fry said just four days prior to game time. "If he's capable of throwing the ball and running around well enough, then he'll start. If he's not, then Mark Vlasic will be the starter.

"I know Chuck," Fry added, "and he's such a great competitor that he's going to show up. But how effective he can be, I don't know."

The answer: an inch from perfection.

With his knee wrapped tight in pregame, Chuck's mobility was not suitable for the start. Enter the six-foot-four-inch Vlasic in place of the NCAA's third-most proficient quarterback.

"With a reasonably healthy Chuck Long in action, Iowa is favored to move one step closer to a second Rose Bowl trip in four years," wrote the *Des Moines Register's* Buck Turnbull. "But without Long, it's anybody's guess as to just how good Iowa's chances are."

The Pennsylvania native had replaced Chuck in the Wisconsin game, helping Iowa preserve a 10–10 tie and an inside track to Pasadena. He had chosen Iowa over Tennessee, Indiana, and Virginia and was considered to have all the natural attributes to be an outstanding college football quarterback.

"He's got everything but experience," bellowed Hayden Fry in the pregame news conference.

Now he was leading the team onto the field in Kinnick while Chuck paced the sidelines trying to loosen a swollen elbow and a bum knee, both reminders of the hard road traveled thus far in another grueling Big Ten campaign.

Meanwhile, the Spartans (5–4) had regained respectability with wins over Minnesota and Northwestern preceded by a hard-fought three-point loss to Ohio State. Coach Bruce Perles, in his second year on the job in East Lansing, was rehabilitating a beleaguered program one game and one position at a time.

They were game for their matchup against Iowa, scoring fourteen unanswered points behind the hard-nosed running of freshman back Lorenzo White after Vlasic had helped guide the Hawkeyes to a 3–0 lead.

By halftime, however, Iowa's offense had sputtered. Trailing 14–3 and with a Rose Bowl berth hanging in the balance, Fry turned to Chuck to start the second half, confident that the quarterback's tight elbow and sore knee were good enough to give Iowa a fighting chance.

Chuck didn't disappoint.

After a sluggish third quarter, the offense began to click in the fourth and into the teeth of a chilly, twenty-five-mile-per-hour November wind, with the quarterback connecting on eleven consecutive passes at one point.

With 9:18 remaining, Chuck engineered an eighty-two-yard drive capped by Owen Gill's two-yard touchdown run. Then, with the clock running out and more than sixty-five thousand fans screaming at the top of their lungs, Chuck hit Jonathan Hayes with a three-yard touchdown strike to culminate an improbable sixty-eight-yard drive.

With the score now 17–16, Hayden Fry had two options. Kick the extra point and score a second consecutive tie or go for the win.

With darkness descending across Iowa City and the full illumination of the portable lighting taking effect, Fry and his quarterback huddled. It was for a moment like this that Chuck had thrown thousands of passes, lifted weights during the off-season, made the most of every practice, and spent nights studying film alone. And it was for a moment like this that Hayden Fry possessed the offensive playbook and play calling.

"I knew right away what we'd call," said Fry. "It was an option play right with Chuck carrying and Gill following close behind."

Chuck took the snap, then began feeling his away along the line, knowing Gill was his safety valve should his forward progress be stymied.

But it wasn't, and for whatever reason, the Spartan defender feathered Chuck inside, effectively taking away any opportunity to pitch the ball to Gill. Then, in a moment that seemed to take an eternity, Chuck searched and probed for any crack in the Spartans' formidable defensive line.

And then, in a flash, he saw it—a sliver of daylight that seemed ripe for the taking. Tucking the ball and bracing for impact, Chuck lunged toward the goal line, confident he'd strike pay dirt.

But several Michigan State defenders converged simultaneously on Chuck as he attempted to punch it in. Then, a mass of humanity piled on.

Several officials leaned in. Their call came quickly and decisively: the two-point conversion attempt was foiled.

And by the nose of a football, Iowa fell by one point, tumbled out of the top twenty, and, for all intents and purposes, saw roses wilt.

Hawkeyes fans, realizing the enormity of the loss, made their feelings known by pelting officials with fruit and beer cans as they left the field.

"I don't know what you [reporters] saw," said Chuck after limping into the postgame interview, "but I thought I broke the plane of the goal line. They pushed me back, but I thought I got the ball over. The hole was there, but they closed it real fast."

As usual, Hayden Fry had his quarterback's back.

"All of our players who were in a position to see the play said that Chuck was over and then he got pushed back. It's unbelievable that not one of the officials was right there to make the call. And it's extremely unbelievable that they waited until after the pileup. They were all looking for someone else to make the call.

"I don't want to sound like sour grapes, though, because we didn't play well enough to win," Fry said, referencing a second-quarter fumble by Gill just three yards short of a touchdown and a blocked punt that led to a Spartan touchdown.

Yet Fry had nothing but praise for Chuck, who had nearly willed his team to victory after sitting out the first half.

His performance, Fry said, "was the most incredible I've seen— unbelievable. We had to put a one-legged man out there. That sore leg, you could see him wince every time he threw the ball."

George Perles didn't mince words as his team vacated Iowa City with a surprising and much-needed win.

"I never expected to see Long in the second half," he said. "In the fourth quarter he was passing as if the wind didn't matter. He threw bullets that cut through the wind.

We were lucky," he said. "We hit Long very hard, within the rules, but he kept coming. He was great. In the second half, he outscored us thirteen to three."

Chuck's line: fourteen of seventeen for 154 yards, two touchdowns, and no interceptions.

Mike Stoops, Iowa's defensive back, was equally amazed, even in defeat.

"Chuck is the only guy who could have done what he did."

Yet the disappointing loss against Michigan State may have been the best thing that could have happened for an Iowa program striving for national respect.

"While they're cancelling holiday reservations to Pasadena this week, Iowa fans can moan all they want about Saturday's disputed last-minute goal-line call that knocked their Hawkeyes out of the Big Ten lead," wrote Bill Jauss of the *Chicago Tribune*. "But quarterback Chuck Long, though he, too, disputed the officials' call, put the thing into perspective when he said, 'We had our chance to go to the Rose Bowl and we blew it.'"

On the other hand, Jauss wrote, the Hawkeyes could ultimately benefit from the decision that produced a 17–16 Michigan State victory instead of an 18–17 Iowa victory.

"That call could influence Long's decision to return to school to quarterback the Hawkeyes in 1985," he surmised.

Chuck seemed to agree.

"It would be tough to come back if we'd gone to the Rose Bowl," he said.

The Hawkeyes, admitted Hayden Fry, were wiped out physically. As Dave Hyde of the *Iowa City Press-Citizen* reminded the Hawkeyes faithful, Chuck had a sprained knee, tailback Ronnie Harmon a broken leg, and Owen Gill an injured shoulder, knee, and ankle. Also, several wide receivers had shoulder separations while others nursed other sprains and similar ailments. All told, nine starters, said Fry, "couldn't do a sit-up or jog the day after the Michigan State game. That would wipe out any team in America."

The injury plague, Fry added, was the worst he had experienced in his five years at Iowa.

With one Big Ten game remaining, the Hawkeye Nation hoped their team would rise from the frozen November turf, right itself, and take care of business. The odds were in their favor: Iowa was a nineteen-point road favorite over 3–7 Minnesota.

Yet fans were restless.

"Iowa is certainly no lead pipe cinch to beat any reasonable opponent at this stage," opined *Cedar Rapids Gazette* sports columnist Gus Schrader. "In fact, the Hawkeyes have been staggering in their last three games since ringing Michigan's bell 26–0."

Ron Maly of the *Des Moines Register* agreed, wondering aloud how the Hawks could be a three-touchdown favorite. "The oddsmakers have been stung in Iowa games the past three weeks," he wrote, citing Iowa's 24–20 escape versus the Hoosiers despite being picked to win by four touchdowns. They were also favored by two touchdowns against both Wisconsin and Michigan State but came away with a tie and a loss.

"It would be a far cry from a year ago, when Minnesota showed up here [Iowa City] with a lame duck coach and a beat-up football team," added Al Grady of the *Iowa City Press-Citizen*. "Eddie Phillips ran 80 yards for a touchdown on the game's first play and Iowa won 61–10 despite the fact that Chuck Long didn't even dress.

"A few weeks after that, Lou Holtz popped up as the new Gophers coach to the astonishment of all," Grady added. "Everyone knew almost immediately that U-M football fortunes were due for a quick rebound."

The forecasted rebound, however, remained a work in progress.

Plenty of $12 tickets remained for the Nov. 17 matchup in the Twin Cities, perhaps just the incentive Iowa fans needed to convoy north.

While fan support was in question, so, too, was the health status of the banged-up Hawkeyes.

"The injury picture has been a nightmare since midseason," Hayden Fry said in his midweek presser, "but this is by far the worst week of the year. Chuck has more swelling in his knee this week than last, but knowing him, he'll bounce back."

Unfortunately for Iowa, the nightmare wasn't over.

Minnesota's rushing game performed well, amassing 197 yards (including a fourteen-yard TD dash by Iowa native Gary Couch), and thwarted several Iowa drives deep into its own territory on its way to stunning the Hawkeyes 23–17. It was a fitting end to a brutal three-game stretch that saw Iowa go winless, lose out on securing a Big Ten title, relinquish the coveted "Floyd of Rosedale," and teeter on the edge of bowl obscurity.

"This is probably the hardest three weeks of my coaching career," said Fry following the game. "I really don't have too much to say."

"Gophers end Iowa's bowl hopes 23–17," read the headline in the *Waterloo Courier.*

Russ Smith, the paper's sports editor, said the upset spoiled Iowa's bowl chances and the day for Tom Starr, another Iowa native and director of the inaugural Freedom Bowl.

"Now, the Hawkeyes may have only their season finale in two weeks (Dec. 1) at Hawaii to look forward to and a battered lineup to contend with," Smith added.

Few could argue with Smith's assessment. Iowa's worst performances came at the most inopportune time. Start out 0–2–1 and finish 6–4–1 and you ride a wave of momentum far into bowl season as people sing the praises of coaches and players for turning around a season on the brink.

But close out the season winless in your last three (or four) games and you have fans muttering for the next eight months about what might have been.

"I don't want to say we don't have any chance left to go to a bowl," said Fry, "but obviously this loss didn't help our chances."

"This was a nightmare, a total nightmare," added Chuck, who admitted to leading an offense that lacked rhythm. "We had trouble moving the ball and scoring. Everything went wrong. I imagine we're not going to a bowl now. No bowl will take us. One might take Notre Dame with a 6–4–1 record, but we're not Notre Dame.

"I guess we'll just have to let the game in Hawaii be our bowl. This is a sad way to finish the Big Ten season."

For whatever reason, Iowa seemed lethargic and uninspired. Perhaps it was the continued absence of blossoming superstar running back Ronnie Harmon, who, years later, Chuck would describe as perhaps the best athlete to ever come through the Iowa football program.

Or perhaps it was a defense that was also gassed and banged up—a defense that had taken hits against Wisconsin but stepped up to shoulder additional responsibilities when the offense began struggling after Harmon and Chuck went down with injuries.

"We went to Minnesota and lost our mojo," Chuck admitted.

Golden Gophers coach Lou Holtz was measured in his praise for his team and offered a respectful sentiment to Iowa and its bowl hopes.

"We played awfully well, but we beat an awfully good team," said Holtz, who was a graduate assistant on the 1960 Hawkeyes team and earned his master's degree at the University of Iowa. "We had a lot of reasons to quit, but didn't.

"It was good to see a hog again," he added. "I hope this loss doesn't hurt Iowa's bowl chances."

Nov. 19, 1984

Dear Mr. and Mrs. Long:

With our regular season about to close, I want to take just a moment to let you know how very much we appreciate Chuck. Although the last three weeks have been extremely disappointing to each of us, Chuck has never given less than 100% of his efforts. He has always worked hard, given his best, and above all has proven himself to be a class individual both on and off the field.

We truly appreciate him.

Warm regards,

Bill Snyder

Offensive Coordinator

The losses stung Iowa. The Associated Press even treated the Hawkeyes like a hot potato, dropping them out of their top twenty for the first time all season.

The losses also soured expectations among fans and reporters that fourth-year players like Chuck Long would return for a fifth season.

Des Moines Register sports columnist Marc Hansen didn't hesitate to offer his opinion, without ambiguity, saying Hayden Fry should tell Chuck Long to take off.

"To do so would be an act of extreme selflessness. It is in Fry's best interests, of course, to have this prize quarterback around for another season," Hansen wrote. "But Long has been battered enough. He's paid his debt in full to the University of Iowa. In four years, he's given Hawkeye fans three glorious seasons."

Hansen surmised that if Chuck decided to continue risking his health, he would do it for more gainful compensation than room, board, and tuition. "If he's going to get his brains bashed in every week, he should do it for a very large paycheck."

The decision to leave the walking wounded for the guaranteed money that came with playing professionally seemed a no-brainer. And the talk only intensified when Iowa went a third consecutive week without a win after falling to Minnesota 23–17.

Much like the *Register's* Hansen, *Cedar Rapids Gazette* sports writer John Millea attempted to give voice to Chuck's conscience when considering coming back for a fifth and final season as an Iowa Hawkeye.

"To put it simply, Chuck, we have absolutely no choice but to make a run at the pros. Loyalty to the old alma mater is a nice thing, and wanting to hang onto a life we enjoy is a nice thing, too. But we must take a look at the bottom line.... Remember, Chuck, this is your conscience. I wouldn't steer you wrong."

Now, smarting from a three-game winless streak, the Hawkeyes made the day-long trek across six time zones to Hawaii for an odd, nonconference, season-ending matchup versus the Rainbows in Honolulu.[19]

Standing at 6–4–1 on the season, the battered and bruised Hawkeyes were far from a festive mood when they boarded the plane, this despite accepting an invitation to represent the Big Ten in the inaugural Freedom Bowl to be played Dec. 26 in Anaheim, California.

Sure, it was a strange occurrence to play a regular season game against an opponent outside of one's conference in December and not have it be a bowl game.

It was a game Hayden Fry had scheduled nearly two years earlier. And it would ultimately prove to be one of the shrewdest moves ever played by the savvy head coach.

Fry had figured that his '83 squad would graduate a lot of seniors and, with them, a whole lot of talent and experience. The chances of making a bowl, he had reasoned at the time, were slim. Very slim.

Therefore, scheduling a game in Hawaii to end the 1984 season would be akin to going bowling. In addition to providing his young Hawkeyes with a much-needed escape from the frigid temps of an Iowa December, it would provide additional reps and on-field competition to help them mature and get a jump-start on what was shaping up to be a one-of-a-kind 1985 season.

The decision could not have been more astute.

Although bowl-bound, Iowa badly needed a chance to redeem itself after a three-game winless streak.

While the Freedom Bowl was paring its list of possible Hawkeyes foes, Hayden Fry and the squad were nursing egos and injuries. Another loss would be painful to the team's psyche. It would also make it that much more difficult for Tom Starr, CEO of the Freedom Bowl, to attract the kind of attention and revenue desperately craved by an inaugural postseason football game.

Not that everyone saw the same silver lining in traveling nearly four thousand miles to play in a game that kicked off at 11:30 p.m. in Iowa City, followed by a trip to Anaheim to take the field in the Freedom Bowl.

"I think it's ridiculous for people to be saying we don't deserve to go to a bowl game," Fry said. "People forget how far we've progressed the last four

---

[19]The idea to play that far away from home that late in the season (in December, no less) was the brainchild of Hayden Fry more than a year before. He scheduled a nonconference game at the end of the 1983 season "thinking the 1984 team may struggle and that that the game may be our bowl game," Chuck later recalled. "It proved to be exactly what we needed."

years. At that time Iowa hadn't had a winning season in nineteen years, and now we're going to a bowl game for the fourth straight year. I feel like I've been kicked at and hit after doing as good a job as possible.

"I'm irritated beyond words," Hayden Fry piled on. "We've put way too much effort into this [football program] to roll over and play dead. Danged if I'll take cheap shots."

In fact, Fry was so irked with the media in the days leading up to the Hawkeyes' season finale versus the Rainbows that he threatened to stop holding his weekly press briefings.

"I'm not obligated by my contract to hold these press conferences or do anything else for the sake of newspaper copy," he added. "My players actually wonder if they're appreciated for what they do."

Fry's grumpiness wasn't unusual. But as *Des Moines Register* staff writer Ron Maly pointed out, it was the coach's first real explosion of the 1984 season and perhaps, just perhaps, not accidental.

"Criticizing the media has paid off for Fry in the past, and obviously the Hawkeyes need a lift now," Maly wrote. "Blasting the media creates an 'us against the world' theme and tends to rally fans around the squad. If not overdone, a plan to make heavies out of the media has helped other coaches at other schools win certain games, too."

And a win was just what Iowa needed.

But Hawaii was more than a worthy adversary. The Rainbows featured quarterback Raphel Cherry, who had flung the pigskin for nearly two thousand yards on the season, completing 49 percent of his passes, and was the team's leading rusher, tallying just a yard shy of 370. All told, Cherry stood eleventh in the country in total offense, while Chuck was twenty-third.

The diversified and mostly mistake-free offensive scheme run by Hawaii concerned Fry, especially given its similarity to the Minnesota Golden Gophers, a team that had just gotten the better of the Hawkeyes.[20]

Of the fifty thousand expected to show in Aloha Stadium, roughly 3,500 would be donning the black and gold—about the same number that would leave the stadium happy at around 2:30 a.m. Iowa time.

Matching the tropical heat, Iowa turned in a red-hot fourth-quarter performance behind the strong running of walk-on freshman running back Rick Bayless and the arm of quarterback Chuck Long. The duo helped Iowa secure a 17–6 victory, halting Hawaii's seven-game winning streak.

But it was an uphill battle from the opening kick.

Trailing 6–3 at the end of the third quarter, little used and lightly regarded Bayless, who hailed from Hugo, Minnesota, stepped up in place of injured running back Owen Gill. He carried the rock thirteen times for eighty-four yards in the fourth quarter.

And Chuck, still nursing a sore knee, hit on six of seven passes in the same frame for fifty-three yards. Two of them went for touchdowns—a three-yard strike to tight end Jonathan Hayes and another for eight yards to Scott Helverson on a fourth-down play.

"To out-condition Hawaii in the fourth quarter is really a tribute," said a relieved Hayden Fry. "And Bayless did a tremendous job. He ran extremely tough. In fact, he gave us a change of momentum we needed to run right back at those people."

Al Grady of the *Iowa City Press-Citizen* piled on the praise in assessing the freshman running back's performance.

"What can one say about Rick Bayless?" he asked. "I guess you can say he's been practicing, waiting for a chance to play. He made the big difference in the fourth quarter thanks to some good blocking and a play series we haven't seen before. Given a chance, under pressure, the young walk-on was terrific."

Pulling out a victory from the jaws of defeat halfway across the Pacific Ocean was just the tonic Iowa needed to mend a season that was beginning to run a fever.

"Just think of this," added Grady. "Despite a crippled offense that has had a terrible time trying to move the football in the last month, Iowa's defense has stayed right there…and on Saturday night [against Hawaii], it did not surrender a touchdown to an offensive team that had been on fire in the last month. So hats off to the Hawkeyes."

---

[20]Hayden Fry pulled no punches regarding the game's importance and proved it by imposing strict limits on extracurricular activities while the Hawkeyes were in the Aloha State. Visits by the players to beaches and bars prior to the game were strictly prohibited.

In what was becoming a tradition in Iowa City, the Hawkeyes were once again playing postseason football, this time in Anaheim, California, versus the Texas Longhorns in the inaugural Freedom Bowl.

As some fans began making travel plans to California, others were already looking ahead to the next season, wondering if Chuck and all–Big Ten tight end Jonathan Hayes[21] would stay for a fifth year or bolt for professional ball.

They weren't the only ones.

"Oh, I may slip in a one-liner now and then just to feel their pulse," Hayden Fry said, "but I wish I was a fly on the wall listening to what some of those agents are telling our guys."

Chuck wasn't rattled by the attention. He kept the focus on goals yet unfulfilled (chief among them, defeating the Longhorns) while underplaying the emotional side of the game.

"It's been bugging me so much that I don't want it to interfere with the bowl game. It's too big a game," he said. "And it doesn't really matter whether we win or lose the Freedom Bowl as far as my decision goes, but a lot could happen from that game. I've talked to different people who have told me different sides. I'm treating this fifth year as an option, kind of like a business decision. I'm trying to work out the options the best I can. It's been a great four years here. And you never know, it could be five."

Not satisfied with the appetizing quotes Chuck had become known for, sports writers sought more meat-and-potato insight.

Marc Hansen of the *Des Moines Register* was one of them. Since Chuck's arrival in Iowa City, the talented journalist had built a strong rapport with the quarterback's father, Charlie.

No novice himself in the ways of the media (he was, after all, a journalism major in college and a public relations practitioner and writer in the "real" world), Charlie Long always made time to visit. His openness and sincerity won over many reporters, including Hansen.

Always mindful not to overstep his welcome, Hansen called Charlie Long from time to time to see how he was doing or to get the inside scoop on how Chuck was faring.[22]

Charlie Long didn't mind. But when asked to handicap the odds of Chuck returning for a fifth year, he was as much in the dark as anyone.

One thing he wasn't doing, he emphasized, was lobbying his son one way or the other.

"We're always there ready to help, but I wouldn't dare try to make his decision for him," said the elder Long. "If he came to me and asked for advice, I wouldn't know what to tell him.

"I'd probably say don't look back," Long added. "The main thing is, if he were to come back for another year, that would be marvelous. … The chemistry has been perfect at Iowa. But I'm one of those sentimental types. I love college football. It's been a great four years. I guess I never like to see it end."

Without a doubt, Chuck loved playing college football. And Coach Fry enjoyed coaching it, especially on the national stage against powerhouse programs.

And few were bigger for Hayden Fry personally than the opportunity to play the Texas Longhorns the day after Christmas.

"Bowls should be a reward for a good season, and I always have looked at 'em that way," he said on the eve of the first Freedom Bowl.[23]

"The number one priority," he added, "is to try to win the game, but it also should be enjoyable and rewarding. The thing about the bowl games I've gone to is that weird things have happened at nearly all of them. Everything from weather conditions, crazy plays, getting sick… Some incredible things

---

[21]Jonathan Hayes was selected by the Kansas City Chiefs in the second round of the 1984 NFL draft. During his first two years at Iowa, he played linebacker, switching to tight end his final two seasons under Coach Fry. Hayes played nine seasons for the Chiefs, three for the Pittsburgh Steelers, and took the field in Super Bowl XXX. He retired from the NFL following the 1996 season. Three years later, he was reunited with Iowa Hawkeyes teammates Chuck Long and Bobby Stoops as an assistant coach for the Oklahoma Sooners (1999–2002), where they won a national championship (2000).

have happened, too. Someday the whole story about the Rose Bowl may even come out."[24]

Fry also respected fans and the sacrifices they made to show up each Saturday.

"I get my paycheck at Iowa, and the people of Iowa are a lot like the people of West Texas. They're good people," said the coach, who possessed deep roots in the Lone Star State.

"You know, when I was coming up the ranks in the church schools [Southern Methodist], you had to pass the plate twice on Sunday to pay for the program. I wanted to work at the 'University Of,' as they referred to Texas. Now I feel that we have the 'University Of' at Iowa."

Chuck Long was a big part of the reason Hawkeyes football was on the national map. And as the clock ticked down to the Freedom Bowl's kick, all eyes were on the experienced signal caller. Everyone associated with the program knew much was riding on the game, not the least of which was Chuck's decision about whether he would return for a fifth season.

"He's one of the most accurate passers in college football," said Hayden Fry when asked what made Chuck an elite player. "Probably his greatest asset is reading defenses and audibilizing at the line, selecting something that has a chance to work.

"He doesn't have a great arm, but he has the ability not to throw the bad ball," Fry added. "He has the great quality of not throwing it up for grabs when he's flushed out of the pocket. He picks up the number two and three receivers for big gains and touchdowns."

And there wasn't a college football game played where those skills were on better display than when Iowa took the field against Texas in a driving rainstorm.

---

[22]Marc Hansen admired Charlie Long. "He was always gracious and friendly. He would give me the 'what's really happening' story," Hansen said. "He was always a very good subject. And while it was sometimes hard for him to open up, he was always cooperative. I often thought in retrospect how well Charlie handled me. He could tell me things and know I would present them fairly. It's difficult to find that kind of relationship in sports today."

[23]The Freedom Bowl would be Hayden Fry's seventh different bowl game. At the time, Fry ranked fifth among NCAA football coaches with appearances in seven unique bowls (Sun, Cotton, Bluebonnet, Rose, Peach, Gator, and Freedom). Tied with Fry were Bear Bryant, Joe Paterno, and Tom Osborne.

To say weather conditions were a sloppy mess would be an understatement. As fans trickled into the cavernous Anaheim Stadium, Chuck was having a difficult time gripping the ball during pregame warm-ups. His passing was erratic, with every other ball slipping from his grasp. Few passes hit their intended target.

"Hey, Chuck, you able to grip the ball? Can you throw it? Can you throw at all?" asked a confused and concerned Bill Happel as the team returned to the locker room following pregame warm-ups to change into dry clothes.

Chuck didn't know. "It's a struggle," he replied to his trusted wideout with a tinge of concern.

"I've never had a victory that meant more to me. Chuck Long is not the picture-perfect passer. All he does is throw strikes. He is so calm and poised and probably reads coverages better than any quarterback in America."

HAYDEN FRY
on Chuck Long's performance in the 1984 Freedom Bowl
("Hawkeyes' Long proves he's good enough for pros,"
Associated Press, *Dec. 28, 1984)*

Oddly enough, the harder it rained on the diehard fans gathered in Anaheim Stadium, the better Iowa's quarterback performed.

On a sloppy track and with just twenty-four thousand brave souls in the stands, Chuck made minced meat of an uninspired Longhorns defense.

While the Texas players seemed afraid of the water, Chuck took to it as if he had gills.

Pass completions occurred almost at will.

Throw left. Complete.

---

[24]Fry suffered from bronchial pneumonia during the 1982 Rose Bowl but ignored doctors' orders and coached anyway. Iowa lost to Washington 28–0.

Throw right. Complete.

Short. Complete.

Same for deep.

Whether passing from the pocket or on the run after being flushed from center, Chuck threw strikes. All night.

It was as if the rainwater turned to glue the way the ball stuck to receivers.

Not long into the evening, Chuck and the Iowa offense were taking big bites of California sod and binging on the Longhorns' secondary. By the time the hour grew late in Anaheim and Texas limped to their locker room, Chuck had thrown six touchdown passes en route to a 55–17 shellacking of the nation's nineteenth-ranked squad.

The final score belied the fact that the contest was a competitive one at halftime, with Iowa leading just 24–17. But thirty-one unanswered points by Iowa in the third quarter—the barrage beginning with a big gainer to sure-handed Hawkeyes tight end Jonathan Hayes—dehorned the team from Texas.

IT'S ABOUT FAMILY

The heartbeat of any relationship is being human and demonstrating a sincere interest in the people you care about. And nowhere is this exemplified better than in the story of Jonathan Hayes and his journey to Iowa.

Hayes got a lot of looks coming out of South Fayette High School—and for good reason. The talented linebacker was a prized recruit. Many college football coaches made their way to the small town just south of Pittsburgh to see him perform and to earn his commitment.

Suitors included the University of Michigan, LSU, Georgia Tech, and Iowa. For good measure, Hayes also paid a visit to the University of Idaho. Nothing serious, he admitted, "just wanted to get out there and get a feel for it since my brother went there." He also paid an unofficial visit to the University of Pittsburgh.

One school he didn't visit was Penn State. Hayes had a feeling that it wouldn't take long for the Nittany Lions coaching staff to transition him from playing linebacker to tight end.

"I wanted to play linebacker, so the thought of moving to tight end didn't sit well with me. Turns out that's exactly what happened at Iowa and probably any other school I would've attended," he said with a chuckle. "Little did I know that these college coaches were right all along. I guess you could say I didn't know as much back then as I thought I did."

Iowa lacked the glitz and glamour of other college football programs. But it more than compensated by being home to quality, sincere football personnel.

"Relationships are very important to me, and that's the thing that attracted me most to Iowa," said Hayes, now in his fifteenth season as linebackers coach for the Cincinnati Bengals. "The relationships with not just the players but coaches and support staff were special. They were so sincere and honest. I knew if I went there I wasn't just going someplace big never to be heard from again. They would nurture me and make sure that I grew as an athlete, student, and, most importantly, as a person."

Coach Barry Alvarez, a trusted assistant to Hayden Fry, recruited Jonathan Hayes. Along the way, Alvarez developed a close relationship with Hayes' mother and father, Joy and Jewitt. That made an impression on Jonathan.

"He knew relationships were important to me even at that age, so he spent time getting to know me and my family," Hayes said. "A lot of the schools and universities I visited had unbelievable facilities and all that stuff. But I knew the relationships I felt the players, coaches, and staff had with each other at Iowa would help me be successful."

He also knew Hayden Fry was building a winning tradition. Hayes just didn't realize it would happen so quickly.

But Jonathan Hayes and this Hawkeyes team was anything but ordinary. Joining him in Iowa City early in the summer of 1981 were new teammates Chuck Long, Hap Peterson, Jay Norvell, Owen Gill, and Nate Creer. Arriving well before the fall semester helped the guys to get acclimated to the facilities, the football workout schedules, and each other.

"It was a great experience, and when fall football started, we hit the ground running," Hayes said. "Now that didn't mean we were starters and had things all figured out when the season kicked. But we knew we had an opportunity to play and get some experience. Along the way, the coaches and staff kept nurturing our relationships with them and with each other."

Key to the camaraderie were team barbecues organized by Coach Dan McCarney and his dad, P. J.

"They would have these barbecues hosted by farmers in the area, and we'd cook a bunch of chicken or roast a pig and play horseshoes," Hayes reminisced. "One of the farms even had a pond, so everyone—players and coaches—had a lot of fun…taking the plunge.

"We didn't think about it at the time, but the barbecues…showed us how to enjoy each other and build relationships and trust. I was glad that we got that opportunity to do those things. It built a foundation so that we would become that Iowa team people really feared—the team that every time someone came up against the Hawkeyes, they knew you'd better pack your lunch pail because it would be a long day, win or lose."

"It wouldn't have made any difference what kind of coverages we were in, whether zone or man-to-man," admitted Texas head coach Fred Akers following the game. "He was the hottest quarterback I'd ever seen in my life. He was everything we saw in the films. He was as perfect as I've ever seen a quarterback be."

The epic offensive display kept statisticians hard at work long into the night.

Chuck set three school records in the contest: touchdowns thrown (six), yards passing (461 of the team's 560 yards total offense), and completions (twenty-nine on thirty-nine attempts).

Iowa's fifty-five-point outburst was the most points a Longhorns defense had allowed since being overwhelmed by Chicago 68–0 in a game played in 1904, almost eighty years earlier to the day.

"Even if the Longhorns had a blanket the size of Texas, they wouldn't have been able to stop Long and his stable of receivers," observed Mark Dukes of the *Cedar Rapids Gazette*. "Texas' secondary, which included two-time consensus all-American Jerry Gray and three sophomores, was a proud unit. Probably too proud because the Longhorns refused to change their man-to-man coverage."

Texas paid dearly for it.

"I was hot and the whole team was hot," said Chuck, who was named the Freedom Bowl's most valuable player. "Their two all-Americans [Gray and defensive end Tony Degrate] weren't on the field as far as I was concerned. In fact, I didn't even know where Gray was."[25]

"I hope it projects him into one of the top players coming back. As far as all-America honors and Heisman Trophy candidates go," Hayden Fry said.[26]

Nothing like trying to plant a seed, eh?

"He probably reads coverages better than any quarterback in

America," the head coach added. "He almost never throws to the wrong guy. For a wet ball and throwing against man-to-man where you have to throw perfect strikes, he was fantastic."

Two story lines quickly emerged following Iowa's record performance in front of a sparse crowd: would the Freedom Bowl survive to see a second year and would Chuck stick around for a fifth?

"I'm going to come to work tomorrow," said Tom Starr, the Freedom Bowl's executive director, when asked if the poor attendance and lopsided score would doom the bowl. "I just hope my desk is still there."

Turned out it was. And Starr had Chuck Long to thank, wrote Marc Hansen of the *Des Moines Register.*

"The Iowa quarterback turned a minor league bowl into a major league spectacle. On one side of the press box sat scouts from the New York Giants. On the other sat scouts from the Los Angeles Raiders."

John Robinson, who coached the Los Angeles Rams, was also a visitor to the press box, as was George Allen, who said the Iowa quarterback was ready for the pros.

But was Chuck? Only he knew for sure.

Sort of.

Prior to the Freedom Bowl, Chuck saw the game as one more opportunity to make a decision. He was, after all, playing with house money. Put up good numbers and head to the pros on a high note or as justification for another year. Struggle and use it as motivation to come back for another year or as justification that the time is right to bolt.

Either way, Chuck had options.[27] And no one was more painfully aware of this fact than Hayden Fry.

"All those good Hawks fans who are listening back home, get those letters coming," Fry quipped after the team's return to Iowa from Anaheim.

---

[25]Gov. Terry Branstad was in Anaheim Stadium and witnessed Chuck's record-setting performance. "I'll always remember that game; it was one of Chuck's best performances and probably Hayden Fry's favorite game," he said. "It was a driving rainstorm for nearly the entire game, but it didn't seem to bother Iowa or Chuck. In fact, the harder it rained, the better Iowa looked. They just clobbered Texas, and given Hayden was from Texas, I'm sure he enjoyed it a lot."

"Write Chuck Long a letter in care of the football department and tell him that you want him to come back next year."

"Dear Chuck: How are you? Please stay at Iowa. We need you. I like you very much. You are a super quarterback. I would like to be like you. I am 8 years old. My friends and I play football. My position is quarterback. I'm sending you my picture. Will you please send one of you?"

KENNY LANDGREBE
Newton, Iowa (one of more than two hundred letters penned by fans to Chuck Long following the 1984 season imploring the Iowa quarterback to play one more year)

AS OF JUNE 2016

Coach Hayden Fry assembled one of the most talented and celebrated coaching staffs in college football history. To this day, many college football fans shake their heads in wonder at the deep bench Fry led during his storied career, an assembly that may never be duplicated.

Former Hayden Fry assistants or players who have taken over as head coach at a Division I-A college football program include (*denotes also a College Football Hall of Fame inductee):

- Kirk Ferentz, Iowa, 1999–present

---

[26]Fry admitted to reporters in his postgame remarks that he never dreamed Iowa would score fifty-five points versus Texas. "I thought the kicking game or specialty teams would decide it," he said.

- Bob Stoops, Oklahoma, 1999–present

- Mike Stoops, Arizona, 2004–2011

- Bill Snyder, Kansas State, 1989–2005, 2009–present*

- Barry Alvarez, Wisconsin, 1990–2005*

- Bret Bielema, Wisconsin, 2006–2012; Arkansas, 2013–present

- Dan McCarney, Iowa State, 1995–2006; North Texas, 2011–2015

- Chuck Long, San Diego State, 2006–2008*

- Jim Leavitt, South Florida, 1996–2009

- Bo Pelini, Nebraska, 2008–2014; Youngstown State, 2015–present

- Mark Stoops, Kentucky, 2013–present

- Bob Diaco, University of Connecticut, 2014–present

Hayden Fry is also a College Football Hall of Famer, elected in 2003.

---

[27]"I had a lot of thoughts swirling around in my head prior to the game," Chuck said. "But when game day arrived, I placed them all on a shelf and went out and played ball." But in the fourth quarter, with game in hand and the outcome sealed, Fry pulled Chuck from the game. "As soon as I stepped on the sideline, Hayden said, 'Charlie, look at all these players coming back. We're going to have a great team. We can contend for a Big Ten championship.'"

CHAPTER 5

Fantastic Fifth

"In college or the pros?"

DEAN CAMPBELL

Texas Longhorns secondary coach when asked if he'd ever seen
anyone match Iowa quarterback Chuck Long's record-setting
performance in the 1984 Freedom Bowl

It was a cold, raw January day in Wheaton. Fresh off his electric, record-setting performance in the Freedom Bowl, Chuck huddled with his family in the relative obscurity of their home tucked just inside western suburban Chicago.

While the brisk north winds blew outside, the Long residence on North Washington Street was warm and comfortable. It was a modest yet stately home with black shutters and a detached garage nestled like so many others under large, bare oak and elm trees with an expansive yard outlined by dormant shrubs and gardens.

Home was Chuck's anchor, and he came calling often. Wheaton and the neighborhoods he roamed as a child were filled with special places, not to mention memories as fresh as the homemade chocolate chip cookies often served by his mother, Joan.

Just up the road and a couple of football tosses to the east was "The Tot Lot," a park the size of a postage stamp but larger than life to Chuck and the neighborhood boys who had frequented it.

The park was a magical place located at the end of the street adjacent Chuck's childhood home. It was open to the west and south and lined with small, stubby bushes along the north and east.

During baseball season, the boys would assemble early in the day with their gloves and bats. Games were played until dusk. A storm sewer cover made do as home plate. Balls that sailed over the fence to the east were "taters." The unlucky boy who retrieved homers had to escape getting scraped by the thickets while avoiding the neighbor's dog.

The Tot Lot was a popular destination for the boys of Wheaton. Chuck and his brother David were always there. So, too, were the Sprenger boys— Tom, Jim, and Patrick (better known as "T-bone," "Rock," and "Reggie")— who lived two doors up from The Tot Lot and adjacent to the Longs. They were often joined by Kent and Danny Graham, who lived in a yellow-painted ranch home located a half-block up the road on the opposite side of the park.

Charlie Long, Chuck's dad, was a regular, too. He wasted no time returning home each day from his place of employment in downtown Chicago. His responsibilities including serving as a substitute for his son at quarterback (with Chuck moving to wide receiver) and refereeing.

The small park was special, as were the boys who played there. Charlie earned the title of "Tot Lot Commissioner," seeing to it that the boys who took the field were between the ages of six and ten.

Charlie and his neighbors so revered The Tot Lot that when the City of Wheaton made plans to convert it into a playground, Charlie and a group of other men were so opposed that they impeded the bulldozers when they arrived to begin excavation. Rumor is that Charlie even lay down in the road.

The bold act of civil disobedience did little to sway city planners. But the intervention of Romelle Graham, a good friend of Charlie and Joan Long and mother to two Tot Lot regulars (Dan and Kent)—well, that was a different story.

Not one to mince words or back down from controversy, Romelle Graham brokered a compromise with the Wheaton City Council. The city scrapped plans to bulldoze the entire park for playground equipment, deciding instead to construct one on just the south half.[1]

---

[1] Romelle Graham's grandchildren are frequent visitors to this day to The Tot Lot, which remains relatively unchanged from the days three future NFL players (Chuck Long and Romelle's sons Danny and Kent) roamed its grounds.

Wheaton in the summer was a great place for kids, according to Joan Long. Chuck and his friends arose each day and played football, baseball, and basketball; there were parks and swimming pools galore; children of families who prepared to take vacations would seek permission to remain home so as not to miss out on any games or possible mischief. And a kid could always find a hot meal at any house in the neighborhood; all they had to do was show up.

Charlie Long was well respected, almost revered, in the community. He was known as a humble and faithful man who was immensely proud of his sons Chuck, David, and Andy.

But he rarely showed it publicly.

Even Chuck's accomplishments on the field, while filling his heart with an unspeakable pride that only a father can know, were downplayed publicly despite continuous adulation and praise from friends, neighbors, and acquaintances.

Charlie's wife, Joan, was a strong and patient woman who fretted over her sons but gave them freedom to fall and fail, only to be there to help them stand and succeed again. Many admired her from afar, using the adjective "saintly" to describe her demeanor. She was soft-spoken, warm, and fiercely protective and loyal to her family. She maintained order in the house and ensured that the boys could come and go as they pleased, without care or concern.

Chuck's father, like many others in the town, traveled roundtrip each weekday by train to his office in Chicago. Rather than complain about the trek, the elder Long used it to his advantage. On the way to work each morning, Charlie planned his day and read. Returning home each afternoon, he caught a short nap so he could be rested and ready to play ball with the boys when he arrived at the front door just after 5 p.m.

Lisa Wells, Chuck's girlfriend, lived just a few blocks away on East Prairie Avenue. There the homes were a bit grander and the yards more spacious. But few noticed. Even fewer cared.

Indeed, Wheaton was an all-American town of about forty thousand featuring wide streets, safe schools and parks, and numerous playgrounds.

Lawns were well kept. A multitude of family-owned businesses added to the town's civic pride—institutions like the Wheaton Bowl and Round-the-Clock, the latter a popular family restaurant in downtown Wheaton.

Strong and loving families found a home in the Chicago suburb, as did Wheaton College, a private interdenominational school founded in 1860 by Lisa Wells' great-great grandfather, Jonathan Blanchard. Once upon a time, the school was a stop on the Underground Railroad. It also graduated Illinois' first African American college student and was where Billy Graham and Ruth Bell met.[2]

The people of Wheaton were diehard sports enthusiasts and supported their high school athletes with tremendous passion. On Friday nights, they filled the football stands from top to bottom to cheer on the Wheaton North High Falcons, who, with Chuck Long as starting quarterback, found much success, including consecutive conference playoff appearances during Chuck's junior and senior seasons, one ending with a state championship.

Now, with his fourth and most successful season as a Hawkeyes quarterback just completed, Chuck was back home in the comfort of the family's modest two-story home. There, he would make the biggest decision of his life: play a fifth year at Iowa or vacate Iowa City and the college football game he loved for an opportunity to play professionally.

For Russ Smith of the *Waterloo Courier,* there was no reason to doubt veteran NFL and US Football League (USFL) coach George Allen. In an interview during the Freedom Bowl broadcast, Allen said with all sincerity that Chuck Long could indeed hold his own as a player in the NFL… and soon.

"The question is, will it be next year?" Smith asked. "Lots of fans, for selfish reasons, of course, hope not. Fry, for similar reasons, has expressed a hope that Long will elect to remain at Iowa for his so-called redshirt fifth year. But it's hard to imagine that Long would not go with Fry's blessings if he is tempted by one of those six- or seven-figure contracts."

---

[2] Billy Graham earned an anthropology degree from Wheaton College. He and Ruth Bell married Aug. 13, 1943. The couple raised five children. Ruth Graham passed away June 14, 2007, at her home near Montreat, North Carolina, with her husband and five children at her bedside.

And why not? Many people who knew football and could properly evaluate talent anticipated Chuck to be a first-round selection.

"There are only two valid reasons for his electing to stay: college football is fun, and the Heisman Trophy is available," Smith penned. "The former probably is true or the pros wouldn't be paying their talented players, such as quarterbacks, in the vicinity of $1 million a year. The latter may not be worth gambling one of those $1-million-a-year contracts on.

"There would appear to be much reason to believe Iowa football would, in fact, be fun next year if Long stays," Smith added.

He undoubtedly expressed the sentiment of every Hawkeyes fan from West Branch to West Okoboji and Corning to Cresco.

To stay or go was a monumental decision, and Chuck wasn't about to rush it. He had much to be proud of. He had donned the black and gold for four years and seen playing time in each of them. He had led Iowa to exhilarating wins and persevered through difficult losses, always with great aplomb and glass-half-full sentiment. He had fulfilled Hayden Fry's "destined for greatness" tag and played the game with conviction and class.

Now the road forked, and the bright-eyed, optimistic, and talented young man from Wheaton faced a tough but enviable choice few would ever have to make.

SMALL LOT. BIG STARS.

The Tot Lot was home field for three boys who would one day play in the National Football League. Kent and Danny Graham were the sons of Vic and Romelle Graham (Charlie and Joan Long affectionately referred to the Grahams as "Wheaton North's first family of football"). The boys frequently joined Chuck in hotly contested baseball and football games. They, along with their older brother Russ, were athletically gifted and, like Chuck, played for Wheaton North before establishing successful NFL careers.

Russ, two years older than Chuck, played college ball at Northern Illinois.

Danny, two years younger than Chuck, led the Wheaton North Falcons to the 1981 state championship. He also attended Northern Illinois and played center for the Tampa Bay Buccaneers and Canadian Football League's Montreal Machine.

Kent, the youngest of the Graham sons and five years Chuck's junior, was a gifted quarterback who possessed a cannon for an arm. As a Wheaton North standout (he led the Falcons to a 1984 state championship), he was successfully recruited by Notre Dame head coach Lou Holtz (who bested Bo Schembechler of the Michigan Wolverines for the Wheaton North prep). Holtz's option-run offense, however, was not a good fit for Graham. After two years in South Bend, he transferred to Ohio State, where he started in 1991, leading the Buckeyes to an 8–4 record. As the top collegiate recruit, Kent Graham was drafted by the New York Giants and played three seasons. He then signed with Detroit for a year, followed by two in Arizona before returning to the Giants. Graham retired in 2002 after a ten-year NFL career.

"Kent had a cannon for an arm, which made him a special player and one of the nation's best quarterbacks," Chuck Long said. "I didn't have that kind of arm. I had to find another way. That meant getting the ball off on time and putting it in the right place. A bomb was a change-up for me; I just couldn't throw it consistently."

Nearly forty-five years after The Tot Lot days, Vic Graham continues to revel in the memories of those special times and the experiences that came with them in the same house just a few blocks away from the park and Wheaton North High.

"People say recruiting is a hassle, but I just loved it," he said while sitting in the comfort of his Wheaton home next to Romelle, his bride since 1957. "I mean, how many people can say that Bo Schembechler, Lou Holtz, and George Perles sat in your kitchen?"

"And Lou always spit when he talked," admitted Romelle Graham with a laugh and nod to the same large oak kitchen table that had hosted Lou and the others. "He was also full of energy. He sat at that table and drew up passing play after passing play. After watching him for a while, Kent came to realize he didn't understand the passing game at all! All Lou did was run the option. He said that's what you do when you don't have as much talent as other teams. But Kent loved Notre Dame and eventually signed with Coach Holtz."

The Grahams traveled to Iowa City more than once to see Chuck play ball.

"He's a special talent, a special kid," Vic Graham said. "And all of Wheaton is still mad that he got ripped off from winning the Heisman Trophy. We wanted an investigation and to this day believe the system was rigged!"

"I think another year at Iowa would be fun. I just don't see the pros as fun."

JOAN LONG
Chuck's mother when asked if her son would leave Iowa after his fourth season to pursue a career in the National Football League ("Chuck says maybe; Mom likes fun of it," Nolan Zavoral, Iowa City Press-Citizen, Nov. 1, 1984)

Those who knew him best understood full well how much Chuck relished the chance to run onto the Kinnick Stadium turf for a fifth season.

As he ducked out of sight following his epic performance in the Freedom Bowl, Hawkeyes fans nervously waited for his decision.

On one hand, they reasoned, Chuck loved Iowa and playing college football. He relished the opportunity few ever earn to play in another Rose Bowl—a distinct possibility given the talent returning.

Still, everyone knew that football was a violent game. With each snap taken, Chuck risked injury. A broken arm. Dislocated shoulder. Torn ACL. A concussion. Anything serious would jeopardize his draft status (if drafted at all), costing him big-time.

It was indeed a million-dollar decision.

"Regardless of whether he returns, Long has become one of the most successful football players in Iowa history," wrote Mark Dukes of the *Cedar Rapids Gazette,* as if anticipating the quarterback would bolt for greener pastures.

"Before 'The Wheaton Nice Man' ever started a game for Iowa, Coach Hayden Fry proclaimed, 'He's gifted. He's intelligent. He's poised. He is destined for greatness.' Fry knew whereof he spoke," penned Duke. "With Long at the controls, Iowa is 23–10–2 dating back to his first start against Arizona in September 1982."

As January passed and the drama escalated, no one was able to sway Chuck's opinion—one he had known from the bottom of his heart since the last snap of the Freedom Bowl.

He would remain a Hawkeye and return for a fifth year.[3]

Under the direction of sports information director George Wine and his assistant Phil Haddy, the idea of a press conference was hatched in late January. The best approach, Wine figured, was to announce the decision

---

[3] "I knew in my heart and mind that I was going back. My dream was to be a starting quarterback for a Rose Bowl team and to be a Big Ten champion," Chuck said. "We really had everyone coming back, with only Jonathan [Hayes] choosing to go pro, which was a good move on his part. But he was the only one. We knew we'd be top five in the country coming into the 1985 season. The way that game [Freedom Bowl] unfolded, we knew we were in for a special year. I knew in that locker room after playing Texas that I was coming back."

publicly so everyone was in the know simultaneously. A decision of this magnitude was national story and required it.

So on Feb. 5, 1985, Chuck strode confidently into the media room in Carver-Hawkeye Arena and took his place at a draped table in front of a gaggle of reporters, coaches, and players.

Without hesitation, he quickly took charge of the moment he had earned.

"I've come to a decision. I'm going to stay at the University of Iowa," he said in the same calm and methodical fashion that he read opposing defenses from the pocket. "I'll continue my education and play football for one more year. A lot of agents talked about big bucks. But if they're there this year, they'll be there next year.

"I have nothing against the Freedom Bowl," Chuck added, "but I'd rather end my collegiate career in Pasadena and the Rose Bowl next Jan. 1. Playing in the Rose Bowl is something I'd cherish forever."

Hawkeye Nation breathed a collective sigh of relief.

Chuck's father, Charlie, said the quarterback's happiness was the main thing. He had also been candid with reporters, saying it would be "wonderful" if Chuck would play another year at Iowa.

"I don't want to see it end," he had admitted to the *Des Moines Register's* Ken Fuson. "He's been leaning all along toward going back to school, and we're happy that he is. I think it was always in his heart to return. He was just trying to convince his mind."

Now it was official. And few were happier than Hayden Fry that Chuck's heart and mind had synched.

"Chuck and his family investigated every possible option before making the decision. I couldn't be more pleased...and believe it's the right thing to do at this time," he said, hardly able to contain his excitement. "Iowa fans across the nation join the coaches and players in congratulating Chuck. He is truly one of the finest quarterbacks in college football. Next season will be another exciting year for the Hawkeyes. Go Hawks!"

Making the decision a lot easier was the purchase of a sizeable insurance policy protecting Chuck from permanent total disability in his final year playing college ball.

"As with most forms of insurance, Long hopes he never has to collect on this particular policy, because it will mean his career as a high-salaried pro won't materialize," wrote *Des Moines Register* staff writer and Hawkeyes beat reporter Buck Turnbull. "But at least it's there if he does have a serious accident the next several months—on or off the football field."[4]

"I was leaning toward coming back all along," Chuck confided when news of the insurance policy was announced. "We have a good team coming back, and going to the Rose Bowl is something we've all been dreaming about."

And as if on cue, Chuck once again sought to downplay the extracurriculars while keeping expectations in check.

"I just hope the fans don't want me to turn pro after my first interception next season," he said with a smile.

'A STORY BOOK CHOICE'

Des Moines Register sports columnist Marc Hansen called Chuck's decision to remain a Hawkeye for a fifth year "a storybook choice," lifted directly from Clair Bee's kiddie sports novels.

"His name is Chip Hilton, the hero of classics like Buzzer Basket, Hardcourt Upset, and the popular Touchdown Pass," opined Hansen. "The latest work should be called Chip Comes Back. It has to be kiddie lit, because the plot is unimaginable in any other form."

---

[4] The insurance policy did have some exclusions. It prohibited Chuck from driving or riding in any kind of race but covered injuries sustained in a riot. Also purchasing a similar policy were quarterbacks Jack Trudeau of Illinois and Purdue's Jim Everett, Georgia all-American running back Herschel Walker, and Virginia basketball star Ralph Sampson.

Hansen wove an interesting tale:

"Chip Comes Back is the story of the football star who passes up a million-dollar NFL contract because he wants to lead his team to the Rose Bowl. Hollywood, of course, turned the script down cold. 'You gotta be kidding,' one producer said. 'Who'd believe that hokey premise? It's the craziest thing I've ever heard.' Isn't it though? Only in an ideal world inhabited by Chip Hilton does the star quarterback come back for a fifth year when the NFL is about to make him a first-round draft pick and a wealthy man.

"But Chuck Long is Chip Hilton," Hansen wrote. "The two look alike—tall, blond—and act alike—polite, humble. Both say please and thank you in the huddle. May I pass the football? You're welcome. Even the names are similar. With [Doug] Flutie signing a five-year, $7 million USFL contract, Long might have been the first quarterback drafted by the NFL. Some scouts preferred him to Flutie. In 1984, he set an NCAA record by completing twenty-two consecutive passes. In the Freedom Bowl against Texas, he passed for 461 yards and six touchdowns. He could have been set for life. But he wouldn't have had that Rose Bowl victory. He might never get it, but only someone like Chip Hilton could appreciate such a longing."

Feb. 8, 1985

Dear Charles, Joan and Andy,

Thank God it's over! Thank God Chuck will return! Thank God for you and the great love you have for Chuck! I'm confident that no one will ever know the amount of praying and studying all of you did in regard to Chuck's decision. The manner in which all of you conducted yourselves in a difficult situation is indicative of the integrity and honesty associated with the Charles Long family. I shall always admire and respect you for the way you treated Chuck during a critical time in his life.

Go Hawks!

Warm regards,

Hayden Fry

Head Football Coach

Chuck was at peace with his decision. So it only made sense that the fifth-year quarterback was the keynote speaker at a Lenten gathering Feb. 23, 1985, in Cedar Rapids.

The ease and confidence Chuck displayed on the football field had been apparent when he sat before reporters and announced he'd return for a fifth season of college football. And it was in plain view once again as he answered questions and shared stories with members and guests of First Christian Church.

A man of faith[5], Chuck reminisced about when he began playing sports as a fifth grader. That included basketball, baseball, and flag football. He had tried out for quarterback in the seventh and eighth grades but was shifted to tight end instead.

"I never caught any passes," he admitted to the group in a story that graced the pages of the Wheaton Journal. "Oh, I might have caught one pass in eighth grade. I was so discouraged I can remember going home almost crying. But I stayed with football, and in the ninth grade, I finally made the team as quarterback. However, we won only one game, and I wasn't sure I wanted to continue playing football.

---

[5] Chuck admitted to being like most athletes and seeking divine intervention. Faith in God, he said, is what sustained players during the good and bad times. "I never prayed for a win. I prayed for everyone on the team to stay well and play well."

"I mean, how can you get excited about a game when you go one for eight?" he asked rhetorically.

But Chuck emphasized to the luncheon attendees that he stuck with the game nonetheless and had more opportunities to throw the ball his sophomore year. Then, his junior season arrived. That's when things turned around. The Falcons won the state championship with a 12–1 record.

"In the championship game, I set a state record that still stands: I completed one of four passes for minus three yards," he said, pausing in just the right places while letting a bit of sarcasm permeate the story's punch line.

The crowd roared with laughter.

But the success in high school, Chuck continued, his voice softening with just a hint of edge to it, didn't mean much to college football coaches—at least not to very many of them.

He had a theory as to why.

When college football coaches and staff arrive at a high school, they want to analyze game film. They like to see a quarterback pass. A lot. But Chuck had only one film to show, and in it, the quarterback didn't do much passing. Not surprisingly, as the team averaged just five or six throws a game.

Yet Iowa signed Chuck "and only the good Lord knows why," he ad libbed to the churchgoers gathered in Cedar Rapids.

"Coach Hayden Fry must have seen something in me. But some of my coaches and friends told me I'd never make it at Iowa. But I was determined to prove the people wrong, and I think it had a lot to do with faith in God. It's been a good four years, but it hasn't come easily."[6]

While Chuck was receiving requests to speak, he was earning accolades from reporters who had witnessed their share of young men whose focus was

---

[6] Gus Schrader of the *Cedar Rapids Gazette* attended the Lenten luncheon and captured one of Chuck's lesser known but equally entertaining stories. Chuck recalled it as if it had happened just days before.

I was in the eighth grade and playing basketball. We had a game with a really tough Chicago city team and we were behind 32–31 when our coach called timeout with ten seconds left. Our coach had us over by the bench outlining a play we were to use to try to win the game, but ol' Chuck was staring around at my folks and friends because I thought we were winning. Our team took the ball out of bounds, and I began dribbling around while my teammates were shouting at me to shoot or pass the ball. The fans were booing me. When the horn sounded, I threw the ball up in the air like we won, only to then look at the scoreboard and discover we had lost by one point. Somehow, everyone knew we were down by a point. Except for me. It doesn't get much more embarrassing than that.

often on the future, not the present. The lure of fame and money was hard to resist, particularly for college athletes whose families craved both.

But Chuck held professional football in its proper context.

As noted by Richard Crabb of the *Wheaton Daily Journal*, there was the chance to be an all-American and set Big Ten records for passing and total quarterback offense. Chuck could also become the first college football player to play in five bowl games, perhaps two of them being the Rose.

"His family, his friends at Wheaton North, and Red Grange will always be proud of Chuck Long for these reasons," Crabb wrote. "At a time when great college passers are being made into instant millionaires by professional teams, Chuck Long told the press conference, 'I'll never have this opportunity again to play another season of college football, and money isn't everything.'

"The reporters didn't believe him, but Wheaton does."

Chuck's reputation was becoming one of authenticity, of being a man of his word,[7] and playing for something more than numbers printed on a bank deposit statement.

"Some might argue that Long is insane. At least he sounds too good to be true," wrote Bob Young of the Arizona Republic.

After examining Chuck's body of work and the demand for quarterbacks at the professional level, it was Young's opinion that the Iowa quarterback didn't need it. He was already a two-time all–Big Ten first-team quarterback, had thrown for almost 7,200 yards, finished seventh in Heisman Trophy balloting, and, in his last season, completed an astonishing 67 percent of his passes.

"For pessimists who wonder if there is a larger sum of money waiting on some unseen bottom line, consider the circumstances," Young offered. "In monetary terms, Chuck had everything to gain by renouncing his fifth year and turning professional. Realistically, only winning the Heisman next

---

[7] Retired Hawthorne School coach and instructor Bernie Hurley was honored at a surprise ceremony during a school honor day March 6, 1985. Hurley was Chuck Long's first coach when the young boy began his athletic play as a grade school student. As part of the event, the story was told by *Wheaton Daily Journal* consulting editor Richard Crabb of the time Coach Hurley traveled to Iowa City hoping to attend an Illinois-Iowa football game. He only happened into Chuck Long and explained his situation. Chuck admitted that tickets were very tight for the game but asked the coach the name of the hotel where he was staying. "In the middle of the night," recounted Crabb, "a messenger rapped on Hurley's door. Upon opening it, he was handed a pair of tickets for the big game."

season would make the wait worth any more money."

Young figured that because of the US Football League's raids on the NFL its first two years, the crop of college quarterbacks was extremely thin, thus putting Chuck in an enviable position.

"It doesn't take a Wall Street analyst to figure out that Long's stock was high this spring. Any broker worth his Alka-Seltzer would have said sell. Bernie Kosar did."[8]

Perhaps.

But Chuck wasn't Bernie.

And Hayden Fry, without having to use Alka-Seltzer, was relieved.

"Getting Chuck to come back was one of the best recruiting jobs we've done," Fry boomed. "You may not believe it, but Chuck actually has fun playing college football. Another thing is that he was so disturbed about us not going to the Rose Bowl last year, he felt a little personally responsible. I don't think he was impressed about all the fantasy of pro football."

"You only live once," Chuck told Robert Markus of the *Chicago Tribune* when explaining his decision to spurn the NFL for Iowa. "It was one I had to make for myself. It had to be from the bottom of my heart, my gut feeling."

He admitted to seeing his coach twice following the Freedom Bowl. Chuck had listened respectfully while "he told me the pros of coming back to school," and then, "I requested that I be left alone. I told him, 'Nothing you say is going to sway me.'"[9]

Chuck's decision to stay put in Iowa City was reaffirmed by the quality of his performances in spring football drills.

---

[8] Bernie Kosar's route to the NFL was not without drama and intrigue. It all had to do with the timing of his declaration of availability to be drafted and NCAA rules regarding his redshirt status and eligibility. After multiple hearings and legal maneuverings, NFL commissioner Pete Rozelle ultimately permitted Kosar to go professional in 1985. Kosar decided to forgo the regular NFL draft in favor of the supplemental draft. On July 3, 1985, he was selected by the Cleveland Browns and signed a five-year contract the same day.

[9] Even as a fifth-year senior, Chuck remained curious about how he appeared on Iowa's radar given he attempted just four passes a game as a wishbone quarterback at Wheaton North. "I always thought I had the ability to play," he confided in Robert Markus of the *Chicago Tribune*. "I just wanted somebody to give me the chance. Luckily, Coach Fry saw something there. I still have to ask him someday how he got my name." Northern Illinois, just one of three schools to recruit Chuck Long, almost landed his name on the dotted line. Then Fry paid a visit to Chuck's home. "Hayden was in my living room and said he was going to turn this program around. He said I could trust him. I did."

"Chuck is having a great spring. He's always the same. It doesn't matter if the weather is bad or what," Fry said. "He attended the off-season workouts, lifted weights and the rest. He's up to about 217 pounds now—at six-foot-four-and-a-half. He's really preparing himself for a good season."

Coach Hayden Fry was a master at keeping football in perspective. It was just a game, after all.

"I don't know. Maybe I'm just fortunate," Fry told reporters after the team's 1985 spring scrimmage. "One reason is because I truly work at trying to make college football a lot of fun. It's never been do-or-die. And I like to think the majority of college football coaches feel the same way."

Fry's love of the Hokey Pokey—a circle dance with synchronized shaking of the head, arms, and legs accompanied by a simple song—became a staple of his coaching era following wins (big and small) and branded Hawkeyes football as a program that celebrated the game along with the wins.

"What Hayden did better than anyone else is that he enjoyed every victory," Chuck recalled about his days as a Hawkeye. "A lot of coaches don't. They don't enjoy the wins you should have won or the ones you scratched out. The beauty of Hayden was that he enjoyed every win."

It was this approach to the game and the young men who played it that were key ingredients to Iowa's winning formula.

Of course, having a Heisman Trophy favorite as your signal caller didn't hurt.

"Chuck is always super," Fry beamed after the QB's spring game performance that included sixteen completions out of eighteen attempts for 283 yards and two touchdowns. "He's just a winner."

As spring ball came to a close, Iowa was a popular top five preseason college football pick. The pieces were all in place: an experienced squad that included Chuck Long, all-American linebacker Larry Station, and all–Big Ten running back Ronnie Harmon. Add to that a gutsy veteran coach surrounded by dedicated assistants and a rabid Hawkeyes fan base and it was indeed a special time in Iowa City.

"If all the optimistic projections about the 1985 University of Iowa football team bear fruit, quarterback Chuck Long will lead the Hawkeyes into the Rose Bowl, win the Heisman Trophy, and promptly be nominated for sainthood," AP sportswriter Chuck Schoffner predicted. "OK, maybe that's being a little too optimistic. Long might only become governor of Iowa instead of a saint."

As summer waned, sports writers were hard at work pecking away at typewriters and handicapping Iowa's odds. Most publications had the Hawkeyes slotted in their preseason top ten.

Football News, so enamored with Chuck's experience and skills, perched Iowa at no. 1.

Chuck Long took the lofty rankings and Heisman hype in stride, keenly aware that performance mattered more than predictions.

"Let's get on with it," he said. "I'm tired of talking about the Heisman Trophy and the national preseason stuff. The national preseason stuff never ends up the way they say, and you know what the odds are of getting the Heisman Trophy.

"There's so many good players across the country, you never know what's going to happen, so I'm not going to worry about it. I'm just glad to be in the running for it. It doesn't put any pressure on me."

In less than three weeks, Chuck would take the field with a group of men he loved and respected like brothers. It was a bittersweet feeling—one last go-around at Iowa but a once-in-a-lifetime chance to do something really special.

The opportunity wouldn't be squandered.

"I'm sure I'm going to screw up, but everybody screws up," predicted Chuck just days before Iowa clashed with the overmatched Drake University (Iowa) Bulldogs.

"You just gotta go on to the next play. You've got to take the good with the bad. And we've had our share of bad moments, believe me. Hopefully, nothing will end up like last year's regular season schedule."

It was a frank assessment. And also true. No player was above making mistakes. Even fifth-year seniors and all–Big Ten and all-American performers.

But few miscues occurred in Iowa's season opener Sept. 14, a home date versus the overmatched Division I-AA Bulldogs.

The Hawkeyes started slow, tallying fourteen points in the first half (including a second score with just seconds to go before intermission) on two touchdown throws by Chuck.

But when quarter three arrived, Iowa's offense lit up the scoreboard with a thirty-seven-point barrage behind a punishing offensive line and the quick feet and elusiveness of senior running back Ronnie Harmon.

When the final gun sounded, Iowa had earned a convincing 58–0 win— Drake's worst loss since a 63–0 rout in 1976—thanks to a bruising running game that led to scores on all five second-half possessions, a determined albeit rebuilt defense led by linebacker Larry Station, and a solid performance by Chuck Long and backup quarterback Mark Vlasic.[10]

Just how good was Iowa's "D"?

Drake managed minus thirty-six yards rushing for the game.

One week later, no. 4 Iowa welcomed Northern Illinois to town.

The Huskies, who had hung with Wisconsin in the season opener, were

---

[10] Mark Vlasic was a prized recruit for Hayden Fry. The six-foot-three athlete from Pennsylvania known for his mustache, tall physique, and strong arm served as backup to Chuck Long for four years. Monaca, Vlasic's hometown, was a thirty-mile drive from Pittsburgh and an area of the state that gave birth to Joe Montana, Dan Marino, and Joe Namath. When reminded by the Arizona Republic's Bob Young of this fact, Vlasic smiled and said, "It would be nice if there would be one more." Despite Chuck Long's decision to return for a fifth season in 1985, Vlasic remained upbeat. In addition to spelling Chuck at QB, Vlasic served as the holder for field goals, including the game-winning kick by Rob Houghtlin in top-ranked Iowa's 12–10 victory in a thriller over no. 2 Michigan.

Following Chuck's departure for the NFL, Vlasic took the reins and had a successful 1986 campaign, helping lead Iowa to a 9–3 record (5–3 in the Big Ten, good for a third-place conference finish). During his early years at Iowa, his strong arm captured the attention of Iowa coaches, including Hayden Fry. "He's got a stronger arm than Long," said Fry, "and he proves it every day by overthrowing his receivers."

Vlasic was selected eighty-eighth in the 1984 NFL draft by the San Diego Chargers and had a six-year career that also included time with the Kansas City Chiefs and Tampa Bay Buccaneers.

coached by Jerry Pettibone, in his first year in DeKalb. Pettibone, the school's third coach in three years, had served as Hayden Fry's recruiting coordinator at Southern Methodist in 1971.

"Hayden gave me my first coaching responsibility," he said, "and I thank him a lot."

Northern Illinois, a member of the Mid-American Conference, was also a familiar and respected foe for Chuck Long. Three Huskies players were Wheaton North grads, including no. 2 tight end Danny Graham, who, as a boy, had run circles with Chuck around The Tot Lot. Chuck had even considered enrolling at Northern Illinois, one of just three schools to seriously recruit him as a high school prep.

"We'd need a perfect game and Iowa would need to be off for us just to have a chance," Pettibone lamented.

Neither happened for the forty-two-point underdog.

Chuck threw five touchdown passes, and Vlasic added a sixth, in a record-setting aerial blitzkrieg that propelled Iowa to a 48–20 rout of the Huskies. Three of Chuck's TD tosses went to wide receiver Bill Happel, whose 207 yards receiving set an Iowa record for most in a game. Iowa's six touchdown passes also broke a Kinnick Stadium record of five set in 1963 against Indiana.

The Hawkeyes rolled up 534 yards of total offense—347 of that through the air—on a rainy day and sloppy track in Iowa City.

Northern Illinois could muster just sixteen yards rushing and eighty-four total.

"I never dreamed we'd be this good this early," said Hayden Fry, despite the team's six turnovers on the day (three fumbles and three interceptions). "We've scored more points and played better defense than I thought we would have at this point in the season."

Pettibone knew his team had taken a lickin' and didn't mind saying why.

"I just finished telling our players I felt we had played one of the really great teams in the country," he said. "I can't remember another team with so many players who can beat you with so many weapons.

"Iowa has all the ingredients to go as far as a good football team can go," he added.

Hayden Fry couldn't help but notice that Chuck's performance in the driving rain was eerily reminiscent of the QB's line in the Freedom Bowl trouncing of Texas. Ironically, that record-setting evening just nine months earlier took place in a steady downpour.

"It's amazing," Fry said. "We've played some good football games in the rain. I'll be happy if it rains every game, because I don't think Chuck Long lets anything bother him."

Chuck, as he usually did, passed the praise right along to Happel.

"The receivers did a great job of hanging onto the ball," he said. "A couple of the touchdowns were thrown high and a couple were outside."

"This was the worst rain I've ever played in," Chuck added. "It was worse than the Freedom Bowl because the field kept getting wetter, wetter, and wetter."

Iowa was cruising after its first two games of the 1985 season, outscoring its opponents by a combined score of 106–20.

Now it was off to Ames to tangle with an Iowa State squad led by head coach Jim Criner and quarterback Alex Espinoza. The Cyclones, with wins over Utah State and Vanderbilt to start the season, were 2–0 and a confident bunch.

And they relished the chance to go 3–0 by defeating the hated Hawkeyes.

Things were clicking for the Hawkeyes. With its win over Northern Illinois, Iowa inched up the Associated Press rankings to no. 3, a spot they hadn't held since 1961.

Sports writers from across the nation couldn't resist the storyline—an Iowa team that was a perennial Big Ten Conference loser sees its fortunes turn behind a swashbuckling coach and on the arm of a kid who was an obscure high school prep turned college football record-setter and legitimate Heisman Trophy candidate.

"Iowa was one of the country's college football doormats during much of the 1960s and '70s," wrote Mark Dukes in a column published in the Sporting News. "When Long was being recruited, the Hawkeyes had just posted their 19th consecutive nonwinning season.

"After Iowa broke that string in 1981, posting an 8–4 record and earning a Rose Bowl berth, a new quarterback had to be found. In August of 1982, when coach Hayden Fry was asked about Long's chances, he said: 'He's gifted. He's intelligent. He has great poise. He is destined for greatness.'"

Chuck Long, of course, had yet to prove himself as a college football quarterback, Dukes noted. But Hayden Fry had followed through on his resolve and proved to be "an accurate prophet."

The breakthrough for the QB from Wheaton was at Arizona in the third game of the '82 season. On that night in Tucson, Chuck rallied Iowa to a 17–14 win. From that point forward, Iowa was 24–8–1 with Chuck as the starter, appearing in the Peach, Gator, and Freedom Bowls.

"The Arizona game was the major turning point in my career," Chuck admitted to Dukes. "It showed me that I had the ability to play at this level."

With each game, Chuck was gaining in the Big Ten record books. His 270 passing yards against Northern Illinois gave him 7,682 for his career, passing Scott Campbell and Art Schlichter as the Big Ten's all-time passing leader. Only Mark Herrmann, who had played for the Purdue Boilermakers before being selected in the fourth round of the 1981 NFL draft, had more (9,946).

In addition, Chuck Long's 250 yards of total offense against the Huskies placed him third on the all-time Big Ten list.

Now, with Iowa State lurking, Hayden Fry was in the enviable position of having to downplay weekly expectations. He also had to balance when to call off the dogs against inferior opponents with protecting his starting quarterback while not muzzling his opportunity to post Heisman-like numbers.

"If I was like a majority of people, I'd be playing him a lot longer than I have," Fry said. "The thing is, those other guys have had to play the whole ball game and we've had a couple of runaways."

Had Chuck played more in his first two games, he likely would have surpassed three hundred yards passing in both contests.

"It's very difficult for me to take him out early," Fry added. "But in addition to winning, our number two priority is to get our people as much experience as we can. We need to get Mark Vlasic as much playing time as possible."

And that was just fine with Vlasic, a tall, strong-armed signal caller from Monaca, Pennsylvania. The bustling community was located just thirty miles northwest of Pittsburgh, an area known for its sports and birthing such gridiron stars as Joe Namath and Mike Ditka, as well as Terry Francona and fellow Hawkeye Jonathan Hayes.

Recruited by Iowa linebacker coach and fellow Keystone State native Barry Alvarez, the six-foot-three-inch quarterback was a prized get for the Hawkeyes despite having to ask "Where's Iowa?" when the black and gold came calling.

The appeal for his talent from the heart of the Midwest was indeed tempting, despite having other suitors. Vlasic, like many kids his age, had grown up being wooed to play for Big Ten and Pac-10 teams by the slate of January bowl games—most notably the Rose. Only those two conferences, after all, could berth contestants to play in "the granddaddy of them all."

So Vlasic, along with a Center High School football teammate, made the flight to Iowa City in February 1982 in the midst of another bone-chilling Iowa winter for a recruiting visit. The weather was so poor in Pennsylvania and across the East Coast that their flight was cancelled after the plane they were to travel on was grounded in Boston.

Undeterred, the pair hopped aboard a four-seater for a chartered flight to Cedar Rapids. With the plane bucking strong headwinds the entire way, the trip took twice as long as anticipated. But the coaches, campus, and players made a great first impression, so much so that Vlasic soon signed.[11]

Vlasic may have lacked experience as a fourth-year player for Iowa, but he wasn't short on confidence.

And neither were the Hawks. In addition to being the highest-scoring team in the nation, they also fielded one of the country's stingiest defenses, giving up an average of just 116.5 yards in their first games (including minus twenty yards rushing).

Iowa State's defensive unit was no slouch, either, giving up 229 yards a game, good for fifth nationally.

Jim Criner, ISU's head coach, didn't exactly ooze confidence in the days leading up to the big in-state rivalry game.

"We've got our hands full," he said. "Iowa has a Heisman Trophy candidate in quarterback Chuck Long, is very physical, and has a strong defense. We're very excited to have an opportunity to play against one of the top teams in the nation."

Coach Fry, as expected, struck a cautious note despite Iowa being pegged by Vegas as a seventeen-point favorite.

"Based on everything I know, it'll be a close game," he predicted. "Iowa State appears to be much, much better than the two teams we've faced. But we won't prepare any differently for ISU.

"Anytime you have Iowa-Iowa State, you don't have to say anything to get motivated."

And when asked if ISU's man-to-man defense might play right into the hands of quarterback Chuck Long, Fry responded with a smile, "Well, we'll see Saturday."

Leading just 7–0 at the end of the first quarter, Iowa poured it on in the second, scoring thirty-four additional unanswered points to take a 41–0 halftime lead. The Hawkeyes added nine more points in the third quarter and cruised from there, winning 57–3.[12]

---

[11] Iowa made an impression on Vlasic for other reasons, too. "I remember watching Iowa play in the Rose Bowl in 1981," he recalled. "I was so impressed by the team and its leadership and the story about where Iowa had come from—how Coach Fry had taken a program that had been down for so many years and returned it to national prominence. I also was inspired to attend a school that was a great college town, and Iowa City was certainly that. And maybe part of it, too, was growing up a Pittsburgh Steelers fan and seeing the Iowa jerseys, which were replicas. It all felt right, right away."

"Hawks humiliate ISU" proclaimed the *Cedar Rapids Gazette*.

It's was Iowa State's worst loss in the thirty-three-game series and their most lopsided defeat in thirty-nine years.

Familiar names wearing black and gold again paced the Hawkeyes. Chuck threw for 223 yards and three touchdowns on nineteen of thirty-two passing while Ronnie Harmon rushed for 103 yards on nineteen totes, scoring twice. Vlasic also got in on the fun, tossing Iowa's fourth touchdown pass while Kevin Harmon added another twenty yards on the ground.

The starters were pulled midway through the third quarter, marking the third consecutive game Iowa's starters had failed to take a snap in the fourth quarter.

ISU's only score came on a fifty-two-yard field goal with 9:21 remaining in the game and Iowa leading 57–0.

"Even as sparkling as Chuck Long is at times, even he could have slipped into an Iowa State jersey at halftime and altered the course of this game not a bit," wrote *Des Moines Register* columnist Marc Hansen. "Consider that a pardon for Cyclones quarterback Alex Espinoza, who deserved better. What he got were dropped passes, missed assignments, and one of the longest afternoons of his life.

"Dan Marino couldn't have turned it around Saturday."

MEETING BO

Jonathan Hayes was a prized high school recruit, drawing the attention of numerous top-tier college football programs, including the Michigan Wolverines led by its flamboyant coach, Bo Schembechler. Michigan wide receiver Anthony Carter was paired with Hayes for his visit to Ann Arbor, providing the

---

[12] In a three-game, three-year stretch (1983–85), Iowa outscored Iowa State 167–34. The fifty-four-point win remains the largest margin of victory in the Iowa-Iowa State series.

Pennsylvania native with a personal tour of campus.

"Anthony was a class act and a real good guy. So he showed me around; I had a great weekend and met a lot of the guys who had already gone to the pros," Jonathan Hayes said.

"So after the tour, Coach Schembechler pulls me into his office and closes the door. He takes a seat behind this huge desk, pulls out his big ashtray, and lights up a cigar. He then leans back in his chair and asks in a voice that only Bo had, he asks me, 'Now, Jonathan, do you want to become a Michigan man?'"

Jonathan Hayes had paused then. His parents had not accompanied him to Ann Arbor, and he wasn't about to answer that question without consulting them first. It was a cold, snowy weekend on campus, and Hayes glanced out the window, then back at Schembechler.

"You know, Coach, it's a little cold up here during these long winters," he replied, buying time. "Some of the other schools had a lot better weather."

Then, with his rhetorical footing solidified, he confidently added, "But more importantly, Coach, the one thing I want to tell you is how important my relationship is with my mom and dad. I'm not going to make a decision without involving them."

It was a surreal moment for Jonathan Hayes and one that he still recalls vividly more than thirty-five years later.

"So Bo is sitting there, and God rest his soul, he's puffing on his cigar. And you're thinking all these things. And how cool it is to be where you are after seeing all the Michigan and Ohio State games over the years as a kid. I mean, that's all you saw on TV as a high school kid, and every one of us who hoped to play one day after high school honestly wished that one of those schools would one day come and recruit you. And now, here they were at my doorstep.

"But there were a couple of things that happened that didn't sit well with me, and that's why I made the decision I did to become a Hawkeye," added Hayes, now an assistant coach with the NFL's Cincinnati Bengals. "They weren't big things, just subtle things that made me choose Iowa. It was also a decision made easier after noticing the camaraderie among the players at Iowa. And it didn't matter if you were a freshman or a senior. Hayden and his staff had created a culture of togetherness, and I wanted to be part of that."

The win was so decisive that the Quad-City Times predicted there would be a new top-ranked team in college football come Tuesday.

And it was a good bet to think that team would be Iowa.

"What the No. 3-ranked Hawks did Saturday to a supposedly improved 2–0 Iowa State team bordered on criminal," wrote the Times' Craig Cooper. "Final toll was 57–3. And it was every bit as bad as that, if not worse."

So began the calls for Iowa to be at the top of the college football rankings.

"Being number one might be the kiss of death," said Hayden Fry. "We're happy where we are right now."

Well, so much for being comfortable.

On Monday, Sept. 30, 1985, the USA Today/CNN Top 25 football poll hoisted Iowa to its top spot. Tallying 774 points, the Hawkeyes bested no. 2 Oklahoma by twenty-eight points and no. 3 Ohio State by more than one hundred.

And as if on cue, Hayden Fry brushed aside the concerns about being no. 1 and instead embraced the lofty status. The no. 1 ranking, he said, would bring prestige to the Iowa program, which he had revived after nineteen consecutive seasons without a winning record.

It was the first time since Oct. 3, 1961, that the Hawkeyes held college football's no. 1 ranking.

"It's not in my wildest dreams that we'd be number one this early in the season," said Fry. "It's an achievement and an accomplishment, but our players are intelligent enough to know that it can last only a few games."

Especially in the Big Ten. While Iowa had throttled its nonconference opponents, the conference schedule now loomed. First up: a home date versus Michigan State, the same Spartan team that had clipped Iowa 17–16 the previous season when a two-point conversion attempt by Chuck on a quarterback keeper on the game's final play came up short of the goal line.

Through the first three games of Chuck's final go-around as a Hawkeye, Iowa had scored 163 points, the most since 1900, when they tallied 172. On the flip side, the Hawks had given up just twenty-three, the stingiest since the 1956 squad allowed twenty.

Iowa also led the nation in scoring average (54.3 points), total defense (154.3 yards), and rushing defense (17.7 yards). The Hawks were fourth in scoring defense (7.7), fifth in passing offense (342.7), sixth in total offense (506.7), and fourteenth in pass defense (136.7).

To Chuck, the numbers added up to long overdue recognition of a program that had been on the rise since he arrived in Iowa City.

"I think about how the Iowa program has come a long way in the five years I've been here," he said. "I've seen about everything—a Rose Bowl, an addition to the stadium, an indoor facility—now we're number one.

"We haven't had a lot of respect in the past," Chuck added. "People thought we were that little farm school. But we've worked hard and gained a lot of respect over the years."

The ranking—and prestige—also wasn't lost on Jim Zabel, who had been sitting atop Kinnick Stadium for thirty-seven years broadcasting Iowa football games on WHO Radio in Des Moines.

For most of those years, and more games than he could count, Zabel had been tasked with making lemonade out of lemons as Iowa was tossed around by Big Ten opponents like a stuffed bird.

In a column authored by Ken Fuson of the *Des Moines Register,* Zabel said the no. 1 ranking "dims the memory of nineteen straight nonwinning seasons.

"I've been through a lot of thick and mostly a lot of thin," Zabel admitted. "I have suffered. I've had people come and tell me they wanted to be buried in the Iowa end zone when they died so nobody would step on them…

"I think this is just tremendous for the morale and the pride of the state," Zabel shared with Fuson. "This calls attention to Iowa in a very positive way. I'm just elated over the whole thing."

Fry confided that the team's meteoric rise so early in the season surprised players as much as fans.

"I told the team about it, and they're very excited," he said. "It's a real honor to the players, the university, and the state of Iowa.

"It's a very nice thing right now for the state of Iowa with all the bad luck the farmers have had and with the economy down," he added. "The Hawks are something they can identify with. I think it [the ranking] is a real wholesome, positive thing. People can take pride in it and forget about their problems."

Everyone, that is, but Hayden Fry.

The Michigan State Spartans were formidable foes and arrived in Iowa City 2–1, their only blemish a 27–10 defeat at the hands of Notre Dame. Fry knew in his heart that the season's first three opponents weren't a true barometer of the talent the Hawkeyes were about to face. Also, being chased was far different than chasing. The nation's top ranking demanded ultimate discipline and perspective—and an attitude.

Once again, Fry's background in psychiatry paid dividends, as did his ability to speak in plain, West Texas English that translated well in the heart of the nation's breadbasket.

"Ignore all the gobble-wobble of the polls and the pressure from the fans and the news media," he said. "Being number one won't make you play any better. It shouldn't make you play any worse, either. Just keep doing what you've been doing."

That mind-set had served Hayden Fry and the Hawkeyes well since his arrival after the 1978 season. Building a program into a traditional winner was more than acquiring better talent. It was about changing a losing mind-set and recruiting athletes who were class people, wanted to be coached, and relished the opportunity to play as a team.

"We corrected a lot of the inadequacies that existed when we got here, whether it was the mental environment or approach," Fry said. "We changed the way we conduct things, organization, and the management. The motivational materials that help stimulate a guy to stay in shape, go to class, as well as on the football field. We have worked more with the total person rather than just as a football player."

The young men Fry wanted on his team were hungry to learn and develop their skills, no matter how raw.

"At times you sacrifice a little talent you might get in a pure athlete who really loves to play football," Fry said. "But he's not motivated to get an education or he's not motivated to be a member of the family. He's so much of an individualist that he doesn't fit in. We stay away from those kinds of people. We phased out the ones that we inherited.

"This is the secret of our success," he continued, "working with quality young men who are not going to give up in the fourth quarter or they're not going to mope or they're not going to do anything to give our program a bad image."

It would now take that same team-first focus to manage the expectations and hype that came with the nation's top ranking. After three easy wins—the kind of stretch that defensive back Nate Creer referred to as "the preseason"—it was time for Big Ten football. And defense of that lofty perch would start when Iowa took the field against Michigan State as a seventeen-point favorite on homecoming in Iowa City.

And wouldn't you know that Chuck, best known for his arm, would use his feet on Iowa's last offensive play to carry the top-ranked Hawks to a thrilling 35¬–31 win in front of more than 66,400 fans.

The play that would end the game almost four hours after it started would befit a bruising, back-and-forth conference grudge match that had Michigan State on the verge of pulling the upset behind the smash mouth running of tailback Lorenzo White (who gained 226 yards on the afternoon) and another 275 yards passing by sophomore quarterback Bobby McAllister.

Actual game time lasted three hours and forty minutes. But to the fans in the stands and millions more watching the broadcast nationwide on CBS, the game was an entertaining roller coaster of emotions and lead changes that flew by in what seemed like three minutes and forty seconds.

The Spartans weren't about to fold against the nation's top-ranked team. Throughout the afternoon, Iowa and Michigan State traded body blows. Iowa scored first on a sixty-yard bomb from Chuck Long to wideout Robert Smith. The Hawkeyes struck again early in the second when Chuck hit tight end Mike Flagg on a seventeen-yard score. A missed extra point made the score 13–0.

But the Spartans responded, scoring a touchdown and field goal to cut Iowa's halftime lead to 13–10. The Spartans also tallied the first two scores of the second half with two touchdown runs by White to take a commanding 24–13 lead.

One minute later, Iowa scored on Chuck's third TD of the day—a three-yarder to Smith—followed by a successful two-point conversion. Moments later, Iowa completed the third-quarter scoring flurry on another Long-Flagg touchdown connection, this one for twelve yards.

The fourth quarter was a grind, with both teams trading jabs. Then, with just four minutes and change remaining, Michigan State freshman running back Craig Johnson, subbing for an exhausted and injured White, broke loose from Iowa's twenty-five-yard line and dashed into the end zone, giving the Spartans a 31–28 lead.

It was now gut check time for an Iowa team that had not been tested all year.

With the inner confidence befitting a fifth-year quarterback, Chuck led Iowa's offense onto the field. Down by three and with less than four minutes to play in the game, the Hawkeyes began a methodical, textbook drive from its own twenty-one-yard line.

A combination of hard-nosed running and precision passing marched Iowa to the Spartans' eleven with less than a minute to play. Two runs by Ronnie Harmon—one for seven yards and another for two—set up the Hawkeyes at the two-yard line. A timeout, Iowa's last, stopped the clock with thirty-one seconds remaining.

It was now strategy time on the Iowa sideline as Iowa faced a third down-and-one from the Spartans' two-yard line.

Hayden Fry, sporting his trademark sunglasses, tussled hair, and mustache, and Chuck Long huddled close as an uneasy current of electricity coursed through Kinnick.

Down, distance, and time were all critical ingredients in determining which plays to call. Given Iowa was out of timeouts, was there enough time to attempt a run if the player was tackled in bounds and short of the goal line? Or should Iowa call a pass play? But what if Chuck was sacked? Would there still be enough time to attempt another play? What was Michigan State expecting? Would they blitz? Or, given that the shortest distance between two points is a straight line, would they clog up the middle of the line anticipating a run up the gut by Harmon?

"OK, Charlie, here's what we're going to do," Fry instructed, pulling Chuck in even closer. "We're going to run an isolation play on the left-hand side of the line of scrimmage. But don't tell anybody. Not a dang person. And don't hand it off to Ronnie. Just put the ball on your hip and go around the right side, and you're going to score a touchdown."

"Coach, have you seen me run?" Chuck quickly retorted as the din of the crowd grew. "What if someone is over there waiting for me? If I get tackled, the game's over. I don't think there's enough time."

The hype built inside Kinnick as the head referee sounded his whistle and prepared to wind the clock. Both teams were signaled to return to the field of play.

Time to make a decision. Just the two of them—Hayden Fry and Chuck Long.

Fry removed his sunglass and poked them directly into Chuck's chest. But instead of uttering a four-letter word, as was usually the case when the sunglasses came off, he remained calm and composed.

"Charlie, I want you to do what I said. I want you to put that dang ball on your hip and do a bootleg back around the right side of the line. You're going to score a touchdown. Just trust me on this."

With just the coach and his quarterback in the know, Chuck turned and lumbered back onto the field and into the huddle.

He barked out the play, and teammates took their place on the line.

The ball was snapped. The play clock ticked down from thirty-one. Chuck turned to Harmon. He tucked the ball into his waiting arms, then pulled it back. He rolled to the right side as an empty-handed Harmon surged toward the line. The Spartan defensive back bit, vacating the left side of the field. There was no one home. Not within five yards. An empty field awaited Chuck as he broke to the far pylon. In a split second, he knew he would cross the goal line untouched.

He gripped the ball tight in his right hand and raised it into the cool air high above his head as he crossed the goal line.

With twenty-seven seconds to go, Iowa scored a touchdown. There would not be a fourth-down play. There would not be an overtime. Iowa would win in a thriller.

"Good call. Great quarterback. Hell of a football game," wrote Mike Hlas of the *Cedar Rapids Gazette*.

Despite giving up 580 yards of total offense and thirty-one points, Iowa was the victor.

In triumph, Chuck completed a school record thirty passes on thirty-nine pass attempts for 380 yards. He also accounted for all five scores, four through the air and the final on a slick, two-yard naked bootleg.

"I feel like I've been run over by a truck," exclaimed an exhausted and exuberant Hayden Fry.

It was perfect revenge for Chuck Long, wrote staff writer Buck Turnbull of the *Des Moines Register*, reminding readers that the QB's last-minute attempt a year earlier to run for a two-point conversion against the same Spartans and from nearly the identical spot on the field had failed.

"They say history repeats itself," Chuck said, "and this sure was a déjà vu thing for me.

"I said to myself, 'Coach Fry, run whatever you want, but don't run that option play [that failed last year],'" Chuck added. "And the play we ran sure worked. Now Michigan State can think about that for a year, like we did.[13]

"It was a gutsy call by Coach Fry. I'll tell you, I wouldn't have made it."

The ability to call great plays by thinking outside the box is what made Hayden Fry a superior coach and an even better leader.

Fry called it "a fantastic football game," telling Turnbull that the team would have never been able to beat back the Spartans had it not been for a quarterback as skilled and poised as his Heisman Trophy candidate.

"The Hawks learned a valuable lesson in life," Fry added. "If you continue to hang together and keep the faith, keep executing what you're supposed to do, then you'll be successful in life. It's something you can't learn in a textbook.

"This was like last year, but with a different ending," he added. "That might have been the greatest fake in the history of football. I think I could have scored on that one, and I'm pretty slow."[14]

"The difference was Long," Spartans head coach George Perles told reporters. "We knew that coming in. Iowa played awfully well today, and I think they'll be favored to win games as long as Chuck Long is healthy," he added. "You're going to see him play for many years on Sundays after this year. He's a great football player. A complete football player."

---

[13] Had the play failed and Chuck Long not scored, Iowa would have had to scramble to attempt a fourth-down conversion. And it wouldn't have been a field goal attempt. Fry said they used the timeout to call two plays—the one that Chuck converted, and another had the attempt failed. "If Chuck was stopped short, we were going to put our field goal players on the field and fake it instead of going for the tie. Thank gosh we didn't have to."

IOWA AND SPARTANS 1985 – THEN AND NOW

The year was 1985, and no. 1 Iowa was battling Michigan State. Trailing by three with just thirty-one seconds to play and no timeouts (and no interest in kicking a field goal, which would essentially end the game in a tie), Chuck Long took the snap and scampered two yards to pay dirt. The bootleg gave Iowa a 35–31 win, revenging a hard-fought loss to the Spartans just one year earlier and on a similar play.

More than thirty years later, the players and coaches who were in position to make plays and change the course of history on that day in Iowa City figure prominently in college football. Starting strong safety for Michigan State was Iowa's current defensive coordinator, Phil Parker. The Spartans' linebackers coach was the late Norm Parker, who coached at Michigan State from 1983 to 1994 before joining the Iowa squad as defensive coordinator (1999–2011). And here's the best part: the defensive coordinator and defensive backs coach that day for Michigan State was…Nick Saban, now head coach of the Alabama Crimson Tide and winner of five college football national championships.

"It's all in the fake," said Chuck Long as fans and sports writers continued to take inventory of Iowa's thrilling 35–31 win over Michigan State. "The 'no. 1' thing didn't bother us this week. We're not accustomed to

---

[14] On the touchdown run, Chuck held the ball above his head as he crossed the goal line. "I noticed he hoisted the ball over his head at the three- or four-yard line, and I was about to have a heart attack," Hayden Fry said after the game. He then tried to scold Chuck when he returned to the jubilant sideline following the score. Chuck would have none of it.

"I just told Coach that, after what happened last year, I was going to make sure that the refs could see the ball cross the goal line."

CHUCK LONG: DESTINED FOR GREATNESS

it, so maybe we don't know how you're supposed to act."

Chuck had completed six of seven passes on the game's final drive that set up his winning two-yard, untouched scamper to the end zone. It was a sweet way to avenge the loss to the Spartans one year earlier, a moment that had validated Chuck's decision to spurn the NFL for more time in Iowa City.

The nifty footwork culminating in a winning score continued to impress Hayden Fry, even with a slugfest versus the Wisconsin Badgers looming.

"We were going into the wind against a very complex defense," he said. "We were fighting the clock and then had no more timeouts when we got down close to the goal line. From an execution standpoint, Chuck throwing the ball, guys getting open, blocking by the linemen, Scott Helverson catching a ball and whirling to make a first down by inches, Bill Happel running a corner route, and Chuck having to throw over the defensive corner back but not far enough that the safety could get it, and the linemen and the fullback picking up all those crazy stunts to give Chuck time enough to throw—all those things, plus that last beautiful fake certainly make it rank with the great ones I've seen."

Everything, Fry added, went as planned, "except Chuck holding the ball up and waving it from about the six-yard line on in. If anyone watched the game doubting that Chuck is a true candidate for the Heisman Trophy, I'm positive he changed his mind after yesterday."

With the win, 4–0 Iowa remained at the top of the USA Today/CNN football poll, edging no. 2 Oklahoma by twenty-nine points.

And with a third of the season in the rearview mirror, Chuck was having a ball.

"What's happened so far this year has been like a dream come true," he said. "It's something you dream about when you're a kid. To think where this team was five years ago and look at where we are now is unimaginable.

"I'll never forget when Coach Fry recruited me. He sat in my living room and told me that he was going to turn this program around, and I believed him."

Iowa was also a believer in how tough it was to play on the road in the Big Ten. The Badgers now loomed on Iowa's schedule. It was already week five of the season, and Iowa had yet to take a snap outside of the state.

Fry confided that there were few places more difficult to play than Camp Randall Stadium.

"It's extremely important to try to take the crowd out of the game there, more so than any other place in the world," Fry said. "It's the worst place to play football. The fans there have the most abusive language I've ever heard.

"Two years ago, we had rotten eggs, beer, and schnapps thrown at us. Our big lineman, John Carroll, caught an egg in the palm of his hand the last time we were up there, or else it would've hit me. We gave him the Golden Glove award after that game.

"One time, I heard the fans yelling, turned around, and they were passing a keg up through the stands. The next time I turned around, I thought the same thing was happening, but instead it was a young girl they were passing up toward the top. They were handing her row to row. The folks up there don't really care too much about the game. They just have a good time.

"My wife's van got broken into and the tires were flattened just because it had Iowa license plates," Fry said, adding that the antenna was also tied in a knot and clothing was stolen just for good measure.

"Wisconsin fans mean well, and there's a lot of real fine people up there. In fact, I got three letters last year from people offering a parking space where it would be safe to park."

Ah, such is life in the Big Ten.

Iowa's first-in-the-nation ranking made the black and gold a tantalizing target for the 3–1 Badgers, who no doubt still relished the 10–10 knot they had tied Iowa with just one year earlier in Iowa City.

Chuck, named the Associated Press's Midwest Player of the Week after his winning performance versus Michigan State, wasn't about to let the team stumble. The Hawkeyes were on a roll, and times like this were meant to last. That's the power of positive thinking, instilled in the team by a coaching staff that knew how to motivate young men of sound character.

Wisconsin coach Dave McClain praised Iowa, saying that he'd never seen a better offense than Iowa's in his eight years at the helm in Madison.

"And I've never seen a better quarterback than Chuck Long."[15]

Wisconsin could move the ball, too, behind two of the best runners in the league—tailback Larry Emery and fullback Joe Armentrout. And they were ready to test an Iowa defense that allowed the Spartans 305 yards rushing.

Fortunately for the Hawkeyes, the Badgers were in a giving mood on a soggy Saturday in Camp Randall. And the Iowa defense survived a scare when Wisconsin drove to its one-yard line late in the fourth quarter, forcing the home team to settle for just a field goal.

Iowa survived 23–13 to remain unbeaten.

Chuck survived, too.

Barely.

The Badgers harassed the Iowa quarterback all afternoon, knocking him down often and hard. On Iowa's first offensive play, Chuck was wobbly as he peeled himself off the turf after sustaining a jarring hit. Later in the first half, he was sacked and, after spending some time looking skyward, walked shakily off the field.

"I don't seem to remember much after the first quarter," he confided to reporters after the game. "At halftime, I felt a lot better. Right now, everything is sore because they really drilled me. I'm just glad to get out of here alive."

Harmon also escaped relatively uninjured against a team that had broken his leg the last time they met.

Chuck completed eighteen of twenty-eight passes for 167 yards and one touchdown while Harmon dashed for 175 while also hauling in eight receptions for sixty-two yards.

When asked after the game if Iowa deserved to keep its no. 1 ranking, Chuck didn't miss a beat.

---

[15] Chuck attended the Wisconsin Badgers Football Camp prior to his senior season as quarterback of the Wheaton North Falcons. Badgers football staff encouraged Chuck to play safety rather than quarterback.

"I don't know if we're number one. That's up to the voters. But I do know we're 5–0."

It was Iowa's best start since 1960.

"I don't know that there's anything I particularly like about coaching against Bo Schembechler," said Hayden Fry. "He's a tough guy, honest, and he's certainly proven he's a great football coach. There's a whole lot of other coaches I'd rather be preparing my team for this week than Bo."

So began one of the most special weeks in the history of Iowa football—six days of sheer craziness leading up to Saturday's clash in Iowa City: no. 1 Iowa hosting no. 2 Michigan.

The records and statistics backed up the significance of the game—the nation's top-scoring offense (Iowa) versus the number-one scoring defense (Michigan).

"Our defense has done it all year, and our defense did it again today," Schembechler said after clobbering Michigan State 31–0. "I don't know when it's going to end. After a while, you get to believe this is a pretty good defensive team, but you've got to play a little better offense to win the championship.

"We may get smashed this week [versus Iowa], but I really don't think so. In my dreams, I'd like to take this team all the way, but we've got six big games left to play."

Bo Schembechler's team was coming to Iowa City having outscored its first five opponents 138–21. Among the five wins were two shutouts (Maryland and Michigan State), a 34–3 drubbing of South Carolina, and an impressive 33–6 pasting of Wisconsin. In those same games, the Wolverines had allowed only three points in the second half while scoring seventy-seven.

Chuck lived for weeks like this, with hype in the air thicker than smoke from a Weber grill. It was the reason he had returned to play a fifth season.

Campus town was alive. Credentialed media were pouring into Iowa City. Local reporters were jockeying for additional coverage in print and on TV. And Iowa farmers, struggling under devastating market prices, appreciated the distraction.[16]

Hayden Fry was equally jazzed. The Texas native told Washington Post staff writer John Ed Bradley that his dream as an Iowa coach was to "come up out of the depths of the cornfield and tee it up against the Wolverines."

In other words, Fry wanted to win some ball games, play for something, put Iowa City on the map, have a sold-out stadium bursting at the seams and lit for nationally televised night games—a program that competed at the highest level.

And now, here he was. Iowa football was at the top echelon of all things college football as the brawl with Michigan loomed.

So, with all the hype and the no. 1 ranking on the line, what was Hayden Fry doing with the press?

Downplaying the significance of the game, a matchup featuring the nation's top two teams for the first time since 1983 and only the nineteenth time in the history of the Associated Press poll of sportswriters dating back to 1936. [17]

"If you put your eggs in one basket, it gets tipped," Fry said. "You are going to be in trouble. It's one victory, nothing more."

Then again, Iowa—a three-point underdog to the Wolverines—hadn't been ranked no. 1 in the nation since 1961, the same year that a gallon of gas sold for twenty-seven cents, Pampers introduced the first disposable diaper, and John F. Kennedy was inaugurated the thirty-fifth president of the United States.

"I put no stock in the polls," said Fry for good measure. "The Michigan game is no more important from a won-loss standpoint than any other."[18]

---

[16] Chuck Long held the farm community in high esteem. "Hayden always said, 'Charlie, to get in good with Iowa, you have to get in good with the farmers first. They are the backbone of the state. If they love you, everybody else will.'" And he was right, Chuck said long after his college playing days were over. "That's one of the reasons why so many people loved Hayden, because he loved the farm community. If you're competitive and you show Iowans respect, they'll come to games and fill the stadium. This begins with showing farmers respect and understanding their dedication and being as competitive on the playing field as they are on the farm fields."

Bo Schembechler was also measured in his diagnosis of the game's importance and heaped praise on the host.

"The last couple of times we played at Iowa, we played our best game and won, and we played our worst game and lost," he told reporters. "This year we're dealing with a precision quarterback who can throw as accurately as anyone in the nation. And we're dealing with a dangerous running back."

And a stadium bursting at its seams.

Musco Lighting of Oskaloosa, Iowa, made sure it was lit for the late-afternoon kick. All sixty-six thousand game-day tickets had been scooped up long ago, and six days prior to kickoff, Iowa's sports information office was turning down requests from media outlets seeking press credentials due to a lack of space in the press box.

Six bowl scouts were in attendance along with fifteen radio stations, seventy writers, and a gaggle of photographers, including three from Sports Illustrated alone.

"It's a real challenge," replied Chuck when a reporter asked if he'd find passing lanes against the Wolverines' vaunted secondary in the self-described biggest game of his career.

"Most of Michigan's defensive backs have faced us the last three years, and we know they're very good. Michigan plays hard, aggressive defense."

With a sellout crowd on its feet, the two 5–0 Big Ten powerhouse programs collided as sunlight faded on an electric fall football afternoon in Iowa City.

It was a game that lived up to the hype.

And then exceeded it.

---

[17] The first time nos. 1 and 2 met in college football was 1948 when top-ranked Notre Dame defeated Iowa 14–13.

[18] Tickets for prime seating at the game cost $14. The *Des Moines Register* reported that some tickets were being sold for $40 by people who were unable to attend, a profit of $26. That included Nathan and Linda Spencer, seniors at the university, who had to forgo the game to be in a wedding. The Spencers sold their four tickets, netting nearly $100. The Spencers said they needed the money but would rather be at the game. "We'll never see this type of matchup again; it's a once-in-a-lifetime game." That it was.

"Concentrate and hit it straight."

Those were the last words Iowa kicker Rob Houghtlin, a sophomore transfer from Miami of Ohio, heard as he jogged onto Kinnick's green turf.

Not that the directive was anything new. They were the same five words Coach Hayden Fry told Houghtlin before every kick.

But this was no ordinary boot, because this was no ordinary game.

With no. 2 Michigan holding a razor-thin 10–9 lead over no. 1 Iowa, the historic college football encounter on a dreary evening in Iowa City was about to be decided by the foot of a twenty-year-old, five-foot-eleven, 180-pound football player from Winnetka, Illinois.[19]

Iowa's offense had just marched sixty-six yards on wet turf and head-on into the teeth of the Wolverines' vaunted defense thanks to several critical third-down conversions by Chuck.[20]

The drive had chewed up more than five minutes of precious game clock after Wolverines kicker Mike Gillette nailed a forty-yarder to lift Michigan to a one-point lead in the seesaw contest.[21]

Now it was up to Houghtlin.

"I was praying," he later admitted when asked what he was thinking as he knelt over the kicking tee in preparation for the game's final play. "I was praying to the Lord, asking for a little strength and direction."

Just minutes earlier, Houghtlin had missed a forty-four-yarder, breaking a string of ten consecutive field goals.

Now, with no. 2 quarterback Mark Vlasic as the holder, Houghtlin lined up the most significant kick of his life and one of the most heralded in Hawkeyes football history.

It was a kick he had attempted and made hundreds of times.

---

[19] Winnetka, Illinois, a suburb of Chicago, is nestled alongside Lake Michigan. It's located just forty miles northeast of Wheaton, Chuck Long's childhood hometown.

[20] Chuck completed twenty-six of thirty-nine attempts on the afternoon for 297 yards. He was intercepted once—a third-quarter pick on a third-and-seven from Michigan's twenty-four-yard line. On the final drive, he started just one of four but hit on his last two to help position Iowa at Michigan's twelve-yard line for the game-winning field goal attempt.

He was ready for the moment.

In a blur, the ball was snapped, placed, and kicked.

And as it sailed through the crossbars, Vlasic and walk-on kicker Houghtlin leaped into the air with arms stretched skyward.

Prayer answered.

Those were the first points scored on Michigan's defense in the fourth quarter on the season. And they couldn't have come at a more fortunate time for the Hawkeyes.

"That's what you call cutting it close," wrote *Des Moines Register* staff writer Buck Turnbull. "When Iowa players review the game and look at the statistics, they can't help but wonder why they didn't do it a little easier than that.

"Six times they prowled inside Michigan's 25-yard line, but even with the nation's No. 1 scoring offense, they got nary a touchdown."

Yet a superhuman effort by Iowa's defense—and four field goals by Houghtlin—were enough to secure a win for Iowa on a gray, rainy afternoon in Iowa City.

"I've never seen so much hugging and kissing in my life," said Iowa wide receiver Scott Helverson.

"The locker room was bananas," added Chuck. "It was maybe the loudest, rowdiest locker room since I've been here."

Coach Fry admitted to also invoking a higher power as the kick sailed through when offering his postgame salutations to reporters.

"Praise the Lord," he exclaimed moments after he and Bo Schembechler met at midfield in the midst of the mayhem. The Wolverines head coach congratulated Fry and even handed him a small gift.

"I told him before the game that the bad thing about this was that one of us had to lose," said Fry. "After the game, I told him he has a great football team. And he looked at me and said, 'Coach, I think you've got the greatest.' And he even gave me a package of chewing gum.

---

[21] While the final score was close, the stat sheets weren't. Iowa ran eighty-four offensive plays on the afternoon to Michigan's forty-one, outgained the Wolverines a whopping 422–182, held the ball for nearly seventeen more minutes, and made twenty-six first downs to Michigan's nine.

"But I'm not going to chew it," Fry added. "I'm going to frame it."

And what did he say to Chuck just prior to the final drive in which he converted three key third downs?

"The greatest thing I could do was grab Chuck by the shirt and tell him to do his thing," said Fry. "And that's exactly what he did."

Rick Brown of the *Des Moines Register* observed that, much like their coach, Michigan players "accepted the loss with grace. There was no yelling, no pounding of lockers. Somber silence prevailed."

"Long is a magnificent quarterback," Schembechler admitted even though his defense had kept Chuck and Iowa out of the end zone. "If it were just Long or just Harmon, we could handle either of them. But with both in there, it's just about impossible."[22]

For once, the hype and hyperbole of a game was prophetic, wrote the *Des Moines Register's* Marc Hansen.

"Most of the time, when two teams get together to play The Football Game To End All Football Games, the game of football ends up dead on the floor," Hansen wrote. "It happens two out of three Super Bowls. But it didn't happen Saturday.

"First-ranked Iowa's last-second 12–10 victory over second-ranked Michigan was a game that was everything it was made out to be."[23]

And the Iowa quarterback's postgame comments, Marc Hansen added, were pure Chuck.

"Then there was the passing," he wrote. "Consider Long's 297 yards and his 26-of-39 accuracy. Remarkably, he told the multitude that gathered before him afterward that he'd had a mediocre day. He was wrong. Iowa 12, Michigan 10 is what Hayden Fry meant when he opened his mouth on a spring day three years ago and remarked that Long was destined for greatness.

"Saturday was another example of manifest destiny," Hansen penned.

---

[22] Hayden Fry had the visitors' locker room painted pink when he arrived in Iowa City. The pastel color, the psychologist-turned-football-coach rationalized, would make opponents feel weak and placid. Bo Schembechler would have none of it when he brought his no. 2 Wolverines to Iowa City to play no. 1 Iowa. The gum-chomping, animated coach had black construction paper taped over the pink walls.

"Almost 300 passing yards in a victory over Michigan is like 900 against Northern Illinois."

The game was more than just a win over a perennial national powerhouse. It was a statement by a program no longer on the rise but an affirmation of a program that had arrived.

With little fanfare and an aw-shucks approach, Hayden Fry had assembled a coaching staff that was player focused yet team oriented. And the winning character of the young men he had made it a point to recruit were now notching big-time victories in front of packed and raucous Kinnick Stadium.

"I'm going to vote for us number one," he exclaimed following the monumental win. "There's no doubt now about who's the daggun best team in the country."

A PILE OF MEMORIES FOR MARK VLASIC

Mark Vlasic was a standout football and basketball player for Center High School in Pennsylvania before arriving in Iowa City in 1982 to compete for the starting Hawkeyes quarterback job.

He chose Iowa because they rarely redshirted players. "So the one thing I didn't expect was to come in and be redshirted in year one," said Vlasic, now a father of three and a wealth management advisor living in Leawood, Kansas. "I was coming in to compete as a freshman—I wanted to play as a freshman."

Yet Vlasic never complained as he backed up Chuck Long for four years.

"All along there was never really a second-guessing that maybe I should have gone somewhere else or what else I should have done," he said. "But

---

[23] Following the win, Iowa became just the second Big Ten school to defeat Bo Schembechler in consecutive seasons during the coach's seventeen-year regime, wrote the Washington Post's John Ed Bradley. Ohio State did so in 1981–82.

there was loyalty there, there was commitment there. And even though you may not be taking the field as the starter, you have to believe in what you can do. It's part of leadership. You focus on preparing and being the best you can so you can make the most of the opportunity when the door opens."

While waiting to take the reins as Iowa's starting signal caller, Vlasic was Iowa's placeholder for field goals and extra points.

Including Saturday, Oct. 19, 1985, when no. 1 Iowa hosted no. 2 Michigan. With just :02 on the clock and Iowa trailing 10–9, Vlasic accompanied Hawkeyes placekicker Rob Houghtlin onto the field to attempt a game-winning twenty-nine-yard field goal in arguably the most exciting game ever played in Kinnick Stadium.

In his own words, Vlasic described how the moments unfolded.

The place was just electric because it was the first time there was a night game in Kinnick Stadium. The game had it all. We're no. 1, and Michigan is no. 2; it's Hayden Fry versus Bo Schembechler; it's Chuck Long versus Jim Harbaugh.

As a player, you have your job to do and you know you have to go out and do it. And the game-ending kick that night was no different. Someone is going to snap it, you're going to put it down, and Rob Houghtlin is going to kick it through the goalposts. We practiced that kick a thousand times, and we practiced it with no time, and we practiced it by running out onto the field with the clock winding to zero.

I remember there was a timeout called, and we're on the sidelines and the place is going crazy. Yet the huddle prior to the kick was as calm as any huddle I'd been in as a Hawkeye. We're all looking at each other in that huddle saying to ourselves, "Let's go kick it through and win this because that's what we're here to do and that's what we're supposed to do." Then we lined up, the ball is snapped, I put it down, and as soon as it was kicked, you expected it to go through the goalposts.

And it did.

As a player, you don't hear all of that noise; you don't see the four players trying to take your head off. You're focused on your job, whether that was running the ball or catching it or kicking it; or catching it and putting it down on a tee that had a nice white cross on it that Rob had taped so you knew right where to put the ball; we practiced it. Once it went through, all of the sudden, it's no longer quiet. You immediately jumped, and the crowd was just incredible.

I remember jumping up and hugging Rob and then the pile. Then I was under the pile. The first thing that flashed across my mind was the Who concert that had occurred a couple years earlier when several people were trampled and killed. I was under the pile and couldn't breathe. I was also bent in a funny position and remember my ribs hurting and being crunched. To this day, I'm not quite sure how I got out from under there. I think maybe it was Dave Croston who pulled me out of the scrum. And it's a good thing he did because I was close to passing out because I couldn't breathe.

I look back on that day and playing for Iowa, and it's a big part of why I'm back in Kansas City and here in the Midwest and why we've stayed here for nearly twenty-five years. It wasn't a group of people in Iowa City that were just so overwhelmed with football and the guys who played it and that's why they liked you. No, it's much more than that. The people in Iowa City were the most kind, generous, and truly honest people I've ever met in my life. And to be in that stadium when that thing just erupted … I honestly have no recall of that moment it went through the goalposts and the pile up and the electricity that was in Kinnick Stadium that night. Fact is, there wasn't an Iowa player on that field that didn't expect to be number one in the country when that game ended.

NO "BIG FISH" STORY

KCRG-TV (Cedar Rapids) sports director John Campbell filmed, edited, and narrated more stories than he can count. Some stand out, and none more than a tale connected with one of Iowa's most memorable wins.

I was out doing a fishing story once with this guy who lived near Iowa City. After we had finished our work near the Iowa River, we met his wife at a nearby boat ramp at the end of day to gather some additional footage. When we wrapped, she said "John, would you be interested in knowing what happened to that football that Rob Houghtlin kicked to beat Michigan in 1985?"

I eagerly took the bait and said, "Yeah, I think I'd be interested in that."

"My father has that ball."

"Really?" I replied.

"Yes, come see for yourself."

So we made our way to see a gentleman that lived not far down the road by a campground near Interstate 80. And he had a football. Said his son was a ball boy for the Iowa football team. His job was to go into the stands and retrieve footballs after kicks because they didn't have nets.

Well, it's Iowa versus Michigan, and he's working the stands. Houghtlin boots the ball through the goalposts as time expires, so the boy goes into the stands and gets the football. He runs back onto the field to give it to Coach Fry, but he says, "Nah, don't worry about it; don't worry about it." So the young boy ends up giving the ball to his dad.

So I ran with the story, expecting that the phone would immediately ring after its airing. I figured someone would say, "John, I've got the ball," or "No, no, John, I've got the football that Rob Houghtlin kicked."

But the funny things is, I never got a call. No one else ever made a similar claim. I even asked Rob Houghtlin and Kirk Ferentz if they knew what happened to the football, and both said, "Nope." I even asked Phil Haddy [former University of Iowa sports information director] and he, too, was stumped.

So I believe that was indeed the game ball that made history that night in Kinnick.

"Michigan this, Michigan that, Michigan, Michigan, Michigan, that's all we heard. We showed the Hawkeyes could play a little football, too."

CHUCK LONG
after no. 1 Iowa outlasted no. 2 Michigan 12–10

Iowa was now the undisputed top-ranked college football team in the country after claiming Hayden Fry's biggest win in his seven seasons in Iowa City.

The win did more for attracting the attention of potential recruits than posters or advertising could have ever accomplished. Iowa, fresh off its 12–10 win over Michigan, was the talk of the town and the nation. Every print publication in the country proclaimed the outcome:

"Iowa tips Michigan at the gun," – *Chicago Sun Times*

"Iowa saves biggest noise for finish," – *Chicago Tribune*

"Iowa Beats Michigan on Last Play, 12–10," – *Washington Post*

"FG at :00 noses out U-M," – *Detroit Free Press*

"No Doubt Now! – :02 left, Houghtlin's FG beats Michigan 12–10," – *Cedar Rapids Gazette*

"Hawkeyes win No. 1 thriller, 12–10," – *Des Moines Sunday Register*

"No. 1 Iowa beats Michigan on last-play field goal," – *The Sunday Oklahoman*

"The Greatest – Hawks' heart-pounding victory has both Bo, Hayden convinced," – *Quad City Times*

"Defense, late field goal lift Iowa past Michigan," – *Norman (Okla.) Transcript*

"If anyone can pull a game out in the fourth quarters, it's the Hawkeyes," said Fry in his Monday comments to reporters. "Our players have a lot of faith in themselves. Being able to pull out two victories in the final seconds in three Big Ten games shows a lot of character under adversity.

"That's one indication we have a great football team."

Now it was prep time for the Northwestern Wildcats, a team Iowa had defeated eleven consecutive times. But backup quarterback Mark Vlasic was questionable.

"The crowd knocked down both Mark Vlasic, who holds for field goals, and Houghtlin," Fry explained to reporters as game day approached. "Vlasic will be in an immobilizer for two or three days because of an injury. I don't know if he'll be able to play Saturday. At this stage, I'd have to think he can, but we'll leave that up to the doctors."

Chuck had made it through the Michigan game relatively unscathed. Quarterbacking the nation's no. 1 team suited him and his coach just fine.

"I ran out of superlatives for Chuck," Fry admitted, while calling him "a superhuman being. When something bad happens, he shakes it off and goes about his business. It's never the other guy's fault. He's what I call unflappable."

But was Iowa?

Now 6–0 on the season, the Hawkeyes prepared to hit the road for Evanston, Illinois, and the surprising 3–3 Wildcats. Fry did his best to keep the players and fans grounded—anything to avoid a letdown in a game sandwiched between Michigan and Ohio State.

"Nobody is going through the Big Ten race unbeaten," Fry predicted with perhaps a dose of reverse psychology. "I think we're going to lose once or twice, and so is Minnesota."[24]

Northwestern wasn't about to sneak up on Iowa. The Wildcats were fresh off an equally hard-fought 17–14 win over the Wisconsin Badgers.

"Northwestern is no longer a sure win," said Fry, who also heaped praise on the Wildcats' head coach Dennis Green.

"I'm Dennis' greatest fan. I can understand the problems he's experienced. I've spent my life turning around sick programs. He's done a super job. His club is fundamentally well coached and he's going to win a bunch of games."

Tickets to the game at Dyche Stadium were selling at a brisk pace thanks to the Wildcats' .500 start and playing host to the nation's no. 1 team, which happened to be located less than a four-hour drive to the west.

Meanwhile, Chuck was managing a constant attack of media requests following the epic win over the Wolverines. Those calling included Sports Illustrated, Newsweek, Los Angeles Times, and Washington Post.

Of course, the Wheaton native attributed the attention to Iowa's no. 1 ranking.

"You try not to think about the reporters and everything," Chuck told Chris McConnell of the Wheaton Journal. "I just hope the club delivers, as we've never had this kind of attention. Even my girlfriend Lisa is getting ink these days. When the guy from Newsweek called me yesterday, he asked me how Lisa was and wanted to set up an interview with her."

So much for distractions resulting in a potential overlook by Iowa. The Hawkeyes would have none of it as they once again feasted on an outmanned Northwestern.

Chuck threw for 399 yards on nineteen of twenty-six attempts and a record-tying six touchdowns (including three to Bill Happel on strikes of

---

[24] Minnesota stood at 5–1 on the season, including Big Ten Conference wins over Purdue, Northwestern, and Indiana by a combined score of 88–32.

twenty-eight, thirty-five, and twenty-five yards). Iowa racked up nearly 540 yards offense in the blowout. Chuck Long also set a new Iowa record with an eighty-nine-yard touchdown pass.

"We knew we could get a lot of big ones on 'em," Chuck said. "They tried to pressure us with about eight people. That's not a bad game plan, but if I get time to throw—four or five seconds—I'm going to find someone open."

For the season, Chuck had amassed twenty-one touchdowns and 1,984 yards.

Dennis Green said the all-American performance by Chuck had more to do with the quality of his arm than suspect coverage.

"I think Iowa is a great team," he said. "The big plays killed us. Long was throwing the ball very well, and we couldn't get the pass stopped."[25]

It was Iowa's twelfth consecutive win over the Wildcats, this one in front of a near-sellout crowd of 47,276, nearly half of whom had donned black and gold.

"It was a good, solid win," said Fry, admitting they called off the dogs at the start of the fourth quarter when they chose to run instead of pass from Northwestern's two-yard line. "I just didn't have the heart to let Chuck throw that seventh touchdown pass. We still have to keep our humility. There's not too many quarterbacks in the history of college football who have thrown for six touchdowns. Obviously, Chuck could have thrown for a few more."

Following the Hawkeyes' rout in Evanston, a reporter asked Chuck how soon he would start thinking about Ohio State. The Buckeyes were Iowa's next opponent and stood tied for second in the Big Ten after handing Minnesota its first conference loss.

"Tomorrow," Chuck said. "I'm just going to enjoy Saturday night first."

---

[25] Denny Green departed Northwestern at the end of the 1985 season. In his five years with the Wildcats, Green amassed a 7–37 Big Ten record (10–45 overall).

"When we came home, the little one, Joe, he was five years old. He said that Daddy was out in the barn and he was out in the machine shed with a rifle. And that's how we found him when we came home from church."

NORMA FETTER
farmer, Chelsea, Iowa

Few places on Earth are more suitable for growing food than Iowa.[26] Rich, organic soil deposited by glaciers thousands of years ago sustain ample grain and pasture production. These feedstocks in turn make Iowa an ideal place to produce pork, beef, eggs, poultry, and dairy. Combined, the food and fiber production overseen by thousands of farm families dispersed across Iowa stimulates processing, transportation, and manufacturing. Nearly one of every four working Iowans owes his or her job to farming.

Despite the many trappings of town life, Iowa City was not immune to the gyrations of the farm economy. Most students came from rural communities—small towns with names like What Cheer and West Bend, Graettinger and Grundy Center, Carroll and Cascade, Atlantic and Arlington, Wilton and Washington.

It wasn't uncommon to see farmers driving their tractors and combines along Melrose Avenue through the heart of downtown Iowa City. They also dined at many of Iowa City's eateries and purchased supplies at area feed and hardware stores.

Hayden Fry understood the importance of farming long before he arrived in Iowa City. He was a product of the country and proud of it. Iowa was like home away from home, but he was always eager to share his family ties rooted in the farm dirt of the Lone Star State.

---

[26] Nearly 86 percent of Iowa's land area is devoted to growing food, the most of any state. It's also been estimated that 10 percent of the world's most productive soil is found in Iowa. All told, less than 7 percent of the earth's surface is arable land suitable for food production. With the global population expected to reach more than 9 billion by 2050, Iowa's ability to grow, process, and transport grain and meat will continue to benefit the state's economy and communities for generations.

"We lived a long way out in the Texas country," he said. "Even after the school bus dropped me off after football practice in the afternoon, I still had to walk nearly three miles to get to the farmhouse."

Fry and his team embraced Iowa's agricultural heritage. They found the work ethic of its more than 150,000 farm families especially appealing. Just like farmers, coaches and players grabbed their lunch buckets each day before going to work. Fry was often more comfortable being around farmers than opposing coaches, program boosters, and political dignitaries.[27]

Game days were also a reminder of the farmer-Hawkeyes interconnectedness. Many of the paying customers who filled the seats in Kinnick on Saturdays were farmers. If caps and jackets weren't sporting the Tiger Hawk, then the chances were pretty good they featured the logo of a bank, farm cooperative, or seed corn company.

This affinity for farm life also made Fry keenly aware of the pain being felt around kitchen tables in farmhouses across the state. Even as the Iowa team rolled through its 1985 schedule and made headlines as the nation's top-ranked team, the coach's thoughts were never far from the struggles taking place daily in farm country.

Reporters didn't miss the connection between farming and the Hawkeyes, either.

"Farmers struggle to survive. Some call it quits. Farm equipment dealers auction off machinery farmers can no longer afford," noted Dave Leon Moore of USA Today. "Yet every autumn Saturday, Iowans escape into the world of

---

[27] Hawkeyes tight end Jonathan Hayes recalled the near reverence Iowa players and coaches had for Iowa's farmers.

When you're a young man, you're unaware of a lot of those things at the time. But as you look back and take inventory of those things you encountered as a player, you become much more aware of how much the community cared about farmers and how much farmers cared about the football program. Iowa City was part of the larger farm community. Everyone affiliated with the program knew the importance of farming to Iowa and Hawkeyes football because each person was touched by farming.

My roommate Hap Peterson's dad worked for John Deere for years. That in a nutshell told you that a lot of people made their living from farming. Many of the people who donated food for our team barbecues were farmers. When you were eating those good steaks and the pork chops or ribs or chicken or whatever it might have been, we knew that the generous people who made all that food available were farmers. They gave of themselves, whether it was food or their property so we could grow closer together as a team. And you got to meet a lot of those farmers and learned what nice and sincere people they were. That will always stay with me as someone who got to experience playing football in an Iowa Hawkeyes uniform.

college football and lavish their seemingly boundless loyalty and enthusiasm upon their Hawkeyes."

Hayden Fry wanted to win to earn an inside track to the Rose Bowl, Moore added. "But Fry also wants to win for the sake of Iowa fans."

"These people are great people, very honest, very loyal," Fry told Moore. "They have a real need to identify with a sports program."[28]

Anything to escape reality.

It was 1985, and Iowa and much of the nation's breadbasket was mired in one of the worst economic disasters since the Great Depression.

The seeds of what was ultimately labeled the 1980s farm crisis had actually been sown a decade earlier.

Remembered to this day as one of the best times for farming, the 1970s was a decade of record exports of US- and Iowa-grown corn and soybeans. Insatiable demand for what Iowa farmers grew boosted the prices they received for every bushel of grain and pound of pork and beef sent to market. Credit flowed. Farm machinery flew off lots and onto farms. Land prices skyrocketed. Record low interest rates encouraged farmers to borrow.

It was indeed a fun and rewarding time to be in farming, and many farmers believed (and even bet the farm) that the good times would last.

But as many would soon learn, what goes boom can quickly go bust.

By 1982, memories of the roaring seventies were a distant memory. High grain and meat prices quickly plunged as production swelled just as a new fed chairman slammed on the monetary brakes, making US farm commodities much more expensive to foreign buyers. Sales plummeted, and land prices quickly followed.[29]

The financial storm inflicted gaping wounds on a state whose economic

---

[28] Hayden Fry was a great teacher, said Chuck. One guiding principle he instilled in every player from the moment they stepped on the Iowa campus was to respect the Iowa farmer.

That's one of the reason why so many people loved Hayden. He loved the farm community real and genuinely. He had a reverence for what they did, what they stood for, and how they conducted themselves. And he told us that Iowans will come to see us play if they love us. It was more than just putting a winning program on the field. Hayden wanted the farmer to bond with the team. Because there was a loyalty to each other—from the Iowa football program to the farmer and from the farmer back to the team. And that's something that sets Iowa apart, even to this day. If you're competitive and work hard, the Iowa fan will respect you and show up on Saturdays to support the team and coaches.

fortunes were tied directly to the balance sheets of farmers. Land prices fell almost 50 percent, and interest rates skyrocketed from the single digits to more than 21 percent. US farm exports declined by more than 20 percent from 1981 to 1983 while the prices farmers received for nearly everything they raised sank 21 percent.

Farmers who had borrowed during the boom of the 1970s quickly found themselves on the wrong side of the ledgers and upside down with their lenders. Many were unable to make the interest payments on their loans, let alone the principal.

By 1985, memories of the roaring seventies were replaced by sleepless nights and nightmares for too many farm families. Gut-wrenching headlines announced farm sales and foreclosures—or worse. Farmers rallied in school auditoriums, libraries, and concert halls to express their frustration to politicians, reporters, and anyone else who would listen.

That same year, the US Department of Agriculture estimated net farm income had declined by 30 percent, and land values were reduced by almost half. One in three commercial-sized farms was unable to pay its bills, and even more were teetering on a financial cliff that grew steeper each day. The financial meltdown proved to be more than many farmers could bear. Farm foreclosures became all too common, and many agricultural businesses struggled to stay afloat.[30]

The despair being felt around kitchen tables throughout the nation's heartland was real and wrenching. Most farmers measured their self-worth against their net worth. When the farm economy went south and their farms' financials turned upside down, many took it personally. Watching the farms they had put their hearts and souls into being sold to the highest bidder was too much to bear for some.

So they jumped from silos.

Or pulled the trigger.[31]

---

[29] The US Department of Agriculture estimated that farmland values dropped as much as 60 percent between 1981 and 1985. Farmers soon owed more for their land than what it was worth (a very similar situation to the housing and mortgage crisis of 2008). One of the primary reasons for the farming catastrophe was the prohibition of American grain shipments to the Soviet Union. This caused global grain supplies to surge and prices for corn and soybeans to plummet.

As the financial pain crippling rural Iowa mounted, Hayden Fry was compelled to act.[32]

After gathering with his coaches, he determined that attention could be brought to the plight of the farmer and rural economy with a simple helmet decal.

The two-and-a-half-inch sticker would carry the initials "ANF," shorthand for "America Needs Farmers," and be displayed on the back of the helmet, just to the right of the player's number. It would make its debut in the nationally televised game at Ohio State.

"In Iowa, the farm economy is very bad, and I understand it's the same way across America," Fry told reporters just one day prior to the much-anticipated matchup against Ohio State in Columbus. "We felt this decal would be a simple and direct way to help get the message across. Three of our remaining four games are on television. Hopefully, these decals will help call attention to the farm crisis."

The surging Iowa Hawkeyes provided the perfect billboard to bring the hurt of farm country to a national audience.

---

[30] Iowa State University Professor of Economics Neil Harl estimated that more than 3 percent of the 2.4 million farmers in the United States were leaving the farming business each year during the 1980s recession. About sixty thousand people were displaced due to the foreclosures. The US Department of Agriculture estimated that agricultural debt in the United States that was forcing farmers to declare bankruptcy reached $216 billion in 1984, of which $17 billion was in Iowa.

[31] The heart-wrenching story of farmer Dale Burr, sixty-three, of rural Lone Tree epitomized the depths of despair that gripped rural Iowa during the midst of the 1980s farm crisis. Struggling under the weight of nearly $800,000 in farm debt, Burr entered the kitchen of his farm home on the morning of Dec. 9, 1985, and shot his wife, Emily, age sixty-four, as she attempted to stop him from leaving the house with a loaded shotgun. Burr then made the short drive to Hills Bank and Trust Company in Hills (a small town located just eight miles south of Iowa City), where he fatally shot Hills Bank President John Hughes, forty-six. Burr returned to Lone Tree, where he shot and killed neighbor Richard Goody, thirty-eight, who had won a judgment against Burr in a land dispute a few years earlier. Burr was traveling back to his farm behind the wheel of his rusting Chevrolet pickup truck when he was approached on a gravel road by a Johnson County deputy sheriff. As the sheriff waited for reinforcements, Burr turned the gun on himself and pulled the trigger. Prior to his death, he left a note addressed to his son, John, thirty-nine, that read, "I'm sorry, I can't take the problems anymore."

> "I don't know if we have proven ourselves to other people yet, but the next few games should show whether we deserve to be number one."
>
> BILL HAPPEL
>
> *Iowa senior prior to top-ranked and undefeated Iowa's Nov. 2, 1985, matchup versus Ohio State in Columbus*

The last time a no. 1-ranked college football team had dared enter Ohio Stadium was Purdue in 1968. The Buckeyes defeated the Boilermakers 13–0.

"That was a long time ago," admitted Ohio State head coach Earle Bruce, who had been a Buckeyes' assistant at the time. "I think they came in here averaging something like forty-one points a game. I do remember it was a great game."

It was now Iowa's turn. Flying high with a record of 7–0, the Hawkeyes were a statistical marvel: they led the country in scoring, were third in passing offense and total defense, fifth in total offense, eighth in rushing defense, and tenth in scoring defense. Chuck led the nation in pass efficiency and stood fifth in total offense.

In other words, the Buckeyes had Iowa just where they wanted them.

---

[32] In an interview for Destined for Greatness, Hayden Fry vividly recalled the events of 1985 that led to a unique helmet decal that would publicize the plight of farmers to the nation.

Nearly twenty-two thousand farmers had lost their farms or had to sell their land or get rid of it or it was taken away from them because they weren't making enough money to make the payments to pay for their farm. So I gathered the coaches and during a staff meeting said, "We have to do something to help the farmers; the farm economy is slumping all across America but particularly here in Iowa." Then it hit me. America needs to help the farmers. And that's where I came up with the idea of "ANF – America Needs Farmers."

We were no. 1 in the nation at the time in the college football rankings. I thought with all the news media and television games, we could give the farmers some exposure and maybe that would rally Congress and other political people who were in a position to help the farmer do something about it. So we put the decal "ANF" on the headgear, and it got a lot of wonderful publicity.

I don't know how much it helped, but according to the farmers, it boosted their morale to know that others were aware of the hardships they were enduring.

The "ANF" decal remains a fixture on the University of Iowa Hawkeyes football helmets today.

To make matters worse, Iowa had lost seventeen of its last eighteen meetings against Ohio State and had not won in Columbus since 1959.

Chuck, however, was confident. After watching reels of film, his attention fixated on the success Purdue quarterback Jim Everett had enjoyed just two weeks earlier against the same Ohio State Buckeyes.

"I watched film of Everett, and he did pretty good, almost five hundred yards," Chuck told reporters. "He threw a lot of underneath passes to his running backs, and they ran a long way."

The Buckeyes were fresh off a surprisingly close 23–19 win over Minnesota and possessed a national best nineteen-game home winning streak. The squad also featured dynamic but injured tailbacks Keith Byars and John Woodridge and linebackers Chris Spielman and Pepper Johnson. The latter helped anchor a defense that gave up yards but surrendered few points.

Hayden Fry predicted the game would be "a toss-up" when asked by reporters to handicap his team's chances just one day prior to kick.

On a gloomy, rain-soaked day in Columbus, Iowa's no. 1 ranking received a cold dose of reality before a record crowd of 90,467 fans. An opportunistic Ohio State team harassed Chuck all afternoon. For whatever reason, Iowa's offense failed to click while its defense couldn't deliver the momentum-turning play.

"It was nice while it lasted, but as the saying goes, all good things must come to an end," summed up *Des Moines Register* staff writer Buck Turnbull. "The setback happened in a way that would never have been imagined—with Chuck Long, the nation's leading passer, playing one of his poorest games as a Hawkeye."

In a loss that Hayden Fry described as "disheartening," Chuck was intercepted four times. The opportunistic Buckeyes also blocked an Iowa punt for a safety and recovered a Hawkeyes fumble.

The net result: a 22–13 win that left both teams 7–1 but the Buckeyes with an inside track to Pasadena.

"This is truly one of the finest victories I've ever been associated with," boomed Ohio State head coach Earle Bruce. "It was just a great effort by our football team."

Chris Spielman ended the day with nineteen tackles and two interceptions. Chuck finished just seventeen of thirty-four for 169 yards.

In the blink of an eye and under dark and gloomy skies, Chuck's dream season had become a bad dream. He blamed himself more than anyone for the substandard performance.

"A guy who Coach Hayden Fry once called 'unflappable' appeared rattled today," wrote Mark Dukes of the *Cedar Rapids Gazette.*

"We pretty much gave the game away," Chuck said, shouldering the blame for Iowa's subpar performance despite breaking the Big Ten's career record for total offense. "I'll probably be sick tomorrow watching this on film.

"I think I might have underestimated Ohio State's defensive backs more than I should have," he added. "Purdue's Jim Everett passed for a lot of yards against them, and I guess I thought I'd be able to do that, too.[33]

"We had open guys and I just missed 'em," Chuck said. "I felt good coming in, but I just don't know what happened."

His poor performance on national TV was also likely to hurt his prospects of winning the Heisman Trophy.

"I'm not worried about it," he said when asked by reporters what impact his performance would have on his Heisman candidacy. "I knew I was a long shot at the beginning of the year, and I was a long shot in the middle of the year. Bo Jackson's probably going to get it anyway.

"I had the best season of my life going, and we had a perfect season going. It was just one of those days."

Fry mused that the crowd noise messed with his team's offensive timing. "We're one of the best teams in America audibilizing at the line of scrimmage," he said. "When we couldn't communicate, it wiped out an awful lot of our offense."[34]

As a result, Chuck for the first time seemed to be flustered. Yet Fry kept the setback in perspective. "It's a disheartening loss," he said, "but not the end of the world, nor the end of the season.

"But it does mean that we've arrived as a national power," he quipped. "Have you ever known of an Iowa team that went into Ohio State favored to win the game? And have you ever been to Ohio State where we have established so much credibility and respect that the people come onto the field and tear down both goalposts?[35] We've come a long way."

But what goes up can also come down.

Iowa's first loss of the season dropped them to no. 7 in the USA Today/CNN college football poll while Ohio State leaped from twelfth to fifth.

And for Iowa's fifth-year quarterback, just three Big Ten games remained in his storied career.

Oh, and one last bowl invitation.

Would the invitation come with a rose?

Illinois, the first of the last three Big Ten contests, would help answer that question. Representatives of the Cotton, Sugar, Fiesta, Orange, and Florida Citrus Bowls would be in attendance should the Hawkeyes stumble.

---

[33] "You always hear from coaches that it's the losses that stick with you," Chuck said. "Well, that Saturday afternoon in Columbus is one of those days that I wish I could have back. I'm in my early fifties, and it still sticks with me.

"I had made it a point during my career to not read any newspapers in the week leading up to a game. But for whatever reason, I did before that one," Chuck admits.

The quarterback's reasoning was sound. Just two weeks earlier, Purdue's Jim Everett had shredded Ohio State's defense by passing for nearly five hundred yards. Chuck zeroed in on the offensive schemes run by the Boilermakers, assuming that the Buckeyes would be similarly confused when Iowa mimicked the play calling.

"I fell in that trap of assuming they were thinking, 'Wow, if Everett did this to Ohio State, imagine what Chuck Long may do.' Well, It didn't turn out that way."

In retrospect, Chuck admits he should have put more emphasis on studying Ohio State's wins, where the defense was playing at its best, rather than one of its lesser performances.

"I made the mistake of honing in when the OSU defense was at its worst. That kind of got me to thinking that I'd have a big day. If I were to go back in time, I wouldn't have read the newspaper. Instead, I would have watched film after film of Ohio State's defense performing at its best."

[34] The Columbus Dispatch reported that before the final Ohio State touchdown, "the stomping and chanting reached almost deafening levels. The two-story press box atop the stadium shook and tables inside swayed. Concession workers inside the press box became frightened. They said no previous crowds had produced such earthquake-like vibrations."

Pregame media attention focused on the strength of the Fighting Illinis' passing attack led by quarterback Jack Trudeau and fleet-footed receiver David Williams. The pair exuded confidence, with Trudeau having thrown 214 consecutive passes on the year—and 282 straight in the Big Ten—without an interception. He and Chuck were 1–1 when facing each other as starting quarterbacks. And Trudeau, like Chuck, possessed a $1 million insurance policy given his NFL potential.

Other fans and pundits referred to the matchup as "gut check" time for the Hawkeyes, who were entering the game as seven-point favorites. The winner would stay in the hunt for a Rose Bowl berth while the loser would be sitting by the telephone waiting for a lesser bowl to come calling.

Illinois had routed Iowa in 1983 33–0. Chuck was sacked seven times and completed just twelve passes. A year later, Chuck had struggled yet again, connecting on only seven of fourteen passes. But a dynamic Hawkeyes running game (313 yards) had helped Iowa gallop to a 21–16 win.

For Chuck, facing off against teams that had an Illinois mailing address was always special. The Fighting Illini was a team that had never called, and its coach, Mike White, wasn't afraid to admit the mistake.

"We let ol' Chuck slip by," he said. "You always regret it when a player like Long slips out of your state."

White's regret was likely cemented by the time he left Iowa City, as Chuck and his Iowa teammates rebounded from their loss to Ohio State with an attitude on a cool, winterlike afternoon. They bolted to a 49–0 halftime lead on their way to trouncing the Illini 59–0. It was the largest point spread ever in the rivalry's history. [36]

While the Iowa defense paced the attack, Iowa's offense sparkled. Chuck hit on twenty-two of thirty passes for 289 yards before giving way to Mark Vlasic in the third quarter. Vlasic added another twenty-seven yards by air on five of eleven passes while the Hawkeyes' ground game gobbled up

---

[35] A security guard for Ohio State said the pregame plan was to let the fans "do whatever they want to do" with the goalposts should the Buckeyes be victorious. Buck Turnbull of the *Des Moines Register* reported that since the game was nationally televised, Ohio State officials determined that restraining fans from on-field celebrations "would look bad."

232 yards, paced by Ronnie Harmon's eighty-eight.

"Wasn't that some kind of game?" asked Fry emphatically in his postgame comments. "Our team was heartbroken and embarrassed last week when we lost to a fine Ohio State team. It took a lot of character for us to come back.

"Like I told President Freedman, this isn't the kind of thing you learn in a textbook. You have to learn it in combat. We were tested in combat, in front of the public eye, to see if we could come back from losing our number one spot against a very fine Illinois team.

"That would not happen again in a hundred contests. Doing what we did today was phenomenal."

The victory was Hayden Fry's fiftieth as Iowa's head coach.

Chuck agreed. In his postgame comments, the senior made it known that the Illinis' yapping, even during the pregame ceremonial coin flip, had gotten under his nerves. What better way to relieve the tension and frustration than by pummeling them on the scoreboard.

"They tend to talk a little bit too much in the press. When they talk like that it makes you angry. I don't know what they were saying, but they were yelling a lot.

"Sooner or later, you have to quit talking and play the game," Chuck added. "When you go out on the field, you do your talking with your football pads and not your mouth. I think that really hurts a team more than it helps, and it gets us mad."

Chuck admitted to knowing the Illinis' fate by early in the second quarter. "We could do no wrong," he said, referencing a first quarter in which the team tallied thirty-five points. "That's probably one of the best halves a college football team has ever played."[37]

"This one was over before we got into our seats," White admitted.

Numerous records fell on the afternoon, including: points-after-touchdown in a game (eight, Houghtlin); TD passes, season (twenty-five,

---

[36] The Hawkeyes pasted Illinois 58–0 in 1899, the same year Ernest Hemingway, Duke Ellington, Alfred Hitchcock, and Fred Astaire were born.

Chuck); TD receptions, season (seven, Robert Smith); and TD receptions, career (thirteen, Smith). The team set a record for most points in a half. All told, eleven records fell. Chuck also needed just 341 passing yards in his final two games to break Mark Herrmann's career passing mark of 9,946.

The record-setting trouncing on Kinnick's cold turf made *Des Moines Register* columnist Marc Hansen a bit nostalgic, as if anticipating the departure of Chuck Long from college ball to the NFL.

"Years from now, when Iowa football fans reminisce about the good old days back in the Hayden Fry era, when the talk turns to Chuck Long and how Hawkeyes fans haven't seen his like at Kinnick Stadium since and probably never will, someone will recall Nov. 9, 1985.[38]

"'This'll give you an idea of how good he was,' the coffee shop experts will say. 'Why, in the first quarter of the '85 Illinois game alone, he completed 10 of 12 passes for 188 yards and two touchdowns and Iowa led 35–0 against a team that was supposed to be very good.

"'But that wasn't the end of it. By halftime, he was 18 of 24 for 256 yards with four touchdowns and Iowa led 49–0. Long demolished the Fighting Illini single-handedly that day.'"

Mike Scully, Illinois' sophomore center, seemed to agree with Hansen, although he put it more bluntly: "We got our butts kicked."

Added White, "He certainly gave a Heisman Trophy performance today. I don't like to make too many definitive statements about this, but I find it hard to believe anyone else in the country has performed as well and meant as much to his team as Chuck Long."

Every kid who has ever played sports dreams of taking (and making) the final shot, orchestrating the final drive, sinking the clinching putt.

---

[37] *Chicago Tribune* writer Robert Markus wrote glowingly about Chuck's performance. "He blew a gaping hole in Illinois' armor with a 49-yard touchdown strike to Robert Smith on the sixth play of the game," he wrote. "Before the first quarter had ended, Iowa was ahead 35–0 and the Illini were drowning in their own ineptitude. By halftime, the carnage had mounted to 49–0 and Long had left both the Illinois defense and the Big 10 record book in tatters."

Few have the opportunity to live the dream, especially when there's a Big Ten Conference championship and Rose Bowl berth hanging in the balance and your name is on the ballot for the Heisman Trophy.

Chuck Long was always prepared to accomplish the impossible—in fact, he reveled in the challenge.

And on a November Saturday in West Lafayette, calm and cool Chuck did just that by marching the Hawkeyes on a sixty-four-yard, twelve-play drive to set up a winning twenty-five-yard field goal. The drive consumed five minutes and twenty-two seconds and enabled Iowa to escape the Boilermakers 27–24.

It was Houghtlin's second game-winning kick in a month.

Iowa's pressure-packed march to victory began at its twenty-eight-yard line. With the scoreboard knotted 24–24 with 6:30 remaining on the clock, Chuck took the reins with the coolness of a fifth-year senior. He completed three of four passes on the drive, including two nifty third-and-long connections (one to Bill Happel and another to Scott Helverson). Ronnie Harmon, who gained 122 yards rushing and another 118 passing on what many would later recall as perhaps his best game as a Hawkeye, helped soak up another two-and-a-half minutes off the play clock, helping set up Houghtlin's boot.

No. 5 Iowa's defense did the rest against talented Purdue quarterback Jim Everett.[39]

"Chuck Long played super with some clutch passing," Hayden Fry said. "We wanted to win, but we knew if we tied we still had a chance to go to the Rose Bowl. So I wasn't that interested in scoring. All we wanted to do is run as much of the clock off as possible."[40]

---

[38] Iowa fans are loyal and were, in the words of longtime assistant athletic trainer John Streif, outstanding even before he took the job of assistant athletic director in 1972.

You look back over the years, even during the nineteen years of losing prior to Coach Fry's arrival, and you'll see that Iowa fans have always been supportive. There would be fifty thousand people for a home game even when we couldn't fashion a winning season. It's this loyalty of fans that makes guys like Chuck Long and Hayden Fry so loyal to this state. Chuck could have gone anywhere he wanted after his coaching career was done, but he picked Iowa, and that says a lot about the people of this state. He had too many opportunities, but he came back here. And that's why Hayden is still so supportive and returned to Iowa City as often as he could. It was about the fans.

Chuck Long finished the day an impressive twenty of thirty-three passes for 268 yards when the stakes were rarely higher.

While Chuck still didn't like his chances to win the Heisman, Iowa continued to raise the bar. For the season, Iowa had tallied 381 points, a school record for offensive output.

All Chuck needed now was just seventy-three yards to claim the Big Ten's career passing mark.

All the no. 4-ranked team in the country needed was a victory over its neighbor to the north to become the first team in school history to win ten games along with earning a trip to college football's most prestigious bowls—the Rose.[41]

At the same time, excitement continued to build over Chuck's prospects to win the Heisman Trophy, college football's most prestigious award.

The 1985 Hawkeyes were also still in the running to finish the season as the nation's top-ranked football team.

With everything on the line, Hayden Fry was still asked if it would be difficult to get his team motivated to play the Golden Gophers.

"I would hope going to the Rose Bowl provides positive motivation," he replied. "It's what we've been working for since spring training. And hopefully we'll go out and win it."

---

[39] Despite being hospitalized much of the previous week with a staph infection and lacking a reliable running game, the soon-to-be NFL first-round pick (1986, Los Angeles Rams) completed twenty-three of thirty-two passes for 315 yards while throwing just one pick. "No doubt, gentlemen, he's the best quarterback in the country," said Purdue head coach Leon Burtnett in his postgame comments. "Give him the same surroundings [as Chuck Long] and the same people surrounding him, and I promise you he'd rewrite the record book. Pound for pound, quarterback for quarterback, I'd take Everett over anybody in the country. Too bad he wasn't well."

When asked about the comparison, Chuck simply responded, "It was fun playing Everett one-on-one."

[40] At halftime, Iowa learned Wisconsin had shocked no. 3 Ohio State 12–7 in Columbus. They had to wait to get the news until they reached the locker room because the public address announcer in Ross-Ade Stadium refused to disclose the score until after the game. *Cedar Rapids Gazette* staff writer Gus Schrader also noted that "Iowa fans helped the Hawkeyes with an altered version of 'tastes great, less filling' with 'Wisconsin 12, Ohio State 7.'

"I was nearly afraid to tell the players about Ohio State at halftime," Hayden Fry admitted. "I was afraid it was hearsay, and I couldn't get anybody to confirm it. That kind of thing could have a good or bad effect. But this is a very mature group, and they didn't show much excitement." The loss was devastating for the Buckeyes. It was their second conference loss, and a road trip to Ann Arbor to play no. 6 Michigan loomed.

For Fry, the emotions were mixed in anticipating the season's final game.[42]

For Chuck, the thought of playing his last regular season game against the Gophers at home in Kinnick was bittersweet.

"I've always wanted to go out a winner," he told reporters. "I know it will be my last game this year, and I want it to be a special game.

"Last year, I wasn't sure if it would be my last game or not, and this year, I know that it is," he added. "This is just what I had in mind—playing at home against Minnesota with a chance to go to the Rose Bowl."[43]

But whether he wins the Heisman or not, wrote Don Doxsie of the *Cedar Rapids Gazette,* "Long's place in Iowa athletic history is secure. He is the single most dominant player in the school's remarkable resurgence. Fry built the airplane, but Long flew it.

"I'll also lay odds that he is the third Iowa football player ever to have his number retired, the first to have it done while he's still alive," Doxsie penned. "The kid Fry once boasted was 'destined for greatness' has reached that destiny."[44]

Indeed, Hayden Fry felt blessed for the good fortune bestowed on the Hawkeyes with just one game remaining.

"I think somebody's reached down and put his hands on us," he told reporters during his weekly presser. "We just have so much to be grateful for. And certainly the coaching staff can't take credit for all those things. There's something more powerful right here that had to be involved in this.

"I thank the good Lord each day for all the blessings."

Even with Fry summoning the strength of the Almighty, Iowa didn't need divine intervention when, on Nov. 24, 1985, Chuck Long played his last regular season game as a Hawkeye.

---

[41] With a record of 9–1 on the season, Iowa's record since 1982—the year Chuck became Iowa's regular starting quarterback—was 34–12–1.

[42] And for good reason. Joining Chuck Long, Ronnie Harmon, and Larry Station as seniors were Bill Happel, Scott Helverson, Devon Mitchell, Nate Creer, Jay Norvell, Hap Peterson, Mike Haight, Tom Humphrey and Kelly O'Brien.

[43] In the early years of the Rose Bowl, the Big Ten had a rule that a team couldn't make consecutive appearances in "the granddaddy of them all." So there were times when the conference's runner-up would make the trip to Pasadena.

Iowa jumped out to a 17–3 halftime lead on a Houghtlin field goal sandwiched by a touchdown run by Harmon and a touchdown through the air by Chuck. The Hawkeyes added fourteen more points in the second half on touchdown runs by Harmon and Rick Bayless on their way to a 31–9 pasting of the Lou Holtz-coached Minnesota Gophers.

When the final gun sounded, Chuck raised both arms and joined players, coaches, and fans in the center of the field.

"Long lifted his arms because he had become one of the few people lucky enough to live their fantasies," wrote the *Des Moines Register's* Marc Hansen.

The game was a bit of redemption for Iowa, which, not needing any additional motivation, got it nonetheless after Minnesota defensive end Joe Christopherson offered several unflattering comments about the Iowa program, its head coach, and fans.

In an article published earlier in the week in the St. Paul Pioneer-Press, Christopherson called Iowa fans "obnoxious" and the Hawkeyes coach "a jerk who likes to run up scores.

"I've always had a deep-down hatred for Iowa people," Christopherson said. "The only thing Iowa has going for it is its football team."

Prior to the game, Fry had accepted an apology from Christopherson and Holtz.

Chuck then went out and did his thing against conference rival Minnesota, completing twenty-one of thirty-one passes for a pedestrian-like 268 yards and a touchdown, the seventy-third of his career.

With the victory came a bronze pig (Floyd of Rosedale) and an official invitation to the Rose Bowl.

And with 268 yards through the air, Chuck reigned as the Big Ten's most prolific passer of all time with 10,142 yards, besting Mark Herrmann's 9,946.

"Breaking Herrmann's record is a great feeling," said Chuck. "I never dreamed I'd even come close. It's something I'll cherish forever."

---

[44] To date, numbers retired by the Hawkeyes football program remain just two: Nile Kinnick (no. 24) and Cal Jones (no. 62). Kinnick is the only player in Iowa football history to win the Heisman Trophy (1939). Jones was the first African American to win the Outland Trophy and the only Hawkeye to date to be named first-team all-American three times. Both Kinnick and Jones were killed in separate plane crashes before their twenty-fifth birthdays.

The victory swelled Iowa's record to 10–1 on the season—the first time in the history of Iowa football that a team had earned double-digit wins.

"It all started this year when Chuck decided to pass up a few dollars from the NFL because he loves college football and wanted to go to the Rose Bowl," said Hayden Fry in the postgame news conference. "I can't say how much I love Chuck Long. He's done so much for this team."

After the game, when the Hawkeyes had come in from the cold of Kinnick Stadium where the snow had been swept from the fake grass and the temperature had descended to fifteen degrees, Fry had accepted a bouquet from the Rose Bowl committee.

"I'm giving these to my quarterback, the greatest quarterback in America," he said.

"As a player, the impact of Chuck Long was first felt in the Arizona game [four years ago]," Fry continued. "That got us started. The way he's handled himself from a personal standpoint, whether it be in class, downtown, or behind the center, has always been first class. We strive to be a class act team and it all starts with your quarterback."

Chuck appeared in the postgame news conference carrying the roses and wearing rose stickers on his cheeks and forehead. He would be joining seven other fifth-year seniors—Mike Haight, Scott Helverson, Hap Peterson, Nate Creer, Devon Mitchell, Jay Norvell, and Fred Bush—for a second trip to Pasadena.

"We're heading to Pasadena for only one reason, and that's to play in the Rose Bowl and win it," said an exuberant Chuck. "We've been thinking about the Rose Bowl all year, ever since the way we played in the Freedom Bowl last year. We helped Ohio State get to the Rose Bowl last year by losing, and they paid us back by losing to Wisconsin last week.

"We knew if we had another chance we weren't going to blow it."[45]

Bob Pille of the *Chicago Sun Times* had followed Chuck's career at Iowa from the first day to the last game. The 31–9 win over Minnesota was the perfect end to a Hawkeyes career and some reprieve for "the land of troubled farms." And it was "one of those fairy tales come true—the quarterback who stayed an extra year to pursue the vision with a coach who told him as a raw recruit he was destined for greatness."

In thirty-eight days, Iowa would play in the Rose Bowl in Pasadena.

Dreams do come true. Goals can be achieved.

Chuck was living proof.

THE BELL COW

Hayden Fry's farm background blended nicely with his psychology degree, to the benefit of the Iowa football program. One example was surfacing team leaders to model a winning attitude to fellow players.

Dad leased a lot of farm ground; I'm not sure how many acres it had, but it was big. We also had quite a few cattle. So each morning before school, I had to feed the cows. I'd fill the old pickup truck with hay and drive out and feed the cows.

One morning I was late getting ready for school, and my dad told me to go feed the cows. I said, "Dad, I don't have enough time for that; if I go searching for those cows to feed 'em, then I'll be late for school." He said I'd have enough time. But I said, "Dad, in all those acres, there's no telling where those cows are; I won't be able to find them in time."

He said, "Son, all you have to do is drive out there, stop and listen. There's

---

[45] "Taking the field at Kinnick for the last time as Iowa's starting quarterback was very surreal for me," admitted Chuck. "I didn't want to leave it. I didn't want to let go of that feeling. Even though I had come back for a fifth year, I still couldn't believe how fast it went. And to know that everything I came back for that last season—for a chance to return to the Rose Bowl and to win a Big Ten championship outright— was riding on us getting that win. That was a big day for the Iowa program. It was a no-brainer that the Iowa football program had arrived. And all I could think after the game ended was how much I wanted to keep playing for the Hawkeyes. And I still feel that way more than thirty years later."

one old cow out there that's the leader. I call her my bell cow. I put a bell around that old heifer's neck. You listen for that bell ringing. When you hear that bell ringing, you'll find the whole herd because they follow her."

Well, sure enough, I drove out there, and I stopped and started listening, and I heard that bell ringing. I drove over to where that sound was coming from and there was the whole herd. I fed 'em and still made it to school on time.

I never explained this approach and how it originated when I was a coach. I just told my assistant coaches to find the leader at each position and that I wanted to visit with them. So they would find the best linebacker that other players appreciated and respected and the best defensive lineman and best offensive lineman, the best defensive back, and so on. Then I would call them one-on-one into my office. I didn't tell the players at the time that they were my bell cows, but I knew that the other players appreciated and respected those players more than any of the others and that they would listen to them.

So when I would talk to my bell cow at each position, I would ask, "What do we need to do in order to win?" and I would get their opinion. Then I would ask, "What do we need to do away with and what are we doing that's keeping us from winning?"

After getting their input, I'd tell them, "The other players really respect you. If you would get across to them what we need to do to win or what we need to stop doing to win, they'll listen to you more than even the old coach."

And over the years, my "bell cow" theory really worked. I never said much about it publicly, but it's one of those things that I learned on the farm and applied during my years as a coach with great success."

> "Chuck's a superstar, and it hasn't changed him a
> bit. It probably made him even more humble. Chuck
> might be the field general for the Hawks, but if his dad
> walks up and says, 'Mow the yard,' Chuck's out
> there mowing."

DR. TOM RICHARDS
Family friend of Toledo, Ohio, following Iowa's Rose Bowl berth-
clinching win over Minnesota in the 1985 regular season finale
("No. 16's dad had a rosy day," Rick Montgomery,
Quad City Times, *Nov. 24, 1985)*

Charlie Long loved his sons. Family was his life. And while he worked hard as a corporate relations specialist for Beatrice Inc. in Chicago, he always made time for Chuck, David, and Andy.

Now he found himself relaxing beside an indoor pool at a motel just down the road from Kinnick. Chuck's last regular season game—a win over Minnesota—had just concluded. Charlie was taking time to reminisce about an incredible season just turned in by his son, Chuck, and a career that would conclude on the famed turf of the Rose Bowl in Pasadena.

"Well, we reached our goal, didn't we," he told Rick Montgomery of the *Quad City Times*. "It's like a dream come true."

And validation of a decision made nearly one year earlier.

Montgomery concurred that Charlie Long had played an important role in Chuck's decision to stay at Iowa for a fifth year.

"Pro football is a business," Long had often told his son. "Like going to the office."

After much discussion and deliberation, Chuck had opted for a fifth year.

"In the end, it was emotion winning over logic, I guess," his father hinted.

Now there were new goals. Perhaps win a Heisman. And maybe a Rose Bowl. Why not? The season had been a dream. No need to wake up now. Transform it from memorable to unforgettable. Ride out of town—Pasadena, that is—on the shoulders of your teammates with a long-stemmed rose between your teeth.

But first, the Heisman.

Most assumed Chuck was a long shot. Then again, maybe not.

There was only one candidate worthy of the Heisman. And that player was Chuck Long, wrote Dennis Dodd of the Kansas City Times on Nov. 25, 1985.

"What the Heisman should not be—and may become—is a tribute to the senior running back or quarterback who has the most yards. Consider Iowa quarterback Chuck Long, who probably will be everyone's runner-up."

Dodd gave voice to what Hayden Fry and many others believed—that someone's word, a commitment to team, a relentless drive to accomplish a goal—should matter more than yards gained or completed passes.

"Long stayed in college when he had a chance to turn pro last year to, he said, lead Iowa back to the Rose Bowl," Dodd wrote. "What's more, he did it.

"Remember, this was not an Iowa team that was supposed to be a powerhouse without Long. The Hawkeyes had already lost running back Owen Gill and faced the usual fight with Ohio State, Illinois and Michigan."

Dodd reasoned that Chuck could have gone out on top, taken the money, and not worried about proving himself again.

"In this day of business as usual at Southern Methodist and Texas Christian, doesn't that put the game back in its place?" Dodd asked rhetorically. "Long showed there's some loyalty left in this game."

And he wasn't done in reminding Heisman Trophy voters that soul, grace, and internal fortitude should count for something when ballots were cast.

"In 1980, Iowans had endured 19 consecutive years of losing football. Five years later, the Hawkeyes are in the Rose Bowl for the second time since then, and they have the first quarterback to throw for 10,000 yards in a career in Big Ten history.

"It seems long ago now, but Long was part of the revolution of the conference. Illinois' Coach Mike White and Fry first brought the sophisticated passing game to the three-yards-and-a-turf-burn conference. Fry and Long merely perfected it."

Unfinished business. A love of college football. Respect for the Iowa fans. A kinship with Hayden Fry and the coaching staff. A passion for the game. These were the factors that had fueled Chuck's decision to return for a fifth year under center for the Hawkeyes.

With the regular season in the books, Chuck took time to reflect on the wisdom of that decision and the hard work that went into that fifth year as Kinnick Stadium was shuttered for another long, cold Iowa winter.

"All last winter I kept thinking about how much I wanted to feel like everything was taken care of," Chuck said in an interview with Karen Allen of USA Today as the squad prepared to face eighth-ranked UCLA in Pasadena. "I enjoy college, and I wanted to be a senior quarterback and lead this team back to the Rose Bowl."

Accompanying his hard work and desire to prove himself again were fortuitous events—circumstances that would have never occurred, in-game thrills that never would have happened, and headlines that wouldn't have been written had he opted to play professionally following the 1984 season.

Like the had-to-be-Hollywood-scripted 35–31 win over Michigan State capped by the play of the year: a Chuck Long naked bootleg around the right end of the line with just twenty-seven seconds remaining—oh, and on third down and with no timeouts left, too.

Or the 12–10 victory over no. 2 Michigan that ended in pure madness when a twenty-five-yard field goal by Rob Houghtlin sailed through the uprights with no time remaining—a kick set up by a clutch drive led by Chuck that began from Iowa's twenty-two-yard line with just 5:27 left on the clock.

Then there was the 27–24 great escape at Purdue. Once again, Chuck engineered a drive that ate clock by converting critical third downs. Once again, Rob Houghtlin trotted on the field and sent a football sailing through the uprights as the clock evaporated.

"This was the season that popped out of Chuck Long's head like a vision come to life," wrote *Des Moines Register* columnist Marc Hansen. "He deliberated over it, debated about it, drew it up like a Broadway choreographer and, finally, orchestrated it to perfection.

"Long—the Iowa quarterback who came back for a fifth year because he enjoyed college (the heretic) and wanted to be a senior quarterback in the Rose Bowl—WILL be a senior quarterback in the Rose Bowl."

Hansen understood that what had happened to Chuck didn't happen to just anyone.

"The rest of us scheme and plot and dream. In the end, we usually come up short. In the end, we're satisfied if a fraction of our scattershot plans turn out the way they're supposed to.

"Not Long. He made it work. It was as if he stood behind a curtain pulling the levers and pushing the buttons. When the Hawkeyes needed a touchdown to beat Michigan State, Long slipped around end, ball on hip, in the last minute to give them one. When Iowa needed a score in the final seconds to beat Michigan, Long ushered them downfield, leaving the rest to placekicker Rob Houghtlin.

"He did the same at Purdue," wrote Hansen. "And when Iowa needed to erase the pain of the Ohio State disappointment and the attendant doubts, Long pieced together perhaps his greatest game as a Hawkeye in the 59–0 thumping of Illinois. And when Iowa needed a game worthy of Chuck Long to tie down a Rose Bowl berth, Long gave them one."

Outwardly, Chuck handicapped the race for the Heisman as a toss-up.

"I really couldn't tell you who's going to win," he told Chuck Schoffner of the Associated Press just ten days before the announcement. "From what I hear, it's a toss-up. Bo Jackson is a very good ballplayer. If he gets it, he deserves it.

"There are a lot of good ballplayers in the country who deserve the Heisman Trophy," Chuck added. "It's like I've said all along, I'm just honored to be considered."

Others felt honored just to know the man who, just five years earlier, was wearing no. 12 for the Wheaton North Falcons.

"When you come right down to it, Chuck Long could be the quintessential Horatio Alger story," wrote Jack McCarthy of the *Wheaton Daily Journal*. "There are hundreds of hot-shot high school quarterbacks throughout the nation with impressive passing statistics. Chuck Long wasn't one of them.

"Scores of elite prep athletes are actively wooed and recruited by the country's collegiate football powers," McCarthy added. "Not Chuck Long. But once in college, few are able to overcome the adversity, persevere and emerge on top. Chuck Long is one of those few.

"And Saturday in New York, the 22-year-old University of Iowa quarterback could grab the biggest prize of them all—the Heisman Trophy—awarded annually to the nation's best college football player."

"Very, very few times in history has anyone been able to point to left field and hit a home run. But the University of Iowa—Hayden Fry and those kids down there—they said at the beginning that they were going to go to the Rose Bowl. There wasn't any question about it in their minds. Usually when people make that kind of prediction, especially when they're 19-year-old boys, it goes astray. But they did it. I think it's just one of the great feats in the history of the game."

BILL REICHARDT
Former Hawkeye and respected Des Moines businessman, on Iowa earning a ticket to the Jan. 1, 1986, Rose Bowl
("On to the Rose Bowl," Ken Fuson and Blair Kamin, Des Moines Register, Nov. 24, 1985)

Chuck's formal invitation to attend the 1985 Heisman Memorial Trophy ceremony came courtesy of the university's athletic department.

Of course, they set up all the logistics, including airfare and hotel. They also helped prepare a detailed schedule of events and activities that would take place in New York City, site of the award ceremony.

Meanwhile, Chuck was enveloped in a whirlwind of activity. In the blink of an eye—and as quick as a quarterback sneak for a touchdown from the half-yard line—a memorable regular season was over. Now there were awards and accolades to accept.

Media requests—several a day—rolled into the University of Iowa athletic department under the close supervision of George Wine and Phil Haddy.

And Hayden Fry.

"The coach controlled a lot of it," admitted Chuck. "He also did most of the talking for me. I'm sure he told Haddy and Wine not to overwhelm me with interviews because I still had a game to play come January."

For most of the season, it appeared that the awarding of the Heisman Trophy to Bo Jackson would be nothing more than a formality. Nagging injuries late in the season, however, had limited the Auburn running back's productivity.

Chuck, on the other hand, had grown stronger as the year grew longer. Dramatic finishes had added to the buzz. Iowa's 10–1 record and a berth in the Rose Bowl had added to his stock.

By the time Chuck joined his family for Thanksgiving dinner in Wheaton,[46] it was a two-horse race—and a dead heat, at that.

"Many observers regard Chuck Long as the favorite to get the Heisman this year," wrote Richard Crabb of the *Wheaton Daily Journal*, "and they have convincing reasons. Jackson, after a sensational season as a junior, has played well this year, but not all the time."

Obviously Crabb had a rooting interest in the vote. But others who didn't agreed that the winner could literally be decided by a coin flip.

For Chuck, the Heisman, awarded to the nation's top college football player, represented more than just a trip to New York City and the opportunity to be recognized with college football's all-time greats.

It was a chance to represent Iowa on a lofty stage, to follow in the footsteps of Nile Kinnick, who had won the award in 1939, and second-place finishers Alex Karras (1957) and Randy Duncan (1958).[47]

The event was also the culmination of years of playing ball, going back to the days of taking on the neighborhood boys in The Tot Lot, to leading

Wheaton North High to an unexpected state championship as a high to accepting a scholarship from Iowa—just one of three that were offered to a blond, curly-haired young man who had a pretty thin resume for a quarterback about to play Big Ten football.

Jackson and Brigham Young quarterback Robbie Bosco joined Chuck in the Big Apple, as did Lorenzo White of Michigan State and Miami quarterback Vinny Testaverde.

Accompanying Chuck and Coach Fry were Chuck's girlfriend Lisa Wells and sports information director George Wine. The peaks and valleys of a five-year run at Iowa had brought Chuck to this place and this moment—a front-row seat for the televised Heisman Trophy ceremony sponsored by the Downtown Athletic Club of New York.

After lots of small talk, speeches, and trips down memory lane, it was time for the announcement. Electricity filled the hall as the lights were brought down and the guests took their seats. The room became silent. Camera operators were in their places. The on-set director gave his cue.

And just like that, NBC began its live coverage of the fifty-first Heisman Trophy presentation.

The fate of the Heisman hopefuls was now up to the collective wisdom of 1,050 voters, mostly sports writers and broadcasters screened to make regional distribution equitable—or at least as equitable as possible.

"You could have heard a pin drop when they said, 'We'll be back right after this to announce the Heisman Trophy winner,'" reminisced Chuck. "You're sitting in the front row with some of college football's most elite players. Your heart is beating like crazy. Waiting for them to return to airing the presentation—it was akin to waiting through the longest commercial ever.

---

[46] Chuck and his Wheaton North High School teammates returned home each year for "Thanksgiving Bowl." There was just one rule, Wheaton North football coach Jim Rexilius told Terry Boers of the *Chicago Sun Times*, "You don't tackle Chuck."

[47] Three Iowans have won the Heisman. Jay Berwanger, a graduate of Dubuque Senior High School, won the inaugural Heisman Memorial Trophy in 1935. After starring as a prep in Dubuque, Berwanger became an all-American at the University of Chicago. Nile Kinnick, who grew up in Adel, Iowa, accepted the Heisman Trophy in 1939. And in 1947, John Lujack of Bettendorf won the Heisman after a decorated stint as quarterback for Notre Dame.

"I just had the feeling my heart was going to beat right out of my chest. Anybody who's been there sitting in those chairs will tell you that."

Viewers taking part in a national telephone poll one week earlier had picked Chuck as their Heisman winner. ABC-TV had conducted the survey and reported that Chuck had received 104,825 votes to Jackson's 99,789.

Veteran TV commentator and Hawkeyes agitator Beano Cook even sided with Iowa fans by casting a vote for Chuck.

"I think Jackson will win, but I voted for Long," he said. "I voted for Long on the basis of what he did for Iowa this year, winning the Big Ten outright, and I think he's a heck of a kid for coming back for another year."

Hayden Fry was also rooting for his star.

"As a football coach, I can tell you there's no question that the most important player on the field, offense or defense, is the quarterback—if he's a good one," he told Bernard Fernandez of College and Pro Football Newsweekly. "You can ask any coach if he'd rather have a great quarterback or a great running back, and he'll take the greater quarterback. Every time.

"As an athlete, Chuck's statistics speak for themselves," he added. "And it isn't all the records he's set. A quarterback has to be a leader, and Chuck Long has the most unflappable poise of any player I've ever seen. He may be the finest quarterback at the line of scrimmage in terms of calling audibles to ever play the college game."

And Hayden Fry wasn't finished.

"But beyond that, he's simply everything you look for in a Heisman Trophy winner. Mention 'Heisman Trophy' to the average football fan, and he thinks about someone who represents the best in college football—as an athlete, as a student, as a good citizen. And that's Chuck Long."

That, along with Chuck's prowess in the pocket and ability to succeed under pressure, had earned him Al Grady's vote. The *Iowa City Press-Citizen* columnist wrote that on three occasions during the season, with the clock winding down in the fourth quarter and Iowa trailing or tied with a lot of field to cover, the Iowa quarterback had delivered.

"Yes, Chuck Long did it all this season, and he did it under pressure, and he did it almost all season in the wettest fall Iowans can remember," he lobbied. "I wonder what he might have done under sunshiny skies, with a dry ball and with good footing? He got my vote for the Heisman Award."

Chuck's high school coach Jim Rexilius—who Chuck admitted had been on the other end of the telephone line at least once a week during his time at Iowa—wasn't surprised that on a Saturday night in New York, his former quarterback was just one of three college football players to have a front-row seat for the Heisman Trophy ceremony.

"I thought he could be a great one when he left here," Rexilius said. "You know we won twenty-three of twenty-four games with him, and he did set one passing record that might never be broken. In the '79 state championship game, he was one of four for minus three yards, but we won the game."

But on this night in New York, Chuck would come up just short of winning the most coveted hardware in college football.

In what was at the time the closest balloting ever in the fifty-one-year history of the famous award, Bo Jackson edged Chuck Long by just forty-five points—1,509 to 1,464. Robbie Bosco came in a distant third with 459 points while Michigan State sophomore running back Lorenzo White rounded out the top four with 391.

It was the second Heisman claimed by an Auburn University athlete–Tigers quarterback Pat Sullivan had captured the coveted trophy in 1971.

"I figured it would be close, down to the wire," Jackson said immediately after accepting the twenty-five-pound bronze statue from Downtown Athletic Club president Eugene Meyer.[48] "I was prepared for whatever the outcome might be.

"I felt like my heart was going to jump out of my shirt," he added when asked what he was feeling in the moments just before the announcement. "It's the first time since I've been in college that I've been nervous. I think the people in the next row could hear my heart beating."

Then the humble man from a humble family owned the moment: "It means a great deal to me to win this award," said Jackson, a McCalla, Alabama, native, the eighth of ten children and the first in the family to graduate from college.[49] "It's something that I've looked at over the years... It's tradition, and I'll do everything I can to uphold that tradition."

Chuck, who later admitted that the suspense during the final hour leading up to the announcement "was worse than the Michigan football game," congratulated Bo and expressed relief that a decision had been rendered.

"It was a lot of fun. I enjoyed the race, especially the last few weeks. But I also feel a sense of relief that it's over," Chuck said. "It was heady for me that I was even in the conversation. I knew I was going to finish second at least. So it was special just to be here."[50]

Added Chuck: "I didn't grow up or go through my Iowa career thinking I was going to win the Heisman Trophy. Just being considered was the accumulation of hard work and having great teammates and coaching staff. It encompassed the whole program and everything it stood for.

"When they announced that Bo won, I was OK with that because I had finished second to a great player," Chuck added. "He really has had some good years, and he's been a great athlete. He deserves it.

"I'm proud it was the closest race," he said. "It's a heck of a lot better being second than not being in the race at all."

After congratulating his star, Auburn coach Pat Dye took Chuck aside. "In this situation, there just ain't no justice," he told Chuck. "Good luck in the Rose Bowl. You've been an inspiration to a lot of people."

Chuck's brothers hadn't made the trip. But as usual, they weren't far from Chuck's mind.

---

[48] Meyer was extremely poignant in his remarks that evening. In his invitation for Bo to come forward and deliver his acceptance speech, Meyer said this:

"As you all know, the recipient of the 1985 Heisman Memorial Trophy is Bo Jackson of Auburn. Winner in a close race over Chuck Long of Iowa; the closest race ever. It was clear during the day last Saturday when I knew the answer and neither Bo nor Chuck did—but I spent a good deal of time with them anyhow—both athletes expected the vote to be close and both had prepared themselves for the possibility that they might finish second, not lose, finish second.

Well, Chuck Long handled that reality as it became for him with style and character. But may I assure you that this young man, Bo Jackson, would have done the same, such is his character. So therefore it is my real great privilege tonight on behalf of the members of the great club, the Downtown Athletic Club that I represent, to present the fifty-first Heisman Memorial Trophy to Bo Jackson of Auburn."

"I dedicated this season to Andy, my other brother, David, my parents, and my girlfriend, Lisa." Chuck confided, "I'm just happy that they were behind me."

As was his coach.

After the lights dimmed and the room began to clear and the media became focused on filing their stories, Hayden Fry quietly approached his quarterback and, with a hand on his shoulder, pulled him close.

"You're still number one with us," he whispered discreetly.[51]

"I usually get a sweater and maybe a pair of jeans.
This is one I'll remember."

CHUCK LONG
*after receiving the Maxwell Award on Feb. 18, 1986, his twenty-third
birthday ("After a Long wait, an all-American boy," Ray Didinger,
Philadelphia Daily News, Feb. 19, 1986)*

Not everyone took Chuck's runner-up finish to Bo in the awarding of the Heisman as well as Chuck.

"If the basis of the award is pure unadulterated athletic ability and potential, Bo is my choice," wrote Don Doxsie of the *Quad City Times*. "But if character and personality are among the criteria, as the Heisman people would have you believe, I think they got the wrong guy.

"He's a guy who dreams of victories," Doxsie continued, "not an NFL paycheck, who plays football because he loves it, not because it will someday make him a millionaire. A lot of us would have been tempted to tell the Heisman folks what to do with their 25-pound chunk of bronze," Doxsie

---

[49] Bo was the thirteenth running back in the previous fourteen Heisman Trophy selections.

[50] Long, Wells, and Wine occupied the same row of the airplane on the flight from Saint Louis to New York. As reported by Mark Dukes of the *Cedar Rapids Gazette*, twenty minutes before landing, the captain of the aircraft told passengers, "We're pleased to have aboard Heisman Trophy candidate Chuck Long from Iowa and his coach, Hayden Fry." Dukes reported that passengers applauded politely.

wrote. Instead, Chuck "smiled for the cameras, talked about all the fun he was having, and noted that he was relieved the whole episode was over.

"There were no recriminations, no regrets, no excuses, no pointed fingers, no sour grapes. He took what one suspects was a bitter pill and swallowed it without a whimper."[52]

Hayden Fry, as was his way with the fifth-year quarterback, had nothing but praise for Chuck and his second-place finish.

"He's the kind of guy that will never break stride," he said. "He's like that on the football field; if he throws an interception or takes a loss, he shakes it off and on the next play tries to win."

Those qualities may not have given Chuck the edge in the Heisman, but they were good enough to earn him the forty-ninth Maxwell Award, announced Dec. 19. The annual recognition is given to the nation's most outstanding college football player.

"In our view, Chuck, the Maxwell Trophy is the first best thing to the Heisman," said Maxwell Club President Francis Bagnell. "We not only take into consideration your ability on the field, but also your standing as a student and generally what kind of a guy you are. We've checked into all that, and I think you'll be quite surprised how much we know about you."

The honor met with Hayden Fry's approval.

"You gentlemen in Philadelphia can pop your buttons," he said. "This is probably one of the most positive things that's ever happened to our program. You made one great choice in Chuck Long."

For Chuck, the honor—as with most superlatives that had come his way as a Hawkeyes quarterback—was taken in stride.

"I found out two days ago about this, and I was shocked," he told reporters while wearing a stark-white billed cap featuring the Rose Bowl insignia. "I never dreamed of winning this, and I never really heard much about the Maxwell until this year.

---

[51] Chuck and his coach bonded while hitting the parade of award ceremonies after the season finale versus Minnesota. "We went on the banquet circuit—there was the Heisman, Davey O'Brien, and Maxwell Awards," recalled Chuck. "That was a special time. I got to know Hayden a lot better during that time. It's always a lot of fun to really get to know your head coach after the playing career is basically over. He let his guard down and wasn't quite so demanding."

"But Coach Fry told me the last four guys who won the Maxwell also won the Heisman. If that's the case, then it's quite an honor."[53]

Tom Russo, director of public relations for the Maxwell Football Club, said Chuck's emphasis on remaining at Iowa for a fifth year in pursuit of a Rose Bowl appearance rather than opting for the NFL was noted by the selection committee.

Other factors included Chuck's high regard for Coach Fry and his stellar on-field credentials, Russo added.[54]

Now the only credentials that mattered to Chuck, Hayden Fry, and the Iowa Hawkeyes was a Rose Bowl victory.

Iowa was pegged as a slight favorite to defeat UCLA (8–2–1)—by one-and-a-half points to be exact. The last time Iowa had been favored to win a Rose Bowl (by a field goal over Washington in 1982), they got rolled 28–0.

Equally concerning was the Big Ten's lack of success in the granddaddy of them all, having lost fourteen of the previous sixteen.

"We have to go out to Pasadena and do something out there," said Chuck. "Everything's happening so fast. It really hasn't hit me that we're going out to the Rose Bowl yet until we get there."

But he was on his way.

And Iowa fans didn't want to miss out.

With just two weeks until game day, Iowa athletic ticket manager Jean Kupka was again waving the white flag. More than ten thousand people who had submitted applications to the university for Rose Bowl tickets would remain empty-handed.

Kupka told the *Cedar Rapids Gazette* on Dec. 18 that her office had received more than thirty thousand ticket requests. The school's allotment was twenty thousand.[55]

Fry expressed concern about Iowa's ability to handle the Bruins, who were a mirror image of the black and gold.

---

[52] Many college football fans agreed. The awarding of the Heisman to Jackson irritated a good number of folks, and they made their feelings known courtesy of letters to the editor that swamped newspapers across the state. Like L. E. Marshall of Estherville. "Bo Jackson, to many of his fans, is a good player," he wrote in a letter published Dec. 15, 1985, in the Sunday *Des Moines Register*. "But to me (and millions of others), Chuck Long is a heck of a lot better."

"We feature throwing the ball and they feature running it, but our diversified offenses and multiple defenses are very similar," he said. "UCLA is the fastest team we've seen."

After celebrating Christmas with family and friends, the Hawkeyes boarded their charter plane and departed Cedar Rapids for Pasadena Dec. 26. The Iowa players and coaches ducked into accommodations in Industry Hills, California, more than an hour's drive from the Rose Bowl's party atmosphere and practice at Mount San Antonio College near Los Angeles. One tradition they kept was participating in the famous Beef Bowl.[56]

Hayden Fry's approach to the festive New Year's Day bowl was so workmanlike that *Chicago Sun-Times* reporter Ron Rapoport referred to the Iowa coach as "the Grinch who stole the Rose Bowl."

And that was OK with Iowa's boss, a man who wanted his team to reflect the work ethic of the state it represented.

Fry took extra pride in the fact that Iowa's run to the Roses happened during one of the darkest years for the state's farmers and rural communities. The Hawkeyes' winning ways were a "tonic," as he called it, for the financial challenges afflicting farm families in the worst economic bust to hit farm country since the Great Depression fifty years earlier.

---

[53] Chuck became the second Iowa Hawkeye to win the Maxwell Award. Nile Kinnick received the honor in 1939, the same year he won the Heisman. The four Maxwell recipients prior to Chuck Long were also Heisman Trophy winners: Marcus Allen of Southern California, Herschel Walker of Georgia, Mike Rozier of Nebraska, and Boston College's Doug Flutie.

While Chuck was announced as the recipient in December, the Maxwell Award ceremony would not be held until Feb. 18 in Philadelphia. Coincidentally, it was presented on Chuck's birthday. "It'll make a pretty nice birthday gift," he told reporters.

[54] In addition to finishing runner-up for the Heisman and winning the Maxwell Award at the conclusion of his senior season, Chuck was named the sixty-second recipient of the Big Ten's Most Valuable Player Award and was presented the Davey O'Brien Award as the nation's most outstanding quarterback. Chuck was also a first team all-American pick by the Associated Press, Football News, Walter Camp, Gannett, Mercedes (writers) and Kodak (coaches), and Football News College Player of the Year. During his career at Iowa, Chuck was a three-time consensus first team all–Big Ten quarterback and graduated as the Big Ten's all-time leader in career passing yards and total offense. He also held the NCAA record of twenty-two straight completions (against Indiana in 1984) and held Iowa records for yards passing, completions, touchdown passes, and total offense in a game, season, and career.

Oh, and prior to his final game as a Hawkeye, Chuck had completed more passes (732) than any previous Iowa quarterback had attempted. He finished his career as the third-ranked quarterback in NCAA history for passing efficiency.

"The farmers, bless their hearts, haven't had just one bad day, they've had three years of bad days," Fry told reporters. "These are Czechs and Norwegians, Irish and Germans, and they've got tremendous pride. You know they're hurting. So many of them are just hanging on."

It was the reason he had affixed the "America Needs Farmers" stickers to the Hawkeyes' helmets—to bring attention to the plight of rural Iowa and its dedicated farm families.

Support from those rural families was showered on the team throughout the season, and the overwhelming response for tickets was all the more stunning given the poor farm economy.

"You actually have to experience it by living in Iowa," Fry said. "We're the only dance in town. We don't have the professional teams to compete with, so the people can really follow Iowa sports, not just football, all the sports."

All one had to do to verify Hayden Fry's words was look at the support Hawkeyes fans were pouring on their home team. Chris Dufresne, a staff writer for the Los Angeles Times, took note of the nearly $3.5 million that had been raised during the year for the Hawkeyes' athletic program. Every home game in the sixty-six-thousand-seat Kinnick Stadium had been sold out. And while thirty thousand fans were expected to make the trip to Pasadena, another fourteen thousand ticket requests went unfulfilled.

Hayden Fry was accustomed to doing things his way. And for this Rose Bowl, the coach readily admitted that he was much more comfortable than in 1981.

"It was a wonderful experience, except for the final score of the game," he told reporters upon arriving in California after the team's flight out of Iowa was delayed an hour due to ice and snow squalls. "But when we came

---

[55] The face value of the 1986 Rose Bowl ticket was $35. Two weeks prior to the game, ticket outlets in Los Angeles were reportedly asking $135 for end zone seating and more than $200 for prime sideline tickets.

[56] The Beef Bowl is held prior to the Rose Bowl and features the Big Ten and Pac-10 champions. Founded in the mid-1950s, the event was originally a contest to see which squad could consume the most prime rib in a single sitting. It was an immediate hit, loved by both players and media. By the mid-1960s, Sports Illustrated noted that each of the Beef Bowl's first nine winners also went on to win the Rose Bowl. Known today as "Lawry's Beef Bowl," the event has transitioned from an eating competition to one that celebrates the accomplishments of student athletes who play in "the granddaddy of them all."

out here last time, maybe we had gone too far too fast. Rather than going to minor bowls and working our way up to the Rose Bowl, we came head on to the Rose Bowl."

This time around, Fry added, "I'm loose as a goose. I'm ready for the ball game. I want to get it on."

The Hawkeyes faithful who had made the pilgrimage west were ready, too.

They were also optimistic about the team's prospects given Iowa's numerous bowl appearances, success against strong competition, and finding a way to win close games. The team was also loaded with experienced and confident seniors.

None more than Chuck.

"My goal for four years has been to come out to the Rose Bowl. Now that we've done it, my goal is to win the game," he said.

Prior to kick, Chuck admitted to having gone through all eleven of UCLA's 1985 game films, backward, too.

"The quarterback position is ninety percent mental and about ten percent physical," he said. "You've got to get the job done physically, of course, but mentally you've got to know what kind of defense they're in. If you know what kind of defense they're playing and their tendencies, that's half the battle right there."

Fry loved Chuck's commitment to preparation.

"I've never had a quarterback so knowledgeable about his opponent," Fry said. He's as knowledgeable as any coach on the staff in that he puts in hours and hours in preparation, studying the other team's defense, every little tendency, personality traits. He's a master at knowing what to do when a situation arises because he's prepared."

It would take more than preparation to defeat UCLA. Although the Hawks had prevailed 20–7 over the Bruins in 1981, Iowa was 2–6 all-time versus the team from the Westwood district of LA. UCLA's defense against the run was one of the best in the country, and its quarterback tandem of starter David Norrie and backup Matt Stevens were not flashy but poised and consistent.[57]

Fry knew it was a special game and special opportunity for his Iowa squad.

"A team like this doesn't happen a lot of times," he said, referencing the star trio of Chuck Long, Larry Station, and Ronnie Harmon. "It's just the right blend of togetherness, pride, and ability. This team is capable of beating any team in the US on any given day. It's capable of exploding."

"The Peach Bowl was OK. The Freedom Bowl, pretty good. But the Rose Bowl..." Long says, his voice picking up speed, "I got in only two plays in the Rose Bowl my freshman year. But, man, walking out there in front of 100,000 people. It's incredible."

CHUCK LONG
on the drive to come back for a fifth year as Iowa's starting quarterback ("Long, his dedication pays off," Rick Montgomery, Quad City Times, Sept. 1, 1985)

NFL scouts were taking note of Chuck.

Long rumored as a first-round selection, the stock of the product of Wheaton, Illinois, was climbing thanks to a 10–1 senior season and leading Iowa to a Rose Bowl berth.

"Chuck Long has the ability to take a team to the Super Bowl," said Gil Brandt of the Dallas Cowboys in an interview with the Los Angeles Herald Examiner's Tom Singer. "I wouldn't be surprised if he was among the first five players taken."

Added Ron Woolf of the Oakland Raiders, "Long is the ideal size and has received great training at Iowa. If anyone is capable of stepping into a starting NFL job, he certainly is."

---

[57] Prior to the Rose Bowl, there was doubt as to which UCLA QB would get the starting nod (Stevens eventually did, due to a strained quadricep that hampered Norrie). When asked prior to the game to explain the difference between the two quarterbacks from a defensive preparation standpoint, Hayden Fry quickly responded, "About four inches and thirty pounds." (Norrie stood six feet four inches and weighed 212 pounds compared to Stevens at six feet and 191 pounds.)

Mike Hickey of the New York Jets told Singer that the NFL would be better if more kids like Chuck Long were eligible for the draft.

"I wish there were more people like Chuck Long who also have a lot of pro potential," he said. "You never go wrong taking a good player who's also a super person. It's nice to see the good guys win for a change."

"He's a highly dedicated athlete," added Brandt. "He's had to work hard to accomplish what he has. He'd come down at lunch and look at films of the previous day's practice. If there was a meeting at three, he'd be there at noon. He's a lot like Roger Staubach in that way. If you ask him to do five, he gives you ten."

Chuck had been eligible for the NFL draft a year earlier but preferred the smell of roses over cashing a large check. That only made him an even bigger hero to Iowa fans while leaving the NFL scouts out in the cold.

"The NFL will still be there next season," Chuck had said at the time.

And now, on the eve of being one of just a select few college football players to take the field in five postseason bowl games, a prediction made by Chuck nearly twelve months earlier had proven to be just as accurate as his arm.

Chuck had many fans long before he had even won a game at Iowa.

Counted among them were Wally Fuchs and his wife, Bonnie.

The Fuchses and Longs were neighbors in Wheaton, their quaint homes separated by just a few blocks.

Wally Fuchs, like Charlie Long, was a hard worker and dedicated family man. Born in Cedar Rapids, Iowa, Fuchs was the son of a golf course greens keeper. Prior to his senior year, the Fuchses moved to suburban Chicago. A mediocre athlete at Lemont High School, Wally Fuchs turned to turf management, attending Iowa State University in Ames. He soon landed a course superintendent job at the prestigious Medinah Country Club in Medinah, Illinois.

"I didn't know if working at a golf course would be challenging enough, so when the opportunity came along to work for Upjohn instead in their ag division, I took it," recalled Fuchs.

"Soon I was selling a golf course fungicide. But after working for them for nearly four years and writing them plenty of business, I decided I would go into business for myself."

Easier said than done.

It was 1969, and Wally Fuchs was now a father of three with a mortgage. And he needed $10,000 to start the business.

"I had grown up on a golf course as a kid and did my very best to do things the right way," he said. "A person there noticed, and when he found out I was trying to pull together a business, gave me ten thousand dollars with no strings attached. Said he didn't want anything for it. But he believed in me and my dream. I gave him a third of the business because I thought that was the only fair thing to do.

"He also reached out to his banker, who in turn gave me an unlimited credit line," Fuchs added. "I was in business for twenty-eight years and never had to borrow a penny from a bank."

In 1996, Fuchs sold the business, only to start another four years later serving the golf turf and landscape industry.

"We were successful, and people wanted to work with us because we worked hard, could get products to market before anyone else, and were priced competitively," he said. "It was a fun ride."

After moving to Wheaton, Wally Fuchs met the senior Long in the stands following a Wheaton North High basketball game. The families hit it off immediately. Soon they were enjoying burgers and beverages together following football and basketball games.

Humility, said Wally Fuchs, was one of Chuck's most endearing qualities, and it came from his parents, Charlie and Joan.

"They were humble people," he said. "I knew Charlie for at least ten years. In all that time, he never talked about himself. In fact, here was a man who had won a state high school basketball championship but never told me.

"I asked him about that team and how well he played, and he said he was 'all right.' Come to find out that he had won all kinds of honors. But it was not like him or Joan to boast. [58]

"And they would never let Chuck get cocky. They wouldn't allow it."

Fuchs said he'd always remember the first time he watched Chuck play for the Wheaton North Falcons.

"I said he'd play in the NFL, and people laughed at me," he recalled with a broad smile. "But he was a winner. You could just tell that from the moment you met him or saw him on the football field. There are a lot of athletes around, but not a lot of winners.

"But just look at what Chuck accomplished—playing in five bowls, which is unprecedented. The Peach Bowl where he connected on all those consecutive completions and the yards he threw for in the Freedom Bowl versus Texas.

"Heck, even his first play as a Detroit Lion went for a touchdown against Tampa Bay. I think it was for forty yards to Leonard Thompson."

When asked to describe the ingredients for success, Wally Fuchs said without hesitation, "Too often, successful businesspeople get too confident. They think they know everything there is to know and they forget about their business. Those who have studied successful people and looked for a common denominator often find that they have a certain level of insecurity. That can fuel drive.

"Insecurity kept the edge on me, and I think the same held true for Chuck," Fuchs said. "He relished the chance to prove people wrong, including those who said he didn't have what it took to be successful as a Big Ten football player. I think the doubters gave him an edge, like he was always coming from an underdog role. That insecurity drove him to want to prove people wrong.

"With Chuck, it was his humbleness that kept him focused. Even with his success, you never saw any ego with him. He has a great personality and charisma—those attributes that make someone successful."

---

[58] "The quality I admired most in my dad was that he never had a bad day," said Chuck. "He had the right attitude. He came from a good family, and his parents were positive. He loved going to parties, and he loved everybody. He was very humble and very personable and caring."

The Fuchses still live in their comfortable two-story home just a few blocks away from Joan Long. And they continue to cite the importance of faith in achieving great things.

"Rock solid faith is critical," said Wally Fuchs. "I tell my grandchildren today that life is really simple when you look back at the Master's plan. In retrospect, it was never easy making a big decision. But I would pray and then listen and be patient. At the right time, I would feel the confidence to make the decision. That was the Lord. I mean, starting a business with ten thousand dollars and never working with a bank and making eighty-five thousand the first year? These are not normal things. We've had the challenges of life, but having a strong faith makes things a lot easier."

"I dropped to my knees and thanked the Lord."

HAYDEN FRY
when asked by Tracy Dodds of the Los Angeles Times how he reacted when Chuck Long said he would pass up the NFL draft and stay for a fifth year at Iowa ("Iowa believes a win in the Rose Bowl is, well, long overdue," Los Angeles Times, Jan. 1, 1986)

Chuck had been called many things by his coach. "Scary" had never been one.

Until the day before the Rose Bowl.

"He's kind of scary because he's such a gentleman, such a nice guy," the coach told reporters. "I can't even get mad at him. I'd like to. I've grabbed ahold of him before to get his attention. He just grins at me."

Fry, wrote Chuck Schoffner of the Associated Press, said even when Chuck Long does something wrong, it often turns out right.

"He'll come to the sidelines, and I'll be mad at him because he's audibilized out of a great play into a play that I didn't think was good, and what can I say to him because he's just thrown for six," the Iowa coach said. "He's that kind of guy."

But could he win a third Rose Bowl for the Hawkeyes?

UCLA, playing in its tenth, was a respectful opponent. Head coach Terry Donahue, an alum of the school he represented, knew Iowa's offense began and ended with Chuck Long. Not only did he possess uncanny ability with his arm, but his legs could do damage, too. Running back Ronnie Harmon completed the triple threat.

"When you look at the strengths of Iowa's offense, you have to look, number one, at their balance," said Donahue. "They not only have the great passing of Chuck Long, they have the ability to run the ball. Ronnie Harmon is one of the premier tailback athletes in the country.

"We have faced other great quarterbacks who played with passing teams, but we have never faced a quarterback like Chuck Long, who played for a team that has this kind of balance. This team will really stretch your defense."

UCLA's defense had given up just seventy yards rushing per game heading into the Rose Bowl. The goal was to make Iowa one-dimensional and force Iowa to make plays…and perhaps some mistakes.

And the mistakes, well, they happened…and in bunches.

Iowa's normally sure-handed tailback Ronnie Harmon lost four fumbles—all in the first half—propelling the underdog Bruins to a commanding 24–10 halftime lead.[59] It was a lead UCLA would never relinquish on their way to a 45–28 battering of the Hawkeyes in front of a crowd of more than 103,000, many of them Hawkeyes faithful.

Not many saw this one coming. Certainly not Hayden Fry.

"Gentlemen, you just witnessed a complete annihilation of the Iowa football team," said Fry matter-of-factly as he opened his postgame remarks to the media. "UCLA did as fine a job at blocking, tackling, and moving the ball against our defense as any team in the nation."

UCLA freshman and second-string running back Eric Ball[60] scooted through Iowa's defense like he was on skates, streaking 227 yards on just twenty-two carries and a Rose Bowl-tying record four touchdowns.

"I can't tell you why they only won eight games," said Fry after the Bruins scorched Iowa for nearly five hundred offensive yards. "We knew by watching game films that when they were hot, they were very, very good. They [Michigan] couldn't hold a light to this bunch."

Chuck connected on his first nine attempts. For the day, he hit on twenty-nine of thirty-seven for 319 yards and one interception.

"You certainly couldn't fault Chuck for what happened out there today," said wide receiver Bill Happel. "He performed great. Some of the players around him didn't."

Safe to say Happel was referring to Harmon, whose fumbles dug a hole too deep for Iowa to climb out. The running back finished with fifty-five yards rushing and 102 yards receiving on eleven catches.

It was UCLA's fourth consecutive bowl win—three Roses and a Fiesta.

Hayden Fry shrugged off criticism that the Hawkeyes were too tight heading into the game due to his "no frills" approach to the team's week of practice in Los Angeles.

"But do you realize what the score would have been had I allowed the players to honky-tonk out here?" he responded, estimating the team missed twenty to thirty tackles. "I'm dumb but not that dumb to think our preparation was wrong."

Chuck took the stinging loss in stride despite having set his sights on a Rose Bowl victory nearly one year earlier when he chose to return for a fifth season.

"It just wasn't in the cards," Chuck said. "The funny part is, I thought we were really ready to play a good game. Everybody was relaxed and ready to go.

"Yeah, this one hurts a little," a dejected Chuck added. "But it's better to be out here than nothing. It's been a great trip and a great bowl. The Big Ten didn't win again, but it was fun to represent the Big Ten. I thought we were one of the better teams in the country.

---

[59] Prior to the Rose Bowl, Harmon had lost just one fumble all season.
[60] Eric Ball was selected the game's MVP. He was picked by the Cincinnati Bengals in the second round (thirty-sixth pick overall) in the 1989 NFL draft. He played seven seasons professionally, six with the Bengals and one with the Oakland Raiders, running for 586 yards.

"It's not as if we went out there and choked today. UCLA made the big plays on offense, and on defense they did what they had to do.

"The completions didn't mean much if we couldn't win," Chuck added. "It was a great disappointment, a tough finish, but it was a great season, and I enjoyed it."

Steve Bisheff of the *Orange County Register* didn't hold back.

"It was not as if Harmon didn't contribute at all out there," he wrote. "He finished the day with 165 yards rushing and receiving. But no one will remember that.

"No, when they think back to the 1986 Rose Bowl, they'll only remember one thing. They'll only remember that UCLA's leading runner had a ball. And Iowa's leading runner couldn't hold onto one."

Chuck Long's stat sheet, 1985–86 season:
    388 attempts; 260 completions (67 percent);
    3,297 yards; 27 touchdowns
Career:
    1,203 attempts; 782 completions (65 percent);
    10,461 yards; 74 touchdowns

Chuck's plan was to get to the Rose Bowl in his fifth and final season as Iowa's quarterback.

And win it.

But Chuck didn't go sour on the loss as he reflected on his final year under center for the black and gold.

"This was a year I'll never forget. It was great, and I had a lot of fun. It hurt to lose the game, but I would have been more disappointed if we had played in a smaller bowl.

"I have no regrets," he added. "I always wanted to play in the Rose Bowl, and we did. We had a good year. I feel like we did end up on a high point even though we lost the game. Going 10–1 and playing in the Rose Bowl was a pretty good way to finish."

Now, with degree in hand, Chuck prepared for the NFL draft while guessing as to when and by whom he would be selected.

"At this point, I really don't care where I end up playing," Chuck told Chris McConnell of the *Wheaton Daily Journal.* "I wouldn't mind playing in warm weather, someplace in the southern states. The Midwest would be nice because that's where I'm from and I've played my college ball here. Then there's New York, the Big Apple. That would be great. I guess I wouldn't even mind playing for the Packers if I had to.

"Every kid that plays football wants to end up in the pros someday," Chuck added. "It all depends on a team's need. Sometimes you can guess that a certain team will go for a certain player because of their team needs.

"But by the time the draft rolls around, teams do so much trading of draft picks you never know who's picking them."

Chuck also made plans to attend postseason award ceremonies, including the Walter Camp team selection (New Haven, Connecticut), the Davey O'Brien (Fort Worth, Texas), Gold Helmet Player of the Year (Seattle), and the Maxwell Award (Philadelphia).

"It all seems so natural, so right, so inevitable for Long to be in Fort Worth," wrote Paul Hagen of the Star-Telegram on the eve of Chuck's acceptance of the Davey O'Brien Award. "Except that, but for a break here or a twist of fate there, Long could just as easily have been somewhere else.

"If Iowa, unlike most colleges, hadn't decided to gamble a scholarship on the gangly senior out of Wheaton North High School, he might be somewhere else, starting his career in business marketing.

"If the Hawkeye coaches hadn't turned back to him after a less-than-spectacular debut in 1982, he could be somewhere else, wondering what might have been.

"If Long had made a different decision prior to last season, he might be somewhere else reflecting on his just-completing rookie season in the National Football League and planning for next year.

"Each factor, taken separately, might have led him in a different direction. But together, the factors add up to the Davey O'Brien Award," Hagen penned.

He observed that Chuck was able to turn "faintly negative situations, such as not being highly recruited out of high school, into positives."

"I think it has helped me work harder," Chuck told Hagen. "If a lot of schools had been after me, I could have been swayed to coast. I knew I'd never be able to take it easy. I knew that I'd always have to work hard.

"I've seen a lot of players who were highly recruited come in and coast," he added. "They thought they were so good they didn't have to work, and they had a rude awakening. Because I didn't have that situation, it helped me. I've always had to push myself."

———————

"I enjoy people who give all their effort. I've always enjoyed underdogs—guys who weren't supposed to win, but did."

CHUCK LONG
in a conversation with Jack McCarthy, Copley News Service,
Dec. 31, 1985

Chuck's hometown of Wheaton wasn't about to be upstaged by glamorous award banquets held in places like Philadelphia, Fort Worth, and New York. So community leaders planned their own ceremony. "Chuck Long Day" would be held Jan. 24 with festivities at Wheaton North High School and Wilton Manor Restaurant.

More than two thousand were anticipated to attend ceremonies modeled after a similar recognition held years earlier for another Wheaton great, Red

Grange. Attendees would include Illinois Lt. Governor George Ryan, the Wheaton North student body, city chamber and Big Ten representatives, members of Iowa's coaching staff, and WHO sports broadcaster (and voice of the Hawkeyes) Jim Zabel.

"Football is such a team game," said the senior Long when asked to put the planned celebration in context. "I hope it [the day] serves to honor all the players from Wheaton North, Wheaton Central, and Wheaton Warrenville [high schools] who've gone on to make a contribution at the collegiate level."

Chuck Long Day organizers said it would be a celebration of achievement and sportsmanship. There were the coaches who helped mold Chuck as an athlete and the fans who supported him. Then there were the "little kids who play football in a backyard, imagining the roar of a packed stadium and pretending that they are Chuck Long," wrote Jack McCarthy of the *Wheaton Daily Journal*. "They'll all be part of the day."

And what a celebration it was.

Wheaton North rolled out the red carpet, complete with performances by its marching band, as the town welcomed home one of its own for a day of recognition. Chuck was the guest of honor at an all-high school ceremony attended by nearly 1,500 students. There he was presented the *Chicago Tribune's* Silver Football Award, which goes to the league's most valuable player.

"I bring with me numerous congratulation wishes from people around the Big Ten," Jeff Elliott, Big Ten Conference sports information director, told the crowd between long rounds of applause. "The other nine teams think it's wonderful that Chuck is finally graduating and moving to the NFL."

Iowa's offensive coordinator Bill Snyder also made the trip to Wheaton to recognize Chuck in front of his hometown fans.

"You people at Wheaton North have not had the opportunity to know Chuck like I have," he said. "I don't think I've come across a young man as gifted athletically as Chuck Long. But surely I have not come across a finer person than Chuck."

A luncheon hosted by the chamber followed by a dinner, basketball game, and school dance rounded out the day's festivities.

Even Red Grange[61] chimed in, albeit remotely. "I wanted to congratulate Chuck on his remarkable achievement," Grange said from his Florida home during a telephone interview with the *Wheaton Daily Journal's* Richard Crabb. "He has not only been a credit to himself, his community, and his university, but to the game of football.

"In addition, he has proven again what I have always believed, and that is that Wheaton is the most sports-minded town that I have ever known. The families, the schools, and the whole town follow their school teams and encourage the players. I am sure Chuck will never forget this."

High praise from a man credited for single-handedly saving the National Football League from bankruptcy during a nationwide barnstorm of NFL cities during his early years with the Chicago Bears that drew huge crowds (and gate receipts).

For Chuck, it was an unforgettable tribute from the most important fans in the world—those who know you best.

"It felt good to go back to the old gym," he said. "It warms my heart to be honored like I have been today. I was sitting in the gym thinking about all the good memories I had at Wheaton North. All the good times.

"It was a special day in my life," he added. "I will always remember the warmth and kindness extended by so many people. I'll forever treasure the kind words and gifts and the memory of a wonderful day."

---

[61]Nicknamed "The Galloping Ghost," Red Grange starred in football, baseball, basketball, and track for Wheaton High, earning sixteen varsity letters (he scored seventy-five touchdowns as a running back for the Falcons). To earn money for the family, he toted ice and quickly became known as "Ice Man." He played college football at the University of Illinois, earning national recognition when he scored six touchdowns in a much-anticipated 1924 matchup against the Michigan Wolverines (including two kickoff returns). Grange signed with the Chicago Bears and because of his prominence and ability to draw fans was credited with legitimizing the NFL. He was described as a humble man who possessed raw, God-given instincts that allowed him to perform at a high level on the football field. He starred in several movies and was a sports broadcaster and motivational speaker. He died on Jan. 28, 1991, at the age of eighty-seven. Wheaton Warrenville South High School's football field is named in his honor.

"He was a regular visitor at the White House," said Chuck. "Some would even say he was more popular than the president."

Chuck Long already on the move as a young boy in Wheaton, Illinois. *Photo courtesy of Joan Long*

The Long brothers (1975) – Chuck (7th grade), Andy (front) and David in the living room of the family's home in Wheaton, Illinois. *Photo courtesy of Joan Long*

Annual Long family fishing outing to Green Mountain Falls, Colorado in 1974 (from left): Charlie, Chuck (6th grade), David, Joan and Andy. On this day, the family caught 62 rainbow trout and, adds Joan, we "ate them all!" *Photo courtesy of Joan Long*

Long family Christmas (1975): Chuck (7th grade) with brothers Andy and David and mother Joan. *Photo courtesy of Joan Long*

Chuck, 8th grade (1976) stands in front of "The Tot Lot" as a member of the local Pony League baseball team. *Photo courtesy of Joan Long*

The Long family on vacation to "Four Corners" USA (New Mexico, Arizona, Colorado and Utah). From left: David, Andy, Chuck (8th Grade, 12 years of age) with Charlie. *Photo courtesy of Joan Long*

CHUCK LONG: DESTINED FOR GREATNESS

Long family at the Grand Canyon – 8th grade (1976) – Chuck, David, Andy and Charles. *Photo courtesy of Joan Long*

Chuck (third from left) celebrates with teammates after winning the Pony League Championship (8th grade, 1976). *Photo courtesy of Joan Long*

The Long family portrait 1974 – Charlie, Chuck, Andy, David and Joan. *Photo courtesy of Joan Long*

Senior pic -- Wheaton North High School Falcon Chuck Long (1980). *Photo courtesy of Joan Long*

Chuck Long and Lisa Wells pose for a photo before the Wheaton North Senior Prom in Spring 1981. *Photo courtesy of Joan Long*

CHUCK LONG: DESTINED FOR GREATNESS

Wheaton North's No. 12 Chuck Long discussed the next play with head coach Jim Rexilius in the 1979 Illinois State High School 4A championship game. The Long-led Wheaton North Falcons defeated La Salle-Peru 14-6 to claim the school's first state championship. *Wheaton North High School*

Chuck approaches the line to accept his first snap as quarterback of the Iowa Hawkeyes in 1981 versus the Northwestern Wildcats. *Photo courtesy of Joan Long*

IOWA FOOTBALL

HAYDEN FRY
Head Coach

BIG TEN CHAMPIONS 1981

May 6, 1983

Mr. & Mrs. Charles Long
1106 N. Washington
Wheaton, Illinois 60187

Dear Mr. & Mrs. Long:

Now that spring football has concluded and school is about over, I
wanted to drop you a note and let you know again how much we appreciate
Chuck and all that he has contributed to the development of a quality
program here at the University of Iowa. He has worked hard, always done
his very best, and is a quality young man both on and off the field. We
are very proud of him and his achievements. We thank you for allowing
him to be a part of our program.

I hope you enjoy a pleasant summer.

Very sincerely,

Bill Snyder
Offensive Coordinator

BS:da

THE UNIVERSITY OF IOWA

Department of Intercollegiate Athletics   •   Athletic Office Building   •   Iowa City, Iowa 52242

Chuck Long, quarterback, University of Iowa Hawkeyes (1984). *Photo courtesy of University of Iowa Athletic Communications*

Game-on as Chuck Long and Coach Hayden Fry strategize on the sidelines (1985). Their mutual respect manifested itself in wins and bowl appearances. *University of Iowa Athletic Communications*

Enjoying some California sun and a 1984 Freedom Bowl win; from left: Chuck Long, Jay Hayes (visiting); Andy Long, Jonathan Hayes, Hap Peterson and Kelly O'Brien. *Photo courtesy of Joan Long*

IOWA FOOTBALL

HAYDEN FRY
Head Coach

1981 BIG TEN CHAMPIONS
1982 ROSE BOWL
1982 PEACH BOWL
1983 GATOR BOWL

November 19, 1984

Mr. & Mrs. Charles Long
1106 N. Washington
Wheaton, IL 60187

Dear Mr. & Mrs. Long:

With our regular season about to close, I want to take just a moment to
let you know how very much we appreciate Chuck. Although the last three
weeks have been extremely disappointing to each of us, Chuck has never
given any less than 100% of his efforts. He has always worked hard,
given his best and above all has proven himself to be a class individual
both on and off the field.

We truly appreciate him.

Warm regards,

Bill Snyder
Offensive Coordinator

BS:da

THE UNIVERSITY OF IOWA • CARVER-HAWKEYE ARENA • IOWA CITY, IOWA 52242 • (319) 353-5070

CHUCK LONG: DESTINED FOR GREATNESS

It's all smiles at the Junior Iowa Hawkeyes Football Banquet held at Memorial Union (1984); from left: Kelly O'Brien, Andy Long, Jonathan Hayes, Chuck Long, Hap Peterson and Mike Haight. *Photo courtesy of Joan Long*

Chuck Long, joined by Lisa Wells, accepts the Roy Carver MVP award at the 1985 Iowa Hawkeyes football banquet. *Photo courtesy of Joan Long*

Brothers Chuck Long and Andy Long at the family home in Wheaton, Illinois. *Photo courtesy of Joan Long*

IOWA FOOTBALL

HAYDEN FRY
Head Coach

1981 BIG TEN CHAMPIONS
1982 ROSE BOWL
1982 PEACH BOWL
1983 GATOR BOWL
1984 FREEDOM BOWL

February 8, 1985

Mr. & Mrs. Charles Long
1106 N. Washington
Wheaton, IL 60187

Dear Charles, Joan & Andy:

Thank God it's over! Thank God Chuck will return! Thank God
for you and the great love you have for Chuck!

I'm confident that no one will ever know the amount of praying
and studying all of you did in regards to Chuck's decision.
The manner in which all of you conducted yourselves in a
difficult situation is indicative of the integrity and honesty
associated with the Charles Long family. I shall always
admire and respect you for the way you treated Chuck during
a critical time in his life.

Go Hawks!

Warm regards,

Hayden Fry
Head Football Coach

HF:bk

THE UNIVERSITY OF IOWA   •   CARVER-HAWKEYE ARENA   •   IOWA CITY, IOWA 52242   •   (319) 353-5070

With receivers covered, Chuck Long takes to the ground in search of a first down.
University of Iowa Athletic Communications

Chuck Long on the turf in Pasadena stretching before the start of the 1986 Rose Bowl. *Photo by Bob Rasmus*

Chuck salutes the home crowd after another Hawkeyes victory. *University of Iowa Athletic Communications*

THE NATIONAL **FOOTBALL LEAGUE**

410 PARK AVENUE.   NEW YORK, N.Y. 10022 • PLaza 8-1500

January 11, 1985

Dear College Senior:

We just wanted to take time out from our Super Bowl preparation to let you know how highly our NFL scouts think of you.

There are a number of rookies both on the Dolphins and 49ers who were in the same position as you when they finished their collegiate careers last season. Should they stay in school and wait for the NFL draft or should they make a quick decision about their pro football careers?

We are certain those young players on both our teams are glad they waited. Dan Marino was faced with that same question in 1983. He continued his education at the University of Pittsburgh and was selected as the sixth quarterback in the 1983 NFL draft. Dan considered his options and signed the best deal for himself and his family. He set the NFL record for most touchdown passes in a season in 1984. Now, Dan and Joe Montana are considered by many as the finest quarterbacks in pro football.

There are a number of rookies who contributed to our Super Bowl effort including LB Todd Shell and RB Derrick Harmon of the 49ers and LB Jay Brophy and RB Joe Carter of the Dolphins. Each of our players will earn a total of $64,000 in postseason monies by winning the Super Bowl, while the loser will collect $46,000.

If you have any questions regarding the NFL, the Super Bowl or our 1985 draft, please call this toll-free number today: 1-800-NFL-INFO. Our NFL staff will do its best to answer your questions.

We hope the enclosed Super Bowl program will help you enjoy the game. We also have sent you a Super Bowl poster in a separate mailing. WHO KNOWS? MAYBE YOU WILL BE PLAYING IN SUPER BOWL XX IN NEW ORLEANS NEXT YEAR!

Regards,

Don Shula
Miami Dolphins

Bill Walsh
San Francisco 49ers

No. 16 Chuck Long drops back for a pass. As an Iowa Hawkeye, Chuck threw a record 1,203 passes, completing 782 of them (also a record!). *University of Iowa Athletic Communications*

Jennifer Berg tries on Chuck Long's football helmet during the quarterback's visit to Roosevelt Elementary School in Iowa City. The children's student teacher was Lisa Wells. *Photo published in the Iowa City Press Citizen; courtesy of University of Iowa Athletic Communications*

Hayden Fry, Andy Long and "Sweetness" Walter Payton share a few laughs on way to Philadelphia for presentation of the 1986 Maxwell Award. *Photo courtesy of Joan Long*

Mr. and Mrs. Charles Long
1106 N. Washington
Wheaton, Illinois 60187

Dear Charlie and Joan:
What wonderful news! I don't
need to tell you how excited and happy
June and I are, and little old River
City is really buzzing with the good
news. It was indeed, a privilege to
attend Chuck's press conference. That
son of yours is really something; I
would imagine there were 75 to 100
news media in attendance, T.V. cameras
movie cameras, still cameras, a large
assortment of microphones, people
almost hanging from the ceiling, flood
lights on, flashbulb's bursting, Chuck
walks in sits down and starts the
meeting just like it were an everyday
occurance; he made the necessary opening
remarks, and answers every question
in a concise and intelligent manner,
no wonder he is such an outstanding
quarterback. Enclosed are papers passed
out to the media.
Sincerely,
Patrick J. Mc Carney

First-hand account of Chuck Long's January 1985 news conference announcing he'd return for a fifth year as an Iowa Hawkeye… penned by Iowa Assistant Coach Dan McCarney's father, P.J. McCarney.

The stars come out for the Davey O'Brien Award (spring 1986); back row, from left: Todd Blackledge, Doug Flutie, Steve Young, Chuck Long; Brent Musburger (seated) served as ceremony emcee. *Photo courtesy of Joan Long*

1985 Heisman Trophy presentation in New York City; Chuck Long (right) interviewed by broadcaster Bob Costas with Bo Jackson of Auburn University (behind podium) looking on. *University of Iowa Athletic Communications courtesy of Chuck Benson, photographer*

February 5, 1985

STATEMENT FROM HAYDEN FRY

Chuck and his family investigated every possible option before making the decision. I couldn't be more pleased with their decision and believe it is the right thing to do at this time.

Iowa fans across the nation join the coaches and players in congratulating Chuck. He is truly one of the finest QB's in college football. Next season will be another exciting year for the Hawkeyes. Go Hawks!

Statement to reporters by Coach Hayden Fry regarding Chuck Long's decision to return to the Iowa Hawkeyes for a fifth year.

Head Coach Hayden Fry (back row, center) assembled a dream-team staff that included: (front row, from left): Bernie Wyatt, Barry Alvarez, Bill Brashier, Dan McCarney and Bob Stoops; (back row, from left): Bill Snyder, Del Miller, Kirk Ferentz, Carl Jackson, Don Patterson, Bill Dervrich. *Photo by Bob Rasmus*

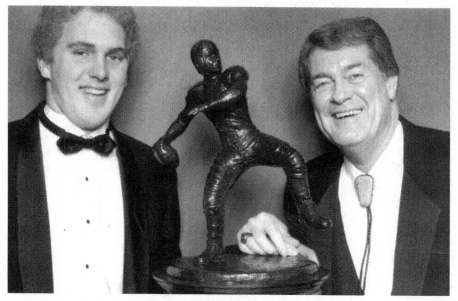

Chuck Long, joined by Coach Hayden Fry, accepting the 1985 Davey O'Brien Award.
University of Iowa Athletic Communications

Many stars gather for presentation of the Davey O'Brien Award to Chuck Long (February 1986). The ceremony was held at the Fort Worth (Texas) Athletic Club. Attending (from left): Brent Musburger, Hayden Fry, Andy, Joan, Charlie and Chuck Long, Lamar Hunt, Lisa Wells, David Long and Charles Ringler. *University of Iowa Athletic Communications*

Awaiting presentation of the Maxwell Award in Philadelphia (Feb. 18, 1986; also Chuck's birthday), from left: David, Joan, Charlie and Andy Long, Coach Hayden Fry, Lisa Wells, Chuck Long. *Photo courtesy of Joan Long*

CHUCK LONG: DESTINED FOR GREATNESS

Chuck Long displays No. 16 in blue and silver. The Iowa Hawkeye was selected by the Detroit Lions as the 12th overall pick in the 1986 NFL Draft. *University of Iowa Athletic Communications*

Chuck's first NFL pass as a Detroit Lion goes for a touchdown versus the Tampa Bay Buccaneers. *University of Iowa Athletic Communications*

The groomsmen and bridesmaids – Chuck and Lisa's closest and dearest friends forever – gather for the couple's wedding day, June 6, 1987. *Photo courtesy of Joan Long*

Topps® rookie card of Chuck Long – 1987.

Dropping back to pass – Chuck Long as a member of the Los Angeles Rams. *University of Iowa Athletic Communications*

The Long children are ready to ring in the New Year 2000 in Iowa City (from left): Zachary, Nathan, Lindsay, Sammy and Maddy.

Lindsay Long's wedding day (July 12, 2014) at Laguna Beach, California; the Long children (from left): Nathan, Zachary, Lindsay, Maddy and Samantha. *Photo courtesy of Chuck and Lisa Long*

Longs at the 2016 Rose Bowl (from left): son Nathan, wife Lisa, daughters Lindsay, Maddy, Sammy, son Zach, son-in-law Sean, Chuck

CHAPTER 6

After Hawkeye

"He's a guy that wins."

GIL BRANDT

Cowboys vice president of personnel, when asked what came to mind when assessing Chuck Long ("The Long Road," Mark Blaudschun, Dallas Morning News, Feb. 17, 1986)

Award banquets had concluded. The "Chuck Long Day" banners that adorned the Wheaton North gymnasium had been removed. The Japan Bowl—a post-season college football all-star game where Chuck had finished eight of eleven for eighty-two yards—was over.

Now the Iowa coaching staff was preparing for spring drills and a 1986 football season that would kick off Sept. 13 versus Iowa State. And for the first time in five years, someone other than Chuck Long would be taking the snaps as the Hawkeyes' starting quarterback.

"I enjoyed the travel and the banquets and recognition, but now it's time to look to the future and get ready for the next challenge," said Chuck as he prepared for life in the National Football League.

Draft scouts and pro personnel were complimentary of the Iowa product.

"Chuck Long is a good quarterback. I don't know if he's going to be a Hall of Famer, but I think he's going to be a decent NFL quarterback," predicted George Young, general manager of the New York Giants.

"He's got a good but not great arm," said Gil Brandt of the Dallas Cowboys. "But he's a good, solid player. Maybe not a franchise player. But someone who is going to be a very good pro. David Krieg took Seattle to the

AFC Championship game, and this guy is every bit as good as him. It just depends on where he winds up. If he gets into a good situation like a Chicago or Miami, he could be a Pro Bowl quarterback right away like [Dan] Marino was at Miami."

Chuck was reflective as the NFL draft loomed. And anxious. "It overwhelms me how far away pro ball used to be in my mind and how fast it has come," he said. "But I'm looking forward to it. It's going to be like my freshman year all over again. I'm going to have to prove myself all over again."

He had no regrets delaying his departure for the pros by a year, even though his final collegiate start resulted in a loss versus UCLA.

"I just wanted to achieve something," he told Paul Hagen of the Fort Worth Star-Telegram. "If I had gone out to the draft last season, it would have left me with an empty feeling."

Now, with his dream career at the University of Iowa safely filed in the memory bank and the tour of award banquets over, Chuck was content to focus on participating in benefit wheelchair basketball games[1] and the NFL draft.

But the NFL scouts stayed focused on him.

"He's a highly dedicated athlete. He's had to work hard to accomplish what he has," said Brandt. "He'd come down at lunch and look at films of the previous day's practice. If there was a meeting at three, he'd be there at noon.

"He's a lot like Roger Staubach in that way. If you ask him to do five, he'll give you ten."

Chuck didn't disagree. But even on college football's biggest stage, he remained humble and receptive to any interest he received from NFL teams. He was also willing to wait his turn if the team that drafted him already had an entrenched starter.

---

[1] Chuck was one of ten Hawkeyes football players who participated in a basketball game against an Iowa Quad Cities area girls' basketball team that finished second in the state as reported in the March 30, 1986, *Wheaton Daily Journal*. Both teams played in wheelchairs with the proceeds of the benefit going to handicapped children.

"I'm excited to go anywhere. I'm a very coachable person. I can adapt to any system," he said.

Hayden Fry agreed and was willing to let everyone know about it.

"He is the most consistent passer ever to come out of college football," he said. "I've never seen a guy with his kind of temperament. He never gets angry—about an official's call, about the fans screaming, about playing eight of eleven games this season in the rain. The only time I've seen him get upset was this year at Ohio State, where he couldn't hear the snap count. He was madder than hell. I was madder than hell."

Hayden Fry continued to believe in Chuck as NFL personnel came calling. Chuck's resiliency, confidence, humility, and work ethic were tangible qualities that attracted NFL scouts like church faithful to a potluck supper.

One of those teams was Indianapolis. In need of a quarterback, the Colts were interested in the two-time all-American.

Fry wasn't sold.

"I wouldn't want to see Chuck thrown to the wolves," he told Ray Didinger of the Philadelphia Daily News. "I'd like to see him go to a strong team that could give him [pass] protection. I hate to see these kids rushed in to make up for weaknesses elsewhere."

Not surprisingly, Heisman Trophy winner Bo Jackson was at the top of most draft lists, both NFL and Major League Baseball. Other top-ranked college players getting a close look by pro football scouts included Tony Casillas of Oklahoma, Keith Byars of Ohio State, Purdue's Jim Everett, and Robbie Bosco of BYU.

The Tampa Bay Buccaneers held the first pick.[2] The Atlanta Falcons, Houston Oilers, Indianapolis Colts, and St. Louis Cardinals rounded out the first five. Out west, the Los Angeles Rams, sitting at no. 23 in the draft, were also giving out vibes that a quarterback was on their wish list.

---

[2] The Buccaneers were vocal in their interest to sign Auburn's Bo Jackson. However, Bo was upset at the franchise for, according to media reports, torpedoing his ability to play college baseball his senior season by purposely flying him to Florida for a team visit prior to the draft (which was against NCAA rules). Bo said he would not sign with Tampa Bay. And he didn't, despite being selected by the franchise as the draft's top pick. The two-star athlete eventually signed with Al Davis and the Los Angeles Raiders due in large part to a pledge by Davis to allow Bo to take the field each season with the Kansas City Royals prior to joining the NFL team halfway through the regular season.

Chuck busily traveled the country, working out and conducting interviews with prospective NFL suitors, including the Cardinals, Rams, and Pittsburgh Steelers. The Detroit Lions, Houston Oilers, and Buffalo Bills were also expected to be in the mix for securing Chuck's services.

As were the San Diego Chargers, who, with veteran Dan Fouts under center, held the thirteenth pick.

If Chuck was still on the board, admitted Ron Nay, San Diego's director of scouting, "Our pick would take a while. It would be practically impossible to pass on him.

"Realistically, he's not going to be around. There are some teams ahead of us that need quarterbacks a lot more than we do. We're not trying to do their business for them, but they'd be foolish if they passed him up."

As rumors floated and teams jostled for pick order, Chuck and his family secured the legal services of A. J. "Jack" Mills, a college classmate of his parents at the University of Oklahoma.

Mills agreed with Hayden Fry that it would be best for Chuck to sit a year. "I would rather him not have to play a lot the first year. It would be better for him to be given a year to become oriented to the pro system," he said. "I've seen a lot of quarterbacks have bad experiences because they had to start their rookie year. Ideally, a guy needs a year."

Many NFL teams, however, were in immediate need of a leader under center. A *Chicago Sun-Times* article highlighted the shortage of passing aces by stating that they had been "limping off the field faster than fair-haired youngsters had ridden to the rescue."

Joining Chuck Long, Jim Everett, Jack Trudeau, and Robbie Bosco in the mix of quarterbacks making draft conversation were Mike Norseth (Kansas), Mark Rypien (Washington State), and Doug Gaynor (Long Beach State). Only Chuck Long and Jim Everett were expected to be selected in the first round, with Bosco and Trudeau likely slated for the second or third.

"Everett will be in the top four. Long won't last much longer," predicted Kevin Lamb of the *Chicago Sun-Times*.

Chuck, he wrote, had a better stat line and possessed the much-sought-after intangibles of poise, durability, and leadership. But Everett was "the better physical specimen. He's two inches taller with a rocket arm comparable to Dan Marino and John Elway. He's also more mobile."

While some sports writers opined that Chuck's standings in the draft had slipped as a result of choosing to play a fifth year at Iowa, the majority of pundits disagreed.

"I admire Chuck Long very much," Chicago Bears personnel chief Bill Tobin told Cooper Rollow of USA Today. "His ambition and his desire to go back to Iowa were admirable. He played awfully well last year.

"He could have legitimately gotten out," added Tobin, whose Mike Ditka-coached Bears held the twenty-third pick of the first round. "But he would have ended up sitting on somebody's bench this year. So many guys want to grab the money and run. They're greedy. I admire Long's character. He helped himself."

Joe Stein of the Sporting News also sang Chuck's praises.

"Long is an extremely smart quarterback, and I'm not talking raw IQ. As far as football smarts go, Long is a lot smarter," he wrote. "I know he wasn't as high on most lists a year ago than he is now. He's gotten better and better."

Meanwhile, Iowa's deep talent pool made it likely that at least two Hawkeyes would be taken in the first round and perhaps five or more in the latter rounds. Ronnie Harmon, Larry Station, Jay Norvell, Hap Peterson, Devon Mitchell, and Mike Haight were just a sampling of the players to appear on NFL draft boards.

Stein had Harmon as a latter first-round pick with Jackson, Byars, Neal Anderson of Florida, and Anthony Toney of Texas A&M competing for early selections.

Station, Haight, and Mitchell were also expected to be drafted in the first four rounds. Peterson, Happel, and Helverson were considered late-rounders.

Chuck, as was his way, had no grand plans for draft day.[3] He was going

---

[3] Hawkeyes great Randy Duncan, who also led Iowa to the Rose Bowl his senior season and was runner-up to the Heisman Trophy, was in Chicago's Midway Airport when he learned he'd been selected by the Green Bay Packers as the top pick in the 1959 NFL draft.

to take in the proceedings from the comfort of his Iowa City apartment with roommate Hap Peterson, former teammate Jonathan Hayes, his brother David, and friends. Whenever asked his preference for where to be drafted, Chuck said he didn't care. If pressed, he admitted favoring an opportunity to play in warm weather, "someplace in the southern states." The Big Apple was also intriguing. "I wouldn't even mind playing for the Packers."

Iowa fans and draft junkies nationwide were looking forward to expanded TV coverage of the draft courtesy of ESPN. The cable channel was set to telecast eight hours of the draft beginning at 7:00 a.m. Tuesday.[4]

The Longs and the Hawkeye Nation would be watching.

SIDEBAR 1

More than thirty years after he took the field as a teammate with Chuck Long, the memories are still vivid for Pennsylvania native Mark Vlasic, who came to Iowa as a freshman in 1982 with the hopes of competing immediately for the starting job.

He was redshirted his freshman year. For the next three, he subbed sparingly. During the 1985 season, he was assigned the role of holder for kicker Rob Houghtlin.

"Sure, at the time, there's frustration when you're not the starter," said Vlasic, reminiscing about his time as a Hawkeye nearly thirty years to the day he made his first start. "But as I look back on those very special years, I'm reminded that we all arrive at crossroads in life—those times when you have the choice to travel in a different direction. We are who and what we are today

---

[4] The 1986 NFL draft was held at the Marriott Marquis Hotel. It began at 7:00 a.m. and, twelve rounds later, concluded at 2:00 a.m. the following day. Today, the draft is a four-day must-see global TV event with hundreds of hours of coverage by numerous networks.

because of the paths we chose to take."

Vlasic said when it's time to make a decision, take your time and trust your gut.

"Today, it's all about immediate gratification. But sometimes success is defined after the fact, when you have a chance to look back and take inventory of what you were able to achieve. Time has a way of making you more aware of what success looks like and appreciative of what you've been able to accomplish."

Vlasic held the utmost respect for his coaches and teammates, a tangible and heartfelt appreciation that resonated from the stories he told of his time at Iowa.

"The guys who wore the uniform during that special time became best friends. You grew up with them. There's really no other environment like that.

"People sometimes ask me how many guys I met in the pros that I still hang out with. And I reply that the best friends I ever had were the guys from Iowa City. We lived in the Slater dorm together for four or five straight years when you're eighteen-plus years of age doing all the same things together."

Vlasic, who today serves as a senior wealth advisor with Mariner Wealth Advisors in Leawood, Kansas, is "excited as heck and grateful" for the opportunity given to him at Iowa. Not because it was easy. But because he persevered.

"How many can say they had the opportunity to start at a Big Ten school and play on a team that's ranked number one in the country?

"But no matter what, the task at hand in the game of football is to step up and be a leader and to do what's best for the team," he added. "To this day, what I find amazing about football is that you're always competing against somebody for a job for the better of the team. It didn't matter whether it was at Iowa or San Diego Chargers or Kansas City Chiefs or the Tampa Bay Buccaneers. Even when you're competing for a job, never once do you withhold any information from the guy who's trying to take your job or the guy whose job you're trying take. I always found that incredible. Nowhere else would you give your competition all the ammo to come around and beat you with it. But that's your job.

"When Chuck would come off the field, I'd say, 'Chuck, here's what I saw.' You share with them because the objective is for the team to come out victorious. It's about putting the team and the others ahead of you. That's not unlike my time spent with the Boy Scouts and teaching a class on leadership. The topic was being a servant leader. And that one just struck me as so surreal because, as a football team, servant leadership is the most important component. And I think it was believing in the team, wanting to be part of a team, a team that was going to be number one in 1985.

"To this day, I take every bit as much pride in the fact that I was a part of that team that was ranked as high as number one in 1985 and played in the Rose Bowl and starting the following year and being named the Holiday Bowl MVP in the 1986 Holiday Bowl. To me, that all was the result of being a good leader. You're not out there for 'me.' You're out there for 'us.' That's a role I embraced."

With the twelfth pick in the 1986 NFL draft, the Detroit Lions selected Chuck Long, quarterback, University of Iowa.[5]

And with that, the boy who had played game after game of pickup football on The Tot Lot in Wheaton, who had received just three scholarship offers to play college football, who was benched following his first collegiate start, was now a member of the National Football League's Detroit Lions.

And no one was more surprised than Chuck.

"It seems like just the other day I was being recruited out of high school," he told the *Detroit Free Press'* Tommy George. "All of a sudden, especially in the last year, I've graduated, gone to the Rose Bowl, and made the pros in the first round. I've gone from eighteen to twenty-three years old, and I'm wondering how did everything happen so fast in-between?"

The Motor City suited Wheaton North's first NFL draft choice just fine.

"Detroit's a great city," he added after his name was called less than two hours into the nineteen-hour marathon. "I've been there a couple of times. I'd love to play for Detroit. They've got that big indoor stadium out of the cold. I love Midwestern fans. I love being in the Midwest. This whole year has been a dream come true for me."

The Lions weren't sure Chuck would drop to twelve, but they pounced when he did. They called him just ten minutes before making the selection.

He was the second quarterback taken in the draft. As anticipated by most NFL scouts, Jim Everett of Purdue went off the board early as no. 3 to the Houston Oilers.

Detroit head coach Darryl Rogers was ecstatic about the selection.

"I believe quarterback is the start of a franchise," he said. "Chuck is our man."

While Chuck didn't expect to start right away (Eric Hippel was the incumbent), he was comfortable to be drafted by a team where he could develop without the heat of trial by fire.

---

[5] The Lions selected three Iowans in the 1986 draft. In addition to Chuck, defensive back Devon Mitchell was chosen in the fourth round; in the tenth round, Detroit chose Trace Johnson, inside linebacker from Morningside College (Sioux City).

"It all depends on the system," he said. "I think it takes a while. Going from college to the pros is like going from high school to college. It's a step up into better competition."

In other words, Chuck was approaching the next step in his "destined for greatness" journey with his lunch pail in hand.

The Iowa grad who always wanted to be his best was the first quarterback selected by the Lions in the first round since 1968 when they chose Greg Landry of the University of Massachusetts–Amherst.

"We're all stunned he's going to Detroit because we had heard so much about him winding up with the Colts," said Joan Long. "Chuck has always been mature, but it seems he went from a little boy to a man overnight."

In addition to his parents, Chuck made sure to share the news with his brothers, David and Andy.

"I talked to him [Andy] today," said Chuck, referring to his teenage brother who has cerebral palsy. "I don't think he really knows what's going on, but he's excited anyway. Andy is the ultimate sports fan. Our relationship is very special.

"I guess the one thing I've learned from him is how football should be a fun game, how it should not become the game of life. I lose a game and walk off the field and it seems like the end of the world," Chuck added. "And then I see Andy outside the locker room smiling. You say, 'What am I down about?'"

For Iowa, the draft was a validation of the team's ascent, with three Hawkeyes selected in the opening round: Chuck at no. 12, Harmon no. 16 (Buffalo Bills), and Mike Haight no. 22 (New York Jets). Others with Iowa ties selected in the '86 draft included Hawkeye Devon Mitchel (fourth round), Jim Luebbers of Iowa State (ninth round), and Tracy Johnson, Morningside College (tenth round).

Having three Hawkeyes selected in the first twenty-two picks was also a validation of Hayden Fry's success in transitioning a program from the depths of despair to a launching pad for pro talent. [6]

"The one word I would select in trying to express my views of three

Hawks getting chosen in the first round is 'fantastic,'" exclaimed Fry to *Cedar Rapids Gazette* sportswriter Mike Hlas.

"It was a fun day with a lot of twist and turns," said Chuck. "I thought maybe Pittsburgh would nab me given we had visited a lot; I thought the Chargers may have also made a pass, but neither did.

"It's always been a dream of mine to be drafted in the first round," he added. "The Lions flat-out told me they didn't think I'd be around when they made their pick. I'm just happy to be going there."

And Hayden Fry couldn't have been more pleased with the fate that awaited the boy he had said was destined for greatness more than five years earlier.

"Chuck's a winner," he told Jack McCarthy of the *Wheaton Daily Journal.* "He has all the ingredients [for success]. From a personal standpoint, I don't have to sell Chuck Long, he sells himself. It might not be the first year or the second, but eventually, Chuck Long will be the no. 1 quarterback in Detroit. He'll also be an outstanding quarterback in the NFL."

While Chuck wanted to get to work, there were a few minor details to work out first. Like the Iowa graduate and the Detroit Lions coming to terms.

Progress on a long-term contract for the league's twelfth overall pick was stalled. NFL owners were reluctant to sign first-year players to lucrative deals. The United States Football League (USFL), launched in 1983 with great fanfare, was beginning to hemorrhage talent and financial resources.

With the USFL on shaky ground, less competition for talent transitioning from college to the pros meant NFL owners could be stingier with signing offers than the previous year.

Jack Mills told the *Des Moines Register's* Tom Witosky that the offer failed to acknowledge "the pay scale for quarterbacks in the NFL." The Lions' ownership countered that its offer was commensurate with salaries offered to other NFL rookie QBs.

---

[6] Hayden Fry's ability to hire quality assistant coaches became legendary. Twenty-nine assistants he hired while serving as head coach at SMU, North Texas, and Iowa became head coaches in either college or professional football. "My father had a lot of words of wisdom," Fry recalled. "When I was nine or ten years old, he told me, 'Son, I don't know what you're going to become or do when you grow up, but if you're going to be successful, if you're going to be a winner, you gotta surround yourself with winners.'" In 2015, two of the nation's top college football coaches—Oklahoma University's Bobby Stoops and the University of Iowa's Kirk Ferentz at Iowa—were former assistant coaches of Fry's.

If the two sides reached an impasse, the Lions would risk losing their rights to Chuck, making him eligible for the 1987 NFL draft.

The pressure was on the Lions. The team was 11–20–1 in its previous two seasons and eager to make the playoffs after a 7–9 campaign in 1985.

"Play Chuck Long right now," wrote Jerry Green of the *Detroit News*. "Rewrite the playbook for him if necessary. Put him through a cram course. Go out and find him some pass receivers who can burn up the sidelines. Give him the football and let him throw."

Green added that for the first time in years, "the Lions have the opportunity to stir pro football excitement in Detroit. They have the chance to rock the town with anticipation and reverie. Chuck Long is a proven winner in the image of a Bobby Layne, blond hair and all. The Super Bowl is not tomorrow for the Lions, or this season. But if Chuck Long is permitted to play now, the Lions will be starting their way there."

Lions fans were hungry for a winner. Overall, they were pleased with the team's draft selections. Now it was time to get them signed and working out. Another NFL campaign was rapidly approaching—a road trip to Minnesota September 7.

Chuck Long was hungry, too.

"It's a brand-new life for me," he quipped. "I'm going to be like a freshman all over again. That's what it's all about.

"I want to come in and learn as much as I can in my first year," added Chuck, who would wear no. 16 for the Lions—the same number he had donned as an Iowa Hawkeye. "I don't feel any pressure now. If I don't feel comfortable with the offense, I don't think I'll play well. As a quarterback, you want to come in and learn the first year, especially with Joe Ferguson and Eric Hipple. They've been around a while. When I'm ready [to start], the coaches will know, the guys will know."

Chuck wasn't the only NFL draftee awaiting a deal. Few contracts were being offered or signed by NFL teams due to uncertainty shrouding the USFL as it struggled under the weight of a $1.5 billion antitrust suit brought by the NFL. As a result, the available talent pool for NFL teams was deepening.

Only four of the NFL's twenty-seven first-round draft picks had received opening offers within a week of the draft: Tony Casillas with Atlanta, Brian Jozwiak with Kansas City, John L. Williams with Seattle, and Joe Kelly with Cincinnati. Agents were working the phones and trying to stay relevant as NFL owners watched and waited for the lawsuit to proceed.

"There's a united effort by all teams to reduce the contracts even more than they reduced them last year," Mills said. "I don't think the owners are all that worried about holdouts. They want to establish some precedents. They don't think there's competition now from the USFL."

CHARGERS PASS

Detroit's drafting of Chuck—and the Chargers' decision to pass—mystified the former Iowa Hawkeye.

Here's how it played out.

San Diego possessed two first-round picks—nos. 8 and 13—and the word was they would seek to sign a breakout player on both offense and defense. They were highly interested in Chuck as the draft approached, summoning him to California twice for workouts.

"They told me they were very interested in drafting me; actually, they showed the most interest of any team," Long recalls. "Dan Fouts, their quarterback, led the most prolific offense in the NFL at the time, but he was aging. So I was excited to go to San Diego. It was an ideal situation and a place I always wanted to play, especially with the chance to learn under Dan and to play in their wide-open offensive scheme.

"Detroit was sitting there with the number twelve pick but with a slew of quarterbacks on the roster. I really didn't give much thought to going to Detroit, and they didn't give any indication that they were all that interested in bringing another quarterback into the fold.

"So I'm sitting in my apartment in Iowa City having a small party with my brothers and teammates and the picks are unwinding, including Leslie O'Neil, who Detroit selected with their first pick. Most thought Pittsburgh needed a quarterback at number nine, but they pass and take a guard. I'm feeling more confident that I'm going to San Diego, and just then, the phone rings. It's San Diego, and they say, "Chuck, if you're still available at number thirteen, we're taking you." And that was the kiss of death because two picks later, the Lions call my name.

"But you take the cards you're dealt and move full bore ahead. And I did. Turns out Detroit was a good place to play and have a career in the NFL."

"I understand enough [about sports] to know that life is going to work out very well for Chuck. He has a lot of energy. He's peppy, really happy, outgoing. When he has an occasional chance to stay home and rest, he never does. He's always out playing golf or socializing. He really likes people."

JOAN LONG
in a conversation with the Chicago Tribune's *Cooper Rollow,*
June 19, 1986

Chuck wasn't one for sitting still. So he kept active while waiting to play for the Lions.

"Chuck was not the type to spend a lot of time in his room," Joan Long told the *Chicago Tribune's* Cooper Rollow when asked the kind of boy he was growing up. "He never had a lot of time to read. He couldn't sit still long enough. Even as a baby, he loved to be moving around."

Given his nonstop motor and interest in all sports, Joan Long knew her son would excel in athletics from the time he could dribble a basketball. Maybe younger.

"We didn't think he was as good as he turned out be," she added. "But he was well coordinated and played everything that moved, including ice hockey.

"I'm not a good judge of talent, just a mom," she told Rollow matter-of-factly. "It's been kind of a surprise that he's been as good as he has been."

Joan Long also told Rollow that the Lions' selection of Chuck was a good one for her son.

"He was very happy when they drafted him. It's a Midwest team, he loves the domed stadium and the opportunity to play inside, and he likes Darryl Rogers and the coaching staff. Right now, he's without a contract, but so is everybody else from what I read."

While contract negotiations continued, Chuck and his longtime girlfriend were planning for the future. And a doting mother didn't hesitate to let everyone know.

"He dated a lot in high school and in college," offered Joan Long in her conversation with Rollow. "And now he's become engaged to his high school sweetheart.

"Her name is Lisa Wells, and she used to live right around the corner from us. She's...just a darling girl with lots of personality. Just right for Chuck. The wedding is scheduled for next June."

With Lisa Wells going to work on wedding plans, Chuck packed his bags in Iowa City and returned to the family home in Wheaton.

"It's kind of sad leaving here [Iowa City]," he told Mike O'Hara of the *Detroit News*. "It's been a good home for me for the last five years. I'm going to miss it. I made a lot of friends here. I'm going to miss them, too."

While Chuck awaited his first snap as a Lion, Bo Jackson was on his way to stardom. After being selected no. 1 by Tampa Bay, he spurned the

Buccaneers and signed a lucrative deal with the Kansas City Royals.

"Money isn't everything," said Chuck when asked if the next pay day would be his.

"It's just a game. In the end, who cares if you win or lose? Ten years from now, who's going to remember? There's more to life than football. I love the game, but I realize that's all it is."

CHUCK LONG
on keeping football in perspective ("After a Long wait, an all-American boy," Ray Didinger, Philadelphia Daily News, *Feb. 19, 1986)*

Patience and perspective, qualities that served Chuck well as a top-tier quarterback, also came in handy following draft day.

"They [the coaches] told me that they would be patient with me," said Chuck when asked if the delay in signing would hinder his chances to vie for the starting job. "I have a long way to go in learning their playbooks. If I'm going to sign with them, I'd like to do it before they open their regular training camp."

The Baltimore Stars of the USFL weren't as patient. Despite the league's ongoing war with the NFL, the champion Stars wanted to do business. So Chuck traveled to Baltimore to meet with Stars management and visit Memorial Stadium, home of the USFL franchise.

Memorial Stadium, also home of the MLB's Baltimore Orioles, was a big-league stadium where another record-setting quarterback named Johnny Unitas had held court for the NFL's Baltimore Colts.

While holding a short press conference near home plate (it was baseball season, after all), Chuck assured reporters that he was not using time in the Monument City as leverage against the Lions.

"I'm just exploring my opportunities," he said.

Interest from a professional team like the Stars was gratifying for Chuck and other NFL draftees in similar predicaments. But uncertainty about the USFL's future made many players anxious about signing. Would the USFL defy the odds and reign victorious over the NFL? If so, would the USFL grow in stature, and would a bump in player salaries come with it? Or would the USFL go under, leaving players scrambling to find work?

It was anyone's guess. But deep down, Chuck was fond of his Midwestern roots. Detroit was a quick drive from Wheaton. And playing in the climate-controlled Pontiac Silverdome was an enviable attraction, especially considering the rigors of playing against the likes of the Vikings, Bears, and Packers come November and December.

While the situation played out, Chuck continued to win awards. This time, it was the Big Ten Conference Men's Athlete of the Year. Chuck edged out Purdue quarterback Jim Everett.

Lifting weights and playing basketball, racquetball, and golf were getting tedious. Nearly three months had passed since draft day. And with July quickly waning, Chuck and the Lions had still not come to terms.

"Chuck Long, despite all his college credentials and clippings, is not coming to the Lions as a savior. He is coming only as a talented young man with untapped potential."

CHARLIE VINCENT
Detroit Free Press *("Long negotiations over, a career about to begin," Aug. 19, 1986)*

"I'm glad to be in camp and glad to have it over with."

The former "Tot Lot" star, Illinois state high school football champ, and record-setting Iowa Hawkeyes quarterback was officially a Detroit Lion.

"I'm happy to be here and get started," said a relieved Chuck Long after stepping to the microphone for a rare weekday afternoon news conference shortly after agreeing to a deal. "I think it's going to be the start of a good, long relationship."

Chuck, who was accompanied by his fiancée Lisa Wells and agent Jack Mills, had given the thumbs-up to a four-year deal.

Following a physical and signing the required paperwork, Chuck was finally taking snaps under the dome with his new teammates.

"I've only been here a couple of hours, and some of the guys are calling me 'new meat,'" Chuck laughed. "As a matter of fact, I've been practicing singing. I've got a feeling that tonight I'm going to have to do some singing at dinner."

In addition to learning new songs, Chuck needed time to familiarize himself with the playbook, lose the rust, and get into football shape. But he was up to the challenge.

"I knew I'd be in camp sooner or later," he added, saying his fiancée had predicted the deal would happen after scanning the day's horoscope that said some sort of business deal would be consummated by week's end. "I'm glad to be here, and I'm happy to play in a sports town. I can't wait to get started."

Now it was all about getting into the flow of a pro football program and earning the trust of the players and coaches.

"I'm probably a little bit out of shape, and I still have a lot of playbook time to get in," Chuck admitted as the team prepared for its third preseason game versus Indianapolis. "As a quarterback, you've got to get your timing down, and that takes a while. That's probably the one thing I lost, but it will come around sooner or later.

"I don't expect the coaches to bend over backward to take me aside and teach me the plays I missed," he added, acknowledging that he had missed forty-one practices. "They're just gonna keep going with the veterans. I'll watch the veterans as much as I can and pick up where they are. They're probably pretty far ahead, so I've got a long way to go."

Most sportswriters assumed that whatever chance Chuck had to compete for the starting job had evaporated due to the tardy signing. But that also assumed the Lions would be playoff contenders.

A more likely scenario based on recent history, however, was a team that would struggle to be competitive. In fact, the Lions' frequent struggle to be competitive seemed to be an ideal and familiar one for Chuck, wrote Curt Sylvester of the *Detroit Free Press*.

"My freshman year we went to the Rose Bowl, and we've been going to bowl games ever since. This is the same thing. They bring in a new coach; he's real low key, and you get the feeling he's going to turn things around.

"That's the kind of program a lot of athletes like to be a part of," Chuck added. "When you go to a winner all the time, like maybe the Raiders or the Dolphins, you're probably under a lot more pressure to win. Here, there's pressure to win, but it's an up-and-coming team. It's a team that needs to be turned around to start going to the playoffs. That can be done."

No doubt, a dream of Chuck's had been realized. But now it all boiled down to performance.

"The novelty of me being around will wear off. People get excited about the number one draft pick, but the novelty runs out. You've got to win for 'em. It's either win or lose."

So could he turn it around in Detroit?

Not likely, wrote Jerry Green of the *Detroit News*. He mused that once again the Lions had managed to fumble and bumble a good thing—the twelfth-pick selection of Chuck Long.

"The Lions keep creating their own tragedies," Green lamented. "On draft day last April, there was excitement gripping the Lions." But with Chuck relegated to the sidelines in sweats and not ready to play, "the Lions will enter [the new season] with nothing new. They'll enter it without glamor, without some magic, without much to stir the emotions of their fans."

Lions coaches agreed it would likely be five or six weeks into the regular season before Chuck would be seasoned enough to take a game-time snap.

Only time—and a lot of hard work—would tell.

> "When a team scores only seven points, maybe it's time to think about getting someone else in there."

HAYDEN FRY

when asked about Chuck's lack of playing time in Detroit following the Lion's 31–7 loss versus the Dallas Cowboys in the second game of the 1986 NFL season

It had been a long time since the 1960s, when the Lions played hard-nosed football and had something to show for the effort. Little was expected of the 1986 version of the Detroit Lions given the competitiveness of its division and a modest budget that limited the team's ability to attract big-time playmakers.

For better or worse and through thick (and mostly) thin, Detroit fans were a loyal bunch. But they were also growing hungry for respectability and a winning pedigree. Chuck Long, it was hoped, would be the guy to help change Detroit's fortunes.

A 13–10 win over Minnesota to begin the season was a nice start, but reality bit in week two when the Cowboys came to town and stomped the home team 31–7.

Detroit Free Press' George Puscus wrote that fans began chanting "We want Long! We want Long!" midway through the third quarter.

"It began as a chant from a throng of 73,812 and quickly swelled into a crescendo that engulfed the Lions and head coach Darryl Rogers.

"We want Long! We want Long!"

Long, however, stood on the sidelines holding a clipboard.

"There'll be a day I'm in there," Chuck said after the game, "and they'll be chanting for somebody else."

And maybe sooner than later. Chuck was improving with each practice. It was now mid-September, and in just one month under the tutelage of Detroit's staff, his timing was improving, he was releasing passes more quickly, and his arm was strengthening.

"As I get more comfortable with the offense, I think maybe I'll be ready to play sooner than you think," he told Curt Sylvester of the *Detroit Free Press*. "Not that they'll start me, but I'm learning a lot quicker than I thought I would."

Much of Chuck's time was spent throwing one-on-one drills with receivers and helping break down and replicate opponent pass plays. He was also watching game film on his own.

"I have a lot of confidence in my ability, but I don't have a lot of confidence in my ability to run the offense now," Chuck confided in Sylvester. "That's a big difference.... If he puts me in now, I wouldn't set the world on fire. If he puts me in now, we'd probably call all running plays."

Perhaps. But truth be told, the running game wasn't exactly setting the house on fire for the Lions, either.

The Bucs, considered one of the weakest teams in the NFL, came to Detroit in week three, jumped out to a 24–6 lead and left a 24–20 winner. Less than thirty-nine thousand fans showed up, the smallest crowd to see a regular season game since the Silverdome opened in 1975.

Charlie Vincent of the *Detroit Free Press* was convinced that fans knew Chuck wouldn't quarterback the team for months. But if just the thought of the former Hawkeye taking the field gave them a reason to show up in the Silverdome, well, so be it.

"If it helps you get your $15.50 worth to scream for Chuck Long, feel free. This is a free country," he penned. "But you really ought to know you're wasting your time and vocal chords. And you ought to know, too, that Chuck Long is among those who think what you're doing is counterproductive."

"I wish they wouldn't," admitted Chuck. "I think it's really getting annoying to the other guys."

Eric Hipple took the serenade in stride.

"I asked him [Chuck] if I could borrow his jersey," Hipple said with a laugh and a broken nose courtesy of a Tampa Bay defender.

Chuck admitted he was initially flattered to hear his name chanted from the stands. "It was nice at first," he said. "Now it isn't."

With Detroit's hopes fading with each Sunday loss, the question wasn't whether Chuck would go under center his first year, but when.

"Detroit has the only NFL team with a wide receiver whose surname fits its offense. Carl Bland."
TERRY BOERS
Chicago Sun Times, *Oct. 6, 1986*

Detroit fans were a dejected bunch. The home team had had just two winning seasons in the previous thirteen. Things didn't look to improve anytime soon as the 1986 campaign was off to an abysmal 1–3 start.

With betting odds favoring yet another losing season, the quarterback of the future hadn't taken a regular season snap. The closest Chuck had come to zinging a pass across the Silverdome's fake grass was versus Dallas. With the game out of reach and the fourth quarter growing long in the tooth, Chuck began warming up in anticipation of taking the field. Much to the disappointment of the hometown crowd, however, the Cowboys ate the remainder of the clock. Chuck remained anchored on the sidelines. The Wheaton boy's first snap in the pros would have to wait for another day.

"Forget any outside chance for the playoffs," surmised Bruce Johns of Pro Football. "Who cares about respectability? This team's future rests entirely with the talents of one Charles Franklin Long, and the time is now. Do whatever it takes to get their No. 1 draft choice ready as soon as possible.

"Let's face it," added Johns, "Long was drafted to be the Lions' quarterback for—like his name says—a long time. He brings talent, skill, and ability at a position that has handicapped the Lions for many a season."

Then, Detroit surprised. Wins versus the Houston Oilers (24–13) and Green Bay Packers (21–14) improved the team's record to 3–4.

But a 14–10 loss at the Los Angeles Rams blunted the momentum, stalling the Lions at 3–5 at the season's halfway point.

A level-headed Chuck Long took it all in stride, content with watching and learning.

"If everybody's patient, things will work out in the end. If we get a good winning streak or if we start to lose some games, maybe I'll see some time. It depends on a lot of things. I want to play. I want to win."

———————

"When things aren't going very well, he'll say, 'Don't worry, everything's going to work out.' And it always does. He's always right. But I'm the ultimate pessimist. I always think it's going to end someday. He thinks it'll never end."

LISA LONG
commenting on her husband's uncanny ability for seeing the best in every situation ("With lady luck at his side, Chuck Long faces the challenge of his athletic career," Tom Kowalski, Oakland Sunday Magazine, July 26, 1987)

It was Nov. 10, one day removed from the Lions' seventh loss in ten games, a 24–10 loss against conference rival Minnesota.

"He's much closer now than he was before," said Coach Rogers when asked for the one-millionth time if Chuck was ready to play. "Every day and every practice, he gets closer. But it always depends on who you're playing and what the circumstances are."

Just six regular season games remained—visits to Philadelphia, Tampa Bay, and Pittsburgh and home dates versus Green Bay, Atlanta, and the world champion Chicago Bears.

Syndicated sports columnist Mitch Albom, visiting with Chuck over lunch prior to the Eagles matchup, was impressed with the rookie's candor when asked if he should be starting.

"I think Darryl's done the right thing," said Chuck while enjoying an order of chicken fingers. "He has to decide if I've earned my starting role, he has to be fair to players who didn't miss camp like I did."

"Are you at all worried that when you finally do play you'll disappoint?" asked Albom.

"Well, everyone wants to see the new guy. They have to realize I'm human. I'm not comfortable with every situation yet. I may not be the savior they're looking for right off the bat.

"There'll be a point in my career here when they'll be calling for the other guy, too. That's just the way it is."

No doubt that he would play, mused Albom after he picked up the check. "He will get his feet wet. He will wake up sore on Monday mornings sooner or later."

With Detroit all but eliminated from the playoffs, most every fan, writer, and NFL junkie expected the rookie to see playing time when the team faced the Eagles in its next game. All indications were that he was getting closer to being shoved from the nest.

Then, on Nov. 12, Chuck's stock as the Lions' potential starter took another step forward, if only for a day, when Hipple sat during practice with a sore elbow. Chuck ran the offense, sharing time with veteran Joe Ferguson.

Yet the Lions' next game versus Philadelphia came and went with no Chuck Long sighting. Instead, veteran Joe Ferguson led the team to a 13–11 victory over the Buddy Ryan-coached Eagles. The victory was capped by a forty-one-yard field goal by kicker Ed Murray.

The win only added to the starting quarterback rumor mill as the team prepared to travel to sunny Florida to face the Buccaneers.

"For 11 games, three quarters, 12 minutes and 54 seconds of his first NFL season, Chuck Long waited. And then, with one swing of his right arm, the Lions rookie quarterback made the wait worthwhile."

CURT SYLVESTER
Detroit Free Press, *Nov. 24, 1986*

"Let's go downtown, guys."

And with that, the Lions broke the huddle with just over two minutes remaining versus divisional rival Tampa Bay.

Chuck was about to take his first snap in the National Football League. The score was 31–17, and the ball rested at the Buccaneers' thirty-four-yard line. Just a few thousand of the nearly thirty thousand fans who were present at kickoff still remained in the sun-drenched stadium. Tampa Bay quarterback Steve Young[7] had gotten tossed around by the Lions, ultimately finishing the game twenty-two of thirty-two for just 218 yards.

But now the ball was in Chuck's hands, and after three successive handoffs to fullback Scott Williams, his first pass would come on, of all things, a fourth-and-four.

In his NFL debut—playing for a total of twenty-three seconds—Chuck managed one pass, a strike to wideout Leonard Thompson that went the distance for a thirty-four-yard touchdown strike.[8]

The team mobbed the rookie as he made his way to the end zone.

For a boy who didn't care when he took his first snap with the Lions, he certainly made it count when it happened.

"One pass. One catch. One touchdown," wrote Mitch Albom.

"It felt good just to go back on a football field," Chuck admitted enthusiastically to a swarm of reporters gathered for postgame interviews.

---

[7] Young was a 1985 draft pick of the Bucs. However, the team could muster just two wins in each of his first two seasons while the quarterback compiled a record of just three for sixteen as a starter. Young's resume included nearly twice as many interceptions (twenty-one) as touchdowns (eleven) while completing just a whisker better than half his pass attempts. On the others side of the country, San Francisco 49ers head coach Bill Walsh thought the BYU and Salt Lake City, Utah, product was just what his team needed. After the 1986 season, Tampa Bay was ready to move on and traded Young to San Francisco and selected University of Miami quarterback Vinny Testaverde as the first overall pick in the 1987 NFL draft. Young went on to play thirteen years with the 49ers. He was a three-time Super Bowl champion, Super Bowl MVP, seven-time Pro Bowler (including three-time first team), and was twice the NFL's Most Valuable Player. His no. 8 49ers jersey was retired Oct. 5, 2008.

[8] "It was a typical bomb on a go route on the left side and it went flawlessly," recalled Chuck. And although it was his first NFL touchdown pass, it wasn't the only memorable throw that afternoon. As was customary, Chuck was tossing pregame warm-up throws with fellow QB Joe Ferguson. All was going well until Joe's attention was momentarily diverted. In that split second, a sharp throw by Chuck was on target, nailing the veteran quarterback squarely between the eyes. Ferguson dropped to the ground. Chuck quickly approached. Joe, shaking his head, retorted, "Damn, boy, if you want to play that bad today, why didn't you just tell me!" It was a humbling experience, Chuck said. "When I saw Joe drop to the ground, all I could think was 'Oh my God, I just put our starting quarterback out of the game.' But he ended up playing a pretty good game, and we left Tampa with a win."

"After they called that pass, I said, 'Thank God it's a bomb.' I went into the huddle and told everybody, 'Let's go downtown.' They wanted me to. It felt great.

"It's a big thrill," Chuck added. "I didn't really see the catch. Then I saw the referees, and I said, 'All right! Yeah! I like that.'"

Shelby Strother, sports columnist for the *Detroit News*, liked what he saw.

"In the final 1:43 of a game long since decided, the Detroit Lions unpacked the future and let him start happening," he wrote. "Chuck Long's first official pass as a pro stuck in the chest of Leonard Thompson. A touchdown. It's OK if you don't wipe your feet on the welcome mat. But shouldn't someone who's never been on the premises before at least ring the doorbell once?

"How do you like him so far, Detroit?" Strother asked rhetorically. "In your eye, Jim Everett. Hey, Mr. Rozelle, is this all there is to it?

"It was the first pass in the Chuck Long Era, and it blazed through the balmy Florida sky, surely scorching the ozone, definitely piercing reality, positively splitting perspective in two," Strother continued, as if unleashing a bevy of pent-up superlatives to describe the frosh QB. "Now, gravity has lost its grip. Motown is somewhere over the rainbow. The kid has landed. And taken off. And we're all soaring through the clouds with him, holding onto his kite tails, drunk with wild expectations."

What else was there to say?

With the Chuck Long era in Detroit officially started, albeit with a heavy dose of hyperbole (the headline on the front page of the Nov. 25 *Detroit Free Press* sports section read, "He's perfect! So start him!"), many now wondered if he would be tabbed the starter.

The Lions, as much a mainstay on Thanksgiving Day as turkey, stuffing, and cranberry sauce, prepared to host the Packers for some holiday football.

That idea, however, disappeared as quickly as a piece of pumpkin pie.

"I told Chuck if he wanted to play to just ask me."

Lions' starting quarterback Joe Ferguson after suffering a circular bruise on the bridge of his nose courtesy of an errant warm-up throw by Chuck Long in Detroit's win over Tampa Bay. Moments later, Chuck hit wideout Leonard Thompson for a thirty-four-yard touchdown on his first NFL pass attempt.

"If Chuck Long helps us win, we'll play Chuck Long. If it won't help us, we won't play Chuck Long, no matter what the people upstairs say," replied Lions' coach Darryl Rogers when asked if Chuck was ready to be Detroit's starting quarterback when the team took the field against Green Bay Thanksgiving Day.

Chuck wanted to play. But he also respected the chain of command.

"There's no reason to be any change," he said. "Joe [Ferguson] is on a winning streak. Just because I threw one pass late in the game doesn't mean I should play automatically."

And he didn't. A 44–40 loss in a shootout versus the Packers followed by a 27–17 defeat at the hands of the Steelers in Pittsburgh left Detroit at 5–9 on the season. Playoff aspirations were vanquished.

Just two games remained, and both were at home—a rematch versus the world champion Chicago Bears on Monday night and the season's capper versus the Atlanta Falcons.

Rumors that Chuck would start versus Chicago began the day after Detroit's loss to Pittsburgh.

And fans and sports writers were almost giddy at the thought.

"The Lions' 1986 season is broken beyond repair," wrote Mike O'Hara of the *Detroit News.* "But they could use a fix at the box office. Only one player can pump any life into the end of the season: Chuck Long.

"Let's forget football for a while and think about putting on a show," he suggested. "It's time to give the home fans a little action. Get the crowd out of the doldrums. Put some life in the Silverdome— for a change."

O'Hara admitted that the decision had nothing to do with football strategy but everything to do with sports entertainment.

"Lions' fans don't get much to cheer about. So start the kid."

Rogers, who promised to decide on a starter by Thursday at the latest, admitted that starting Chuck would "give the guys on Monday Night Football something to talk about."

Adding to the uncertainty was an intestinal flu that had gotten to Chuck while in Pittsburgh.

O'Hara and others scoffed at the notion that Chuck should be protected from the likes of Bears defensive starters Richard Dent, Dan Hampton, Steve McMichael, William "The Refrigerator" Perry, and Mike Singletary. True, the fearsome fivesome and its supporting cast had made minced meat of many quarterbacks. And no doubt they relished the opportunity to hit "new meat"—a.k.a. QB Chuck Long.

Yet on-the-job training against the league's best football team was just what the rookie wanted and needed. Even if the opponent was the Mike Ditka-led Bears who stood at 12–2 on the season and were poised to win a second Lombardi Trophy in as many years.

By midweek, Chuck's health had improved. He felt strong and was ready for battle, even if it would be against the league's top-ranked defense and potentially lethal pass rush that had racked up forty-nine sacks on the season.

"You've got to start somewhere," he told O'Hara. "Sometimes it's good to start off against the best. You've got to play them sooner or later.

"The game's on national TV," he added. "If I get to start, there'll be a lot of people watching."

By Thursday, the waiting and wondering were over. Chuck, who had played just four professional downs in mop-up, would take the field for his first professional start Monday night versus Chicago.

"It's nice to know," quipped Chuck, who, surprisingly, had not been much of a Bears fan as a youngster despite growing up less than an hour away from Soldier Field. "The pressure will be off because we're five for nine and out of the playoffs. It will be a big challenge.

"I'm going to need a lot of help," he admitted. "But it would be a dream come true if we can go out and win against the Bears."

The prime-time start didn't appear to affect Chuck, reported Bill Halls of the *Detroit News*. Nor did the prospects of failure.

"If I throw some interceptions, so be it," he told Halls. "I'm not going to worry about it. I've always got the next play or I can learn from the game films. I'll never have a firm foundation unless I get experience. You can practice all you want, but you can't trade anything for experience."

For Chuck, football remained just a game. The kid from Wheaton had an uncanny ability to keep the game and the big moments it contained in perspective.

"I'm trying not to get caught up in the whole situation," Chuck told O'Hara of the *Detroit News*. "I'm staying away from the telephone, the newspapers, and the sportscasts that are getting caught up in it. I'm trying to keep the right mental frame of mind.

"Every game's a big game, especially at the pro level. But I'm just going to take it like another game. Football is a game, if you make it fun, win or lose."

Ditka, the leader of the flamboyant yet supremely talented Bears, was pleased for Chuck.

"It's a great opportunity," said Ditka, who himself was mired in a quarterback controversy involving second-year players Doug Flutie and Mike Tomczak. "Joe Ferguson has played well for Detroit, but I guess he's banged up. It's an opportunity for Darryl to see what Long can do. I just hope he doesn't do too much."

Added Dan Pompei of the *Chicago Sun-Times*, "Long's assignment against the Bears isn't a matter of comfort so much as it's a matter of survival. Young quarterbacks are delicacies to the defense."

Lisa Wells had waited a long time to hear the five words.

However, "Lisa, will you marry me?" just didn't seem to be part of Chuck's vocabulary.

For thirteen years, they dated.

For thirteen years, Lisa Wells traveled the long (no pun intended) and winding road that comes with dating a star athlete.

For thirteen years, she endured stops and starts in their relationship. Something other than getting engaged always came up—like the end of one football season and the start of another. Graduations. An NFL draft. And moves to a new city and state.

Thirteen years was indeed a long time.

But for those thirteen years, love blossomed. There were little league games and walks along the sidewalks of Wheaton. There was high school prom. Lisa Wells enrolled in Iowa State University in Ames, only to transfer to Iowa to be closer to Chuck and attend game days in Iowa City with Chuck and their families.

She loved Chuck; his sense of humor, his personality, and how he could walk into a room and make it light up.

"He's just like his dad," she often said. "And he has a lot of his mom's qualities, too."

Now, thirteen years later, with a college football career, bowl games, and the NFL draft in the rearview mirror, Chuck posed the question in the privacy of Lisa Wells' Iowa City apartment.

"Lisa, will you marry me?"

It was about time.

She didn't hesitate to say yes.[9]

On June 6, 1987, Chuck Long and Lisa Wells were married in an afternoon ceremony at Trinity Episcopal Church in Wheaton. A reception at the Evanston Golf Club in Skokie, Illinois, followed. The couple soon established a home in Bloomfield Hills, Michigan.

Fast forward thirty years. A lot had happened, and fast. Plenty of moves and five children later, Lisa Long still fondly recalls those special years in Iowa City.

---

[9] When asked what ultimately led him to propose, Chuck didn't hesitate. "I always knew we were going to marry. I was just dragging my feet a little bit. I broke up with her three times while dating. She said, 'Break up with me again and it's over.' Sometimes you need a little nudge."

"There were lows but mostly highs," she said. "But no matter how you look at it, Chuck's five years as a Hawkeye were very special.

"It was like living in Disneyland every day," she said. "There were times that were so great, and there were close and disappointing losses that tore you up emotionally. But what I'll always remember was the warmth and love of the Hawkeyes coaching staff directed to the players.

"Coach Fry was always bigger than life. Yet he proved to be the most caring and wonderful man. And the same could be said for Coach [Bill] Snyder. He was always so gracious and wise. Both men will always hold a special place in my heart."

As will Chuck.

It was a mid-December Monday night in Wheaton, Illinois, and not a creature was stirring.

Surprising, given that Christmas was just weeks away.

Yet the downtown streets and shops were all but deserted, with neither bells nor cash registers ringing.

Rumor had it that the Wheaton North theatre had sold just one ticket for its 8:15 p.m. show.

And over at Ron's Television on Hale Street, where thirty-eight sets were turned on but not one tuned into the Bears/Lions game, salesman Angelo Port winced at the oversight.

"His mother's gonna kill me. I'll turn it on right now, I will," he said, scurrying to twist a knob.[10]

The reason for the lack of traffic, whether on the streets or in the shops throughout Wheaton, was because one of its own was about to take the field for his first NFL start, and under the bright lights of Monday Night Football, no less.

---

[10] "Wheaton watches as Lions throw Long to Bears," Barbara Mahany and Rudolph Unger, *Chicago Tribune*, Dec. 17, 1986

But not every fan was anticipating the matchup.

A nervous Joan Long was nestled in the family's home on Wheaton's Washington Street. She was too uptight to watch, choosing instead to work on Christmas cards.

"I'm too upset about the whole thing," she told a reporter from the *Chicago Tribune* by telephone. "For his first starting game in the NFL, to be against the best defense in the league, I just don't think it's fair. But then, they didn't ask me."

On one side of the line of scrimmage were the 5–9 Detroit Lions.

On the other, a red-hot Chicago Bears team that overwhelmed and devoured lesser opponents while steamrolling its way to postseason play.

Every fan (well, every fan except Joan Long, perhaps) was eager to see the fresh-faced boy with blond hair play. While Joan Long penned Christmas cards to keep her mind occupied, Wheaton North football coach Jim Rexilius was hunkered in the basement of his home just a few blocks away ready to cheer on his former quarterback.

Meanwhile, more than seventy thousand Lions faithful were packing the Silverdome to the rafters. Parking lots overflowed. Not a seat could be found at area restaurants throughout greater Detroit.

It was a moment many in Wheaton, Iowa City, and Detroit had been waiting for since Chuck arrived in Pontiac to play professional ball.

The anticipation was eclipsed only by Detroit's spirited performance— an all-out scrum and slobber-knocker that nearly ended as one of the greatest upsets of the NFL season.

Almost.

In a game that actually lived up to the hype, Chuck performed well despite being sacked six times for a loss of sixty-three yards and running for his life nearly every time he attempted to throw.

And the Lions' defense more than held its own, helping the home team build and retain a lead for most of the game.

But a fairy tale ending wasn't to be. Trailing 13–3 after three quarters, the Bears spoiled Chuck's professional debut. The rally included a four-yard touchdown run by running back Matt Suhey and two field goals by kicker Kevin Butler, the latter sailing through the goalposts as the game clock expired. Bears 16, Lions 13.

Chuck started—and most importantly, finished—the game, connecting on twelve of twenty-four passes for 167 yards. He threw one interception and one touchdown.

Meanwhile, Doug Flutie of the Bears finished thirteen of twenty-four for 130 yards and an interception after starting quarterback Tomczak left with a leg injury during Chicago's opening series.

When asked what the best moment of the game was, Chuck didn't hesitate: "The touchdown pass," he replied.[11]

Little wonder. The strike helped Detroit to a 13–3 lead over the defending Super Bowl champions. Hope and electricity careened through the Silverdome. Even Chuck was feeling it.

"I thought we had a helluva chance right then," he said. "The crowd was definitely in it, that's for sure. That's the way a crowd should be."

"I'll get better," he told columnist Mitch Albom of the *Detroit Free Press*. "I have to learn that these defensive ends in the NFL are faster than the ones in college. I used to be able to outrun those guys. But I'll learn."

And when asked by Albom about the next—and last—game of the season (at home versus the Atlanta Falcons), Chuck didn't skip a beat.

"To be honest," said the bruised and battered rookie QB, "this game really drained me. I really wanted to win this one, Monday night, the first start, all that.[12]

"But tomorrow's another day," he continued after a long sigh. "I'll start thinking about next week tomorrow, and then after that next year."

Still, Chuck couldn't help but dwell in his postgame comments on what had just happened. And how close the Lions had come to pulling off the unimaginable.

---

[11] Chuck's first completion as a starter came in the first quarter when he hit Carl Bland up the middle for nineteen yards and a first down.

[12] The matchup was the second-most watched Monday Night Football telecast of the season. Only the Sept. 22 Chicago Bears–Green Bay Packers game ranked higher. The Detroit-Chicago game had a 50 percent share of the viewing audience in Detroit and a 68 percent share in Chicago.

"I've been waiting for this chance ever since I signed my Lions' contract," Chuck said. "It was a game we should have won. I used to feel sorry for Eric [Hipple] after games like this. A loss is a loss, no matter how well you play.

"I made a lot of mistakes. The Bears knew I was young. They knew I hadn't seen everything. They kept teeing off on me. Blitzes. Every time I looked up, there was Gary Fencik or Dave Duerson."

Other observers, including Joe Falls of the *Detroit News,* were impressed by what they saw.

On the nineteen-yarder to Carl Bland, it was easy to see what made Chuck such an outstanding passer, he wrote. "He did what all effective quarterbacks must do. He dropped back quickly and released the ball quickly.

"It's the one trait a quarterback must instinctively have because it is something that is never really learned. You have it or you don't. Long has it."

Meanwhile, Chuck's former coaches were also basking in the glory of Chuck's solid debut as a starter in the National Football League.

Nearly 490 miles to the west of Pontiac, Michigan, Hayden Fry and his 8–3 Hawkeyes were readying to face San Diego State in the Holiday Bowl. Yet the Iowa coach wasn't too busy to watch his former pupil's debut as an NFL starter.

"I was extremely proud of Chuck," he said during a news conference in Iowa City the very next day. "I thought he did a fantastic job considering the opponent, the Chicago Bears.

"I don't think they could have picked a more difficult defense to go against in a rookie's first assignment as quarterback," he added. "The big thing about Chuck, he kept his poise. He audibilized. He threw the ball well most of the time. I was just tickled to death."

High praise from a former coach and a man who would forever be one of Chuck's dearest friends and closest confidants.

STARTING CALL

Chuck Long will always remember his first start as a pro. The Lions, coming off a 27–17 loss against the Steelers, were ready to take the field. It was week fifteen, and there was pressure from owner William Clay Ford to get the rookie on the field.

[Coach] Darryl brought me in Monday and said he had some good and some bad news to tell me. "The good news is we're starting you, and that should be pretty exciting for you. The bad news is it's Chicago, and they're pretty good."

He wasn't lying. I recall watching game film of this great Chicago Bears team, fresh off a Super Bowl victory. The team boasted arguably the best defense in NFL history—Richard Dent, Steve McMichael, William "The Refrigerator" Perry, Dan Hampton, Otis Wilson, Mike Singletary, and Wilber Marshall, to name just a few. And they were vicious and mean and fast, and they hit you, and when they did, they hit you hard.

So I'm watching tape of these guys, and they are scary good. And after watching quite a bit of film, I notice that every team that played the Bears would end the game with a different quarterback than the guy who started. So I kept looking at the other quarterbacks who were in the film room watching tape with me and I asked, "What in the world is going on?" And they looked at me because we all knew what was going on. The Bears' defense was injuring the starting quarterbacks and sending them out of the game. And with that, [Eric] Hipple looks me square in the eyes and says, "Good luck, Chuck!"

When game day finally arrived, I remember just asking the good Lord to get me through this game alive. It was Monday Night Football and the place was very electric; the stadium is sold out; fans are jacked; it was an incredible atmosphere. And then the hitting started.

On what I think was my first pass play from scrimmage, I remember a bone-jarring hit. It was Hampton and Dent that sacked me. It was like they were waiting for me at the top of my drop. I remember asking myself at the moment of impact, how in the world did they get here so fast? So Hampton, one of their great defensive linemen, picks me up off the turf and I'm thinking, holy cow, what a nice league; these NFL guys are real gentlemen. Because if you know anything about the NFL, defensive linemen never help a quarterback to his feet. So he picks me up and pulls me right into him by the jersey. I'll save the curse words, but suffice it to say that he wasn't going to share pleasantries. He pulls me close and says, "Boy, you're in for a rough night. A long night. We're going to crush you. And we're going to hit you pretty good. You'll be sore, really sore, for a week, but at least you'll survive. Maybe."

Well, that gets your attention. And Hampton was right. They hit me hard all night. But it was a good kind of sore. I would have felt better had we managed to win, but we lost on a last-second field goal by Kevin Butler. It was my first start and one I'll never forget.

CHAPTER 7

The Next Snap

"He's very lucky. Why do you think I married him? He's the luckiest guy in the world."

LISA LONG

a bride of fifty days, when asked to describe her husband's knack for always smelling like roses after every turn in life ("With lady luck at his side, Chuck Long faces the challenge of his athletic career," Tom Kowalski, Oakland Sunday Magazine, July 26, 1987)

Chuck's first season—and his second start—with Detroit ended with a 20–6 loss versus the Atlanta Falcons. The Lions finished the season with a record of 5–11.

"The Lions aren't putting this much time into Long's development to have him sit on the bench next season," observed the *Detroit News*' Mike O'Hara.[1] "With three consecutive seasons of finishes below .500, they need a lift. Going with a young quarterback with potential is the most obvious place to make a change."

Chuck admitted that delays in signing following the NFL draft stunted opportunities to learn the offense and make an immediate impact for the team.

---

[1] Chuck didn't shy away from making himself available to reporters. "I embraced the media," he said. "That came from my father. He was a journalism major in college, and public relations and journalism were a big part of his career. He taught me the importance of those professions and to respect those who practiced them. At times they would blast me, but I didn't have a problem with that because when they did, they were correct in doing so. If they were fair and talked about the good when it happened, I didn't have a problem when they came to me with tough questions when bad things were happening."

"Last year, I was just trying to get to know everybody," he said. "I didn't say that much. You're a little nervous about everything. I've gotten to know most of the guys.

"I have higher expectations this year of myself and the team as well. If I start, I feel my job ought to be to have us in the playoff race."

This attitude, reported O'Hara, didn't surprise head coach Darryl Rogers.

"That sounds like Chuck; that's good," he said. "Our expectations are a lot higher than last year at this time. He always says he's going to carry us to the playoffs. That's Chuck.

"I won't say we're handing the job to him," Rogers added. "He's going to earn the right to be the starter."

And that was just fine with Chuck.[2]

With the season opener versus the Vikings looming, the quarterback didn't mind being under the gun, or being told that it was his job until he screwed up. The kid from Wheaton had never backed down from a challenge, and he wasn't going to start now.

"I like it," he said. "It's the ultimate challenge. I like it when everybody's against you. The schedule's against us. The fans. Some of the media. Last year's record. I like the underdog role."

Jeff Chadwick, starting wide receiver and one of Chuck's closest confidants, was impressed by the young quarterback's development.

"When he first got here, you could tell he needed a lot of work," he told Rich Roberts of the Los Angeles Times. "He was just trying to throw a spiral. But he's very patient. He doesn't get uptight and worry. He'll carry that onto the field.

"The thing that really impressed me about Chuck is that in the three preseason games we had, he was throwing balls that I'd never seen before," Chadwick added. "I'm coming out of a twenty-yard crossing route, and as I make my break, the ball's right there—like, I never saw him throw it. That's the way it's supposed to be done, but most of the time the quarterback will be

---

[2] In his last 1987 preseason tune-up versus the Philadelphia Eagles, Chuck went fourteen of eighteen for 248 yards and two touchdowns in just three quarters of play on the way to a 36–3 win.

late with it and the defensive backs will converge and the receiver winds up getting nailed."

In what would ultimately prove to be his best season as a pro statistically, Chuck connected on 232 of 416 passes during his sophomore campaign for 2,598 yards and eleven touchdowns. Baked inside the numbers was arguably Chuck's most impressive game of his professional career, a thirty-three of forty-seven performance good for 362 yards, three touchdowns, and no interceptions in a heartbreaking 34–33 loss versus the Green Bay Packers in week six.

Unfortunately, the 1987 NFL season was marred by a twenty-four-day players' strike called after week two.[3] Games scheduled for week three were cancelled while "replacement" players (along with some NFL players who crossed the picket line) took to the field the next three consecutive weeks.

In the blink of an eye, Detroit was underwater. Owner William Clay Ford called the team "lousy" and made it known that coach Darryl Rogers was on the hot seat. Players were frustrated.

Said ten-year veteran and defensive end William Gay, "If I owned a dog, he'd be in trouble. I'd kick him."

Despite a 1–6 record and some suggesting the team would lose out, Chuck maintained his poise and positive outlook.

"I'm not going to worry about it," he told O'Hara. "All the turmoil's going to iron itself out. The pressure's there every game. I still have my confidence. I'm not worried about that being broken."

And then, out of nowhere, came a shocking 27–17 win over the Cowboys in week eight.

"It was a win that felt great because it came over the great Dallas Cowboys," said Chuck. "Growing up, you remember the Super Bowl champion team with [Roger] Staubach and [Tom] Landry and them playing against the Steelers. Those were America's teams. To beat America's Team in my first start meant the world to me."

---

[3] Chuck stuck with the NFL Players Union and sat during the strike. "There's no way I was going to come back before the rest of the players," he said. "Every once in a while you have to stand up for what you believe in."

However, the success was short-lived, and the team in turmoil was never able to right the ship.[4] Detroit's chaotic 1987 campaign ended 4–11.

Chuck finished the season completing 56 percent of his passes and was the NFC's fifth-leading passer in yards (2,598). However, he tossed twenty interceptions and compiled a 63.3 quarterback rating, good for next-to-last in the NFC.

"Good teams have trouble winning without good quarterbacking. Winning will be an impossible task for the Lions if Long doesn't have a good year."

MIKE O'HARA
Detroit News, *July 15, 1988*

Big changes were in store for Chuck Long as he entered his third season in Detroit.

On June 29, Chuck and his wife, Lisa, became parents with the birth of a baby girl.

"Lindsay is the best thing that's happened to me," said Chuck. "I have a family to support now. It makes you play a lot harder."

While Chuck and Lisa's family changed, the Lions' success on the football field didn't.

Despite renewed optimism thanks to top draft picks Benny Blades (defensive back, Miami), Chris Spielman (linebacker, Ohio State), and Pat Carter (tight end, Florida State), Detroit's fortunes didn't improve in 1988.

Attendance in the Silverdome, which had peaked at nearly fifty thousand per game in 1982, averaged just thirty-two thousand in 1987.

And prospects for improvement in 1988 were dealt a major setback when Chuck sustained a right elbow injury during the third week of training

---

[4] The victory over the Cowboys in the Silverdome was Chuck's first win as a starting quarterback. He completed fifteen of twenty-eight passes for 217 yards and a touchdown.

camp. The gimpy elbow kept him sidelined for all four preseason games. Not surprisingly, the Lions went 0–4 in the preseason (ending with a 27–9 loss versus the Eagles).

It was difficult to find reason for optimism. Even hometown sports writers were all but throwing in the towel.

"The face the Lions present to the public is one of a loser," wrote O'Hara of the *Detroit News* in his season preview. "Last year's 4–11 record did not represent a sudden falloff. It was not a one-time aberration. The team has been on a steady decline since its last playoff season of 1983.

"Declining respect—and downright abuse—in the community has become a burden for the Lions."

And it remained that way. Despite a season-opening 31–17 thumping of the Atlanta Falcons in the Silverdome, the Lions' season quickly hit the skids. They lost six straight before earning a second win—a 7–6 victory over the Chiefs.

"We're boring and we're losing," said owner William Clay Ford.

Surprisingly, the pep talk did little to turn Detroit's fortunes.

The team struggled, with Chuck sustaining a severe knee injury in the sixth game of the season, a 24–7 loss to Chicago in Soldier Field.

Things didn't improve during the second half of the season. Head coach Darryl Rogers was fired.[5] Chuck experienced his first benching of his NFL career after a forgettable start against the Minnesota Vikings in week ten (Detroit lost the game 44–17).

In 1989, the Lions drafted Oklahoma State running back and Heisman Trophy winner Barry Sanders as the no. 3 overall pick. They also began to transition from the prototypical drop-back quarterback to a spread offensive scheme, thanks to their pick of quarterback Rodney Peete of USC as the 141st pick in the 1989 NFL draft.

---

[5] Lions defensive coordinator, and former University of Iowa assistant football coach, Wayne Fontes was named interim head coach upon Rogers' dismissal. The Massachusetts native and former NFL player served as head coach for seven years. In 1991, he was named the NFL's Coach of the Year after leading Detroit to a 12-4 record and the NFC Championship game (losing to the eventual World Champion Washington Redskins, 41-10).

Sanders, who fit the offensive scheme perfectly, was an immediate impact player (and franchise maker) and instantly made the team respectable, amassing a record of seven for nine that season.

Chuck, on the other hand, was no longer needed in the Music City.

"I should have retired right then."

CHUCK LONG

after being traded to the Los Angeles Rams, reflecting on his first pass as a Detroit Lion that went for a thirty-four-yard touchdown to wide receiver Leonard Thompson ("New system, forgotten man: Long's sentence ends, period," Mitch Albom, Detroit Free Press, May 4, 1990)

Used only sparingly in his fourth year with the Lions, Chuck was traded to the Los Angeles Rams in spring 1990. Ironically, he was signed to a two-year contract to serve as backup to the Rams' starting quarterback and Purdue graduate Jim Everett—a rival from Chuck's playing days as a Hawkeye.

"There was a time when I was very happy with Detroit. I was excited to be here," said Chuck. "It was an up-and-coming team. It reminded of my college team [Iowa]. I felt good about things. All of the sudden, it turned around 180 degrees on me."

Mitch Albom, who had shared many meals and interviews with Chuck during his time in Detroit, couldn't blame the quarterback for wanting a change of scenery.

"Hell is over for Chuck Long," Albom wrote upon news that Chuck was setting sail for Los Angeles. "He goes free now."

For Chuck, the trade provided a much-needed fresh start.

"If I learned one thing in my time in Detroit, it's that there is no future in the NFL," he told Albom. "Teams can't really wait four or five years. If you don't win in two years, three tops, heads will roll. I'm just glad this whole thing is behind me."

As he prepared to leave for California, wife Lisa was in Detroit expecting the birth of the couple's second child. Eventually the Longs made the move to LA as a family. But they never really unpacked.

In a promising start, Chuck completed seven of ten passes in a preseason game versus Philadelphia totaling 155 yards and two touchdown passes. In four preseason contests, he was fifteen of thirty-one for 293 yards.

But playing time never materialized as Everett's backup. Chuck appeared in just four games and completed only one pass for four yards.[6]

After just one year in Los Angeles, he boomeranged back to Detroit for the 1991 season, though he never attempted another pass in the NFL.

He officially retired as a professional football player in 1994.

During his NFL career, Chuck played in twenty-seven games, completed 331 of 607 passes (55 percent) for 3,747 yards and nineteen touchdowns.

Not bad for a kid who honed his raw talent playing ball in a park the size of a postage stamp in Wheaton, Illinois, received hardly a look by college scouts upon graduating from Wheaton North High School, and was benched after his first start as an Iowa Hawkeye.

———

In 1995, Chuck Long transitioned from the playing field to the sidelines, returning to Iowa as defensive backs coach for Hayden Fry.

The move paid dividends for both Chuck and the Hawkeyes. Despite playing every down as quarterback in high school, college, and the pros,

---

[6] At the first hint of a possible trade to Los Angeles, Chuck wasn't all too thrilled. "I wanted to make it work in Detroit." But after a bit of thought and study, the Rams appeared to be a better fit. The Lions were adopting the run-and-shoot offense. That wasn't Chuck's game.

"Getting traded was a lot different back then than it is now," he said. "There was no such thing as free agency, so when teams sent you on your way, you truly felt like you weren't wanted anymore. All of the sudden, you feel human again."

"But my time in Los Angeles had a silver lining to it off the field. It was where I learned the West Coast offense. That served me well later on as it was the base system for my coaching philosophy."

Chuck's insight had an immediate impact on the defensive side of the ball. Iowa's defense quickly improved against the pass. It led the nation in interceptions returned for touchdowns in 1995. And in 1997, the Hawkeyes led the Big Ten in interceptions.

In Chuck's three seasons as defensive backs coach (1995–1997), Iowa amassed a 24–12 record and played in bowl games three consecutive years— the Sun twice with the Alamo in-between.

The defensive success helped Chuck become a well-known and respected assistant by coaches around the country.

"Being an older quarterback, I knew coverages and tendencies of the signal caller," Chuck said. "I just had to brush up on my technique. I had a mentor—Bob Elliott. He taught me everything I needed to know."[7]

In 1998, Chuck became Iowa's quarterbacks and special teams coach. One year later, when Hayden Fry retired, Chuck was considered for the job. However, Fry's ultimate successor proved to be Kirk Ferentz who, nearly twenty years later, was still at the helm of an Iowa program fresh off a Rose Bowl appearance.[8]

Chuck was retained by Ferentz and continued to serve as an assistant. One year later (and after five years at Iowa), Chuck jettisoned Iowa City for his native state of Oklahoma. There he took the coveted job of pass game coordinator and quarterbacks coach for former teammate Bobby

---

[7] Elliott, a native of Iowa City and graduate of Iowa City West High School, earned three letters as a defensive back for the Iowa Hawkeyes (1972, 1974, 1975). He was an elite football coach, serving as a member of the Iowa athletics department from 1987 to 1999. He served on Hayden Fry's staff from 1987 to 1994 and from 1996 to 1998. The son of former Iowa athletics director and Michigan head football coach Bump Elliott, Bob Elliott served as secondary coach at Iowa from 1987 to 1994 and returned as defensive coordinator from 1996 to 1998. He coached seven first-team all–Big Ten selections and eight second-team all-conference players at Iowa. During his eleven seasons as an assistant coach at Iowa, the Hawkeyes were 74–52–5 (.584) and played in seven bowl games. Opposing quarterbacks completed less than 52 percent of their passes and averaged only 177 yards per game during Elliott's tenure at Iowa He also coached at Iowa State and Kansas State and was the first hire by San Diego State University head football coach Chuck Long. In 2012, he joined the Notre Dame football coaching staff, serving as special assistant to the head coach. In 2017, Elliott was named safeties coach at the University of Nebraska. He died July 8, 2017, after a nearly twenty-year bout with cancer. He was sixty-four.

[8] The call to Ferentz came while serving as head coach of the University of Maine. He owned a 12–21 in his three years as coach of the Black Bears. Iowa lost to Stanford in the 2016 Rose Bowl 45–16 and finishing the year 12–2.

CHUCK LONG: DESTINED FOR GREATNESS

Stoops, who was in his second year as head coach of the perennial national powerhouse Sooners.[9]

"My parents both graduated from the University of Oklahoma and were Sooner fans long before I went to play at Iowa," Chuck said. "My father always wanted Barry Switzer and Oklahoma to recruit me, but they never did."

Bobby and Chuck quickly bonded, and an Oklahoma squad that began the 2000 season ranked nineteenth didn't take long to get on a roll. In its first four games, the Sooners outscored the University of Texas–El Paso, Arkansas State, Rice, and Kansas 176–51.[10]

Then came a much-anticipated matchup versus no. 11 Texas in a nationally televised game in the Cotton Bowl in Dallas. A packed house totaling more than seventy-five thousand fans was gathered under a dreary, threatening canopy to witness the latest episode of a grudge match called the Red River Rivalry.

"It's one of the biggest games of the country—you have red on one side of the stadium and orange on the other," said Chuck. "I recall hopping on the bus after the morning meal for the ride from the hotel through the Texas State Fair. There were throngs of fans and they were booing our bus like crazy and just letting us have it. And we're focused and thinking about the battle that looms.

"We get to the stadium and work through our pregame drills. And just before kickoff, Bobby comes up to me as the rain starts coming down, and he

---

[9] Chuck had a unique habit as a quarterbacks coach:

I never let them (quarterbacks) read the paper. I kept all of the clippings about them and stored them in a shoe box. They got to read about themselves at the end of the season. Reading the paper from game to game sent players on an emotional roller coaster, so I did whatever I could to keep them from reading it. Call it superstition. Call it what you want. The one time I did as a player at Iowa, I got burned. Reading the paper wears you out as a player, so I decided that my quarterbacks would never read the paper during the season.

[10] The Sooners were 4–0, but the assistant coaches were on edge. "We're a struggling 4–0. And after getting past Kansas despite it being a close game at halftime, Coach Stoops comes in Sunday after the game," said Chuck. "And we're all getting ready to spend the day and night breaking down the Kansas film, expecting to work until midnight to get ready for the next game versus Texas, arguably Oklahoma's most anticipated rival. And out of the blue, Bobby tells all of us to go home. And we're looking at him like, 'What?' And he says, 'Guys, we're going to whoop 'em.' And we're looking at him, and offensive coordinator Mark Mangino asks, 'Coach, have you seen us play?' And Bob says, 'I don't care, we're going to whoop 'em good.' He knew something we didn't."

asks, 'What's this game remind you of, Chuck?' And without missing a beat, I yell back, 'The 1984 Freedom Bowl!' And he says, 'Dang right it does!'"

The words would prove prophetic. Just like the Hawkeyes did sixteen years earlier in Anaheim, Oklahoma rolled the Longhorns 63–14.

The Sooners proceeded to win the next eight games, the last coming against the Florida State Seminoles in the 2001 Orange Bowl, earning the national title.

"Dad was on cloud nine," Chuck said. "He had just retired, so you could say it was the best retirement gift he could get that year when his alma mater won the national championship with his son on the coaching staff."

Also that year, Chuck coached quarterback Josh Heupel to a second-place finish in the Heisman Trophy balloting.

After the 2001 season, Chuck was promoted to Oklahoma's offensive coordinator position. Ironically, Oklahoma did something that Chuck couldn't do in his years as a player at Iowa: it won the 2003 Rose Bowl.

That's because the odds of a Big Twelve team playing in the Rose Bowl were extremely remote.

Yet the stars aligned in 2003. Iowa was selected to play in the Orange Bowl versus USC (losing 38–17) while Ohio State competed in the National Championship game (defeating no. 1 Miami 31–24 in double overtime). That meant the Rose Bowl had the opportunity to pick whichever team it wanted. It chose Oklahoma.

"It was a proud moment when I coached Nate Hybl to the 2003 Rose Bowl MVP," Chuck recalled. "It was also quite unique and special to coach a Rose Bowl quarterback at Oklahoma.

"It was special because it was the Rose Bowl," he added. "In many ways, it helped make up for the loss I experienced in the 1986 Rose Bowl.

"Almost," Chuck quickly added. "I only wish we could have achieved a Rose Bowl victory for Coach Fry."[11]

But more memories were yet to be made in Norman.

---

[11] "What are the odds that I would have been on a Rose Bowl champion team with a Big Twelve school and four former Hawkeyes—Long, Hayes, and Bob and Mike Stoops?" asked Chuck. "We were all part of a losing Rose Bowl with Iowa and then won it in 2003 with Oklahoma."

With the arrival of the 2003 college football season, the Sooners were prepared to put their faith in an injury-prone quarterback named Jason White.

The gritty and resilient White was not the popular choice. After two reconstructive knee surgeries that sidelined him for two years, almost every coach and player (even the team's strength and conditioning coach) had written him off. And White, whose dad owned and operated a concrete company, questioned his own ability prior to the start of the 2003 season.

"After his second reconstructive surgery that spring, he came to me and asked if he should hang it up," Chuck recalled. "I said, 'No, let's play this out and see what happens.'"

Chuck believed in the guy. He was tough and gritty. Despite missing all of spring ball and sitting out fall practices, Chuck lobbied—and Stoops agreed—to put him under center.

"His knees were so bad that he couldn't even drop back to pass, never mind scramble," Chuck said. "In other words, every snap we called was in the shotgun formation with no sprint out passes or bootlegs. And yet he excels, throwing forty touchdown passes to just six interceptions on his way to a 12–2 season."

Jason White capped the season by winning the 2003 Heisman Trophy, besting Pittsburgh wide receiver Larry Fitzgerald and a senior quarterback from Mississippi named Eli Manning.

"It is a season I'm very proud of," Chuck reminisced. "I liked playing the game but I also liked coaching and mentoring and seeing stories like Jason White unfold. I didn't win the Heisman, but I coached a kid who did, a kid who would have fit right in at Iowa—from a good, hard-working family and raised in a small town of maybe a hundred people [Tuttle, Oklahoma].

"Helping him win the Heisman meant more to me than winning the Heisman."

ALL IN THE FAMILY

Chuck Long felt right at home with Bob Stoops in Norman, Oklahoma.

Coaching for a guy you played with means you already have his respect and can make decisions a lot quicker because you have some familiarity, according to Chuck.

"Then there's the toughness that came from the blood, sweat, and tears we shared together as Hawkeyes. Add it all up and you gain respect for each other. I also had a better understanding about how he thought, and that enabled me to help the younger guys understand more quickly what Bob was all about.

"He's a no-nonsense guy," Chuck added. "Tough, fair, and wants you to have a family life. He figures if you have a happy home, you'll be happy at work and be a better worker. He wanted the staff to have high energy every day on the practice field. There was no room for being tired or not feeling it. You had to have high energy. It's part of the successful equation in Norman."

"After Detroit, I didn't know where football stood with me anymore. But coaching brought the great game of football back to me with a tremendous amount of satisfaction— the teamwork, the chemistry, the unselfishness. And the chance to be part of an undefeated Oklahoma team, the only undefeated team I've been a part of in nearly forty years of organized football as a coach and player."

CHUCK LONG

Chuck coached at Oklahoma for six seasons, including four as an offensive coordinator. During that time, the Sooners compiled a 67–11 record, losing just twice on their home field.

After the 2005 season in Norman, which included a win over Oregon in the Holiday Bowl, Chuck and the family moved west when he took the reins at San Diego State University. The Aztecs went 9–27 during his three seasons as coach.

After a year removed from football, Chuck joined the Kansas Jayhawks in 2009 as offensive coordinator under first-year head coach and former Nebraska Cornhuskers quarterback Turner Gill. Following Gill's departure as coach in 2012, Chuck Long became receivers coach with the Norman (Oklahoma) High School Tigers to watch his son, Zach, play quarterback his senior year.

In 2013, Chuck joined the staff of Holmes Murphy, a national brokerage company offering various lines of property and casualty insurance with offices in Cedar Rapids, Iowa.

One year later (November 2014), he was named CEO-executive director of the Ames, Iowa-based Iowa Sports Foundation. The nonprofit, launched in 1986, provides sports, recreation, health, and wellness opportunities for Iowans of all abilities with the goal of making Iowa the nation's healthiest state.

Chuck and Lisa are the proud parents of five grown children: Lindsay, Samantha, Nathan, Zachary, and Maddy.

––––––––––––

Make your way to Wheaton and you'll find The Tot Lot. It's where it's always been…at the end of East Hawthorn Boulevard, sandwiched between Wakeman Avenue and Parkway Drive.

Just like Chuck and the boys who once played there, it's changed with the times. Much of what used to be an open field ideal for playing ball has been overtaken by swings and slides and other assorted playground equipment.

The trees are much larger. The park seems smaller.

And while little children still make their way to the park, the baseball and football games that once were played from sunup to sundown are mostly a thing of the past. A small park that reverberated with the voices of young boys pretending they homered at Wrigley Field or tossed a touchdown at Soldier Field sits mostly silent.

A park just isn't the magnet for youth that it once was.

But what happened there once upon a time was magic.

"Let's go play some ball," Chuck the boy would say to his friends.

Soon, other children would be galloping around him, including future NFL stars Danny Graham and his younger brother Kent. And T-bone, Rock, and Reggie Sprenger.[12] And of course Chuck's dad, Charlie.[13] They were soon joined by other neighborhood kids, and together they would play each day like there was no tomorrow…only to return the next day and do it all over again.

Before every child's eyes were glued to a screen, there were places like The Tot Lot where children competed, burned energy, learned the importance of teamwork, sharpened their skills and experienced the thrill of winning and the pains and good-natured ribbing that accompanied defeat. They were destinations for youth where parents knew their children would be safe and where they would be playing until it was time for lunch. And supper.

Sure, The Tot Lot has changed over the past forty-five years.

---

[12] The Sprenger boys (a.k.a. Tom, Jim, and Patrick) lived in a two-story colonial home located just two doors up from The Tot Lot and next door to the Long family while Chuck attended Hawthorne Elementary. "For whatever reason, we'd always end up at the Sprenger home as kids after every Halloween and trick-or-treating and watch a scary movie. Great memories," Chuck recalled. Dorothy, who still lives in the family home, is always ready for a visitor and doesn't mind offering a thought or two about the days the boys careened their way around Wheaton. "Joan (Chuck's mother) was a saint," she said matter-of-factly. "And those boys…not sure if they ever slept a wink. Lots of energy, that's for sure. But good kids and a whole lot of fun to have around."

[13] Charlie Long passed away in 2008. "He was a role model and the best people person I've ever known," said Chuck. "Will Rogers coined the phrase, 'I never met a man I didn't like.' That was Dad. Everybody loved him. I never saw him get angry or raise his voice. I never saw my dad have a bad day. He had the most positive attitude of any role model I've ever had."

But what it stands for hasn't.

Everyone starts somewhere. We're all from someplace. What we do moment by moment and day by day makes up life.

Chuck is a humble, content man.

"Who knows, if Iowa and Hayden hadn't come after me and recruited me, one can only wonder how different my life would be. Sure, there are things you'd always like to change. I'd love to have that Ohio State game back. And that '85 Rose Bowl, too. But I was blessed to have the career I had."

Does he have a yearning to relive those days? Of course.

"They were magical and fun-filled. You got up each day and played football, baseball and basketball. My buddies and I still talk about going back to Wheaton and playing a game or two in The Tot Lot and laughing it up and playing on that grassy field again.

"There's a sense of reliving those days, especially as you get older. But at the same time, I'm very happy with where I am today. I wouldn't change a thing. I was part of some great teams, some championship teams.

"But most important," Chuck adds, "I was around the great game of football that gave me the opportunity to get to know some wonderful people from all around the country, people who made a lasting impression on me and have become very good friends."

It doesn't get more complicated than that.

"That's how I grew up," recalled Chuck, now fifty-four and an analyst for the Big Ten Network and color man for Westwood One Sports in addition to his duties as Executive Director of the Iowa Sports Foundation. "Gosh, I loved that Tot Lot. We'd play game after game there. We'd swing for the fences and throw touchdown pass after touchdown pass.

"I'd select the least athletic kid on my team just to make sure he was included. I wanted everyone to feel part of the game. Never wanted anyone to go home without the chance to step to the plate or catch the winning touchdown. The more kids you could include the more fun it was. No one really cared about the score. It was about having fun and getting better."

He paused, reflecting on the "destined for greatness" prediction made by

Hayden Fry almost 40 years ago.[14]

"What's the definition of greatness? That's a good question because it can mean so many different things," said Chuck. "When Hayden said it at the time, I had finished my first spring scrimmage as a freshman at Iowa. For him to say that after just one scrimmage, well, I wasn't quite sure what he meant other than he was giving me praise and I felt good about it....I thought maybe he knows something that I don't. I was always one to live for the moment, play hard for the moment, and give one hundred percent effort each time.

"Kirk Ferentz often talks about getting a little better every day in what we do and how we go about doing it. It's up to each one of us to get up and get after it."[15]

That philosophy, Chuck said, helped him exceed expectations and warrant the "destined for greatness" tab.

It's an approach—and a journey—that each person can take.

"Hayden had it in his mind what greatness was, and I didn't want to let him or my teammates down. That's a very broad definition, but greatness can mean different things to different people.

"We are all blessed with God-given talent," he added. "What makes us unique is how hard we work at it each day.

"Good things happen to those who work hard. Because one day, when we each look back, we can say we didn't waste anything. We didn't squander time

---

[14] Chuck Long was a big piece of the puzzle that helped Hayden Fry turn around an Iowa program that had nineteen consecutive winless seasons, said John Streif, who served as Iowa's assistant athletic trainer from 1972 to 2012. "Going to a Rose Bowl in his first year, then taking Iowa to four more bowl games, including the Rose after deciding to return to Iowa when he could have gone professional; that was vintage Chuck.

"Today, a lot of people talk about Desmond King and his decision to come back to Iowa for his senior season," Streif added. "But here's Chuck who did that back in the 1980s, and a fifth year, no less. He made a lot of commitments to this institution and took it to new levels. Chuck will forever be remembered as a leader and the kid who helped Hayden turn an Iowa program around. And deservedly so."

[15] Much of the same characteristics that defined Coach Fry could be seen in Coach Ferentz, said John Streif. "You learn from the people you work with. His time away from Iowa working with Bill Belichick and others made him the kind of person he is. He also learned a lot from Coach Fry because Iowa is a special place and setting, and you have to be a special type person to be at Iowa. His attention to detail and the little things are also well known and respected."

Streif remembers to this day the moment Coach Ferentz arrived at Iowa as the new head coach. "I told him that there probably wouldn't be another Hayden Fry—coaches working twenty-plus years at one school anymore—because people want change too much in athletics.

"He sure proved me wrong."

CHUCK LONG: DESTINED FOR GREATNESS

or talents or relationships. That we were indeed destined for greatness, and that we achieved greatness because we were a bit better each day and made the people around us better, too. There's no legacy more impactful than that."

BROTHERLY RESPECT

Wheaton was the perfect neighborhood to grow up in as a kid, said Chuck's brother David.

Now a Northern Trust estate settlement attorney living in Phoenix with wife Tya and children Addy and Gavin, David still recalls the sense of safety and security the children experienced growing up in the quiet Chicago suburb and with parents who loved their children.

"We could just run around the whole neighborhood if not the whole community without any supervision and have tons of fun," he said. "It was a safe neighborhood. For the most part, everybody really knew each other. It was all about sports, and there was always a game being played."

Younger than Chuck by three years, David said the two always had a bond.

"We're close as brothers to this day and always have been. But as typical brothers, we also spent a lot of time in childhood fighting each other," David said. "Three years' difference meant we were in elementary school and high school together. And even though I was only a freshman when he was a senior in high school, we still had a lot of fun with our friends getting together to play games."

David, who also graduated from the University of Iowa where he was a liberal arts major, added, "We had different interests—his were clearly in sports.

And while I was interested in sports, I had other hobbies, too. My friends and I would get together and build go-karts and tool around with more engineering and computer-type stuff."

Because the boys had different passions, there was never a big competition between them. Just the contrary.

"I very much enjoyed watching him in his career. He was obviously very talented in football and at quarterbacking and in sports in general," David said.

Chuck's proficiency on the football field, baseball diamond, and basketball court was obvious at an early age, David said. But it wasn't until high school that the thought arose that perhaps, just perhaps, Chuck had what it took to be a scholar athlete in college.

"We knew he was good. But at the same time, it was hard to think as a child or even early in high school that even someone with talent could make it a career, especially with such intense competition," David recalled. "Chuck didn't have the chance to throw the ball much in football. But as a starter his junior and senior year for the [Wheaton North High School] Falcons, he really put it all together. He had poise and good coordination and the physical attributes to make something of it."

Charlie and Joan Long cared deeply about their children, David said, and promoted the role of the family unit and the importance of being together.

"They loved each other to the day my father died. It was a deep commitment and love for each other. Having that as parents growing up is part of Chuck's success, mine, and ours as a family.

"They also gave us freedom, particularly when it came to the careers we wanted to choose," David said. "There wasn't a lot of pressure to do one thing or the other. But at the same time, scholastics were extremely important."

While Charlie took the train each day for his job in Chicago, Joan was the CEO of the home, managing its daily affairs and the comings and goings of Chuck and David and their youngest brother, Andy. The blend of two talented parents was the perfect complement for the boys.

"Mom played the role of encouraging Chuck and me to keep up with our studies and keeping our grades up," David said. "Mom was at home, always there for us, and kept our noses in the school books. Meanwhile, Dad nurtured our sports interests and did it tremendously well. He probably coached more of my teams than Chuck's. He was always coaching both of us and giving us great advice. It was a passion of his.

"A big part of that, a positive takeaway for Chuck and me, is that we never felt the pressure to be something or someone we didn't want to be. There was never any animosity between us," David added. "Yet there would be times when people and reporters would come to me concerned that either I was jealous or hurt because I couldn't be a starting quarterback or there was competition between me and Chuck. I was always shocked and surprised that there were such questions and that people felt that way.

"But my first reaction was always, 'Uh-oh, this person really doesn't understand our family and me and Chuck and that there is no animosity and that I have no desire or interest to be a star quarterback.' Whether in high school, college, or the pros, I just enjoyed being in the stands and watching him flourish."

Still to this day, David said there are those who wonder if he's OK having a "star" brother.

"I can't tell you how exciting it was to have Chuck as talented as he was to get into football and have the kind of success that he had," David said with the utmost sincerity. "For me, it was a great experience. I was OK with it from the start. It's just been nothing but exciting to see him go through his career, from playing high school, college, and pro ball to coaching. To be at those games during those years, especially at Iowa when the Hawkeyes did so well—it was one of the best experiences of my life. It was just great having Chuck do what he did. I love him today for that. Always will."

———————

"Except for war, there is nothing in American life—
nothing—that trains a boy better for life than football."

ROBERT F. KENNEDY

———————

SALUTING THE STORYTELLERS

BY CHUCK LONG

When I say that I appreciated and enjoyed working with media and sports information staff during my time in Iowa City and Detroit, I mean it.

Really.

Too often, sports reporters—members of a largely thankless profession—get the arrows. They also make storytelling, collecting the sights and sounds of games and press conferences, delivering the play-by-play or capturing sidelines reports look far too easy.

It's not. Capturing what takes place on and off the football field takes dedication and discipline, as does deciphering coach speak, interviewing athletes, working under continuous deadlines, dealing with angry coaches and players, and taking some shots in the chops for a quote or the context of that quote not told just right.

And then rising the next day to do it all over again.

Sports reporting and managing the grind of sports information departments is not a job for the faint of heart. As the son of a journalist, I hold an unwavering appreciation for those who covered my career and the teams I took the field for. Here's a salute to the work you did, stories you told, and the entertainment you bring to millions of passionate fans.

- Mitch Albom, *Detroit Free Press*
- Taylor Bell, *Chicago Sun-Times*
- Bob Brooks, KHAK Radio, Cedar Rapids

- Bob Brown, *Fort Dodge Messenger*
- Rick Brown, *Des Moines Register*
- John Campbell, KCRG-TV, Cedar Rapids
- Gene Clausen, KXIC Radio, Iowa City
- Rick Coleman, KWWL-TV, Waterloo
- Gary Dolphin, WHO Radio, Learfield Sports
- Don Doxsie, *Cedar Rapids Gazette*
- Mark Dukes, *Cedar Rapids Gazette*
- Bob Dyer, *Des Moines Register*
- Kevin Evans, *Waterloo Courier*
- Ken Fuson, *Des Moines Register*
- Paul Galloway, *Chicago Tribune*
- Ron Gonder, WMT Radio, Cedar Rapids
- Al Grady, *Iowa City Press-Citizen*
- Phil Haddy, University of Iowa Sports Information
- Marc Hansen, *Des Moines Register*
- Pat Harty, *Iowa City Press-Citizen*
- Mike Hlas, *Cedar Rapids Gazette*
- Tom Kowalski, *Oakland Press*
- Hal Lagerstrom, *Dubuque Telegraph Herald*
- Ron Maly, *Des Moines Register*
- Robert Markus, *Chicago Tribune*
- Frosty Mitchell, WMT Radio, Cedar Rapids
- Marc Morehouse, *Cedar Rapids Gazette*
- Mike O'Hara, *Detroit News*
- Randy Peterson, *Des Moines Register*
- Bob Pille, *Chicago Sun-Times*
- Eddie Podolak, WHO Radio, Learfield Sports
- Gary Richards, *Quad City Times*
- Steve Roe, University of Iowa Sports Information
- Chuck Schoffner, *Des Moines Register*
- Gus Schrader, *Cedar Rapids Gazette*

- Russ Smith, *Waterloo Courier*
- Curt Sylvester, *Detroit Free Press*
- John E. "Buck" Turnbull, *Des Moines Register*
- Maury White, *Des Moines Register*
- George Wine, University of Iowa Sports Information
- Jim Zabel, WHO Radio
- Nolan Zavoral, *Iowa City Press-Citizen*

"My best experiences through football have been with people. You make great friendships, the camaraderie of the team, that's what has been really special. It's still a lot of fun. And there is absolutely nothing like the roar of the crowd."

CHUCK LONG
when asked what was most memorable from his years as an Iowa Hawkeye ("Long reflects on season, ponders football future," Jack McCarthy, sports editor, special section, Wheaton Daily Journal, Jan. 23, 1986)

Good company

Charles Franklin "Chuck" Long grew up Wheaton, Illinois, a suburb of Chicago. The small town has also been the home of many notable Americans, including Rev. Billy Graham, astronomer Edwin Hubble, sports standout Harold "Red" Grange, journalist Bob Woodward, and the Belushi brothers—Jim and John.

First completion

On Oct. 3, 1981, Chuck Long completed his first pass as a college football quarterback versus the Northwestern Wildcats. It went for fourteen yards as Iowa rolled 64–0. The Cats were coached by Dennis Green, who, in his first year as a college football coach, became just the second African American to coach Division I football. Green was also only one of three coaches to offer Chuck Long a scholarship. The others: Northern Illinois and Iowa. Following the game, Green sent a letter to Chuck's parents, Charlie and Joan, saying his performance in the game had proven that Chuck was going to be "a tremendous quarterback."

In the money

On the eve of Iowa's first Rose Bowl appearance since 1959, third-year Iowa coach Hayden Fry received a $10,000 salary boost after a meeting of the Iowa Board of Athletics. The increase raised Fry's base salary to $65,000. It also included an eight-year extension on his contract, securing him as the Hawkeyes coach for ten years or until age sixty-two. In addition to his base salary, Fry also received a $20,000 yearly payment from the University of Iowa Foundation for speaking engagements on behalf of the school. In addition, he made $25,000 annually from his TV show.

Ground to air

Quarterback Chuck Long threw the ball just ninety-two times as a senior at Wheaton North High (Illinois). Five years later, he held the record for most passing yards ever recorded by an Iowa Hawkeyes quarterback.

Over at nineteen

In 1981 (Chuck Long's freshman year at Iowa), the Hawkeyes football program ended nineteen consecutive losing seasons when it defeated Purdue 33–7 on its home turf Nov. 8 in Iowa City. It also ended what was, at that time, the Big Ten's longest losing streak of one school to another. Prior to the victory, Iowa had lost twenty consecutive games to the Boilermakers dating back to 1960. Iowa hadn't finished a season above .500 since 1961.

A dry spell

Chuck Long was the third-string quarterback when the Iowa Hawkeyes (8–3, ranked thirteenth in the country) met the 9–2 and twelfth-ranked Pac-10 champion Washington Huskies in the 1981 Rose Bowl. Prior to taking the field in Pasadena, Iowa's last postseason appearance had been in 1959, or more than four years before Chuck Long was born (Feb. 18, 1963). For the record, the Hawkeyes prevailed in the 1959 Rose Bowl, defeating California 38–12.

No gamble

On the eve of Iowa's 1981 Rose Bowl appearance versus the Washington Huskies, University of Iowa athletic director Bump Elliott announced he was extending Fry's contract (which had two years remaining) by eight years. "Everything is a gamble," Elliott said. "But in my opinion, this is no gamble at all. Hayden's first two years the team went five for six and four for seven, but there was no question the program was in very sound, solid hands."

The decision meant stability for Chuck Long and for the Hawkeyes program. Fry took the announcement in stride. "I think there will be a sigh of relief and thanks to the Lord," he said. "I was raised poor. I always found it easier to take off clothes than it is to put them on." Fry went on to coach the Hawkeyes through 1998 (twenty seasons), compiling a 143–89–6 record while winning three conference championships and six bowl games. (From the Dec. 27, 1981, *Wheaton Daily Journal,* Dan McLean, Copley News Service)

Then there were six

Going into the 1982 season, six quarterbacks vied for the starting job: Tom Grogan, Chuck Long, Dave Chambers, Dennis Klapperich, Charlie Humphreys, and junior college transfer Cornelius Robertson.

About time

The Hawkeyes recorded their first win of the 1982 campaign—a 17–14 upset versus the Arizona Wildcats on the road in Tucson. The victory was believed to be Iowa's first at night over a team in the Pacific time zone since a 20–14 win over Southern California played in the Los Angeles Coliseum in 1950.

Wildcats are wild

Chuck Long's first two wins as the Iowa Hawkeyes' starting quarterback came in back-to-back weeks and were both against Wildcats. The first was a 17–14 upset on Sept. 25, 1982, in Tucson, followed by a 45–7 win in Iowa City versus the Northwestern Wildcats.

Sneaky

Prior to a 21–16 victory over the Minnesota Gophers Oct. 23, 1982, Coach Hayden Fry had prided himself on never calling for a quarterback keeper in twenty-one years as a head coach.

"We don't have a quarterback sneak in our offense," Fry said in an Oct 20, 1982, interview with the *Cedar Rapids Gazette*. "Why should you do that when you've got all those big, strong guys back there whose job it is to carry the ball on running plays?

"No, in my twenty-one years as a head coach, I've never had a quarterback sneak. I learned that as an assistant coach under Frank Broyles at Arkansas and from other coaches.

"You'll never see me using a simple dive play, either. I believe in getting an extra blocker into that hole before the ball carrier."

But that changed in the week heading into the game versus the Golden Gophers.

"We did put it in last Monday night," Fry told *Des Moines Register* sportswriter Buck Turnbull following the Hawkeyes' victory in the Metrodome that also resulted in reclaiming Floyd of Rosedale. "We did put it in, and we worked real hard on it. I knew Coach Joe Salem has a pipeline down here and knows just about everything that we say or do by reading the papers. So we used the quarterback sneak three times, and it worked every time, once for a touchdown and once on an important fourth-down play.

"Shoot, I like to do things with a little flair. It was good fun, a lot like me putting on my bib overalls and straw hat to talk to the news media after the game."

Closing strong

In Chuck Long's first five wins as starting quarterback, Iowa outscored Arizona, Northwestern, Indiana, Minnesota, and Illinois by a combined second-half score of 58–16. Hayden Fry and his staff were credited for making effective halftime adjustments. "That's what coaching is all about," he said. "You have to be able to think when the bullets start flying. A lot of guys can coach during the week, but they can't think one play ahead during a game."

During the same stretch, four of Iowa's five wins were won by five points or less.

From seven to three

Preseason pundits picked the Iowa Hawkeyes to finish seventh in the Big Ten's 1982 football campaign. Instead, Iowa, led by sophomore quarterback Chuck Long, completed the regular season 7–4 (6–2 in the Big Ten), good for third place behind Ohio State and Michigan. The team earned its second straight bowl trip—a ticket to the Peach Bowl against Tennessee.

Third love

Basketball. Then baseball. Then football. Those were the sports Chuck Long loved—and in that order. He played basketball as a youngster and excelled at baseball in his early high school years. It wasn't until Chuck's senior year at Wheaton North High School that he "fell in love" with football.

Like the pressure

In Chuck Long's sophomore season as starting quarterback, the Iowa Hawkeyes won seven of their final nine games of the season, five of them by one touchdown or less. The strong finish led to a berth in the Peach Bowl, the team's second consecutive bowl appearance and a first in the school's history.

Pack your suitcases

The Hawkeyes' 28–22 win over Tennessee in the 1982 Peach Bowl was the start of something big for the Iowa brand. Nearly fifty-nine thousand tickets were sold for the game played in Atlanta, Georgia, on Dec. 31, 1982. Immediately following the game (by the way, Chuck Long threw three touchdown passes on his way to being named the game's most valuable offensive player), Peach Bowl Executive Director George Crumbley was ecstatic. "…With all things considered… yes, this was our number one bowl, our best ever." Crumbley's assessment was due in large part to the migration of fans from Iowa to Georgia.

In his postgame summary, *Cedar Rapids Gazette* sports writer Mike Chapman reported that Peach Bowl officials were a "little less than amazed at the way Iowans came in and took over the city." Chapman wrote that the Thursday evening prior to the game, thousands upon thousands of Hawkeyes fans "deserted the headquarters at the downtown Marriott, marching through the streets, chanting and singing." He added that the Iowa band "marched through the streets, and the Iowa alumni bash uptown was one of the biggest parties seen here in a long time." To this day, Hawkeyes fans are credited for how they travel to cheer on Iowa bowl game appearances.

MVP style

In his first postseason start, Chuck Long began the 1982 Peach Bowl with eleven consecutive completions and ended the first half with 231 yards passing, both Peach Bowl records. The 231 first-half passing yards (fourteen of seventeen) were six more than anyone had finished with in the previous fourteen Peach Bowls. Chuck Long was named the game's most valuable offensive player, leading Iowa to a 28–22 win over Johnny Majors' Tennessee Volunteers.

One for the guv

Iowa's Gov. Robert D. Ray was in the stands at Atlanta-Fulton County Stadium for Iowa's 28–22 win over Tennessee in the 1982 Peach Bowl. With only two weeks remaining of his fourteen-year tenure (Lt. Gov. Terry Branstad had been elected just two months earlier as Iowa's thirty-ninth governor), Ray had never witnessed a bowl victory by a team from the Hawkeye State. "I don't think I've missed many big athletic events involving Iowa, Iowa State, or Drake," Governor Ray told *Cedar Rapids Gazette* sports columnist Gus Schrader, "and I had never seen one of our teams win a bowl game. I followed Iowa State to the Sun Bowl, the Liberty Bowl, the Peach Bowl. They lost them all. I was in Pasadena when Iowa lost in the Rose Bowl. Even when I followed

Iowa to the NCAA Final Four in basketball, and Drake to the NCAA tournament, we didn't come away on top." But Ray's beloved state did against the Volunteers in what many described as the best edition of the Peach Bowl in its fifteen-year history.

Inflation

Chuck's parents, Charlie and Joan Long, were in the stands when their son took the field for the 1982 Peach Bowl Classic, leading the Hawkeyes to a 28–22 win over Tennessee. The cost of their ticket: $15. The median ticket price for the 2016 Chick-fil-A Peach Bowl was $289.

Counting down

The twenty-five-second play clock was used in the 1982 Peach Bowl, much to the frustration of Iowa's coaching staff. Fry said its use was unsettling for quarterback Chuck Long. *Cedar Rapids Gazette* sports columnist Gus Schrader reported that Fry finally told Chuck to "forget the time limit and call signals as usual." He did. Iowa was called for only one delay of game as it upended the Tennessee Volunteers 28–22. The twenty-five-second game clock was adopted by the Big Ten the following year.

No sophomore jinx

During his second season at Iowa (1982), Chuck Long was the only sophomore starting quarterback in the Big Ten. He led the league in completion percentage (.652), threw for 1,678 yards, and tallied fifteen touchdowns (eleven passing, four rushing). He also set ten school records, was selected to the Big Ten first team, received all-American mention, and was named Iowa's most valuable offensive player.

And then there were twelve

In August 1983, Iowa received approval from the Big Ten to play a game Dec. 1, 1984, in Hawaii. Coach Hayden Fry brokered the game (with Iowa guaranteed a $50,000 pay day plus expenses) after being given the scheduling reins by athletic director Bump Elliot. "The game will be a real bonus for our players," Fry said. "It will be like another bowl game for them." The game was scheduled to be played two weeks after the close of the regular eleven-game season.

Offensive "state"ment

Iowa scored ninety-three points in its first two games of the 1983 season with Chuck Long starting as quarterback (51–10 over Iowa State University and a 42–34 victory against the Penn State Nittany Lions). That was the most since 1914, when the Hawkeyes tallied 144 points against the likes of the Iowa Teachers and Cornell. The forty-two points scored by Iowa against Penn State were, at the time, the most given up by a Joe Paterno-coached team at Beaver Stadium. In that game, Chuck threw for a school record and personal best 345 yards and also tossed two touchdowns. In two starts to begin his second season as Iowa's starting quarterback, Chuck completed twenty-nine of forty-seven passed for 549 yards and three touchdowns with no interceptions. Following the Penn State victory, Chuck was also named United Press International's Big Ten Player of the Week.

A first of sixteen straight

Chuck Long outplayed Ohio State University's signal caller Mike Tomczak in a 20–14 victory in front of more than sixty-six thousand fans gathered for the top ten showdown in Kinnick Stadium Sept. 24, 1983.

No. 16 connected on sixteen of twenty-six attempts for 276 yards and two touchdowns, helping the Hawkeyes break a streak of sixteen consecutive losses over the span of twenty-one years versus the Buckeyes. The key play of the game came with just 4:25 remaining on the clock and Iowa clinging to a 13–7 lead. Coach Hayden Fry, thinking that Ohio State would play the run, gambled on a second-and-eight at its own twenty-five-yard line by turning Chuck loose. The third-year quarterback delivered with an on-point, seventy-three-yard scoring pass to receiver Dave Moritz that sealed the victory.

A winning "state" of mind

The Hawkeyes began the 1983 season with consecutive wins versus Iowa State, Penn State, and Ohio State. It was the first time since 1964 that Iowa had begun a season 3-0. In the season's first three contests, quarterback Chuck Long was a combined forty-five of seventy-three passes (62 percent) for 825 yards, five touchdowns, and just one interception.

Top gunner

With Iowa's 61–21 rout of Northwestern in the fifth game of the 1983 season, Hawkeyes quarterback Chuck Long became the nation's leading passer—the first time he had attained such an honor. Chuck, a junior, had completed eighty of 133 attempts for 1,469 yards and eight touchdowns.

Six broken, one tied

In Iowa's 34–14 win over Wisconsin on Nov. 5, 1983, Iowa quarterback Chuck Long went sixteen for twenty-one (completing his first eleven passes) and throwing for 231 yards. The Hawkeyes also scored four touchdowns on their first five possessions. When Chuck exited the game late in the third quarter against the Badgers and their thirteenth-ranked pass defense, the Iowa signal caller had broken six Iowa records: yards passing in a season, yards passing in a career, touchdown passes in a season, career touchdown passes, single-season total offense, and career total offense. The eleven straight completions tied another—Chuck's own mark established just ten months earlier in the Peach Bowl. "I just felt good when I got up this morning," Chuck told reporters after the game.

Ferentz arrives

Kirk Ferentz arrived at Iowa in 1981, hired by Hayden Fry as offensive line coach. Ferentz joined a few other well-known coaches who were on the Hawkeyes sidelines, including Bill Snyder (offensive coordinator), Dan McCarney (defensive linemen), and Barry Alverez (linebackers).

Five years

In January 1984, the NCAA ruled that freshmen who did not play in more than two games in 1980 and 1981 could receive a redshirt year. Thus, Chuck Long immediately had the option of returning for another year following the 1984 season. "I'd say right now that I'm leaning toward taking another year because I need that fifth year to graduate," he said following the NCAA's announcement. "I probably won't decide until after next season because I want to see how it goes. The [Iowa] coaches haven't let me know when they want me to make a decision, but I'm sure we'll talk about it pretty soon. I know I have to make a decision sooner or later." (as reported by Mark Dukes, *Cedar Rapids Gazette,* March 25, 1984)

Sight unseen

Iowa recruited Chuck Long without ever seeing him play in person. In a 1984 interview with *Cedar Rapids Gazette* assistant sports editor Mark Dukes, Iowa offensive coordinator Bill Snyder said the staff watched eleven game films of Chuck's performances as a senior at Wheaton North High. And even with that limited body of work, they were satisfied with his ability to pass. In Chuck's senior season, he passed for less than one thousand yards and threw only ninety-two passes in twelve games.

Twenty-two beats Young

In Iowa's matchup versus the Indiana Hoosiers in 1984, Chuck set an NCAA record for completing twenty-two consecutive passes in a game, besting eighteen straight by former BYU Cougars quarterback Steve Young. Chuck didn't realize the record-setting performance until postgame locker room chatter. "We were just fighting for our lives to win the game," he said. "After the game, someone told me I broke the record. I thought, 'Great. I just did that?'" Chuck's performance— twenty-six of thirty for 227 yards and two touchdowns—helped lead the Hawkeyes to a 24–20 win and a 6–2 mark overall for the season, keeping Rose Bowl dreams blooming in Bloomington, Indiana.

One more inch

Hobbled by a knee injury sustained the previous week in a 10–10 tie versus Wisconsin, Chuck Long took the field in the third quarter Nov. 10, 1984 in relief of redshirt sophomore Mark Vlasic in a matchup versus the Michigan State Spartans. In doing so, the ailing quarterback came within an inch of pulling off one of the most dramatic comebacks in Iowa football history. When Chuck took his first snap of the game in the third quarter, Iowa trailed 14–3. Four sacks later, Chuck and the Hawkeyes found themselves down 17–3 with just one quarter to play. With fifteen minutes remaining on the clock, Chuck put together what coach Hayden Fry dubbed one of the greatest performances he had witnessed by a college quarterback.

Standing tall in the face of a twenty-five-mile-per-hour wind and playing on essentially one leg, Chuck threw strikes on fourteen of seventeen passes (including eleven consecutive during one stretch) totaling 154 yards and two touchdowns. Trailing 17–10 and with just forty-four seconds to play, Chuck scrambled to find tight end Jonathan Hayes alone in the end zone. Down 17–16, Chuck ran the option and was stopped just short of the goal. "I saw the hole and went for it," Chuck said. "I thought I was in. I thought I broke the plane of the end zone and they pulled me back. The officials waited forever to make the call." Despite the heartbreaking setback, the game may have just been the added incentive Chuck needed to play another year in Iowa and made what would be an Iowa win the following year versus the Spartans that much sweeter.

Coordinating coordinates

So what's the scoop about Coach Hayden Fry and his signature white pants? In a column authored by Ron Maly of the *Des Moines Register* (Dec. 16, 1984), the engaging and entertaining coach was asked that very question on the eve of the Hawkeyes' 1984 Freedom Bowl appearance. Turns out that the origins of the habit, one that ultimately became a signature of Fry's twenty-year career at the helm of the Hawkeyes football team, could be traced to his high school (Odessa, Texas) coach Joe Coleman. Fry said Coleman was very superstitious. After winning the Texas high school championship in 1946, Fry became a believer in wearing the same clothes the day of the game for good luck. "I have worn white pants only at Iowa," Fry said. "Once again, I am aware of not only our football uniforms' impression, but also the coaching staff. I wear the white pants because they go well with the black-and-gold Iowa sweater."

I wear my sunglasses at night

Coach Hayden Fry was known for many things, including the donning of sunglasses regardless of the time of day. The Iowa coaching legend said the use of sunglasses became a necessity after years of watching game film. "I've looked at so many films through the years that my eyes are weak," he said. "The lights hurt my vision, so I have worn dark glasses for the last twelve years. The glasses have become a trademark, but I wear them only out of necessity."

29–39–0, 461, 6 touchdowns

In the inaugural Freedom Bowl played Dec. 26, 1984, in Anaheim, California, Iowa Hawkeyes quarterback Chuck Long threw six touchdown passes, helping lead Iowa to a 55–17 rout of the Texas Longhorns. After leading 24–17 at halftime, Iowa scored thirty-one unanswered points in the third quarter to win going away. Chuck completed twenty-nine of thirty-nine passes for 461 yards; Iowa rolled up 560 yards of total offense in the contest plagued by heavy rains throughout. The twenty-nine completions and six touchdown passes were school records. Also, the six TDs tossed by Chuck were believed to be at the time the most in any bowl game, besting five thrown by Steve Tensi of the Florida State Seminoles in a 36–19 victory versus Oklahoma in the Jan. 2, 1965, Gator Bowl. It was the most points allowed by the Texas program since a 64–0 pasting by the University of Chicago in 1904.

Chuck Long set three school records in the contest: six touchdown passes broke five thrown by Fred Riddle versus Indiana in 1963; twenty-nine completions surpassed the school mark of twenty-seven thrown by Mike Cilek in 1967 versus Illinois, and 461 yards shattered his own career best.

"This is definitely the biggest win of my career," Fry said following the contest. "Being from Texas, you don't get the chance to beat the University of Texas very often. I have never had a victory more meaningful to me."

One additional note: Coach Fry pulled Chuck from the game after the first play of the fourth quarter in favor of redshirt sophomore Mark Vlasic. However, after completing one pass, Vlasic sustained a broken thumb and had to exit the game. Re-enter Chuck, a move Fry couldn't avoid but later apologized for after the game. "We weren't trying to run up the score on Texas, but I had to put Chuck back in when Mark Vlasic broke his thumb," he said. "We didn't have any other quarterback as we've been using Kevin Harmon at running back. He hasn't practiced, so he might drop the ball or run the wrong way."

Tough record to beat

Wheaton North won the Illinois high school football championship in 1979 with a 14–6 win over La Salle-Peru, finishing the season with a 12–1 record. Chuck Long, a junior and the team's signal caller, set a record in the state championship game that likely still stands today. He completed just one of four passes for minus three yards.

The swarm

Hayden Fry instituted a number of changes at Iowa when he arrived in 1978 from North Texas State. In addition to fashioning the Hawkeyes uniforms after those worn by the Super Bowl Champion Pittsburgh Steelers in 1979, he also introduced "the swarm." Hawkeyes teammates took the field at the start of each game holding hands while proceeding in a slow and methodical fashion. Hayden liked the unity and togetherness it demonstrated. "It also allows us to come out calm, cool, and slow so we keep our emotions in check. I think it also has an impact on the other team when they see us come out like that." The ritual of the swarm continues to this day.

Lofty perch

When Football News picked Iowa no. 1 in its preseason college football ratings in August 1985, it was the first time the Hawkeyes were slotted in such a lofty perch in twenty years.

In 1965, Playboy magazine had not only ranked Iowa first, but also chose Jerry Burns as its preseason coach of the year. Playboy also predicted the Hawks would finish 9–1. Instead, Iowa turned in a 1–9 performance and Burns was fired. Despite being just thirty-eight years of age, Burns had earned the respect of the Hawkeyes players, who hoisted him on their shoulders and carried him off the field in his last game as head coach. Burns held no ill will toward the Hawkeyes. Later, he moved on to the Green Bay Packers as an assistant coach to Vince Lombardi, where he won two Super Bowls, then eventually to the Minnesota Vikings, where he served as both an assistant and head coach. "I didn't get it done at Iowa, but Hayden Fry has done a great job," he told the *Des Moines Register's* Bob Dyer upon hearing the news that Iowa had garnered the no. 1 spot in the 1985 preseason poll. "The football program there is in as fine a shape as it's ever been."

"Boiling" hot

Tied 24–24 with 6:30 on the clock, starting on the Hawkeyes' twenty-eight-yard line and clinging to first place in the Big Ten standings, Iowa quarterback Chuck Long engineered a twelve-play, sixty-four-yard drive ending with a twenty-five-yard Rob Houghtlin field goal and a 27–24 victory over Jim Everett and the Purdue Boilermakers. Chuck completed three of four passes on the drive, including two crucial long-distance gains on third down (one being a third-and-fifteen). Entering the game, Chuck was a top candidate for the Heisman Trophy and helped his cause before a national audience courtesy of CBS-TV completing twenty of thirty-three passes for 268 yards. "I don't know what Bo did today, and I'm not worried about it right now," Chuck said. "I'll start thinking about the Heisman after the Minnesota game [Saturday]."

What a deal

The cost of a Rose Bowl ticket for the Iowa versus UCLA matchup Jan. 1, 1986, was $35. When Iowa took the field Jan. 1, 2016, in a matchup versus Stanford, the average ticket price was more than $400.

Out with the old

Hayden Fry instituted numerous changes when he arrived in Iowa. The first thing he did was order new uniforms modeled after the Super Bowl Champion Pittsburgh Steelers. Then he ditched the loveable "Herky the Hawk" in favor of the "Tiger Hawk." But Fry wasn't done. He painted the visitors' locker room in Kinnick pink, told players to mind their manners by saying "yes, sir," "no, sir," and "thank you," and ordered the players to "dress for success." As reported by Randy Harvest of the Los Angeles Times ("Fry Aid," Oct. 28, 1985), Hayden Fry also did away with the individual entrances onto the field, telling the team that running out of the tunnel, jumping up and down, and high-fiving each other was "an insecure type of energy." Instead, he told them to trot onto the field "strong and confident." "The swarm" was born, and that tradition continues today.

"Too much Long"

The people of Wheaton welcomed news about Chuck Long's progress as a quarterback and Iowa's success on the football field. Well, almost everyone. the *Wheaton Daily Journal* published an anonymous letter to the editor Oct. 28, 1985, courtesy of its "Open Line" forum. The disgruntled reader figured something must be done about the numerous sports articles in the journal, "many of them full-page in length, praising the Iowa football team. This must be because local boy, Chuck Long, is the Iowa quarterback.

"But my daughter goes to the University of Illinois, which is our own state school, and she is just as important and successful to me as Chuck Long is to his family. Also, I want my boy to go to Illinois in another couple of years. So can we drop all this Iowa jazz and start running some full-page stories on the Illini. I thank you."

The *Wheaton Daily Journal* editor took the advice in stride.

"Sure," the editor replied via an editor's note, "as soon as we can convince Chuck to switch schools."

Unforgettable

John Streif, Iowa's longtime respected assistant athletic trainer, can recite many special memories during his more than forty years with Hawkeyes sports.

"The first of everything is great," he responded glibly when asked to share his personal favorite, "so the 1982 Rose Bowl with Coach Fry will always be special to me."

But the most memorable event for Streif was also one of the saddest and darkest days for Iowa athletics.

On Jan. 19, 1993, Iowa men's basketball junior power forward Chris Street was killed in an automobile accident following a team meal at the Highlander Inn located on the outskirts of Iowa City. A crowd favorite and Indianola, Iowa, native, Street's sudden and tragic death left the Hawkeyes community emotionally numb.

"It still gets to you. It's still emotional to talk about it to this very day," said Streif, his voice cracking. "I know it is for Coach [Tom] Davis, too. You don't forget those events. They are the first things that come to mind, the impactful and emotional things. The loss of Chris was certainly that, and much more."

Following the loss of a teammate, friend, and emotional leader, the Iowa men's basketball team resumed its season twelve days later with renewed intensity. Led by Acie Earl's twenty-seven points and sixteen rebounds, Iowa scored an emotional overtime win over the heavily favored Michigan State Spartans. Iowa advanced to the second round of the NCAA tournament and finished the season 23–9.

Who's on the box?

Travel to Kinnick and you'll notice the names and numbers of nine Hawkeyes greats affixed to the press box located above the west stands. It's the Kinnick Stadium Wall of Honor, and those who keep company there are members of the National College Football Hall of Fame and consensus all-Americans (or two-time consensus all-Americans if not elected to the Hall of Fame). Those recognized are: Aubrey Devine, Randy Duncan, Calvin Jones, Alex Karras, Nile Kinnick, Gordon Locke, Chuck Long, Duke Slater, and Larry Station.

Iowa Heismans

Iowa has unique connections to the Heisman Trophy.

The first recipient of the prestigious award was John Jacob "Jay" Berwanger of Dubuque. Berwanger was presented the first Downtown Athletic Club Trophy in 1935 (the following year the award was renamed the Heisman Trophy) on a vote of 41–20. After graduating from Dubuque Senior High School, Berwanger played halfback for the Chicago Maroons of the University of Chicago, where he became known as the "one-man football team" and referenced by some sports writers as more talented than Red Grange (of Wheaton, Illinois) and the most gifted athlete since Jim Thorpe. In a 1934 game versus the Michigan Wolverines, Berwanger gave Gerald Ford his distinctive scar beneath the future president's left eye and, in 1936, became the first player drafted by the National Football League. Berwanger was inducted into the Iowa Sports Hall of Fame in 1951 and passed away June 26, 2002, at the age of eighty-eight.

Just four years later, Nile Clarke Kinnick Jr., a student and college football player at the University of Iowa, won the Heisman Trophy as a consensus all-American. He was killed during a training flight while serving as a US Navy aviator in World War II. The University of Iowa renamed its football stadium Kinnick Stadium in his honor in 1972 (it remains the only college football stadium named for a Heisman Trophy winner). His maternal grandfather, George W. Clarke, also a graduate of the University of Iowa in 1878, served two, two-year terms as governor of Iowa from 1912 to 1916. A bust of Governor Clarke is situated behind Governor Branstad's desk in the Iowa Capitol.

Ode to ISU

After losing his lunch on Coach Hayden Fry in his first start on the road versus the Nebraska Cornhuskers in 1982, Chuck Long was benched on the spot. The benching remained in force the following Saturday when Iowa hosted the Iowa State Cyclones. "He probably thought I was a little too young," Chuck recalled, "so he put the junior quarterback in instead. All he had to do was win the game and he's probably the starter at Iowa that year and the next, which means I'm sitting on the bench for two more years." But the Cyclones won the game 19–7. "Hayden says, 'You know what, let's just play the young guy and live with him,'" Chuck recalled. "So he inserted me back into the starting lineup in week three against Arizona, we won, and I started the rest of my career at Iowa. So I owe the Iowa State Cyclones my career."

"His Airness"

When Chuck arrived in Detroit, the Lions shared the Pontiac Silverdome with the National Basketball Association's Detroit Pistons. It was a cozy situation in favor of the Pistons. When the "Bad Boys" began practice, the Silverdome would be divided, allowing the Pistons to rep on one side, the Lions on the other.

"We'd go out to practice, and we only had fifty yards of space," Chuck remembered. "We weren't the number one ticket in town; that was the Pistons. We hadn't won much, and the Pistons were competing for an NBA championship every year. They had Chuck Daly as head coach with stars like Vinnie Johnson, Joe Dumars, Isaiah Thomas, John Salley, Bill Laimbeer, and Rick Mahorn. They were the talk of the town, eventually winning back-to-back NBA titles in 1989 and 1990.

"Sometimes we'd shoot buckets with them where they were practicing," said Chuck. "One day, a young Chicago team came to town and had the floor for practice. Michael Jordan was on the court, and somehow Coach Darryl Rogers had him come over to meet the team. So after introductions, he told Michael to go out for a pass. I grabbed a football, motioned for him to go down the field fifteen yards or so, and do a quick out. I threw the ball a little high, but he leaped up and snapped it right out of the air like he'd been doing it his whole life. I thought he'd be a great receiver in the NFL. He was just so athletic, and it showed, even on the football field."

IN THEIR OWN WORDS

These quotes didn't find a home in the storyline but were too good not to share!

"Chuck was always good at everything he did. Life is going to work out very well for Chuck. He has a lot of energy. He's peppy, really happy, outgoing. When he has an occasional chance to stay home and rest, he never does it. He's always out playing golf or socializing. He really likes people. Chuck is not the type to spend a lot of time in his room. He never had time to read. He couldn't sit still long enough. Even as a baby, he loved to be moving around."

JOAN LONG
in a wide-ranging interview with Cooper Rollow
("Football star's mother long on blessings," Cooper Rollow,
Chicago Tribune, *June 19, 1986)*

"For a guy who has an unlisted telephone number,
a lot of people are sure finding me. Everybody I ever
knew or coached is crawling out of the woodwork,
looking for tickets to our Rose Bowl game."

HAYDEN FRY
*Iowa coach after Iowa clinched a berth in the 1982 Rose Bowl after
defeating Michigan State 36–7 before an overflow crowd in frozen
Kinnick Stadium ("Rose Bowl fever strikes Iowa," Ron Maly,*
Des Moines Register, *Nov. 23, 1981)*

"I've watched people closely. I think I could go into
a high school locker room and guess who played
offense and who played defense just by the way they
hang up their equipment. I think I could be right 80
percent of the time. Offensive players are neater. Tell
them to straighten up their shoulder pads and they
will. Tell that to a defensive player and he won't even
hear you. He'll just throw them in the locker the same
ol' way."

HAYDEN FRY
*("There was more to be thrown in the Iowa fire besides discipline,"
Mike Lopresti,* Iowa City Press-Citizen, *Jan. 1, 1982)*

"That's got to be one of the best sophomore performances at quarterback in college football that I've ever seen. And he didn't have all of those Anthony Carters and Duane Guinns and Willie Gaults to throw to. He's just phenomenal."

HAYDEN FRY
Iowa football coach recapping the performance of signal caller Chuck Long in the Hawkeyes' 28–22 win over the Tennessee Volunteers in the 1982 Peach Bowl (Associated Press, Jan. 3, 1983)

"I'm not worried about pressure as long as Athletic Director Bump Elliott keeps giving me ten-year contracts. I've never asked for a contract in my life or sought out a job. My philosophy has been that if a man does a good job, he'll be compensated."

HAYDEN FRY
Iowa Hawkeyes head football coach (as quoted by Tom Horvath, sportswriter, The Daily Journal, *July 31, 1983)*

"I think I put on the weight because I ate my mother's home cookin'."

CHUCK LONG
explaining how he managed to add ten pounds to his frame during the 1983 off-season

"People were surprised that a Big Ten school would want him. Everyone knew he had great leadership, brains, he was a take-charge guy—all of that. But they questioned if he had the tools."

TAYLOR BELL

Chicago Sun Times, *assessing the lack of interest in Chuck Long by notable college recruits ("A battle of 2 QBs," Brian Chapman, Cedar Rapids Gazette, Sept. 23, 1983)*

"[I don't read newspapers during the season] because I have to deal with you people, and I don't want to read what you're writing. My secretary and my wife may cut out clippings for me to read later. I tell my players if they want to keep a scrapbook, ask their girlfriends to do it and then read it after the season."

HAYDEN FRY

("Tight ends, ex-wrestlers big at Iowa," Gus Schrader, Cedar Rapids Gazette, *Aug. 24, 1984)*

"I always regretted it and always hated my coaches for it. I didn't like rejection. Not at all. Some kids could take it. I couldn't. I wanted to be the quarterback."

CHUCK LONG

on being rejected for the starting quarterback position on his seventh-grade football team at Franklin Junior High School ("Chuck Long: An eye on greatness," Ken Fuson, Des Moines Sunday Register, *Sept. 2, 1984)*

"I have been around great, great people all of my life. I've associated with great players and great coaches. I've taught history and I know a little about the qualities of great people in history. It was just so evident to me that Chuck Long had all the qualities you find in great people."

HAYDEN FRY

on his decision to recognize Chuck as destined for greatness before the young man had even thrown a pass as an Iowa Hawkeyes quarterback ("Chuck Long: An eye on greatness," Ken Fuson, Des Moines Sunday Register, Sept. 2, 1984)

"When you lose 33–0, you tend to stay up later in the spring and summer preparing for the next game you play against that team."

HAYDEN FRY

admitting to spending much time in the off-season preparing for a rematch against the Fighting Illini. Iowa defeated Illinois 21–16 to even its mark at 2–2 on the 1984 season ("Win over Illinois gives Hawks big lift," Des Moines Register, Oct. 1, 1984)

"Chuck Long is the most confident player I've ever been associated with, the most easy-going kid I've ever known. All the kid did yesterday in practice was hit twenty-five of twenty-six passes like it was nothing. Lord, I couldn't do that in pregame warm-ups. He thinks nothing of it, though. Chuck's had confidence since he arrived."

HAYDEN FRY
following Chuck's 370-yard performance in a 40–3 win versus Purdue, Oct. 13, 1984

"In our game at Iowa, at least six of his throws were ones that nobody else in our league—maybe any league—could have made. They were NFL throws... deep, deep outs [sideline patterns] across the field. One had to carry forty yards. He has a gun and carries it high."

GEORGE PERLES
Michigan State Spartans coach sizing up Chuck Long's prospects to play on Sundays following Iowa's 34–31 win in East Lansing ("Brother, roses kept Long at Iowa," Jack Saylor, Detroit Free Press, Oct. 14, 1985)

"My first year we played Oklahoma off their feet but lost in the fourth quarter. Everybody came up to me and said, 'Hey, great game.' I was furious. We lost the game."

HAYDEN FRY

on the first step taken in building a winning tradition at Iowa…and that was no moral victory ("Hawkeyes a tonic for Iowans' ills," Dave Leon Moore, USA Today, Oct. 18, 1985)

"We let ol' Chuck slip by. You always regret it when a player like Long (who is from Wheaton, Illinois) slips out of your state. We established a style to go elsewhere for our quarterbacks because they seemed to throw the ball so much more in those areas. I'm glad Long found the right school. I have a lot of respect for him. Chuck is great for football. By that I mean he's great for the game as a person in addition to his ability as a player."

MIKE WHITE

Illinois coach comparing Iowa's signal caller to Jack Trudeau, his starting quarterback, leading up to a college football showdown in Kinnick Stadium ("Long, foe closely matched," Mark Dukes, Cedar Rapids Gazette, Nov. 9, 1985)

"Colleges today don't give players an education. Classes like 'The History of Rock and Roll Music' just aren't going to help these kids when they graduate. If colleges are going to give kids scholarships, they should be required to make sure they have some way to support a family when they graduate."

VIC ROMELLE
neighbor to the Long family in Wheaton, Illinois, and father of three sons who played in the National Football League

"I knew Chuck Long was a great quarterback, but I've changed my mind. He is a franchise. I have seen many great college passers, but I have never seen a better one. Long is a pinpoint passer with amazing accuracy."

FOREST "EVY" EVASHEVSKI
Former Iowa football coach

"It looks pretty serious to me."

CHARLIE LONG
commenting on the fact that his son Chuck and neighbor Lisa Wells had been dating since sixth grade at Hawthorne Elementary ("The Long Look," Bill Wundram, Quad City Times, Nov. 27, 1985)

"I can't tell you what to write and I'm not threatening you about the press conferences, but it's not specified in my contract that I hold them."

HAYDEN FRY

dwelling on the negative coverage received by the team after a three-game stretch that saw the Hawkeyes go winless against Wisconsin, Michigan State, and Minnesota to close out the 1984 Big Ten season. Fry said unjust criticism by the press had prompted him to consider doing away with his weekly press conferences, adding that similar cheap shots against the Iowa basketball program had driven head coach Lute Olson out of Iowa City. ("Fry lashes out at media 'criticism,'" Cedar Rapids Gazette, Nov. 28, 1984)

"He's the greatest quarterback in America. It all started back when this young man made a decision to pass up a few bucks in the pros because he loves college football and thought, maybe, we had a chance to go to the Rose Bowl. I just can't put into words how much I love Chuck Long as a person. The way Chuck has handled himself from a personal standpoint—whether it be in the classroom or downtown or behind the center awaiting a snap— has always been first class."

HAYDEN FRY

assessing the career of Chuck Long ("Iowa QB Chuck Long has all makings of Horatio Alger," Jack McCarthy, Copley News Service, Dec. 31, 1985)

"We will excuse you this day for destroying Illinois
59–0 Nov. 9…just for today."

JIM THOMPSON

*Illinois Gov. in comments read by Lt. Gov. George Ryan to a crowd
of more than 1,500 gathered at Wheaton North High School for
an assembly honoring Chuck Long. The pomp and circumstance
included presentation to Chuck of the* Chicago Tribune *Silver
Football Award presented annually to the Big Ten's most
valuable player.*

"I'm pleased with the way things have worked out.
It's been a great year. I wanted to play in the Rose
Bowl. It was good to be out there, even though the
game didn't turn out the way we would have liked. I
just wanted to achieve something. If I had gone out
[to the draft] last season, it would have left me with an
empty feeling. A lot of money wasn't going to change
that. Maybe I'm old-fashioned, but I've never believed
you should let money dictate. That's just the way I am.
You only have one life to live. I've never been money-
hungry. It just doesn't mean that much to me."

CHUCK LONG

*on his decision to spurn the NFL for a fifth season at Iowa ("Long's
a natural for awards night," Paul Hagen,* Fort Worth Star-Telegram*,
Feb. 17, 1986)*

"I'm not cocky, I'm confident, and here's the difference: I think someone who's cocky believes they're better than other people. I don't think I'm better than anyone else. I'm very confident of myself in certain situations. I believe I can get certain things done."

CHUCK LONG
reflecting on successes both personal and professional while
preparing for his second year as quarterback for the Detroit Lions
("With lady luck at his side, Chuck Long faces the challenge of his
athletic career," Tom Kowalski, Oakland Sunday Magazine,
July 26, 1987)

Make This Chapter the Start of Your Next Chapter

"I've been kind of underrated ever since I started playing. It's kind of driven me to become better and to show people. Being underrated like that, it just gives you more incentive to become better and to just prove people wrong and to prove to them that you can play."

CHUCK LONG
("Chuck Long: an eye on greatness," Ken Fuson, Des Moines Register, *Sept. 2, 1984)*

Chuck Long's story is not meant to remain static, confined to just ink on paper, a book that's read and placed on a shelf.

It's intended to motivate and inspire, to offer points of reference forged through personal experiences and strengthened by trial and error that can help others do more. Be more.

Where do you want to go? What do you want to achieve? Who do you want to help? What person would you like to meet? What promotion do you want to attain? What relationship do you want to strengthen? What habit do you want to quit? What habit do you want to start?

Take a moment to reflect and anticipate the choices and connections you can make that will position you in the sweet spot when opportunity comes knocking.

Start small, but think big. Dream out loud. Consider your options. Gain the insight and opinions of others you respect, trust, and admire.

Write it down.

It need not be eloquent or detailed. Just write it down.

Studies prove that writing something down increases the likelihood it will happen.

Make this chapter your next chapter by getting involved in the things that matter to you.

Learn a new skill. Try something for the first time. Start a new relationship. Volunteer. Step out of your comfort zone.

Take a chance.

Because you're destined for greatness, too.

– AARON PUTZE

You Are Destined for Greatness

Sixteen game-winning plays to motivate and empower the human spirit

Inspired by the story of

CHUCK LONG

Featuring

Hayden Fry, Suku Radia, Kirk Tyler, Terry Branstad, Miriam Erickson Brown, Wendy Wintersteen, Kirk Ferentz, Terry Rich, Gene Meyer, Jim Knuth, Jonathan Hayes, Randy Edeker and other inspiring leaders!

BY AARON PUTZE

COMING IN SUMMER 2018

Made in the USA
Lexington, KY
14 December 2018